Toshiaki Iwashiro

I like big things.

I especially like big things that are trying to be small and unobtrusive.

No matter how peaceful and quiet you are, I'm acutely aware of your presence...

Toshiaki Iwashiro was born December 11, 1977, in Tokyo and has the blood type of A. His debut manga was the popular *Mieru Hito*, which ran from 2005 to 2007 in Japan in *Weekly Shonen Jump*, where *Psyren* is currently serialized.

PSYREN VOL. 2
SHONEN JUMP Manga Edition

STORY AND ART BY TOSHIAKI IWASHIRO

Translation/Camellia Nieh
Lettering/Annaliese Christman
Design/Sam Elzway
Editors/John Bae, Joel Enos, Carrie Shepherd

PSYREN © 2007 by Toshiaki Iwashiro
All rights reserved.
First published in Japan in 2007 by SHUEISHA Inc., Tokyo.
English translation rights arranged by SHUEISHA Inc.

Printed in the U.S.A.

Published by VIZ Media, LLC
P.O. Box 77010
San Francisco, CA 94107

10 9 8 7 6 5 4 3 2 1
First printing, January 2012

THE WORLD'S
MOST POPULAR MANGA

www.viz.com

www.shonenjump.com

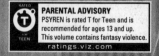

SHONEN JUMP MANGA EDITION

PSYREN

2

BABY UNIVERSE

Story and Art by
Toshiaki Iwashiro

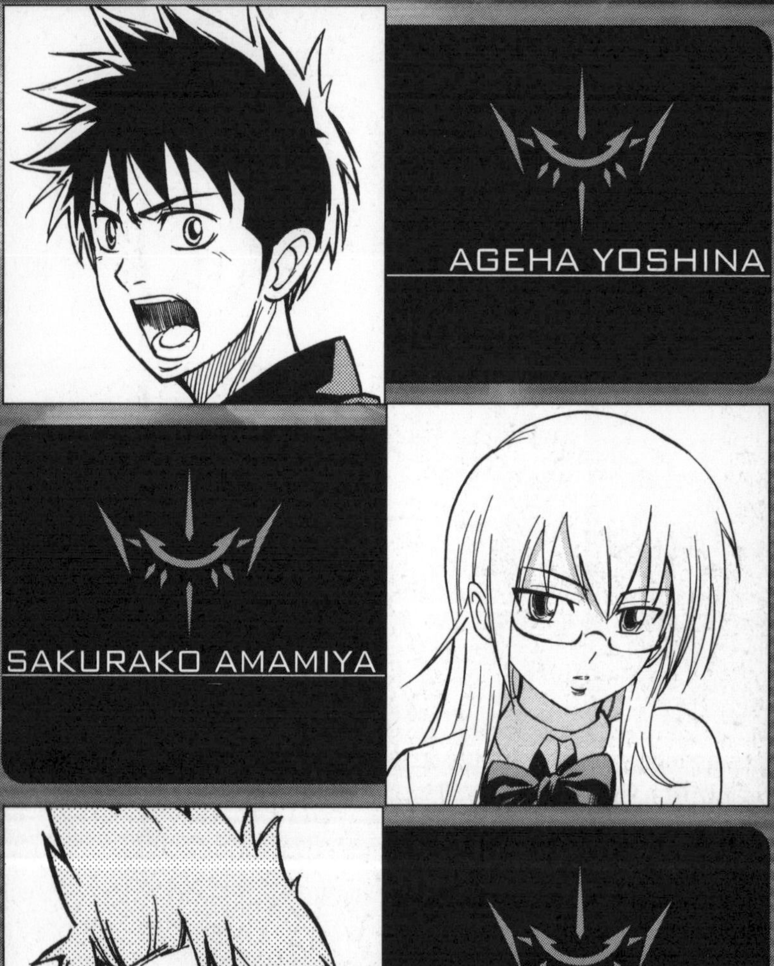
AGEHA YOSHINA
SAKURAKO AMAMIYA
HIRYU ASAGA

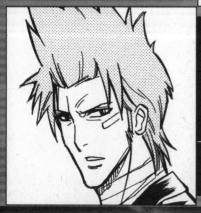

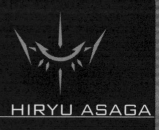

Characters

NEMESIS Q

FUBUKI YOSHINA

Story

AGEHA YOSHINA IS A STUDENT AT SHIRATAKI HIGH
SCHOOL WHO HAPPENS UPON A RED TELEPHONE CARD
EMBLAZONED WITH THE WORD *PSYREN*. SUSPECTING A
LINK BETWEEN THE DISAPPEARANCE OF HIS CHILDHOOD
FRIEND SAKURAKO AMAMIYA AND THE URBAN LEGEND
OF THE PSYREN SECRET SOCIETY, AGEHA USES THE
CARD. THE NEXT DAY, TWO MEN CLAIMING TO BE
POLICE DETECTIVES SHOW UP AT AGEHA'S SCHOOL
AND ATTACK HIM. HOPING TO CONTACT SOMEONE FOR
HELP, AGEHA PICKS UP HIS CELL PHONE AND FINDS
HIMSELF TRANSPORTED TO A STRANGE WASTELAND.
WITHOUT KNOWING IT, AGEHA HAS BECOME A
PARTICIPANT IN A LIFE-OR-DEATH GAME!

PSYREN

VOL. 2
BABY UNIVERSE

CONTENTS

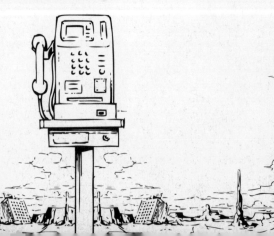

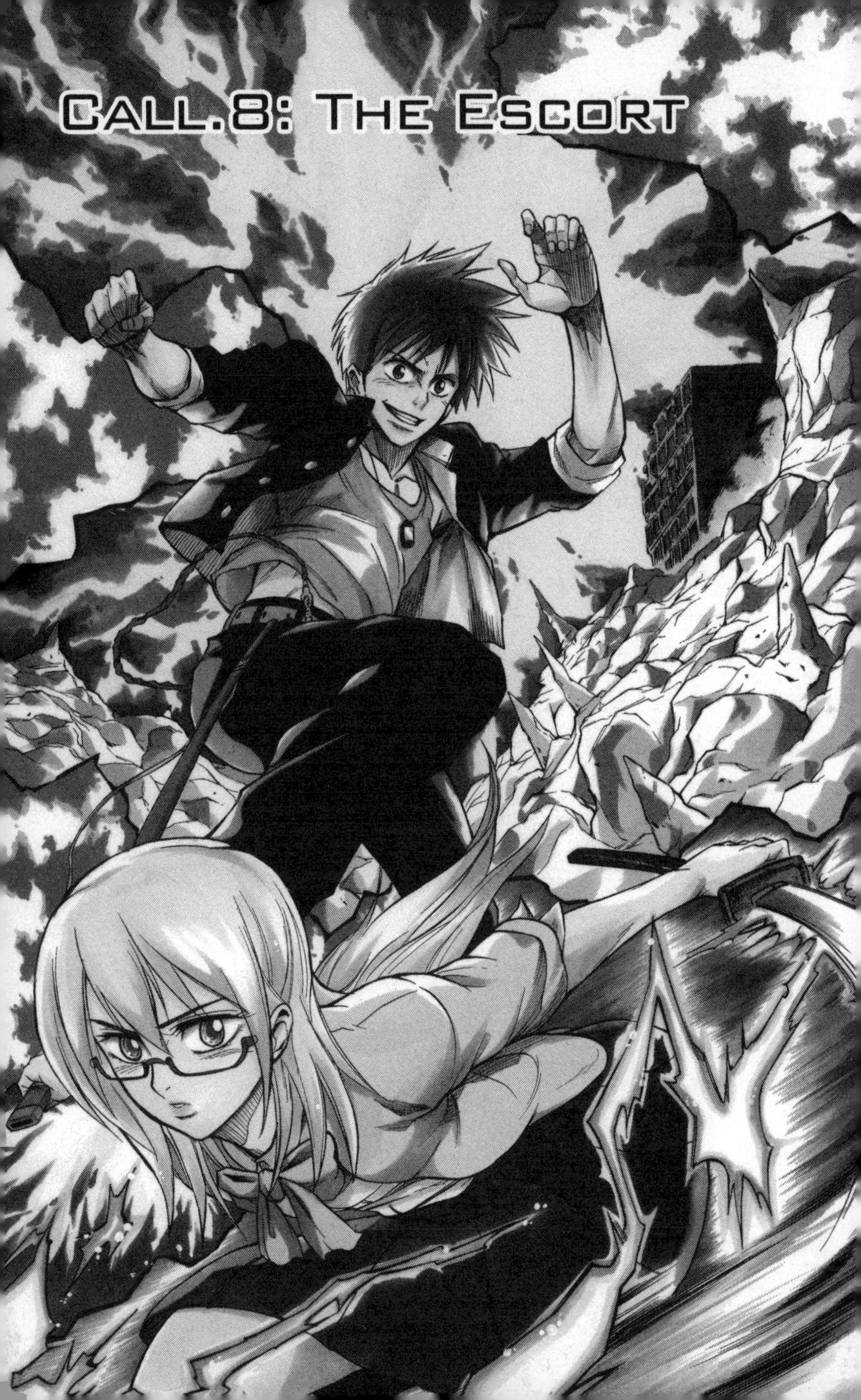
Call.8: The Escort

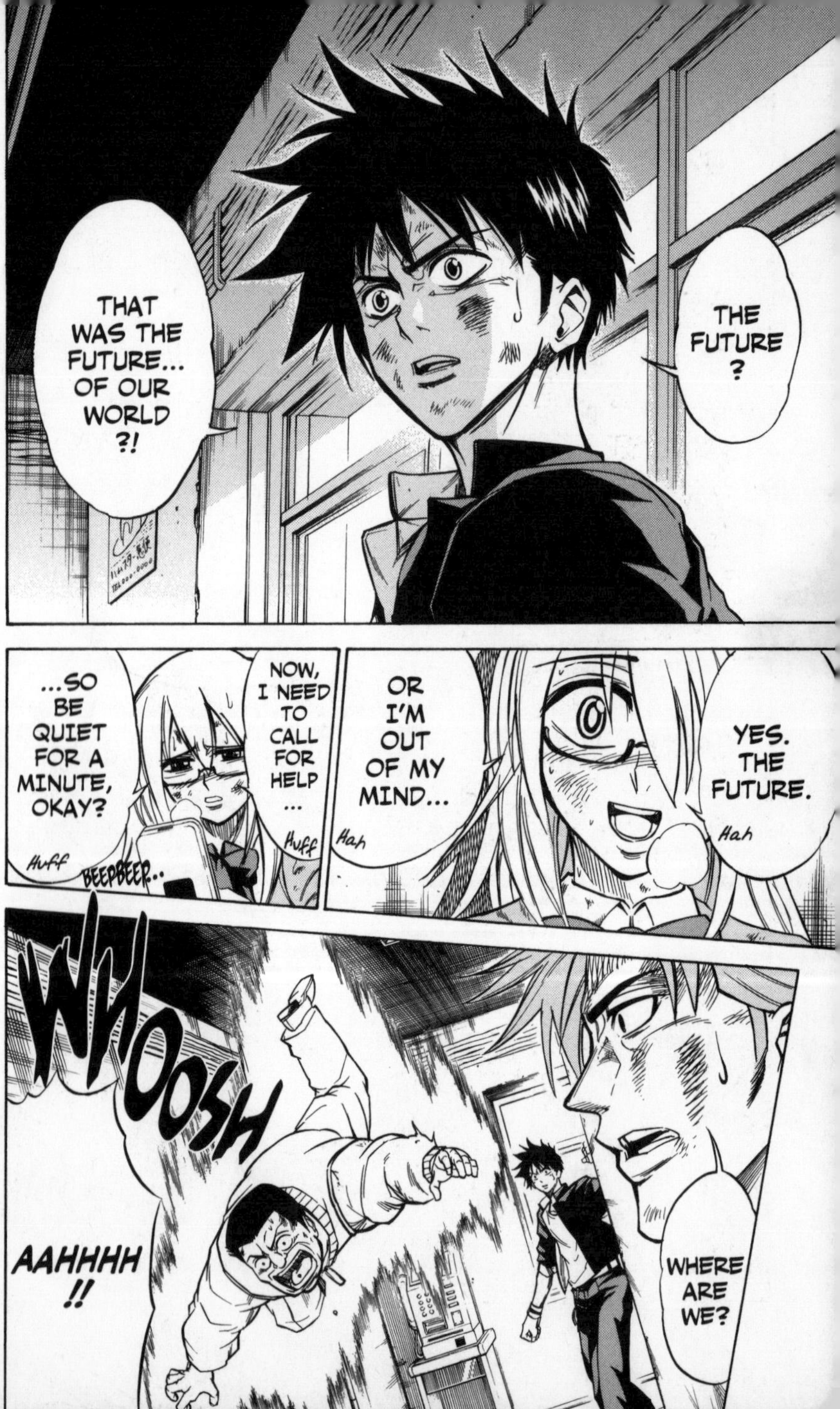
THE FUTURE ?
THAT WAS THE FUTURE... OF OUR WORLD ?!
YES. THE FUTURE.
Hah
OR I'M OUT OF MY MIND...
Hah
NOW, I NEED TO CALL FOR HELP ...
Huff
...SO BE QUIET FOR A MINUTE, OKAY?
Huff
BEEPBEEP..
WHERE ARE WE?
WHOOSH
AAHHHH !!

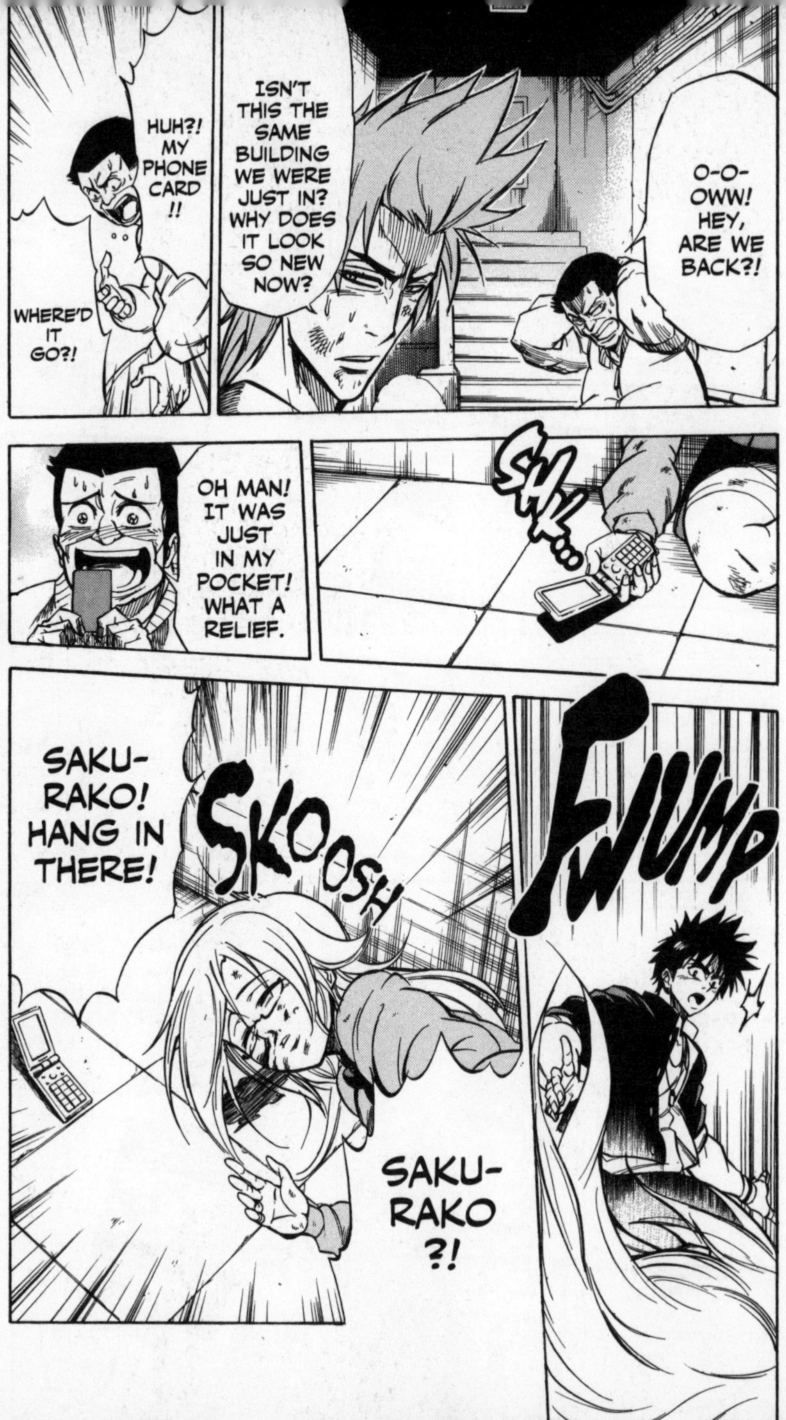
O-O-OWW! HEY, ARE WE BACK?!
ISN'T THIS THE SAME BUILDING WE WERE JUST IN? WHY DOES IT LOOK SO NEW NOW?
HUH?! MY PHONE CARD !!
WHERE'D IT GO?!
SHK...
OH MAN! IT WAS JUST IN MY POCKET! WHAT A RELIEF.
FWUMP
SAKU-RAKO! HANG IN THERE!
SKOOSH
SAKU-RAKO ?!

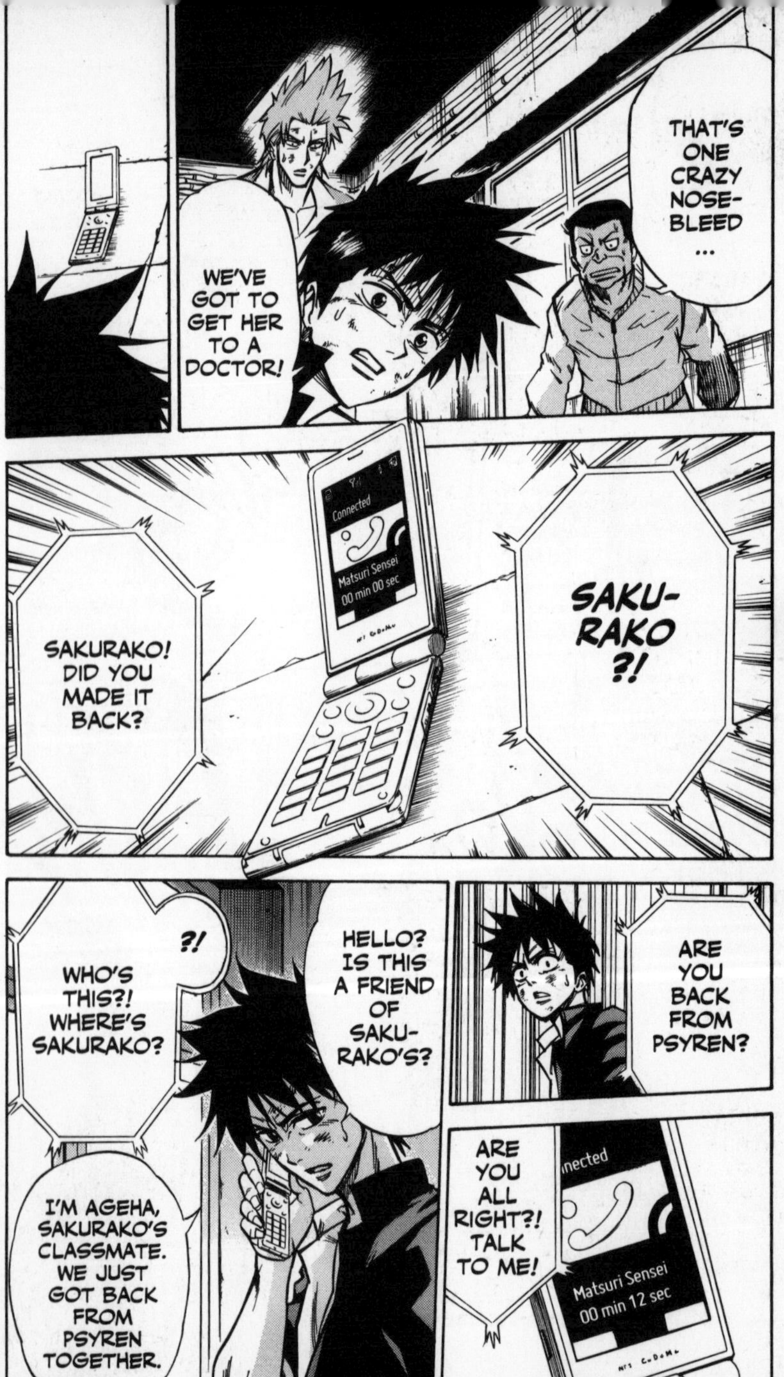
THAT'S ONE CRAZY NOSE-BLEED...
WE'VE GOT TO GET HER TO A DOCTOR!
SAKU-RAKO ?!
Connected
Matsuri Sensei
00 min 00 sec
SAKURAKO! DID YOU MADE IT BACK?
ARE YOU BACK FROM PSYREN?
nected
Matsuri Sensei
00 min 12 sec
ARE YOU ALL RIGHT?! TALK TO ME!
HELLO? IS THIS A FRIEND OF SAKU-RAKO'S?
?!
WHO'S THIS?! WHERE'S SAKURAKO?
I'M AGEHA, SAKURAKO'S CLASSMATE. WE JUST GOT BACK FROM PSYREN TOGETHER.

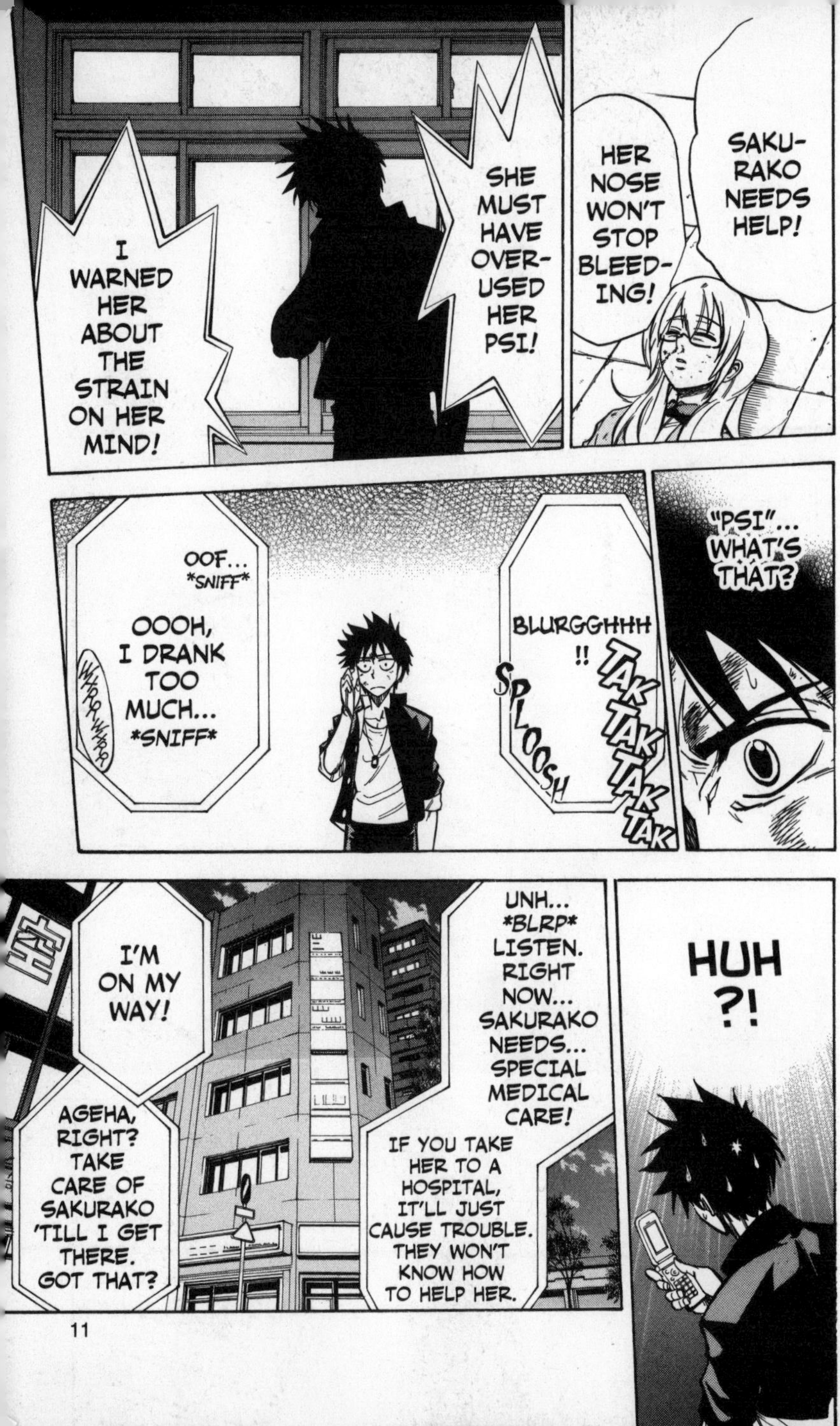
SAKU-RAKO NEEDS HELP!
HER NOSE WON'T STOP BLEED-ING!
SHE MUST HAVE OVER-USED HER PSI!
I WARNED HER ABOUT THE STRAIN ON HER MIND!
"PSI"... WHAT'S THAT?
BLURGGHHH!!
TAK TAK TAK TAK
SPLOOSH
OOF... *SNIFF*
OOOH, I DRANK TOO MUCH... *SNIFF*
HUH?!
UNH... *BLRP* LISTEN. RIGHT NOW... SAKURAKO NEEDS... SPECIAL MEDICAL CARE!
IF YOU TAKE HER TO A HOSPITAL, IT'LL JUST CAUSE TROUBLE. THEY WON'T KNOW HOW TO HELP HER.
I'M ON MY WAY!
AGEHA, RIGHT? TAKE CARE OF SAKURAKO 'TILL I GET THERE. GOT THAT?

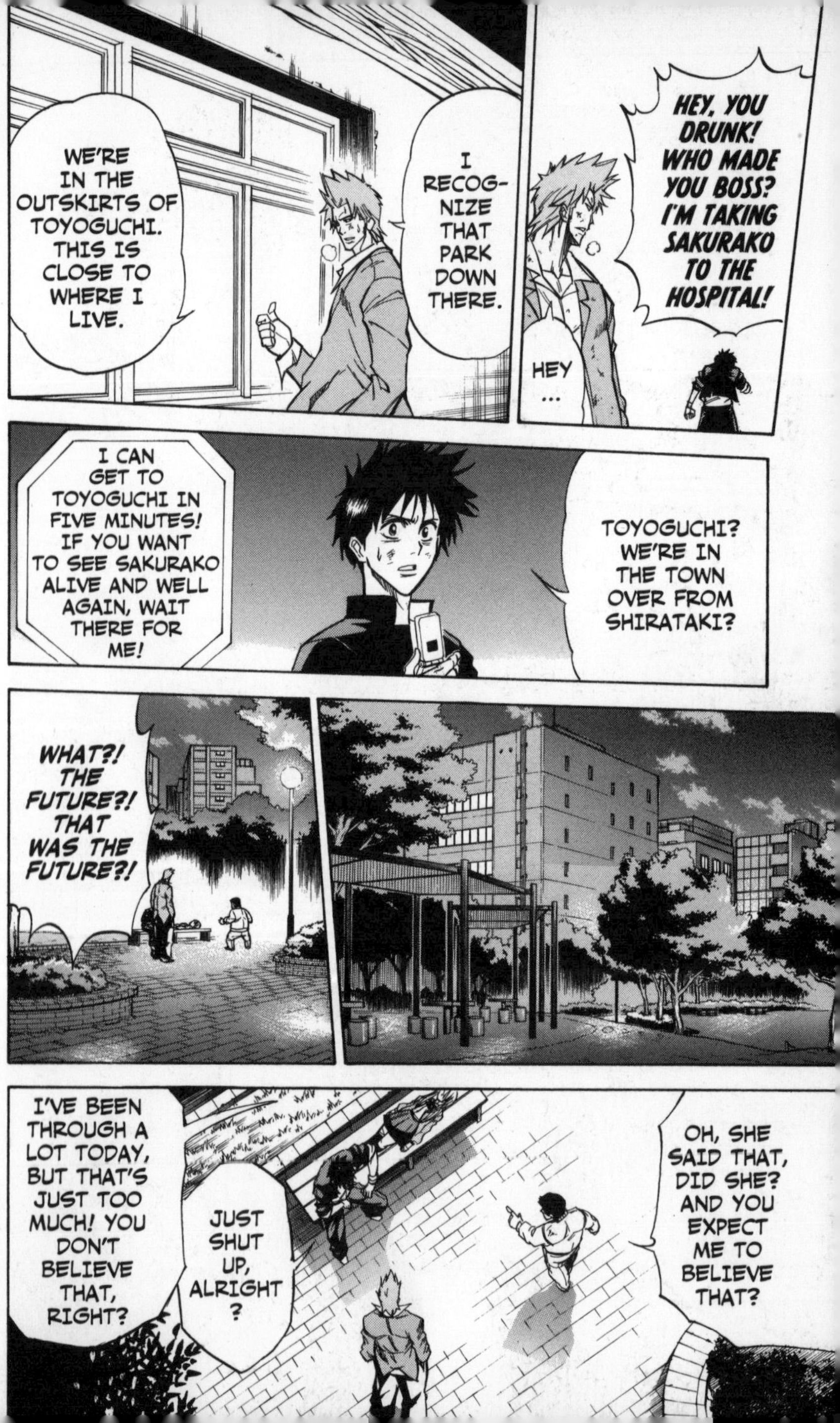
HEY, YOU DRUNK! WHO MADE YOU BOSS? I'M TAKING SAKURAKO TO THE HOSPITAL!
HEY ...
I RECOGNIZE THAT PARK DOWN THERE.
WE'RE IN THE OUTSKIRTS OF TOYOGUCHI. THIS IS CLOSE TO WHERE I LIVE.
TOYOGUCHI? WE'RE IN THE TOWN OVER FROM SHIRATAKI?
I CAN GET TO TOYOGUCHI IN FIVE MINUTES! IF YOU WANT TO SEE SAKURAKO ALIVE AND WELL AGAIN, WAIT THERE FOR ME!
WHAT?! THE FUTURE?! THAT WAS THE FUTURE?!
OH, SHE SAID THAT, DID SHE? AND YOU EXPECT ME TO BELIEVE THAT?
JUST SHUT UP, ALRIGHT?
I'VE BEEN THROUGH A LOT TODAY, BUT THAT'S JUST TOO MUCH! YOU DON'T BELIEVE THAT, RIGHT?

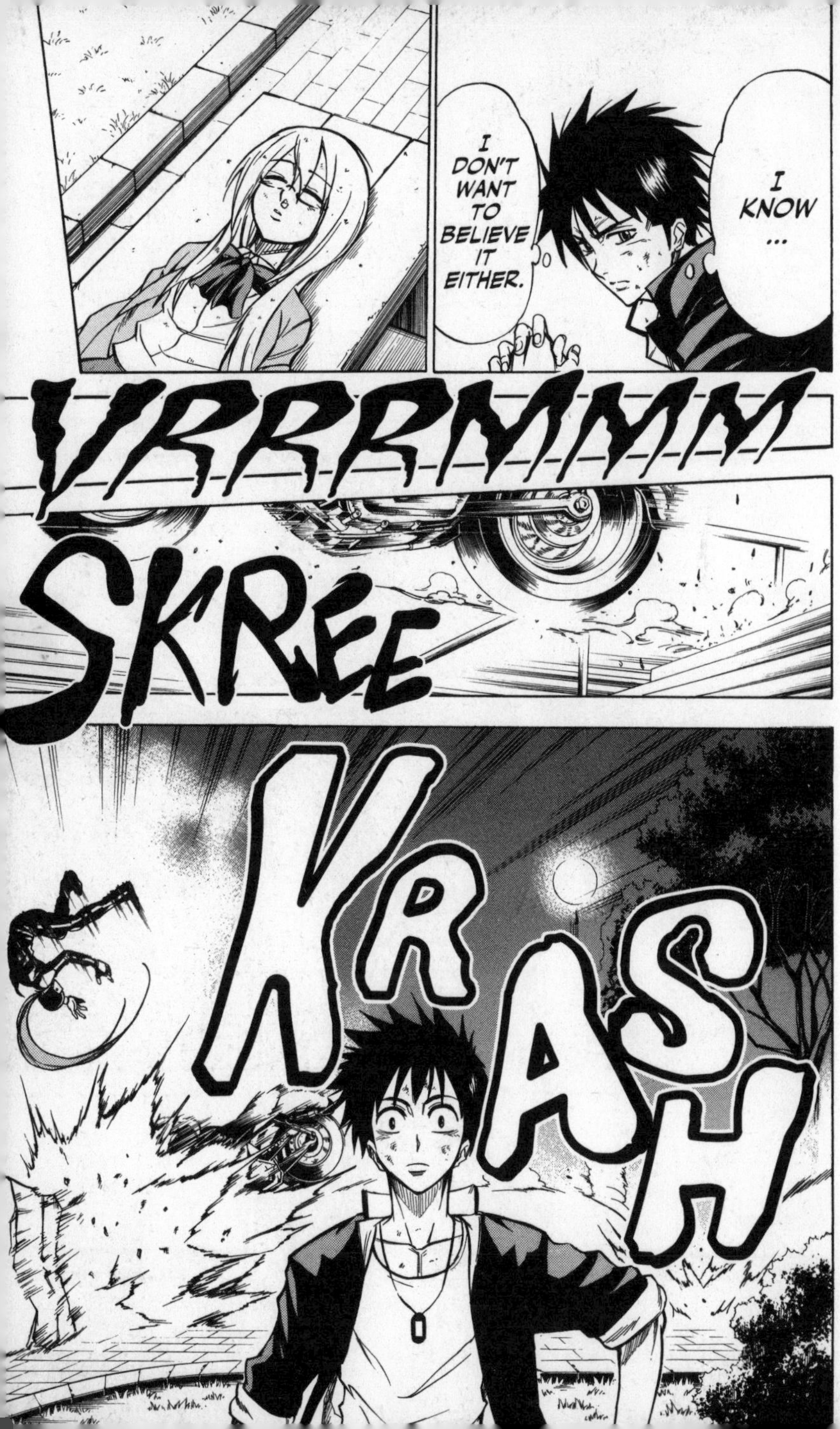
I KNOW ...
I DON'T WANT TO BELIEVE IT EITHER.
VRRRMMM
SKREE
KRASH

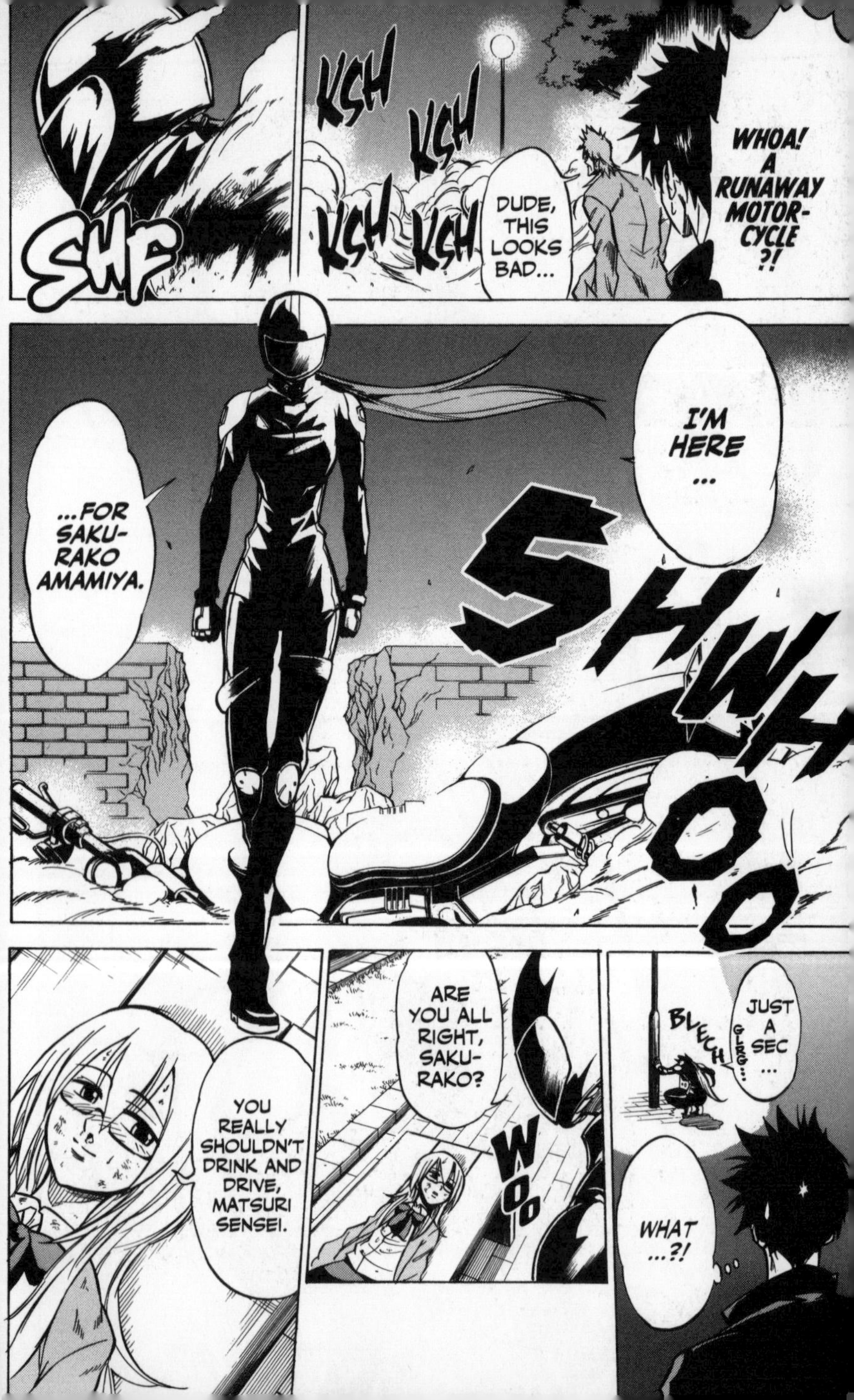
WHOA! A RUNAWAY MOTOR-CYCLE?!
KSH
KSH
DUDE, THIS LOOKS BAD...
KSH
KSH
SHF
I'M HERE...
...FOR SAKU-RAKO AMAMIYA.
SHWHOOO
JUST A SEC...
BLECH
GLRG...
WHAT...?!
ARE YOU ALL RIGHT, SAKU-RAKO?
WOO
YOU REALLY SHOULDN'T DRINK AND DRIVE, MATSURI SENSEI.

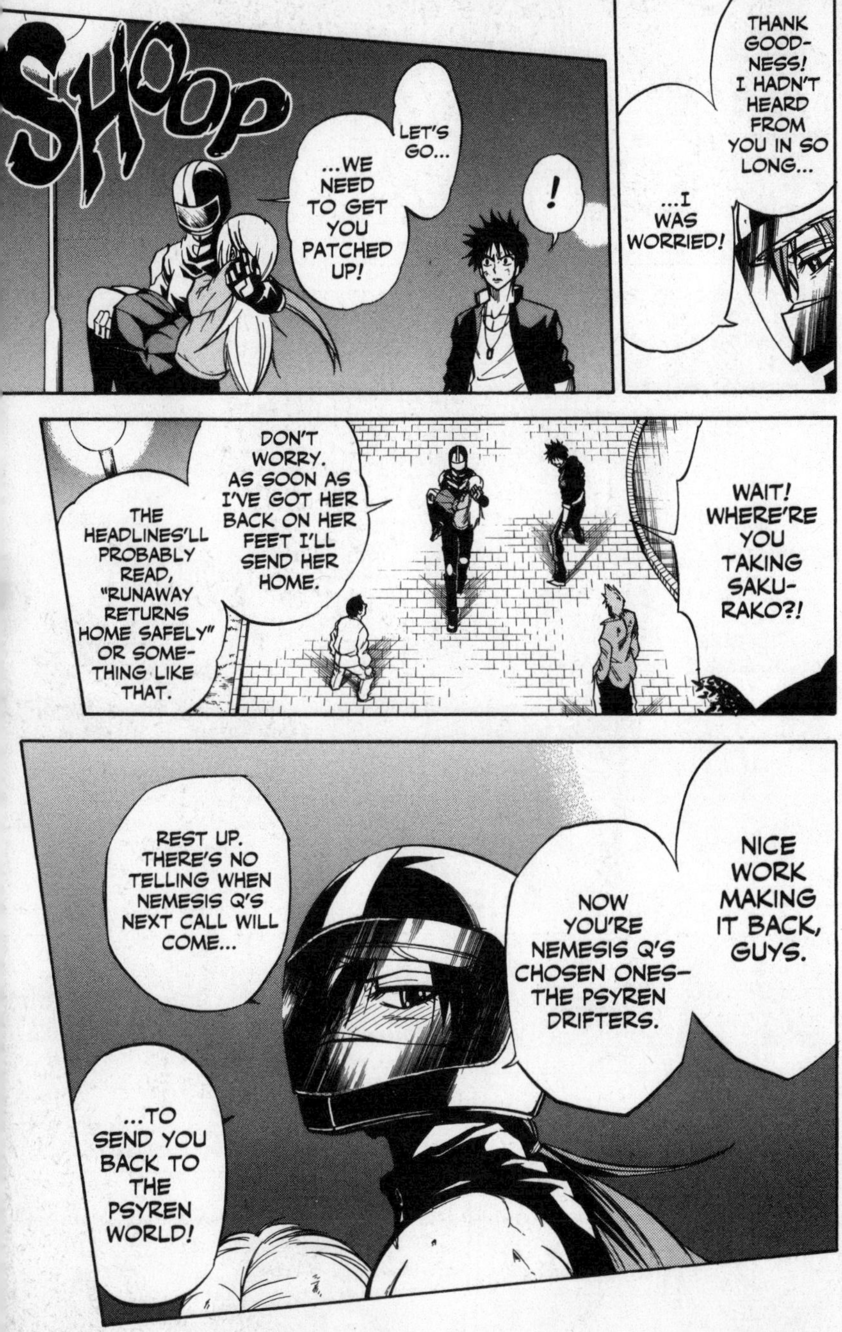
THANK GOODNESS! I HADN'T HEARD FROM YOU IN SO LONG...
...I WAS WORRIED!
SHOOP
LET'S GO...
...WE NEED TO GET YOU PATCHED UP!
!
WAIT! WHERE'RE YOU TAKING SAKURAKO?!
DON'T WORRY. AS SOON AS I'VE GOT HER BACK ON HER FEET I'LL SEND HER HOME.
THE HEADLINES'LL PROBABLY READ, "RUNAWAY RETURNS HOME SAFELY" OR SOMETHING LIKE THAT.
NICE WORK MAKING IT BACK, GUYS.
NOW YOU'RE NEMESIS Q'S CHOSEN ONES—THE PSYREN DRIFTERS.
REST UP. THERE'S NO TELLING WHEN NEMESIS Q'S NEXT CALL WILL COME...
...TO SEND YOU BACK TO THE PSYREN WORLD!

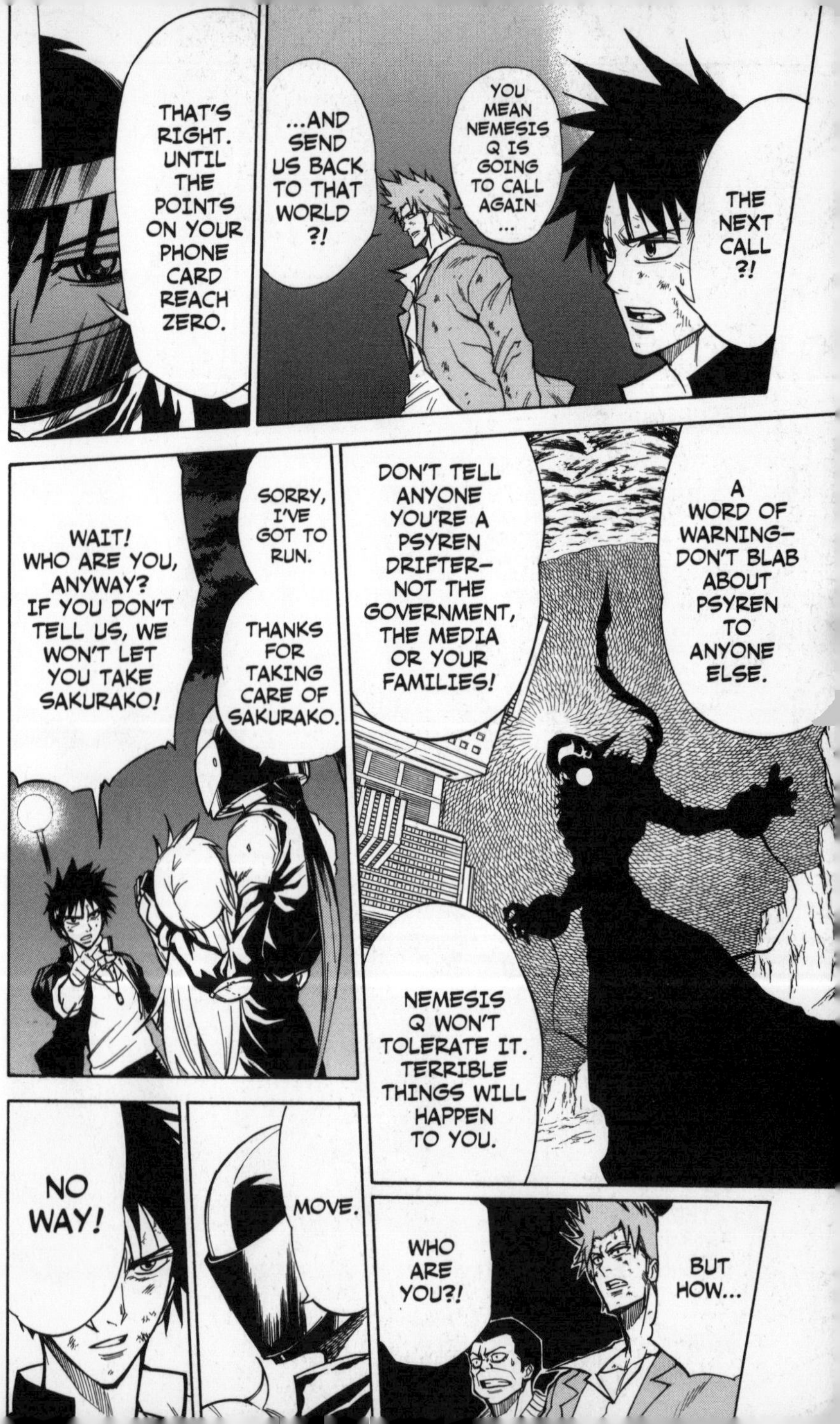
THE NEXT CALL ?!
YOU MEAN NEMESIS Q IS GOING TO CALL AGAIN ...
...AND SEND US BACK TO THAT WORLD ?!
THAT'S RIGHT. UNTIL THE POINTS ON YOUR PHONE CARD REACH ZERO.
A WORD OF WARNING— DON'T BLAB ABOUT PSYREN TO ANYONE ELSE.
DON'T TELL ANYONE YOU'RE A PSYREN DRIFTER— NOT THE GOVERNMENT, THE MEDIA OR YOUR FAMILIES!
NEMESIS Q WON'T TOLERATE IT. TERRIBLE THINGS WILL HAPPEN TO YOU.
BUT HOW...
WHO ARE YOU?!
SORRY, I'VE GOT TO RUN.
THANKS FOR TAKING CARE OF SAKURAKO.
WAIT! WHO ARE YOU, ANYWAY? IF YOU DON'T TELL US, WE WON'T LET YOU TAKE SAKURAKO!
MOVE.
NO WAY!

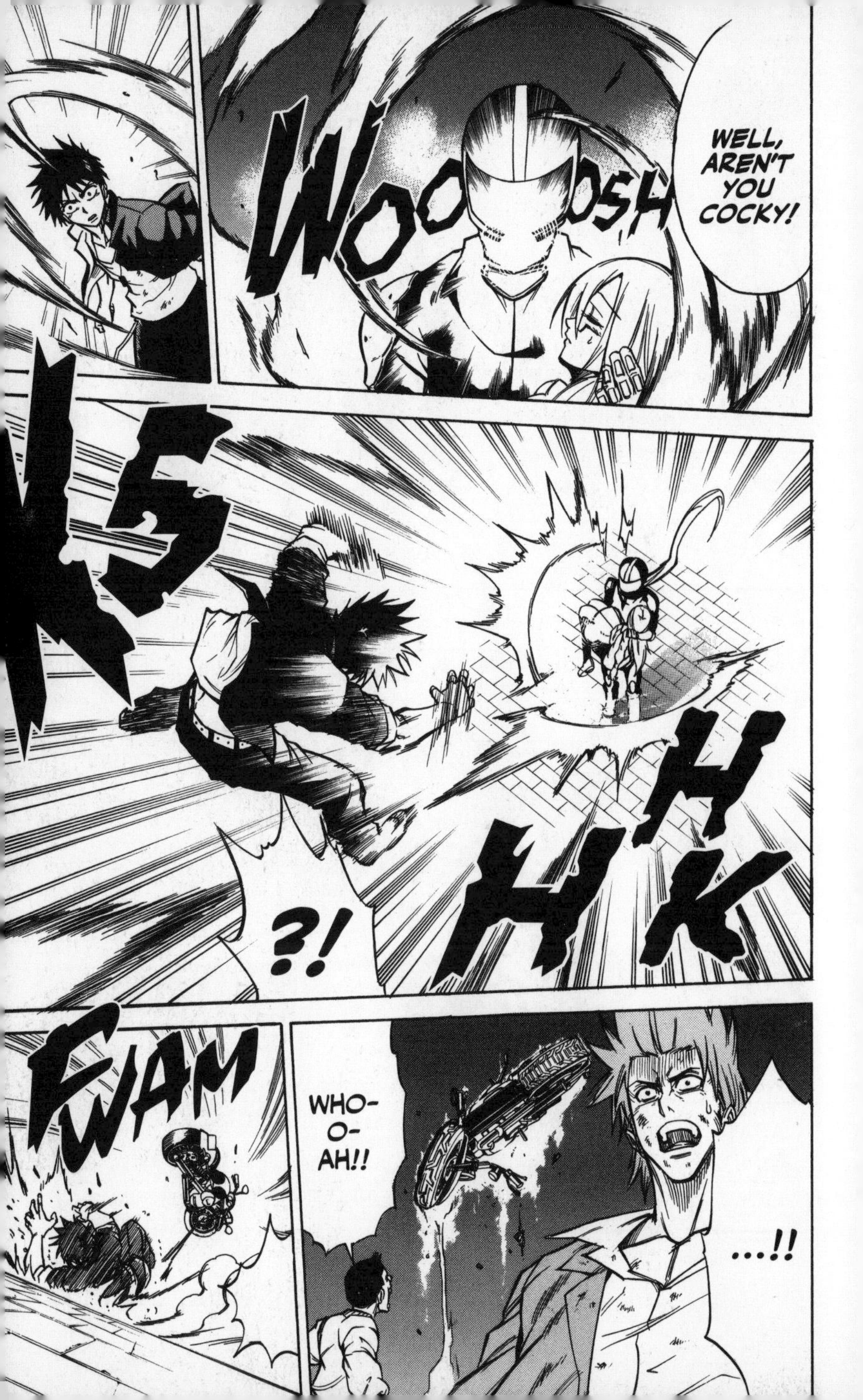
WELL, AREN'T YOU COCKY!
WOOOSH
HHK
?!
...!!
WHO-O-AH!!
FWAM

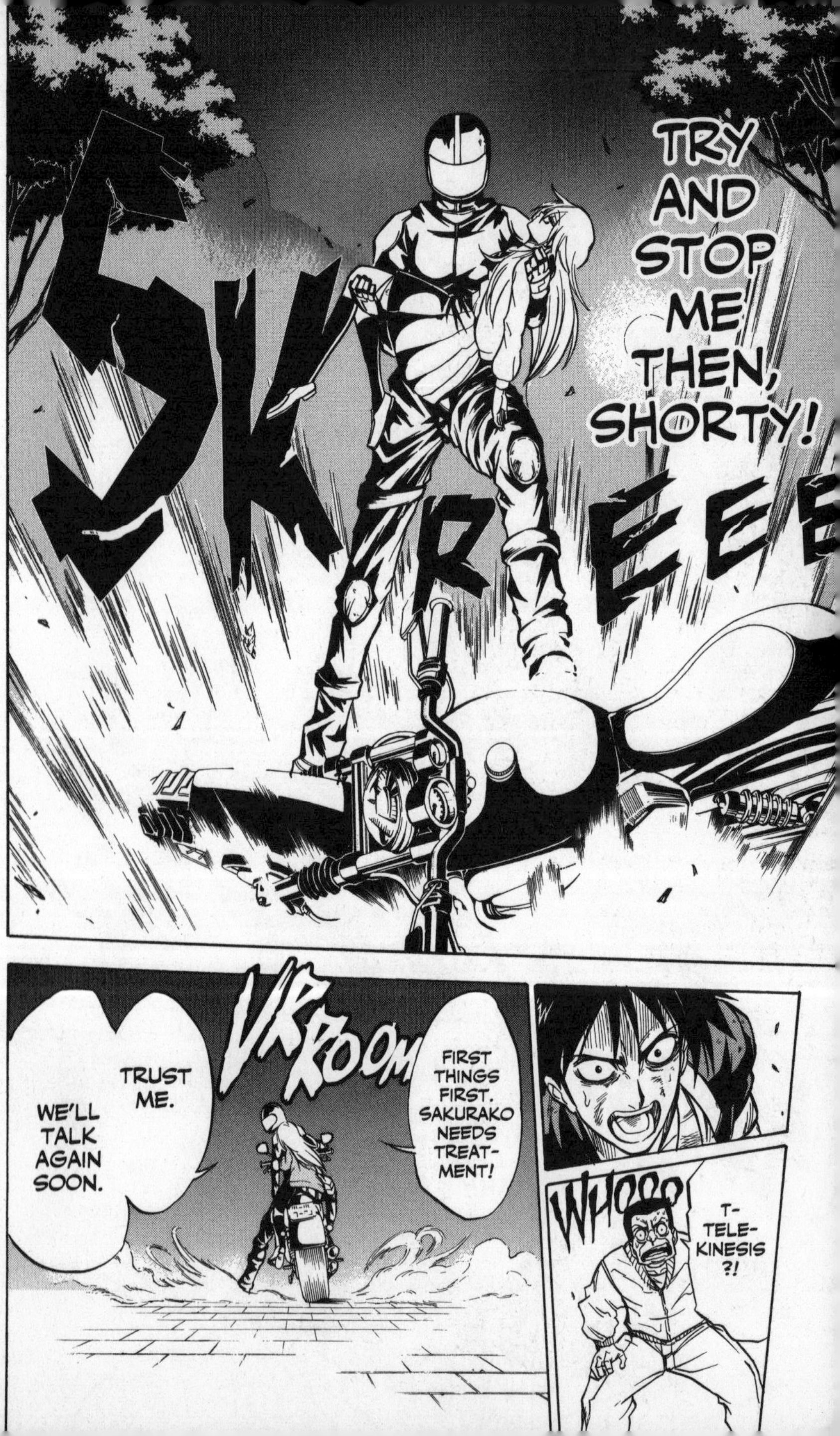
TRY AND STOP ME THEN, SHORTY!
SKREEE
WHOOO
T-TELEKINESIS?!
VRROOM
FIRST THINGS FIRST. SAKURAKO NEEDS TREATMENT!
TRUST ME.
WE'LL TALK AGAIN SOON.

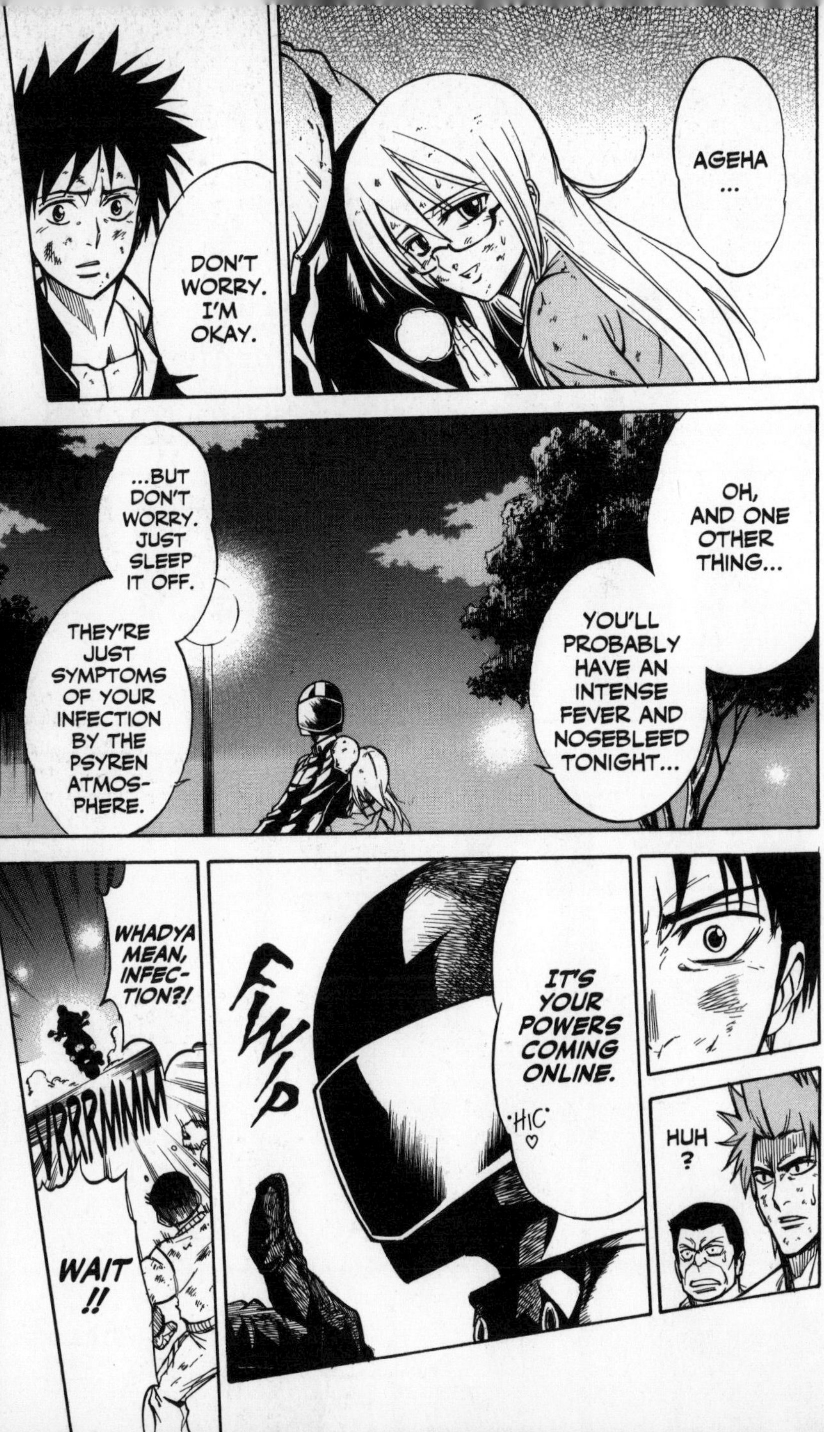
AGEHA ...
DON'T WORRY. I'M OKAY.
OH, AND ONE OTHER THING...
YOU'LL PROBABLY HAVE AN INTENSE FEVER AND NOSEBLEED TONIGHT...
...BUT DON'T WORRY. JUST SLEEP IT OFF.
THEY'RE JUST SYMPTOMS OF YOUR INFECTION BY THE PSYREN ATMOS-PHERE.
HUH ?
IT'S YOUR POWERS COMING ONLINE.
HIC ♡
FWIP
WHADYA MEAN, INFECTION?!
VRRRMMM
WAIT !!

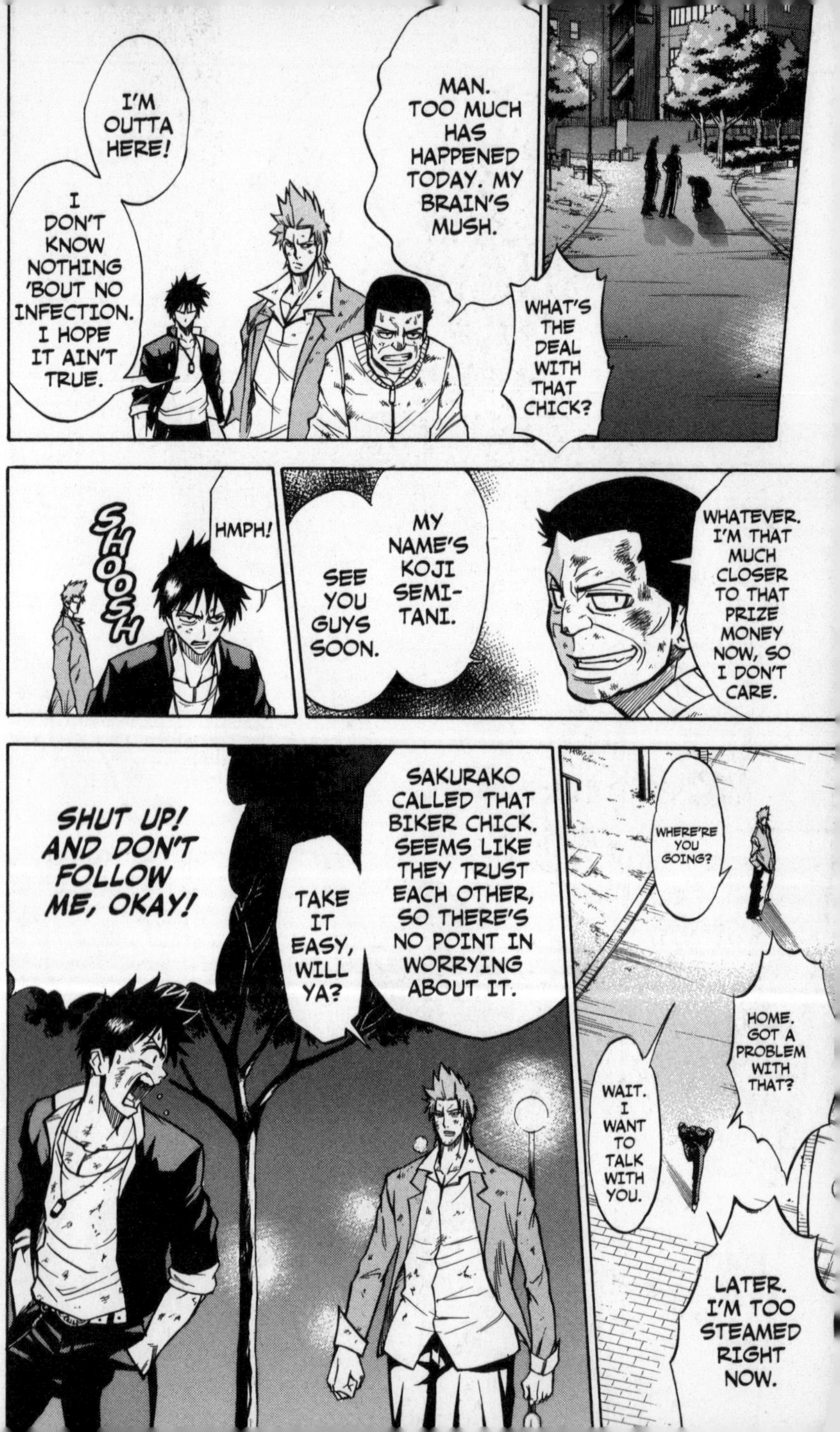
WHAT'S THE DEAL WITH THAT CHICK?
MAN. TOO MUCH HAS HAPPENED TODAY. MY BRAIN'S MUSH.
I'M OUTTA HERE!
I DON'T KNOW NOTHING 'BOUT NO INFECTION. I HOPE IT AIN'T TRUE.
WHATEVER. I'M THAT MUCH CLOSER TO THAT PRIZE MONEY NOW, SO I DON'T CARE.
MY NAME'S KOJI SEMI-TANI.
SEE YOU GUYS SOON.
HMPH!
SHOOSH
WHERE'RE YOU GOING?
HOME. GOT A PROBLEM WITH THAT?
WAIT. I WANT TO TALK WITH YOU.
LATER. I'M TOO STEAMED RIGHT NOW.
SAKURAKO CALLED THAT BIKER CHICK. SEEMS LIKE THEY TRUST EACH OTHER, SO THERE'S NO POINT IN WORRYING ABOUT IT.
TAKE IT EASY, WILL YA?
SHUT UP! AND DON'T FOLLOW ME, OKAY!

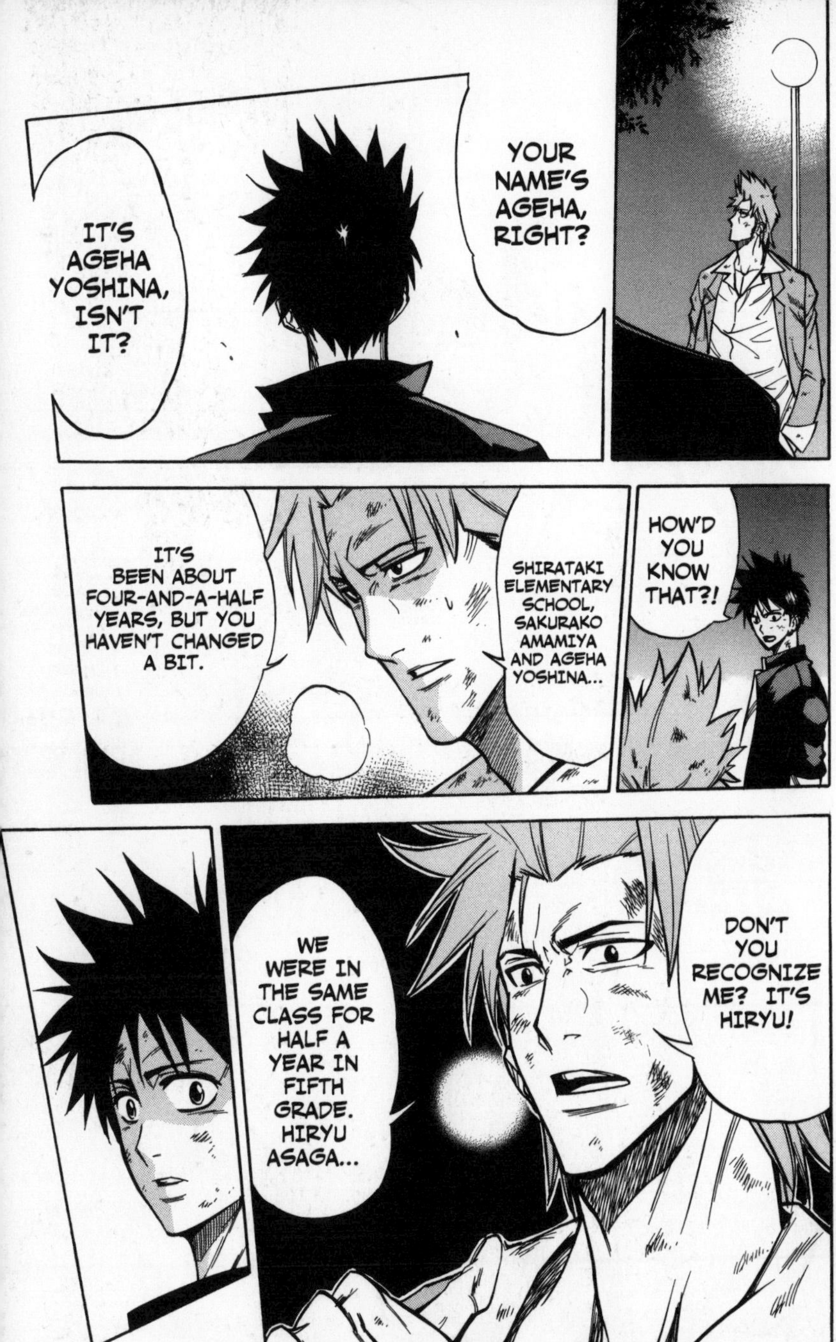
YOUR NAME'S AGEHA, RIGHT?
IT'S AGEHA YOSHINA, ISN'T IT?
HOW'D YOU KNOW THAT?!
SHIRATAKI ELEMENTARY SCHOOL, SAKURAKO AMAMIYA AND AGEHA YOSHINA...
IT'S BEEN ABOUT FOUR-AND-A-HALF YEARS, BUT YOU HAVEN'T CHANGED A BIT.
DON'T YOU RECOGNIZE ME? IT'S HIRYU!
WE WERE IN THE SAME CLASS FOR HALF A YEAR IN FIFTH GRADE. HIRYU ASAGA...

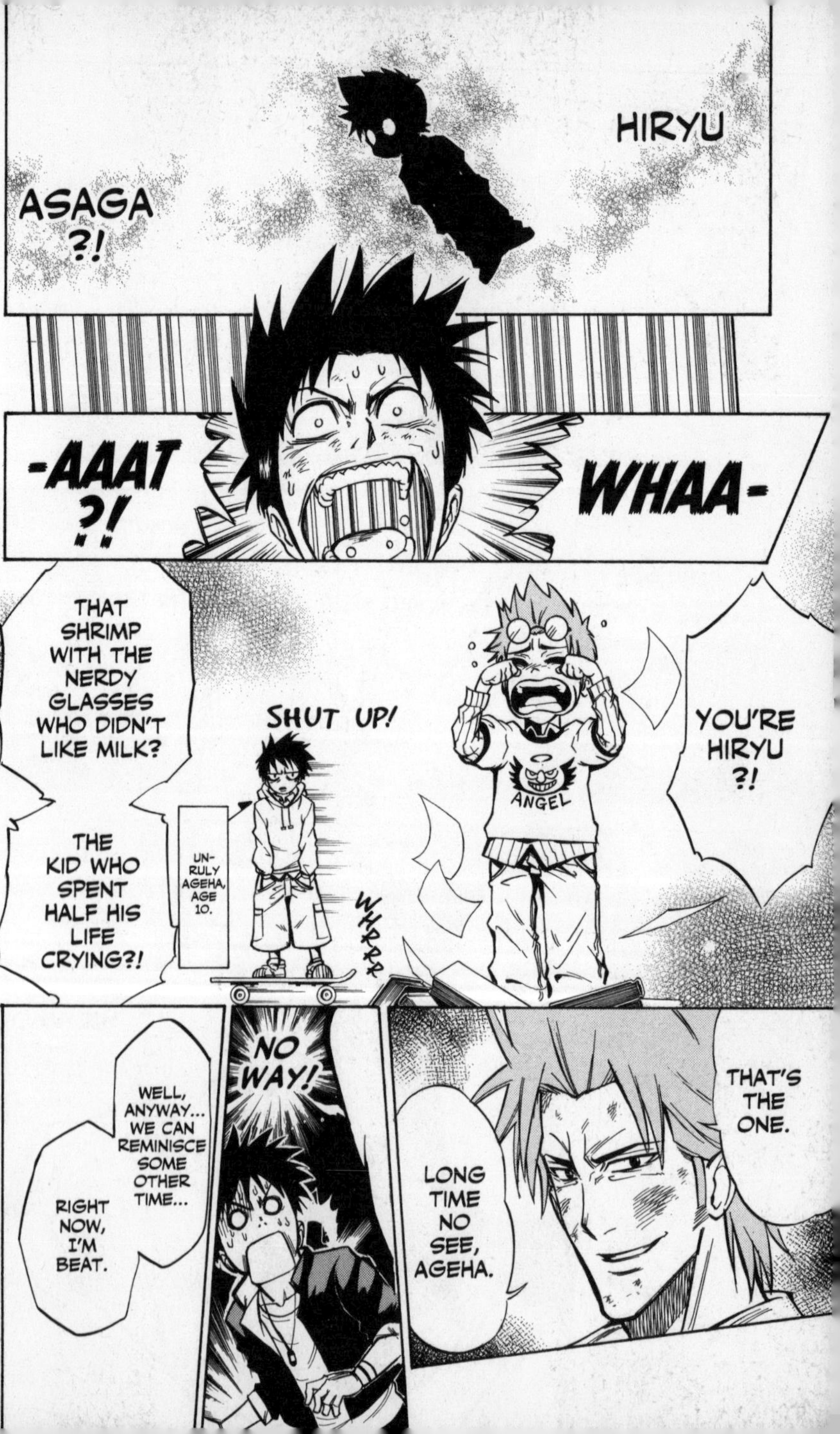
HIRYU
ASAGA ?!
WHAA-
-AAAT ?!
YOU'RE HIRYU ?!
SHUT UP!
THAT SHRIMP WITH THE NERDY GLASSES WHO DIDN'T LIKE MILK?
THE KID WHO SPENT HALF HIS LIFE CRYING?!
UN-RULY AGEHA, AGE 10.
WHRRR
THAT'S THE ONE.
LONG TIME NO SEE, AGEHA.
NO WAY!
WELL, ANYWAY... WE CAN REMINISCE SOME OTHER TIME...
RIGHT NOW, I'M BEAT.

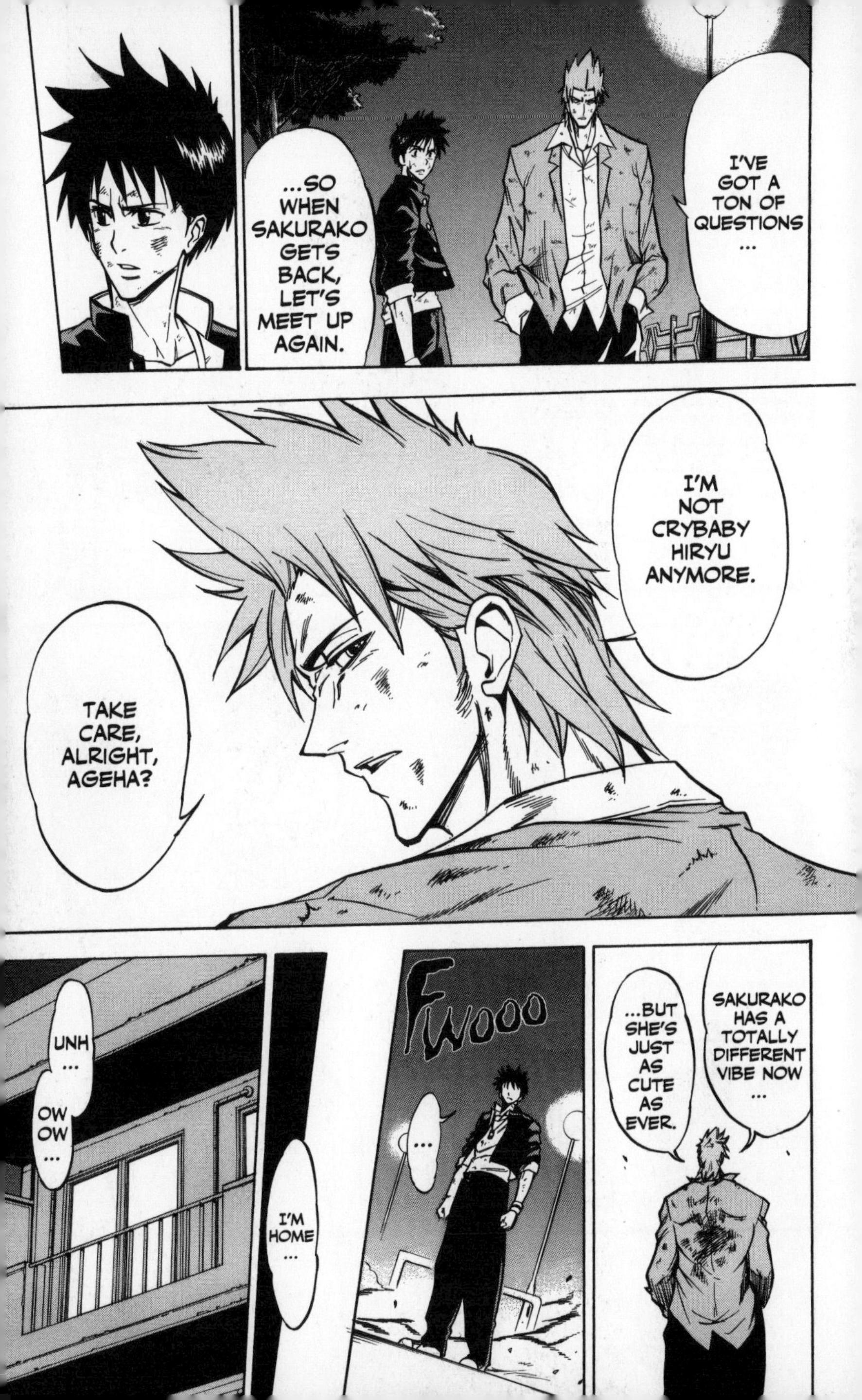
I'VE GOT A TON OF QUESTIONS ...
...SO WHEN SAKURAKO GETS BACK, LET'S MEET UP AGAIN.
I'M NOT CRYBABY HIRYU ANYMORE.
TAKE CARE, ALRIGHT, AGEHA?
SAKURAKO HAS A TOTALLY DIFFERENT VIBE NOW ...
...BUT SHE'S JUST AS CUTE AS EVER.
FWOOO
...
I'M HOME ...
UNH ...
OW OW ...

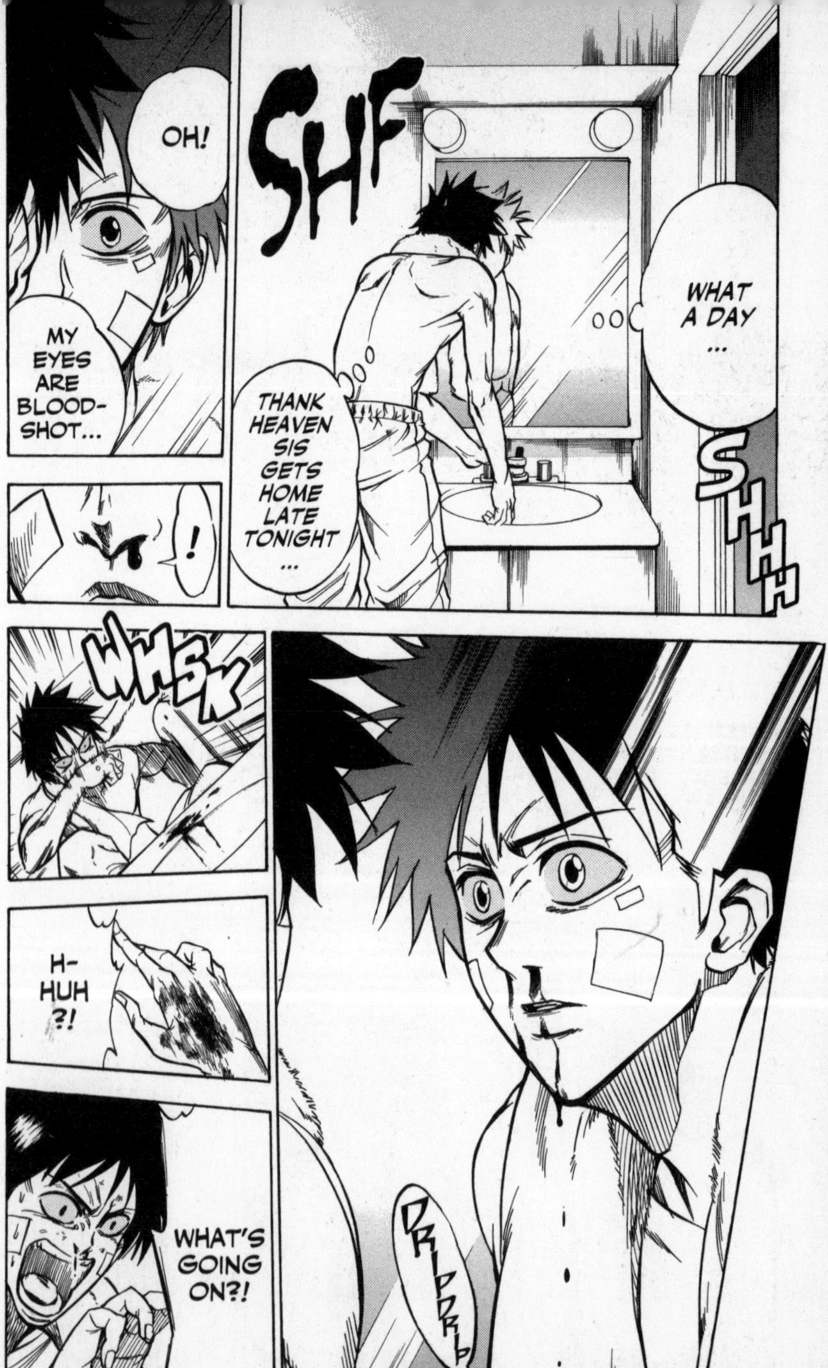
SHF
WHAT A DAY ...
THANK HEAVEN SIS GETS HOME LATE TONIGHT ...
SHHHH
OH!
MY EYES ARE BLOOD-SHOT...
!
DRIPDRIP
WHSK
H-HUH?!
WHAT'S GOING ON?!

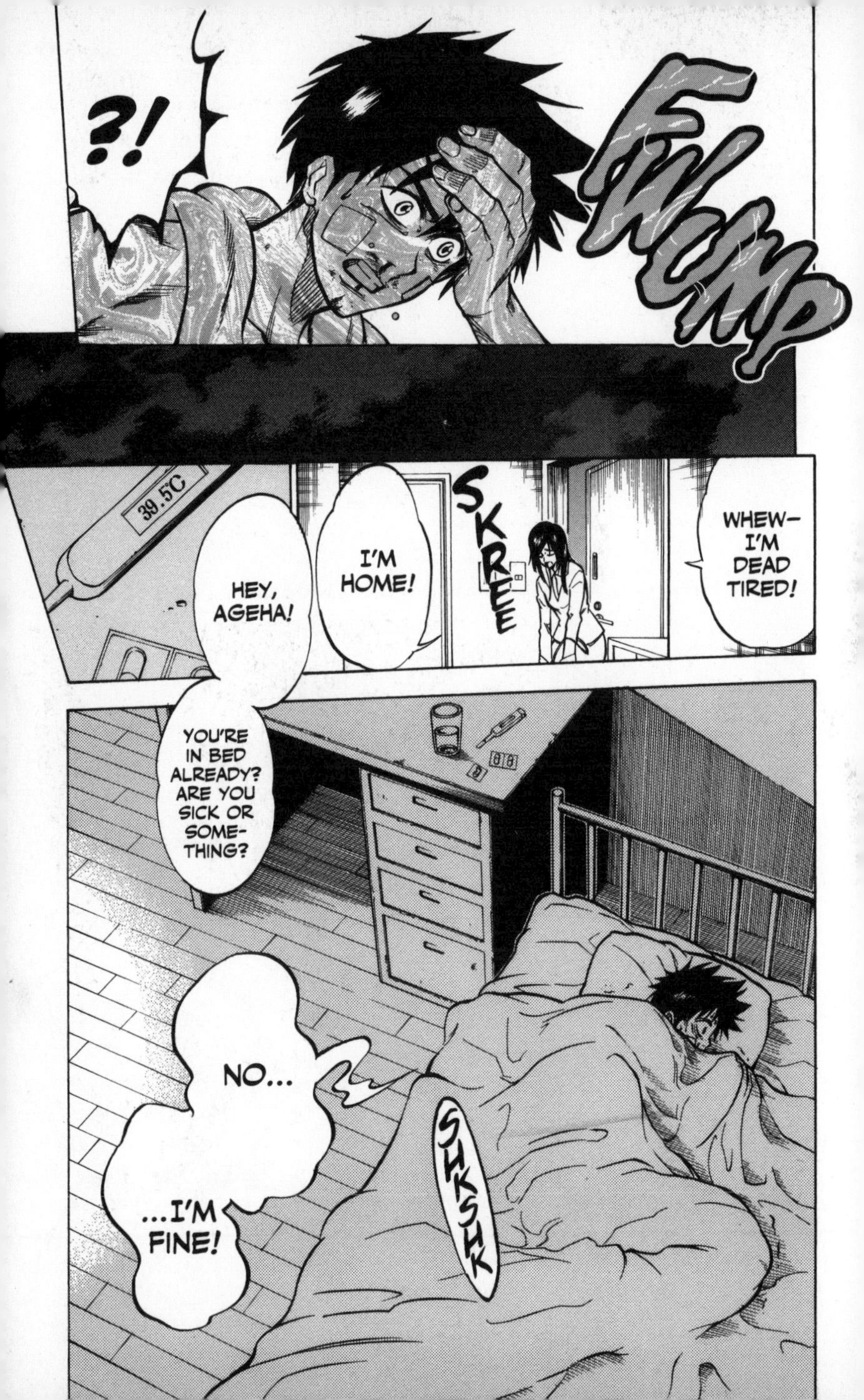
FWUMP!
?!
WHEW— I'M DEAD TIRED!
SKREE
I'M HOME!
39.5℃
HEY, AGEHA!
YOU'RE IN BED ALREADY? ARE YOU SICK OR SOME-THING?
NO...
...I'M FINE!
SHKSHK

AGEHA YOSHINA

AGEHA CAN'T TURN HIS BACK ON ANYONE IN TROUBLE. HE MAKES HIS DECISIONS BASED ON HOW HE FEELS. SINCE HE DOESN'T THINK TOO HARD ABOUT THINGS, HE DOESN'T GET FLUSTERED IN AN EMERGENCY.

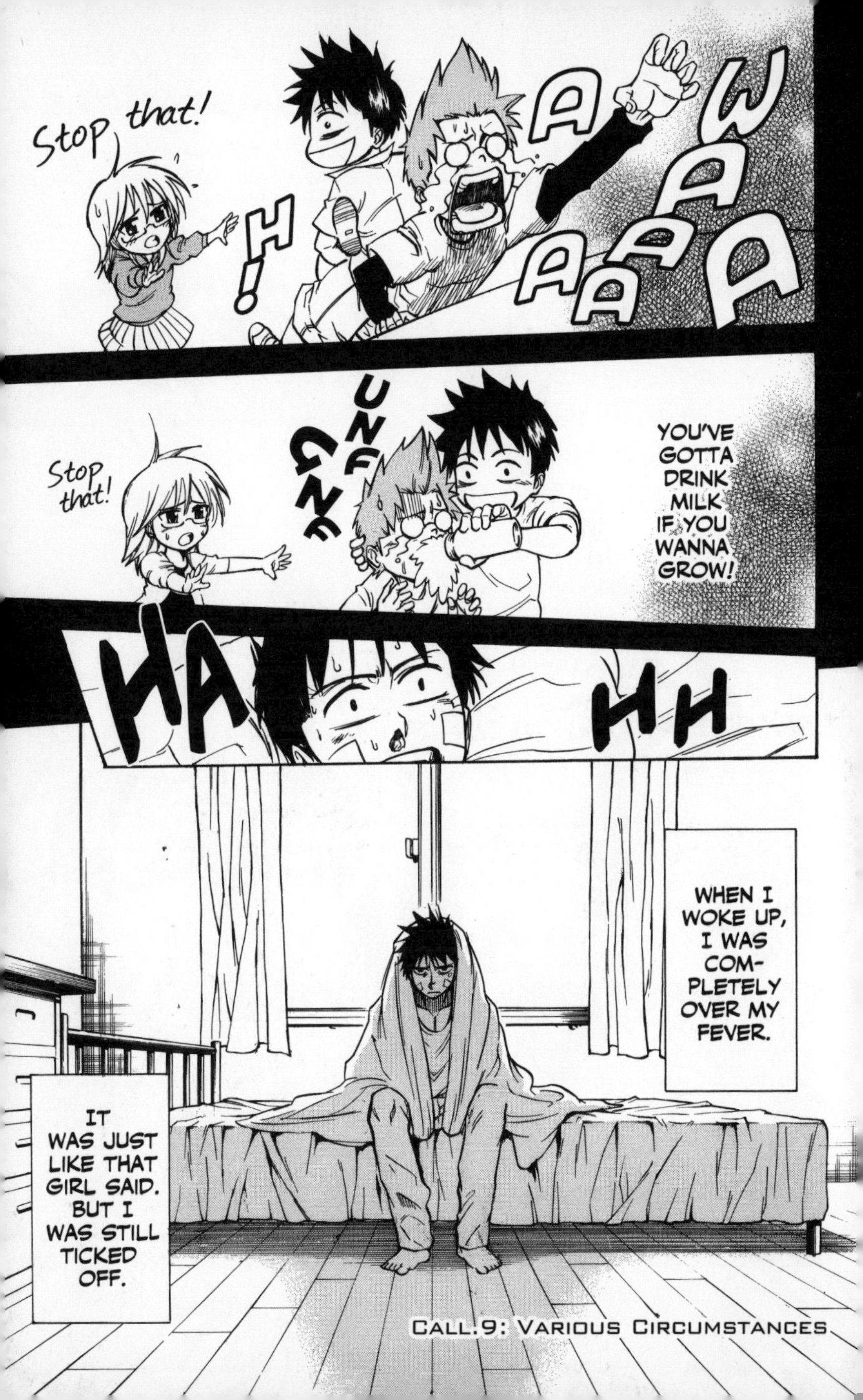
WAAAAAAH!
Stop that!
YOU'VE GOTTA DRINK MILK IF YOU WANNA GROW!
UNF GNF
Stop that!
HAHH
WHEN I WOKE UP, I WAS COM-PLETELY OVER MY FEVER.
IT WAS JUST LIKE THAT GIRL SAID. BUT I WAS STILL TICKED OFF.
CALL.9: VARIOUS CIRCUMSTANCES

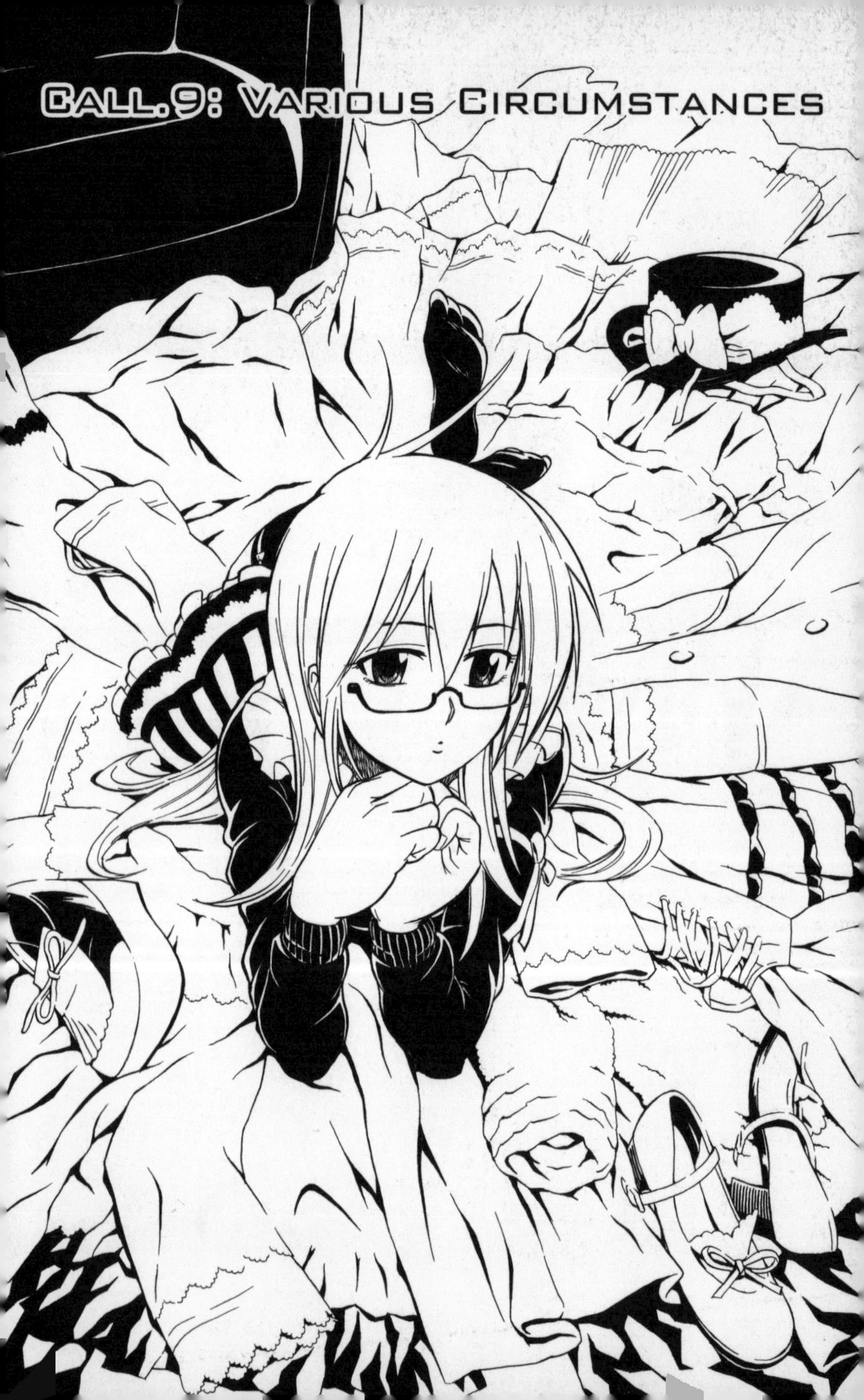
CALL.9: VARIOUS CIRCUMSTANCES

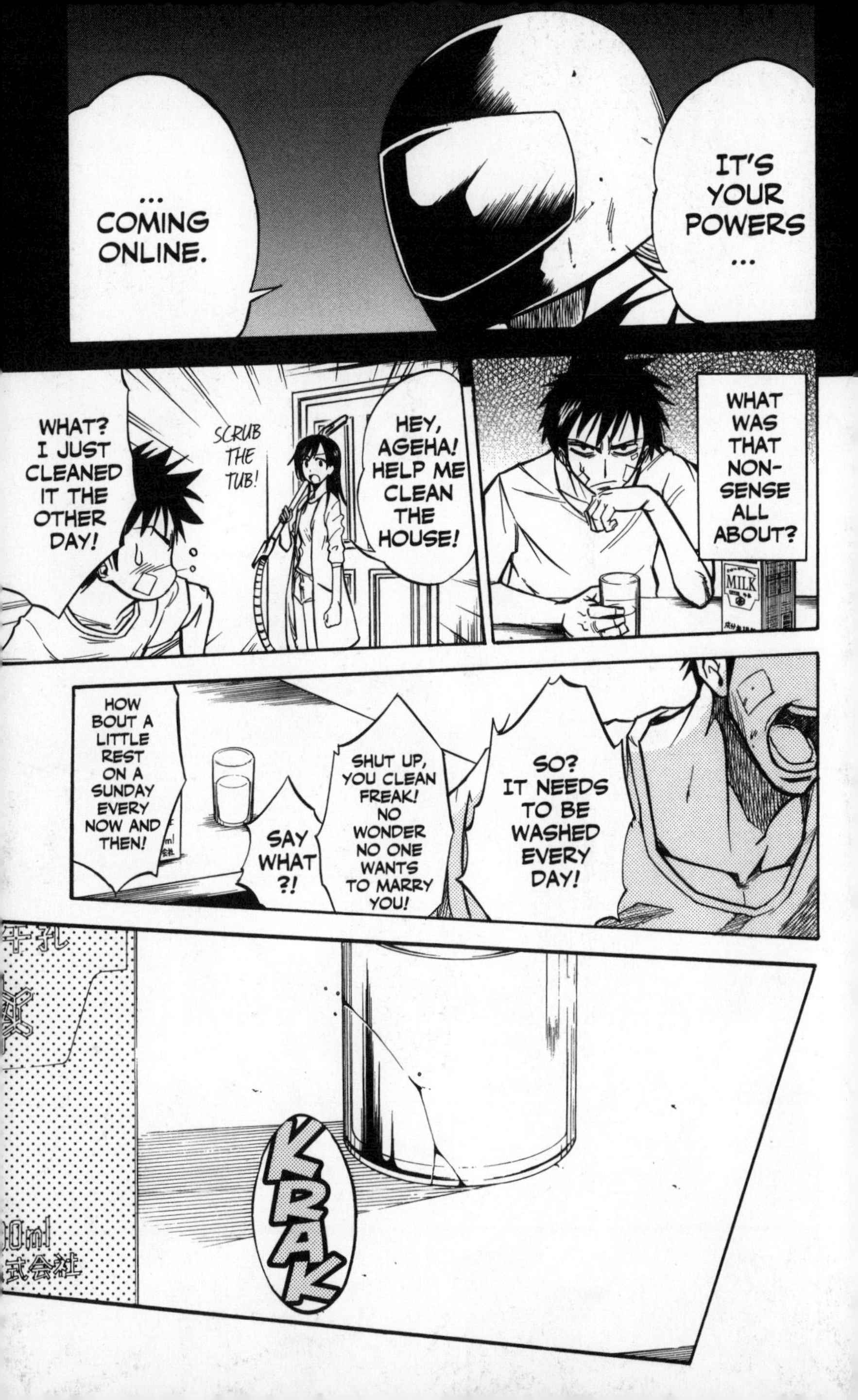
IT'S YOUR POWERS ...
... COMING ONLINE.
WHAT WAS THAT NONSENSE ALL ABOUT?
MILK
HEY, AGEHA! HELP ME CLEAN THE HOUSE!
SCRUB THE TUB!
WHAT? I JUST CLEANED IT THE OTHER DAY!
SO? IT NEEDS TO BE WASHED EVERY DAY!
SHUT UP, YOU CLEAN FREAK! NO WONDER NO ONE WANTS TO MARRY YOU!
SAY WHAT?!
HOW BOUT A LITTLE REST ON A SUNDAY EVERY NOW AND THEN!
KRAK

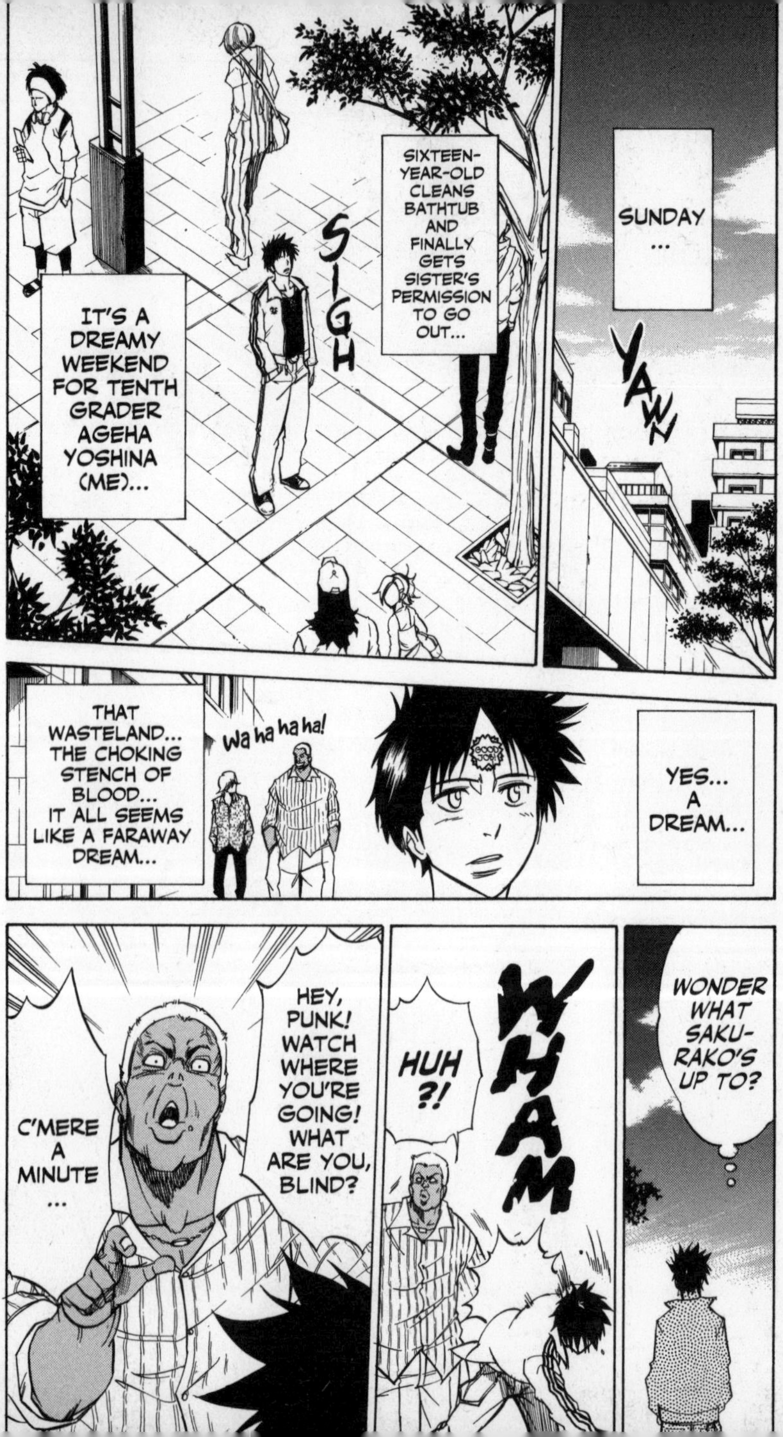
SUNDAY...
YAWN
SIXTEEN-YEAR-OLD CLEANS BATHTUB AND FINALLY GETS SISTER'S PERMISSION TO GO OUT...
SIGH
IT'S A DREAMY WEEKEND FOR TENTH GRADER AGEHA YOSHINA (ME)...
YES... A DREAM...
GOOD JOB!
Wa ha ha ha!
THAT WASTELAND... THE CHOKING STENCH OF BLOOD... IT ALL SEEMS LIKE A FARAWAY DREAM...
WONDER WHAT SAKU-RAKO'S UP TO?
WHAM
HUH ?!
HEY, PUNK! WATCH WHERE YOU'RE GOING! WHAT ARE YOU, BLIND?
C'MERE A MINUTE ...

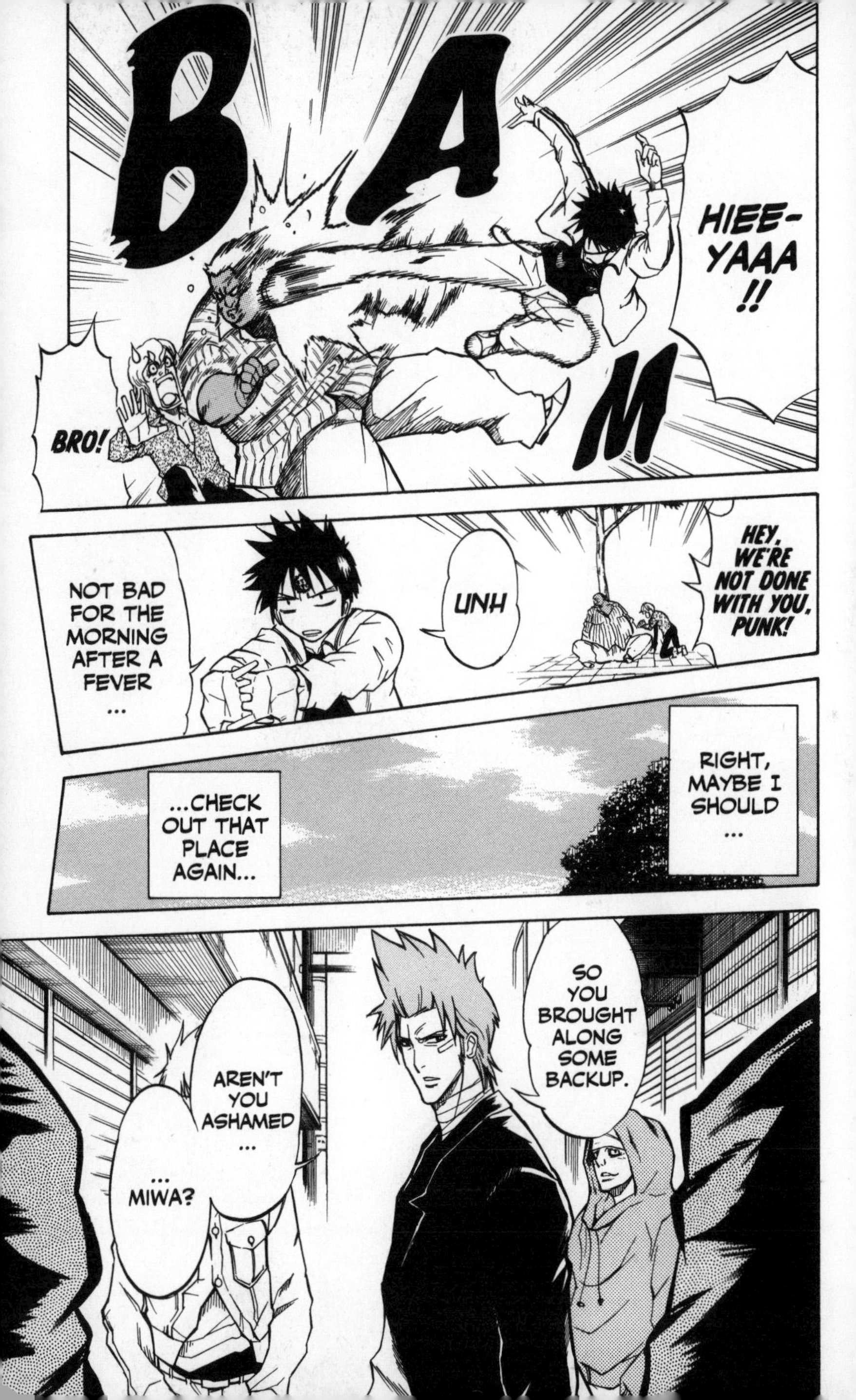
HIEE-YAAA!!
BAM
BRO!
HEY, WE'RE NOT DONE WITH YOU, PUNK!
UNH
NOT BAD FOR THE MORNING AFTER A FEVER...
RIGHT, MAYBE I SHOULD...
...CHECK OUT THAT PLACE AGAIN...
SO YOU BROUGHT ALONG SOME BACKUP.
AREN'T YOU ASHAMED...
...MIWA?

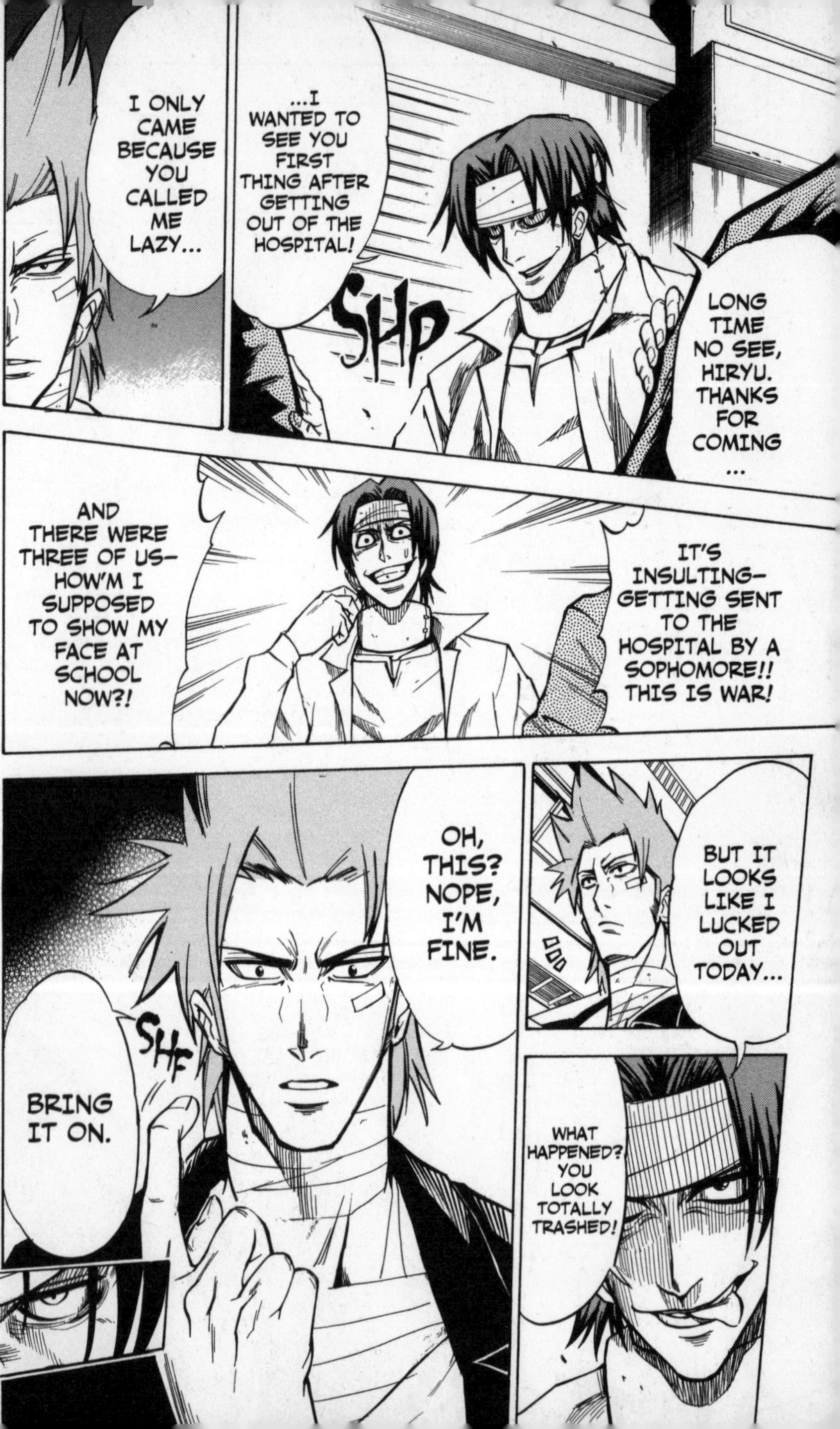
LONG TIME NO SEE, HIRYU. THANKS FOR COMING...
...I WANTED TO SEE YOU FIRST THING AFTER GETTING OUT OF THE HOSPITAL!
SHP
I ONLY CAME BECAUSE YOU CALLED ME LAZY...
IT'S INSULTING—GETTING SENT TO THE HOSPITAL BY A SOPHOMORE!! THIS IS WAR!
AND THERE WERE THREE OF US—HOW'M I SUPPOSED TO SHOW MY FACE AT SCHOOL NOW?!
BUT IT LOOKS LIKE I LUCKED OUT TODAY...
WHAT HAPPENED? YOU LOOK TOTALLY TRASHED!
OH, THIS? NOPE, I'M FINE.
SHF
BRING IT ON.

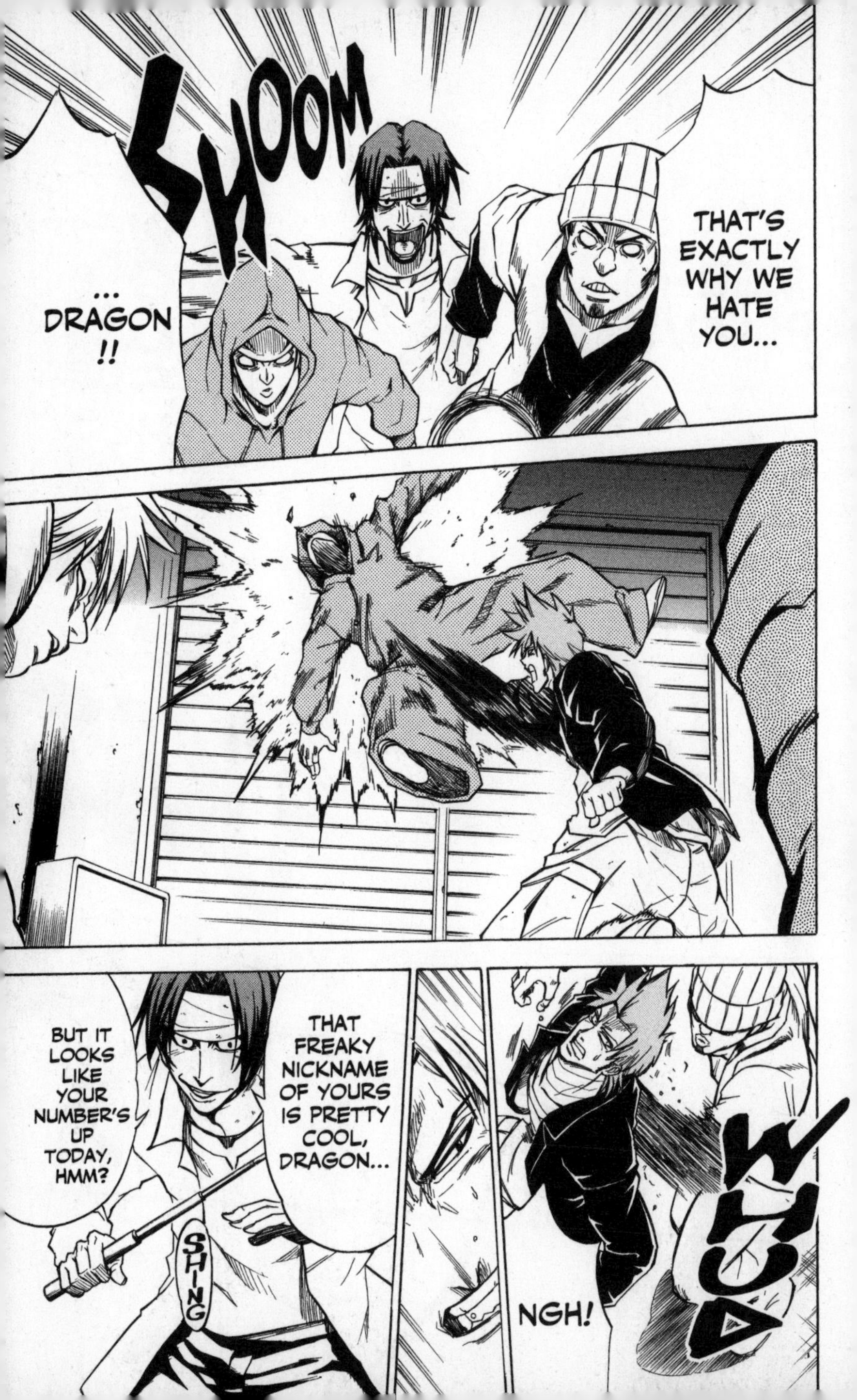
THAT'S EXACTLY WHY WE HATE YOU...
SHOOM
... DRAGON !!
NGH!
WHUD
THAT FREAKY NICKNAME OF YOURS IS PRETTY COOL, DRAGON...
BUT IT LOOKS LIKE YOUR NUMBER'S UP TODAY, HMM?
SHING

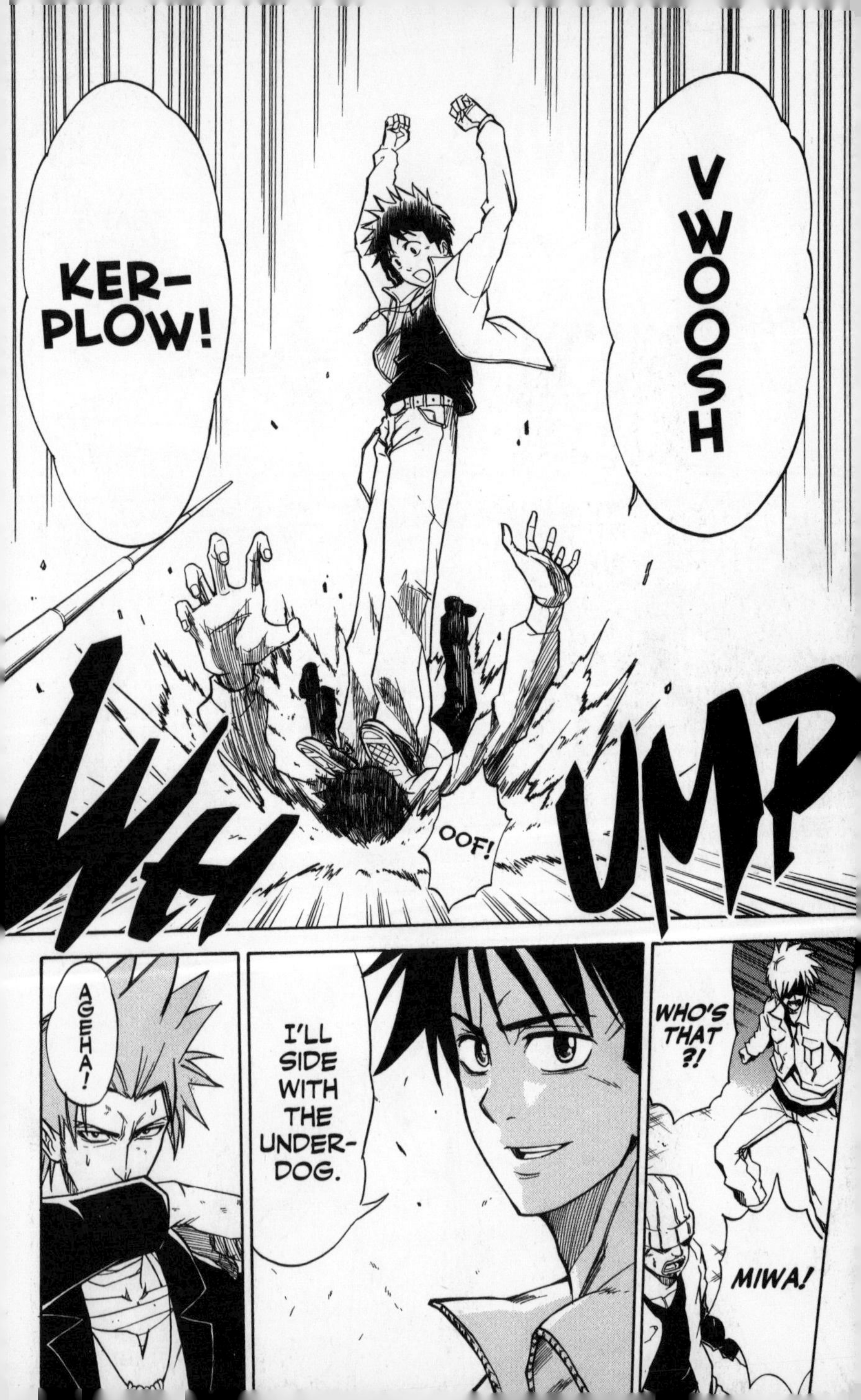
VWOOSH
KER-PLOW!
WHUMP
OOF!
WHO'S THAT?!
MIWA!
I'LL SIDE WITH THE UNDER-DOG.
AGEHA!

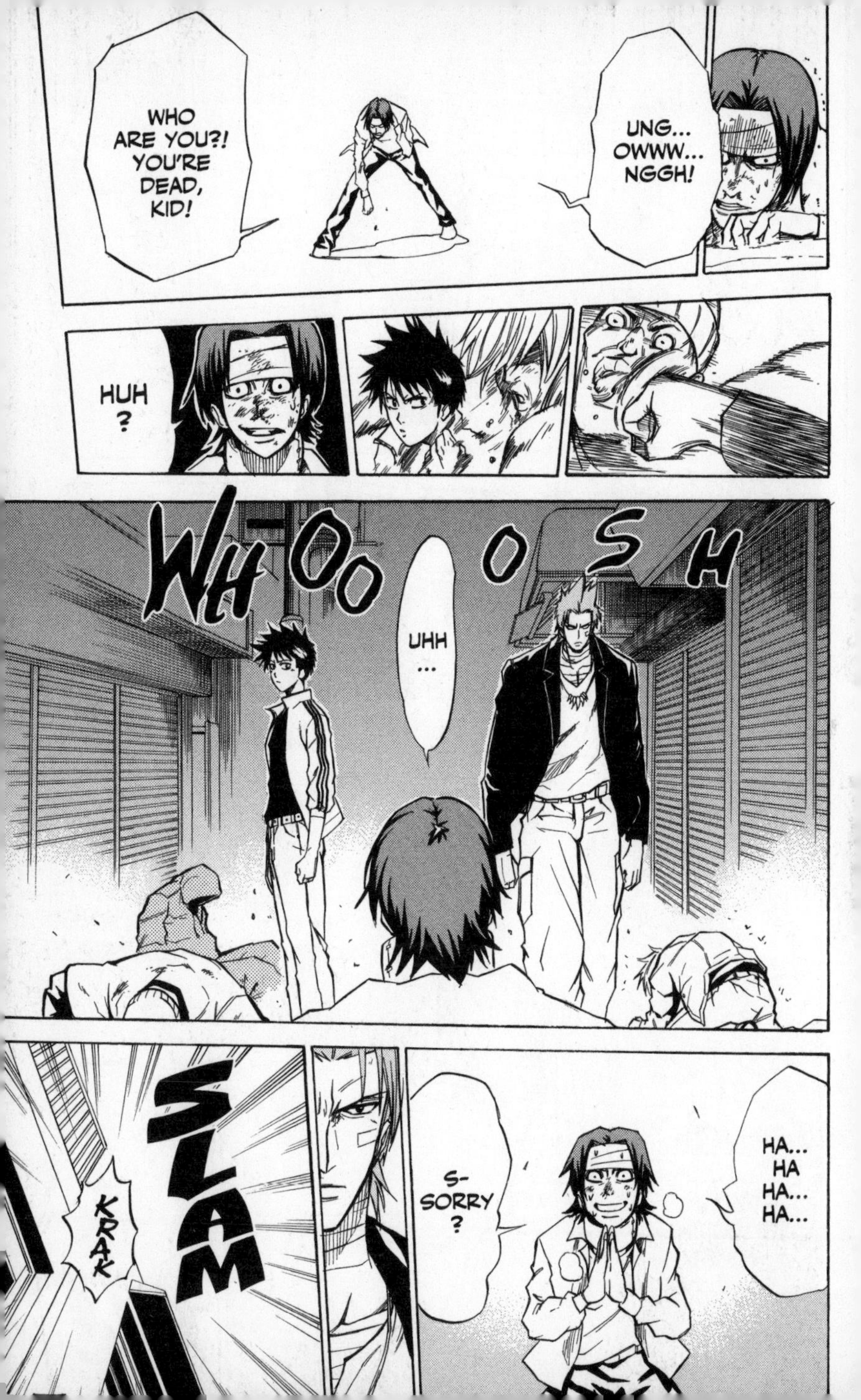
UNG... OWWW... NGGH!
WHO ARE YOU?! YOU'RE DEAD, KID!
HUH ?
WHOOOSH
UHH ...
HA... HA HA... HA...
S-SORRY ?
SLAM
KRAK

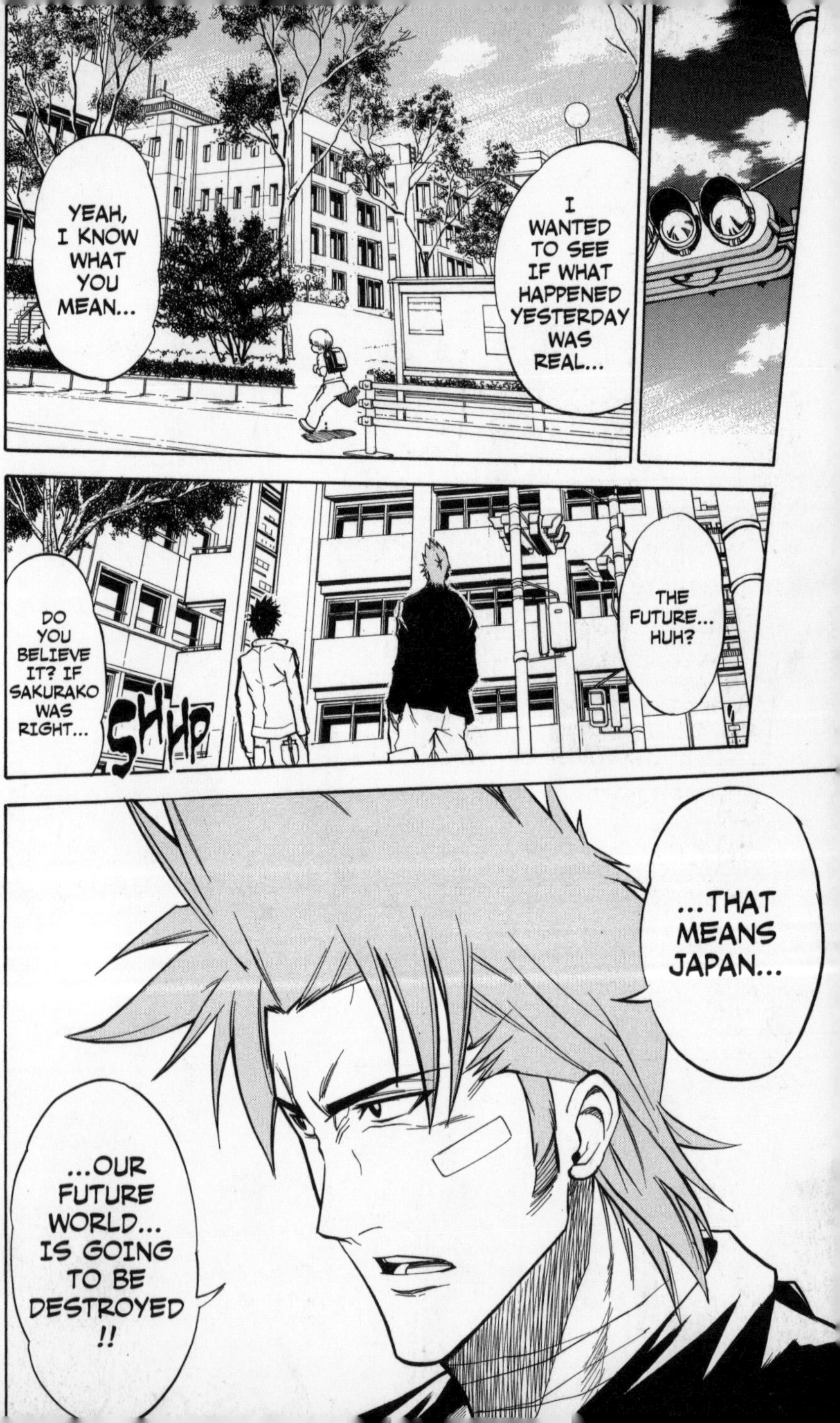
I WANTED TO SEE IF WHAT HAPPENED YESTERDAY WAS REAL...
YEAH, I KNOW WHAT YOU MEAN...
THE FUTURE... HUH?
SHHP
DO YOU BELIEVE IT? IF SAKURAKO WAS RIGHT...
...THAT MEANS JAPAN...
...OUR FUTURE WORLD... IS GOING TO BE DESTROYED!!

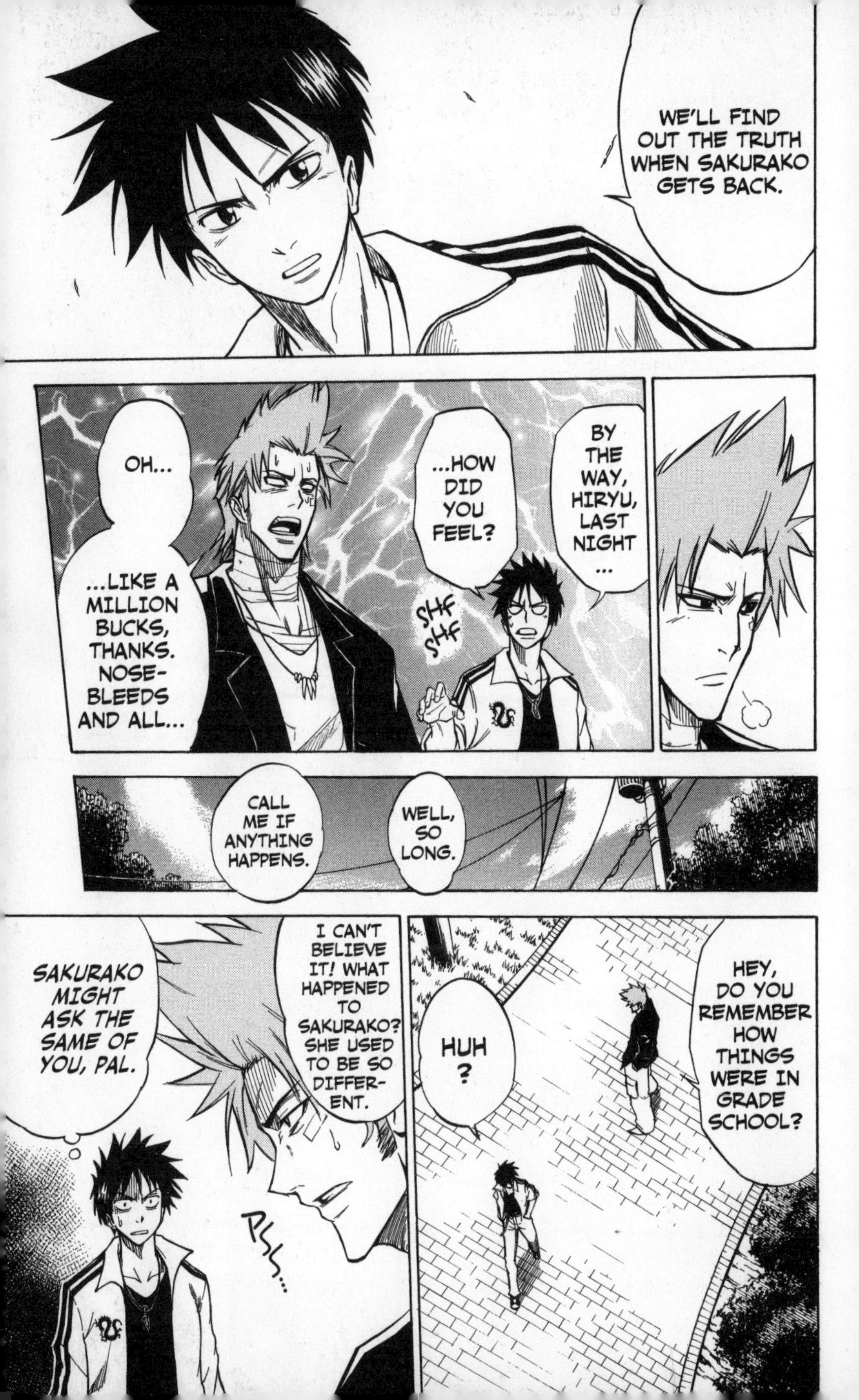
WE'LL FIND OUT THE TRUTH WHEN SAKURAKO GETS BACK.
BY THE WAY, HIRYU, LAST NIGHT ...
...HOW DID YOU FEEL?
SHF SHF
OH...
...LIKE A MILLION BUCKS, THANKS. NOSE-BLEEDS AND ALL...
WELL, SO LONG.
CALL ME IF ANYTHING HAPPENS.
HEY, DO YOU REMEMBER HOW THINGS WERE IN GRADE SCHOOL?
HUH?
I CAN'T BELIEVE IT! WHAT HAPPENED TO SAKURAKO? SHE USED TO BE SO DIFFER-ENT.
SAKURAKO MIGHT ASK THE SAME OF YOU, PAL.

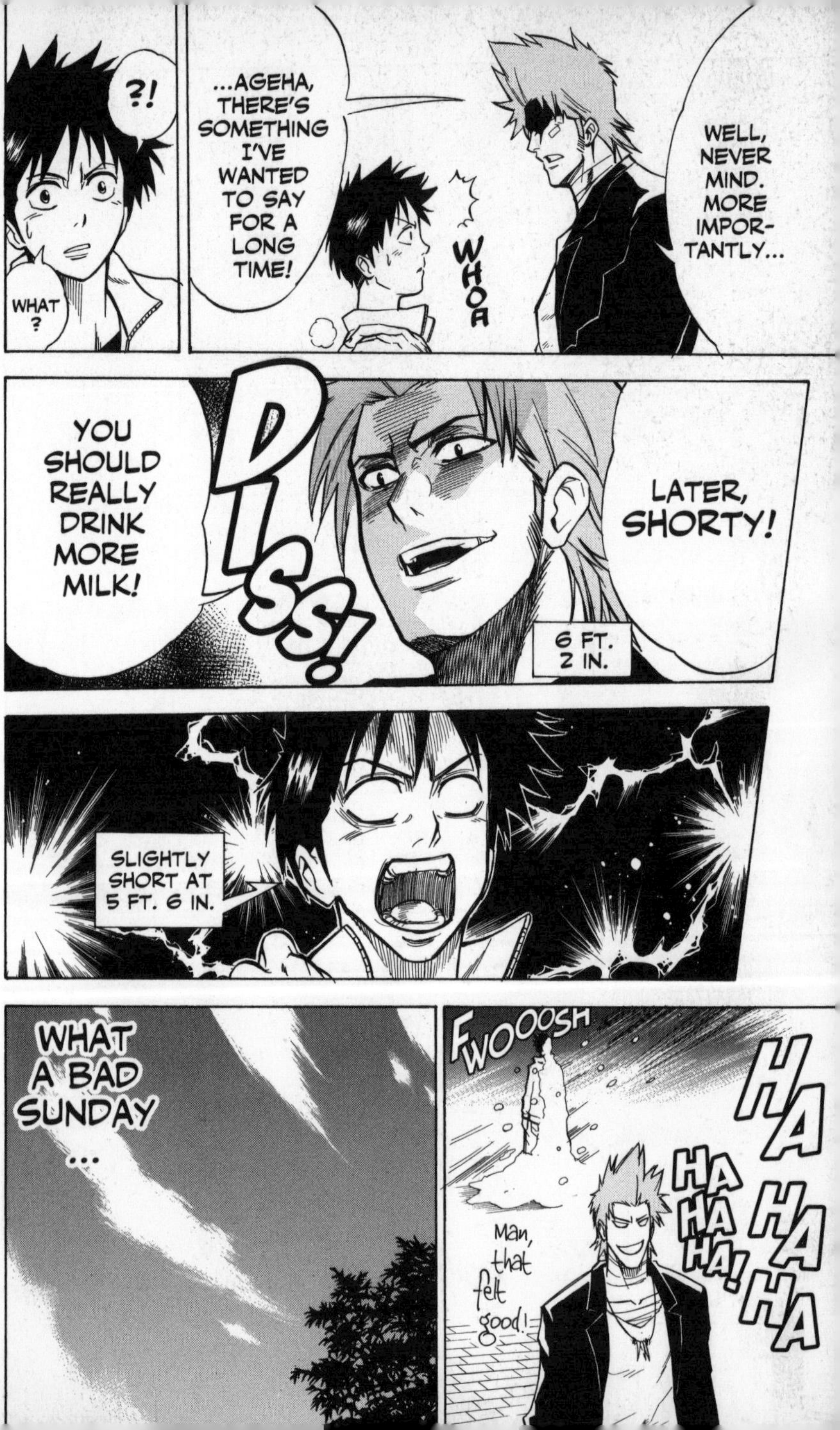
WELL, NEVER MIND. MORE IMPORTANTLY...
...AGEHA, THERE'S SOMETHING I'VE WANTED TO SAY FOR A LONG TIME!
WHOA
?!
WHAT?
LATER, SHORTY!
6 FT. 2 IN.
DISS!
YOU SHOULD REALLY DRINK MORE MILK!
SLIGHTLY SHORT AT 5 FT. 6 IN.
HA HA HA HA HA HA HA HA!
FWOOOSH
Man, that felt good!
WHAT A BAD SUNDAY...

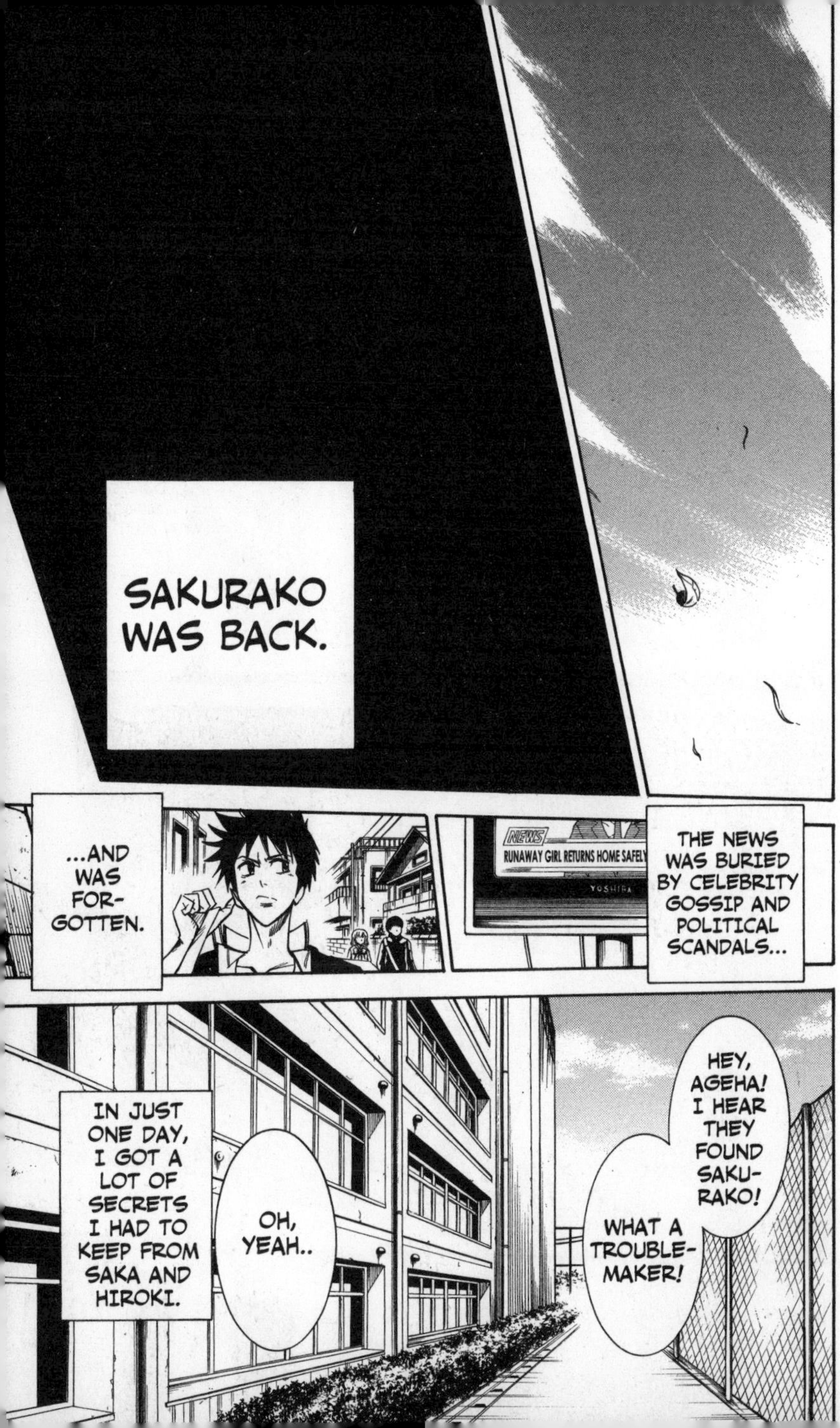
SAKURAKO WAS BACK.
THE NEWS WAS BURIED BY CELEBRITY GOSSIP AND POLITICAL SCANDALS...
NEWS
RUNAWAY GIRL RETURNS HOME SAFELY
...AND WAS FOR-GOTTEN.
HEY, AGEHA! I HEAR THEY FOUND SAKU-RAKO!
WHAT A TROUBLE-MAKER!
OH, YEAH..
IN JUST ONE DAY, I GOT A LOT OF SECRETS I HAD TO KEEP FROM SAKA AND HIROKI.

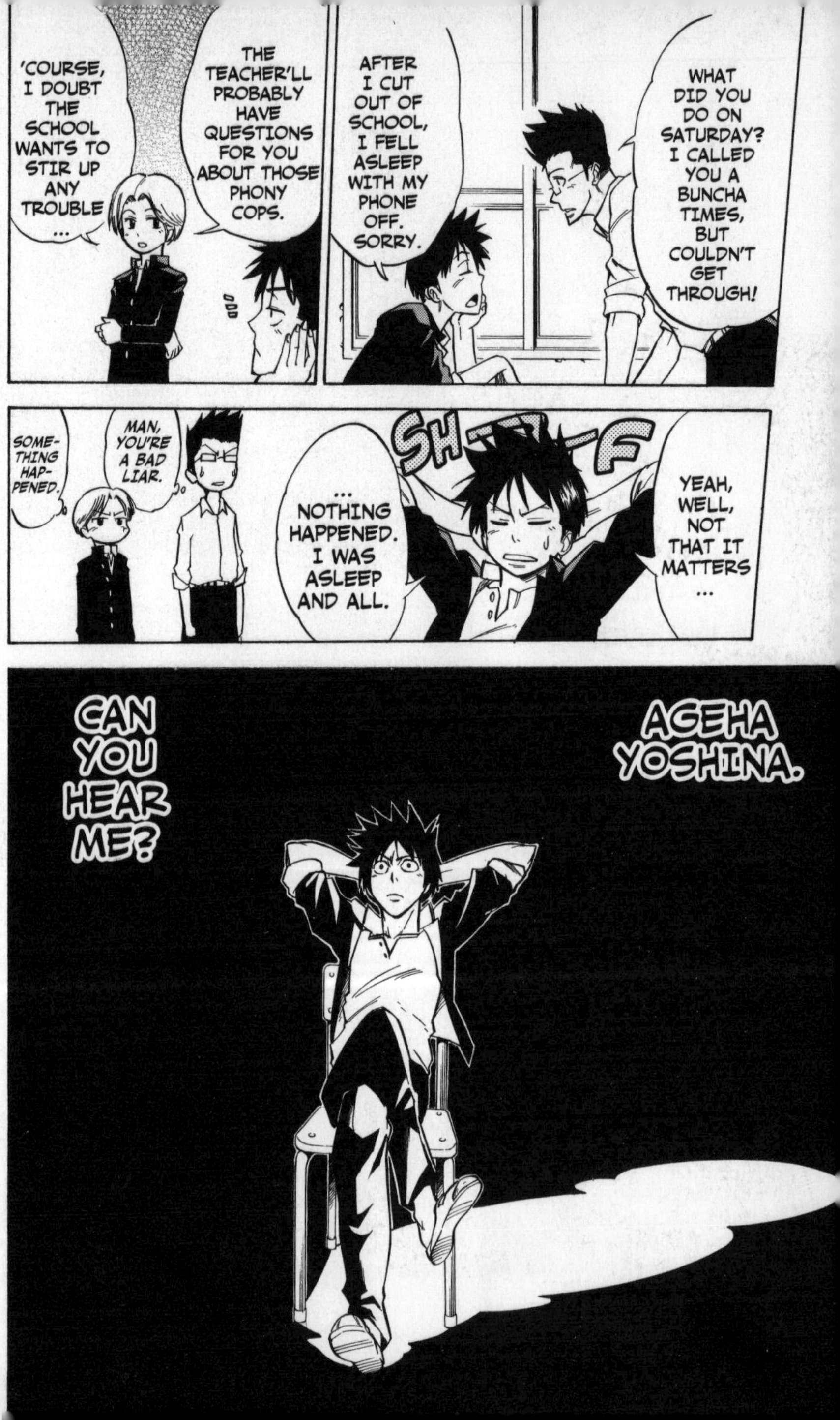
WHAT DID YOU DO ON SATURDAY? I CALLED YOU A BUNCHA TIMES, BUT COULDN'T GET THROUGH!
AFTER I CUT OUT OF SCHOOL, I FELL ASLEEP WITH MY PHONE OFF. SORRY.
THE TEACHER'LL PROBABLY HAVE QUESTIONS FOR YOU ABOUT THOSE PHONY COPS.
'COURSE, I DOUBT THE SCHOOL WANTS TO STIR UP ANY TROUBLE ...
YEAH, WELL, NOT THAT IT MATTERS ...
... NOTHING HAPPENED. I WAS ASLEEP AND ALL.
MAN, YOU'RE A BAD LIAR.
SOME-THING HAP-PENED.
AGEHA YOSHINA.
CAN YOU HEAR ME?

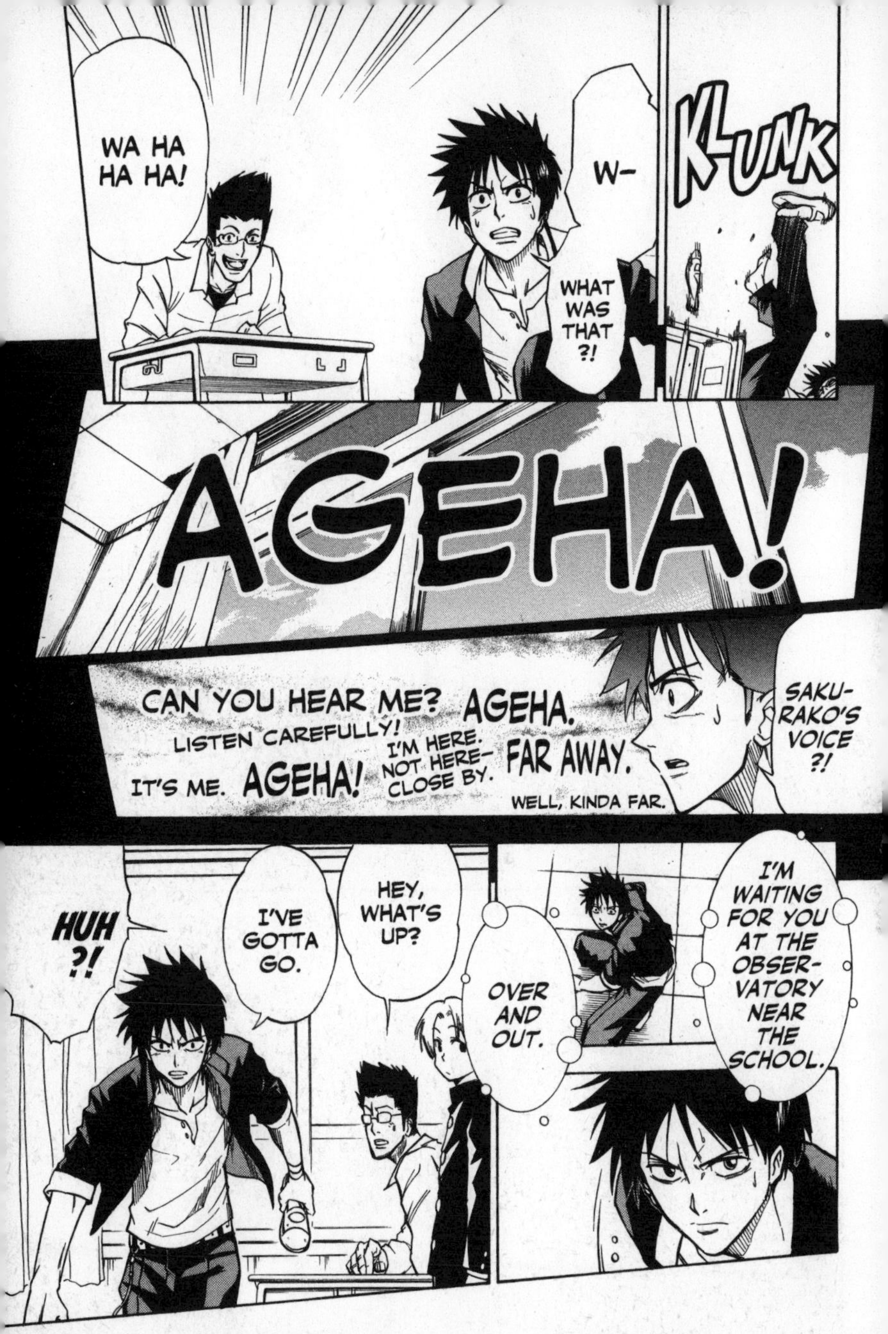
KLUNK
W-
WHAT WAS THAT ?!
WA HA HA HA!
AGEHA!
SAKU-RAKO'S VOICE ?!
CAN YOU HEAR ME? AGEHA.
LISTEN CAREFULLY!
IT'S ME. AGEHA!
I'M HERE. NOT HERE- CLOSE BY.
FAR AWAY.
WELL, KINDA FAR.
I'M WAITING FOR YOU AT THE OBSER-VATORY NEAR THE SCHOOL.
OVER AND OUT.
HEY, WHAT'S UP?
I'VE GOTTA GO.
HUH ?!

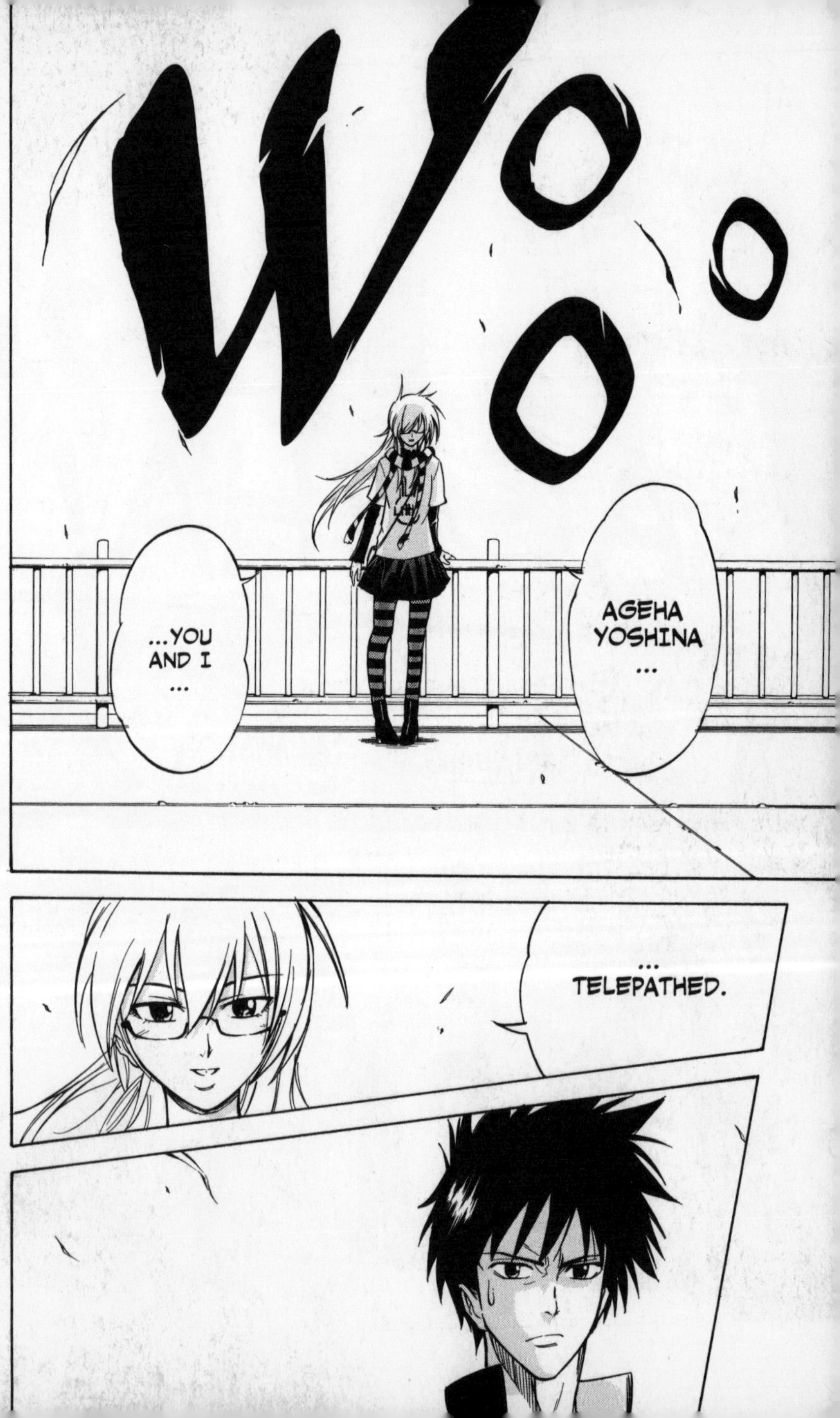
Wooo
AGEHA YOSHINA ...
...YOU AND I ...
... TELEPATHED.

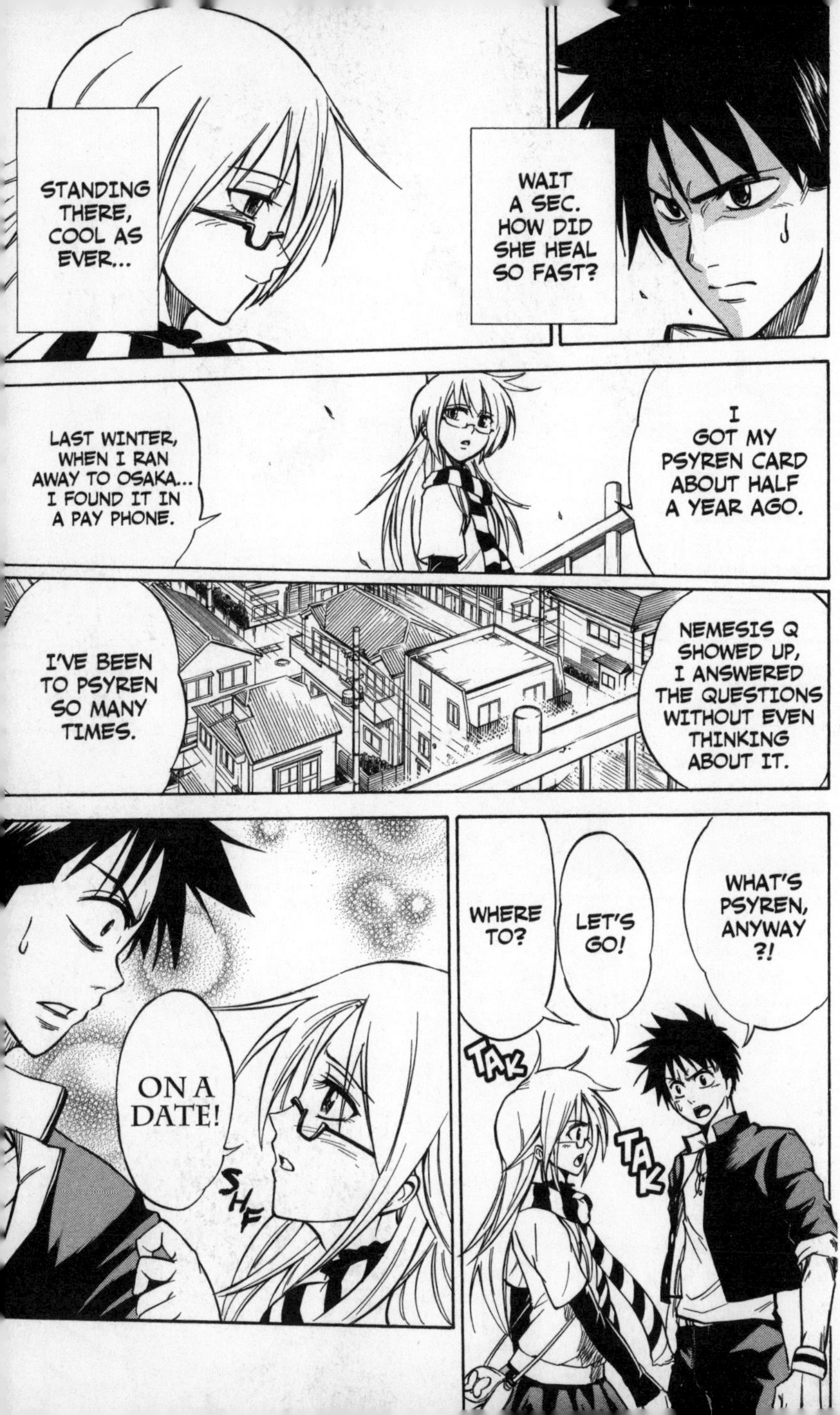
WAIT A SEC. HOW DID SHE HEAL SO FAST?
STANDING THERE, COOL AS EVER...
I GOT MY PSYREN CARD ABOUT HALF A YEAR AGO.
LAST WINTER, WHEN I RAN AWAY TO OSAKA... I FOUND IT IN A PAY PHONE.
NEMESIS Q SHOWED UP, I ANSWERED THE QUESTIONS WITHOUT EVEN THINKING ABOUT IT.
I'VE BEEN TO PSYREN SO MANY TIMES.
WHAT'S PSYREN, ANYWAY?!
LET'S GO!
WHERE TO?
TAK
TAK
ON A DATE!
SHF

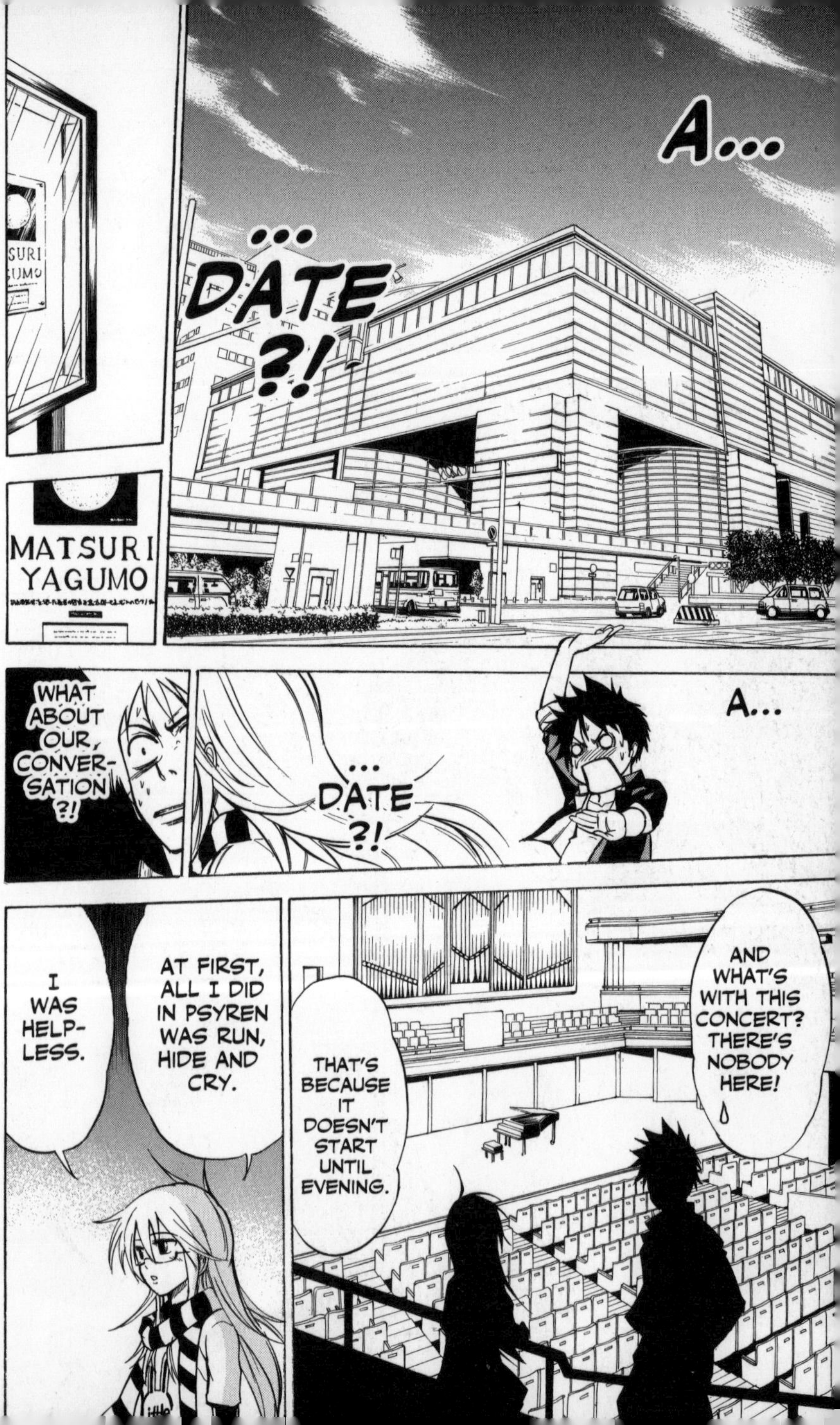
A...
...DATE?!
MATSURI YAGUMO
A...
...DATE?!
WHAT ABOUT OUR CONVERSATION?!
AND WHAT'S WITH THIS CONCERT? THERE'S NOBODY HERE!
THAT'S BECAUSE IT DOESN'T START UNTIL EVENING.
AT FIRST, ALL I DID IN PSYREN WAS RUN, HIDE AND CRY.
I WAS HELPLESS.

READ THIS WAY

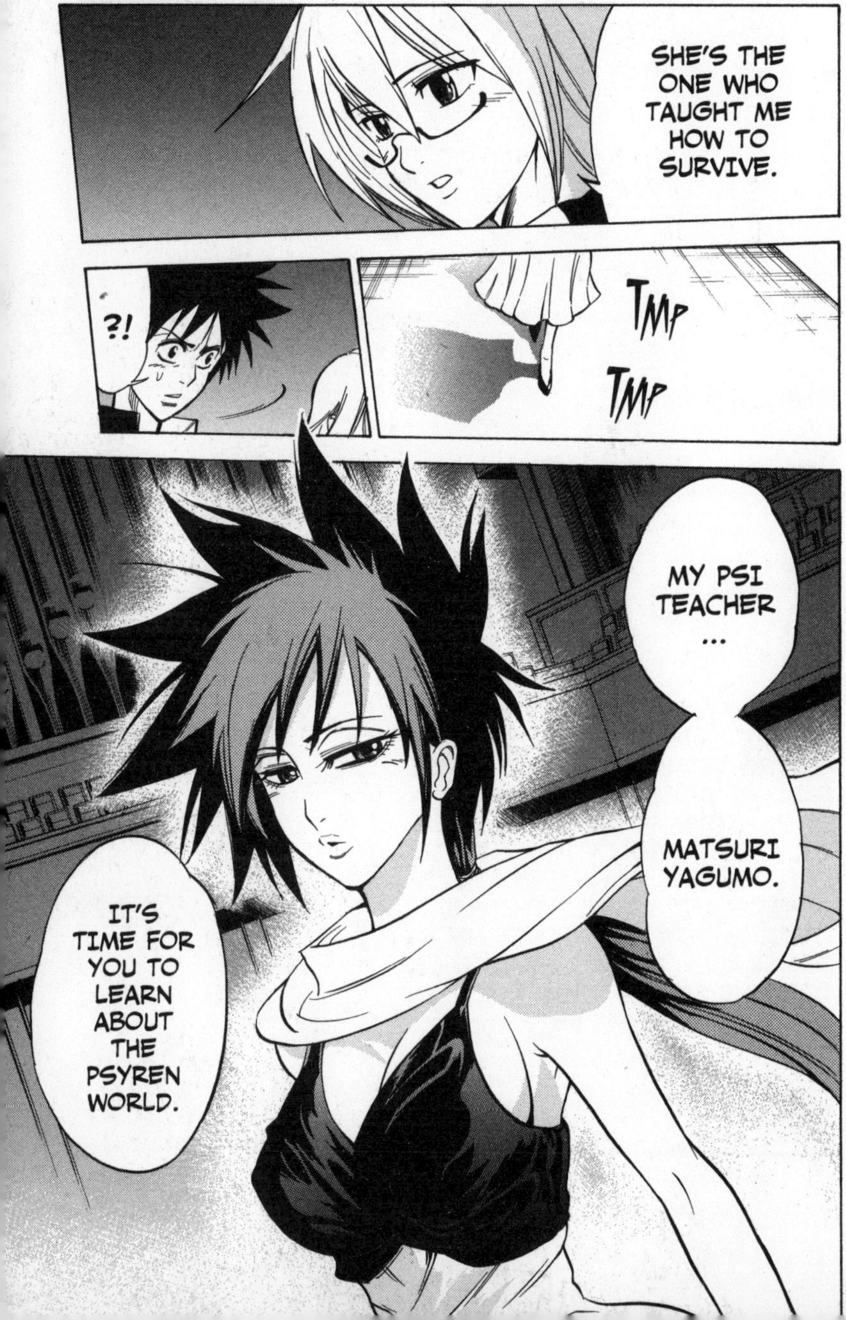
SHE'S THE ONE WHO TAUGHT ME HOW TO SURVIVE.
TMP
TMP
?!
MY PSI TEACHER ...
MATSURI YAGUMO.
IT'S TIME FOR YOU TO LEARN ABOUT THE PSYREN WORLD.

HIRYU ASAGA

STRONG AND TOUGH, HIRYU'S FATHER NAMED HIM HIRYU, OR FLYING DRAGON, IN THE HOPES THAT HE WOULD FLY HIGH IN LIFE. HIRYU NO LONGER HATES MILK. BECAUSE OF HIS GENTLE NATURE, HE'S CONSIDERATE OF OTHERS AND CALMLY THINKS THINGS THROUGH. SINCE HE GENERALLY THINKS BEFORE HE ACTS, HE NEEDS TIME TO RECOVER WHEN UPSET.

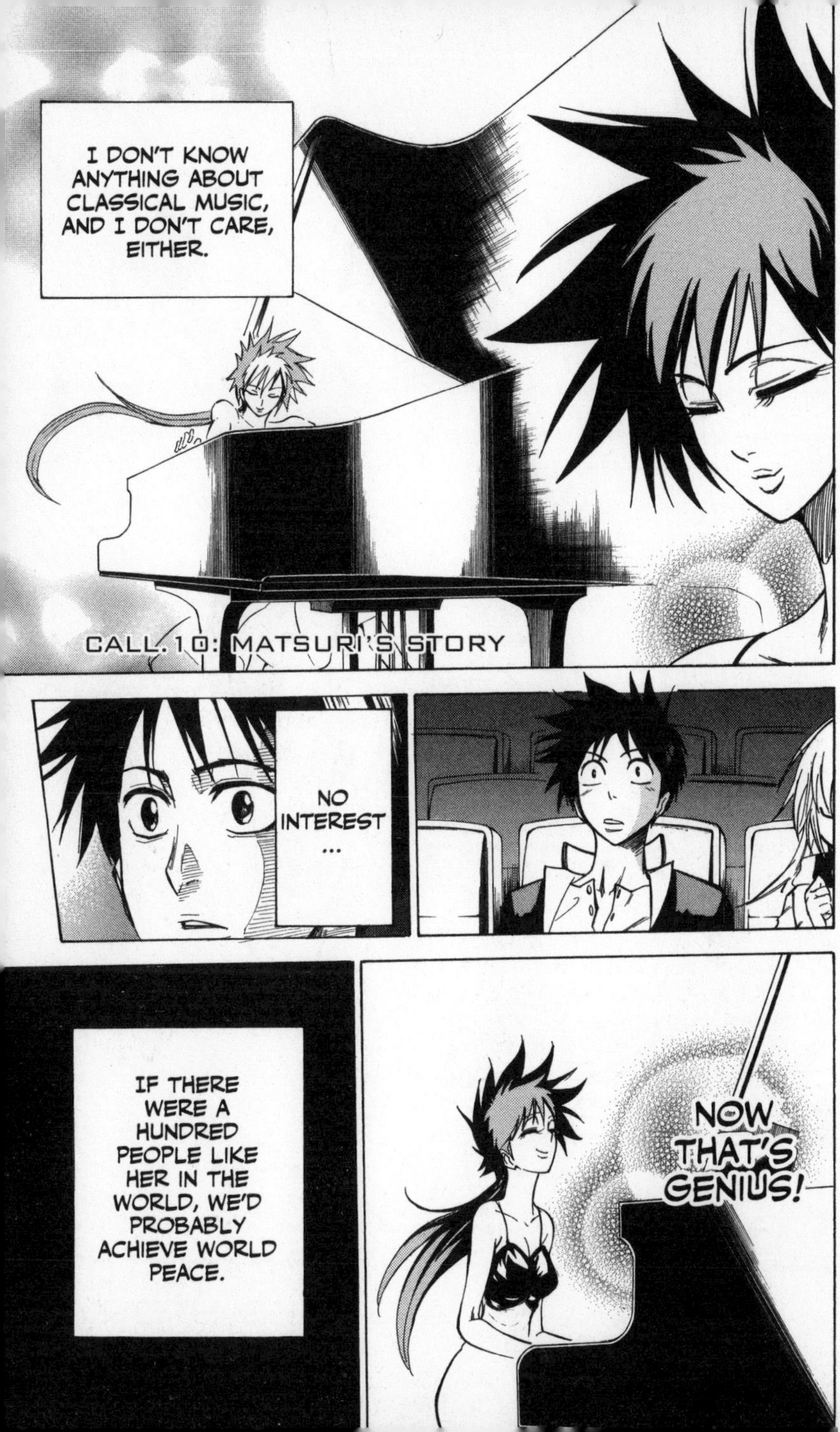
I DON'T KNOW ANYTHING ABOUT CLASSICAL MUSIC, AND I DON'T CARE, EITHER.
CALL. 10: MATSURI'S STORY
NO INTEREST ...
NOW THAT'S GENIUS!
IF THERE WERE A HUNDRED PEOPLE LIKE HER IN THE WORLD, WE'D PROBABLY ACHIEVE WORLD PEACE.

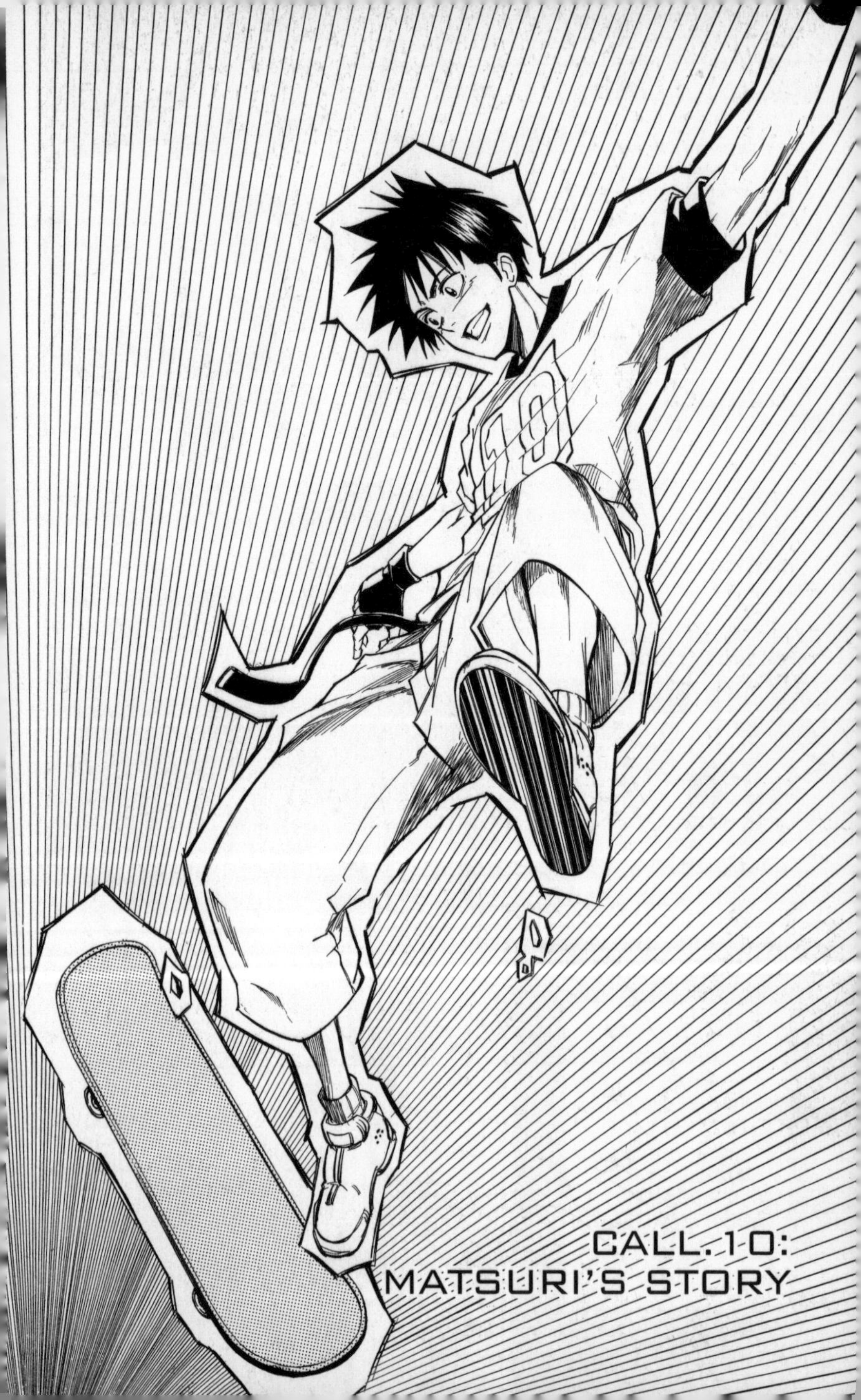
CALL.10:
MATSURI'S STORY

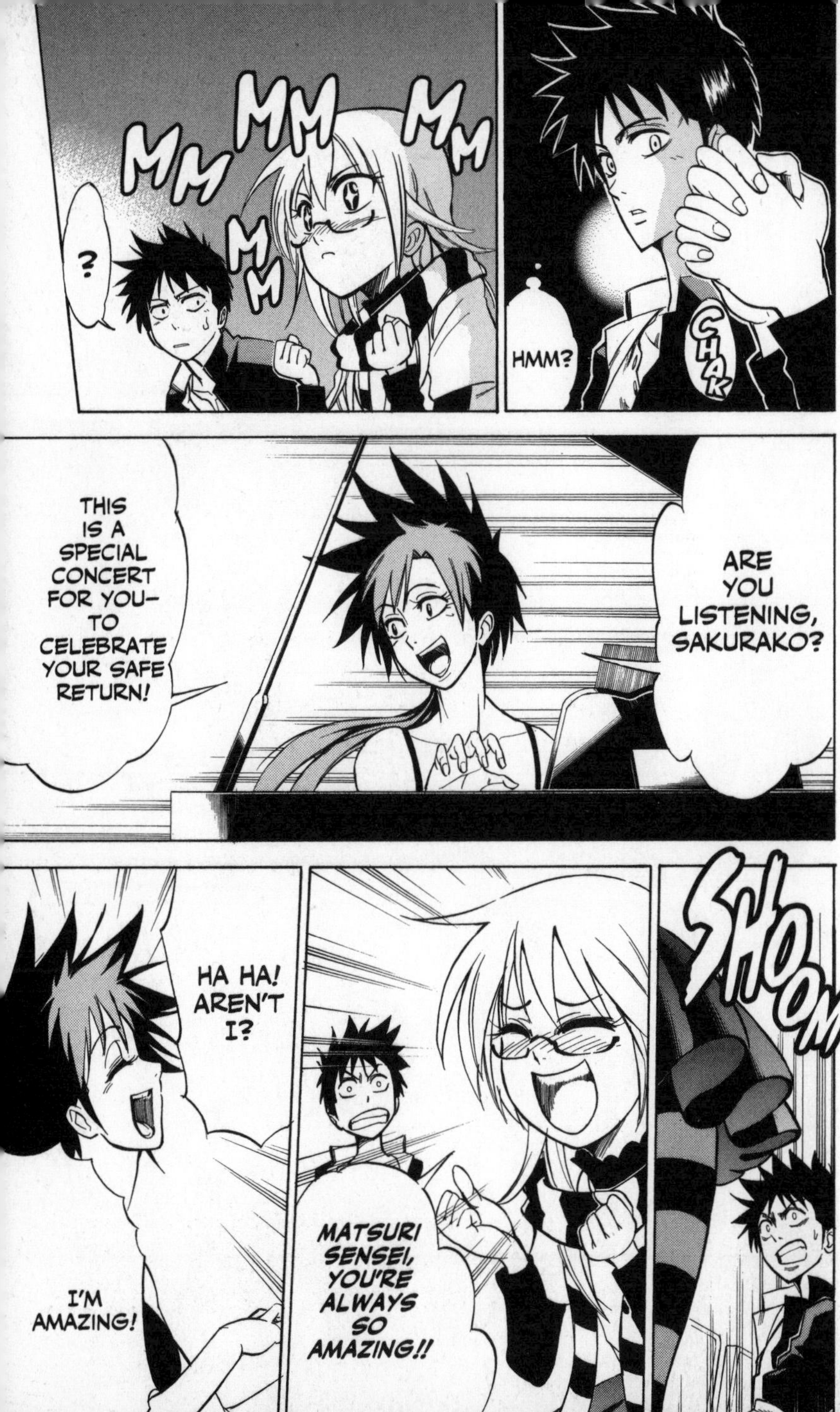
CHAK
HMM?
MM MM MM MM MM
?
ARE YOU LISTENING, SAKURAKO?
THIS IS A SPECIAL CONCERT FOR YOU—TO CELEBRATE YOUR SAFE RETURN!
SHOOM
MATSURI SENSEI, YOU'RE ALWAYS SO AMAZING!!
HA HA! AREN'T I?
I'M AMAZING!

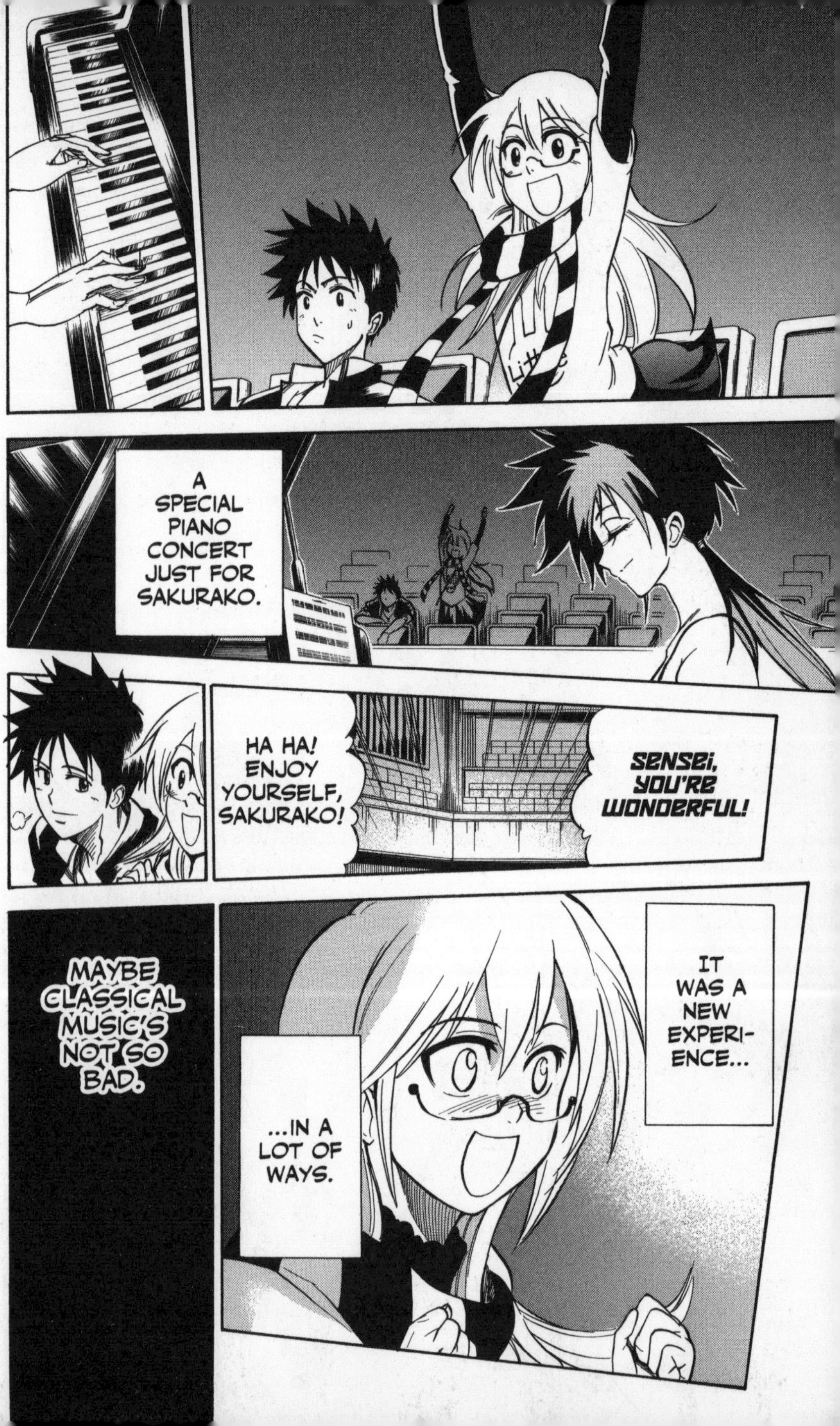
A SPECIAL PIANO CONCERT JUST FOR SAKURAKO.
SENSEI, YOU'RE WONDERFUL!
HA HA! ENJOY YOURSELF, SAKURAKO!
IT WAS A NEW EXPERI-ENCE...
...IN A LOT OF WAYS.
MAYBE CLASSICAL MUSIC'S NOT SO BAD.

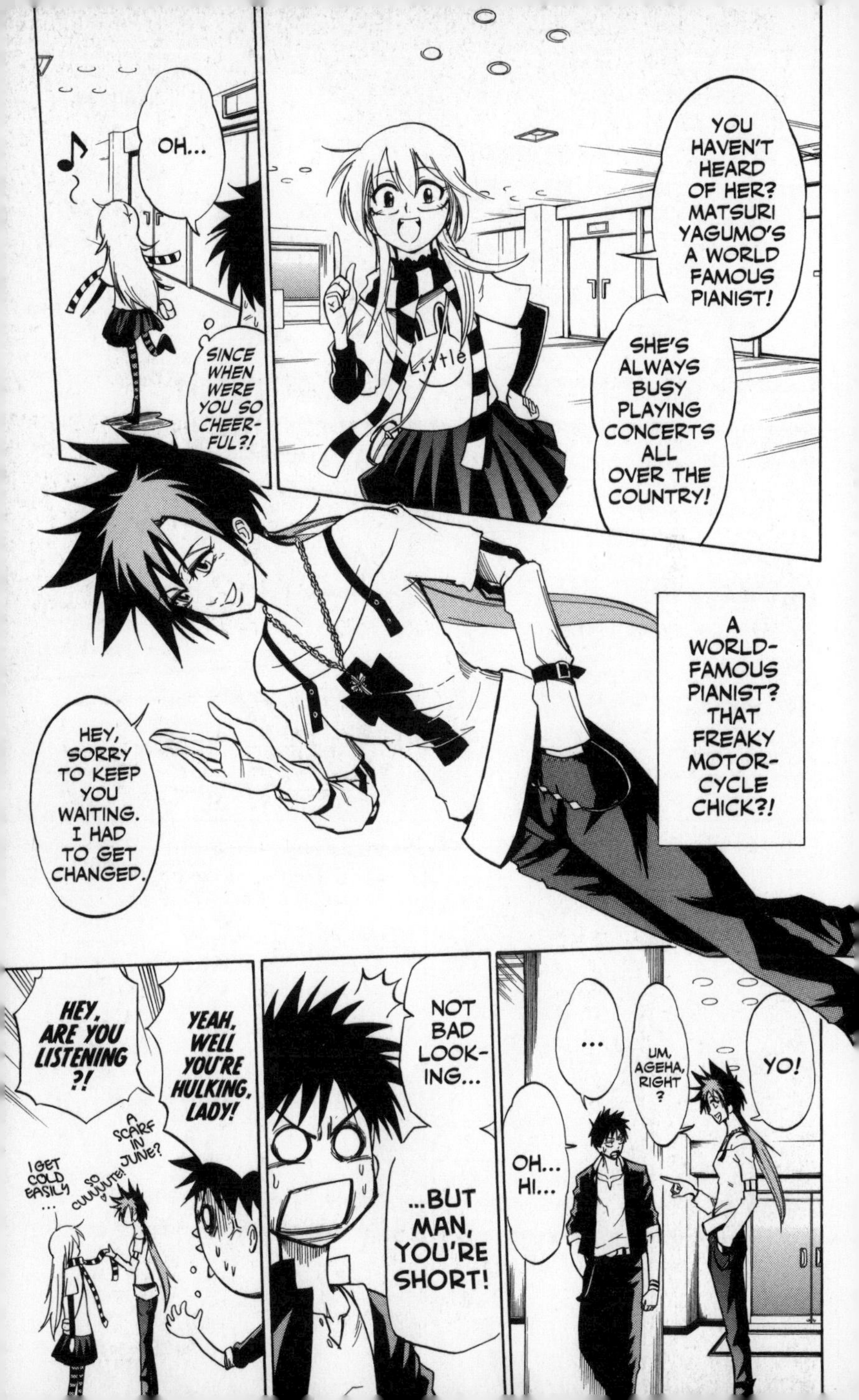
YOU HAVEN'T HEARD OF HER? MATSURI YAGUMO'S A WORLD FAMOUS PIANIST!
SHE'S ALWAYS BUSY PLAYING CONCERTS ALL OVER THE COUNTRY!
OH...
SINCE WHEN WERE YOU SO CHEER-FUL?!
A WORLD-FAMOUS PIANIST? THAT FREAKY MOTOR-CYCLE CHICK?!
HEY, SORRY TO KEEP YOU WAITING. I HAD TO GET CHANGED.
YO!
UM, AGEHA, RIGHT?
...
OH... HI...
NOT BAD LOOK-ING...
...BUT MAN, YOU'RE SHORT!
YEAH, WELL YOU'RE HULKING, LADY!
HEY, ARE YOU LISTENING ?!
A SCARF IN JUNE?
SO CUUUUUTE!
I GET COLD EASILY ...

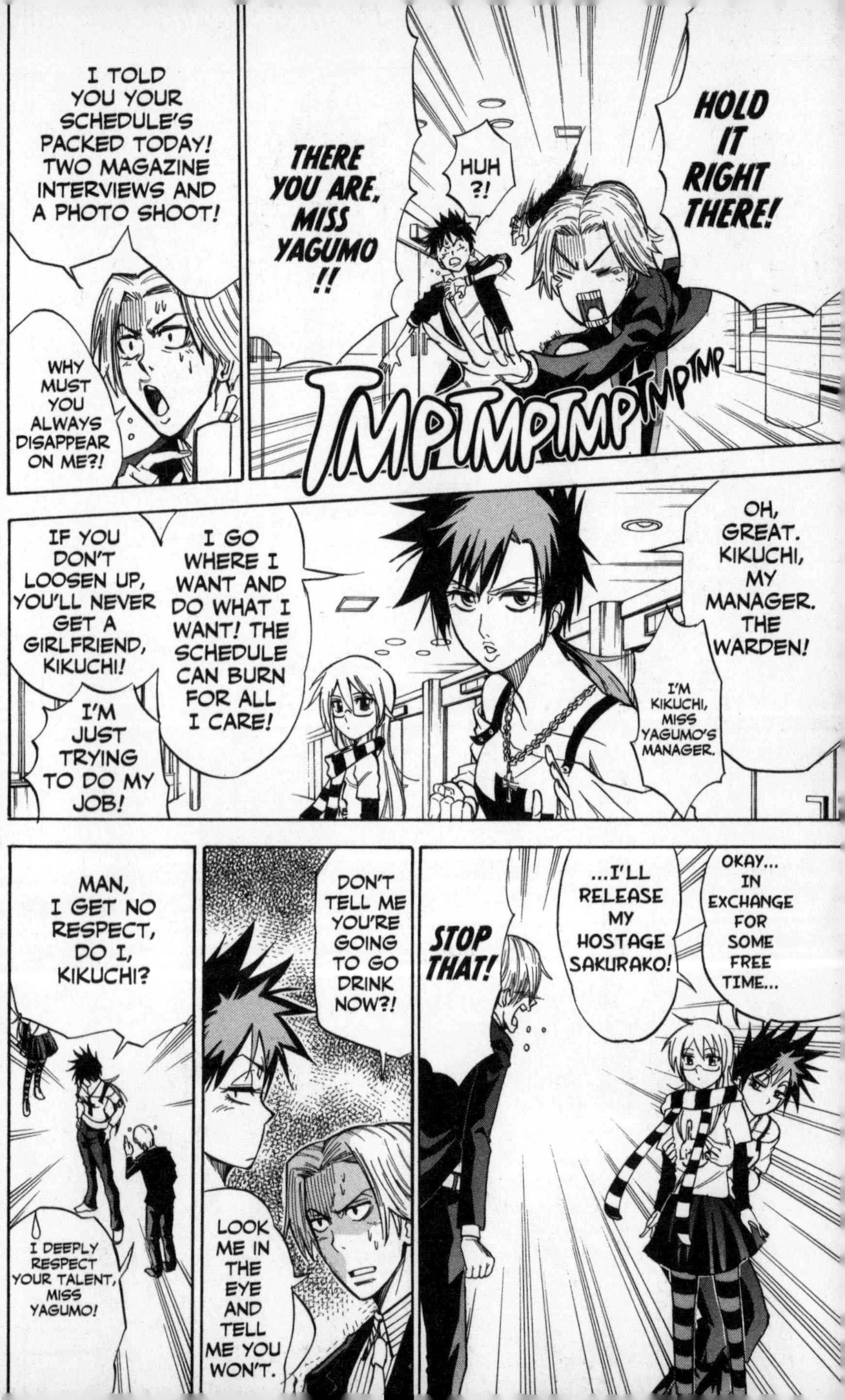
HOLD IT RIGHT THERE!
HUH?!
THERE YOU ARE, MISS YAGUMO!!
TMPTMPTMPTMPTMP
I TOLD YOU YOUR SCHEDULE'S PACKED TODAY! TWO MAGAZINE INTERVIEWS AND A PHOTO SHOOT!
WHY MUST YOU ALWAYS DISAPPEAR ON ME?!
OH, GREAT. KIKUCHI, MY MANAGER. THE WARDEN!
I'M KIKUCHI, MISS YAGUMO'S MANAGER.
I GO WHERE I WANT AND DO WHAT I WANT! THE SCHEDULE CAN BURN FOR ALL I CARE!
IF YOU DON'T LOOSEN UP, YOU'LL NEVER GET A GIRLFRIEND, KIKUCHI!
I'M JUST TRYING TO DO MY JOB!
OKAY... IN EXCHANGE FOR SOME FREE TIME...
...I'LL RELEASE MY HOSTAGE SAKURAKO!
STOP THAT!
DON'T TELL ME YOU'RE GOING TO GO DRINK NOW?!
LOOK ME IN THE EYE AND TELL ME YOU WON'T.
MAN, I GET NO RESPECT, DO I, KIKUCHI?
I DEEPLY RESPECT YOUR TALENT, MISS YAGUMO!

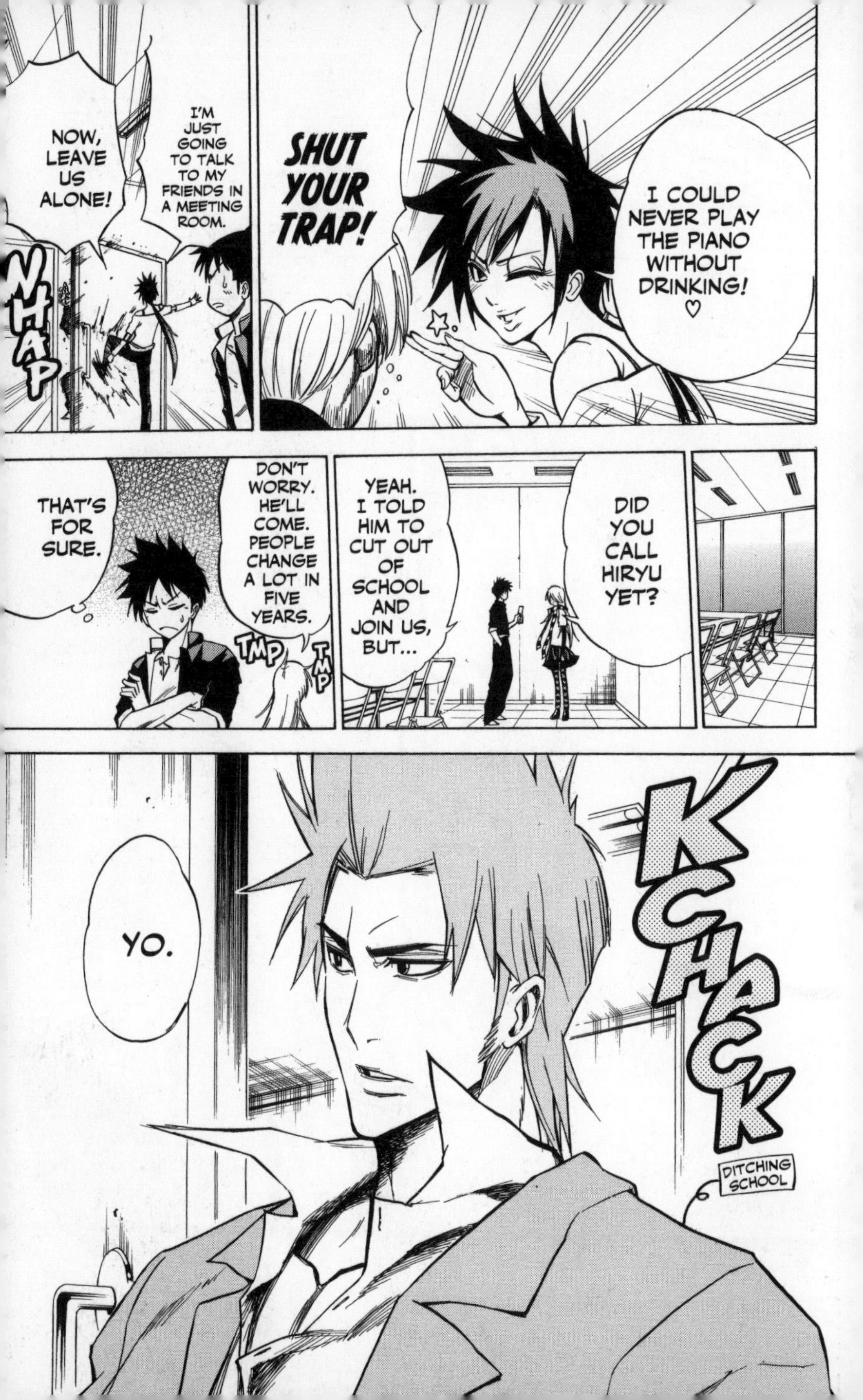
I COULD NEVER PLAY THE PIANO WITHOUT DRINKING! ♡
SHUT YOUR TRAP!
I'M JUST GOING TO TALK TO MY FRIENDS IN A MEETING ROOM.
NOW, LEAVE US ALONE!
WHAP
DID YOU CALL HIRYU YET?
YEAH. I TOLD HIM TO CUT OUT OF SCHOOL AND JOIN US, BUT...
DON'T WORRY. HE'LL COME. PEOPLE CHANGE A LOT IN FIVE YEARS.
TMP
TMP
THAT'S FOR SURE.
KCHACK
DITCHING SCHOOL
YO.

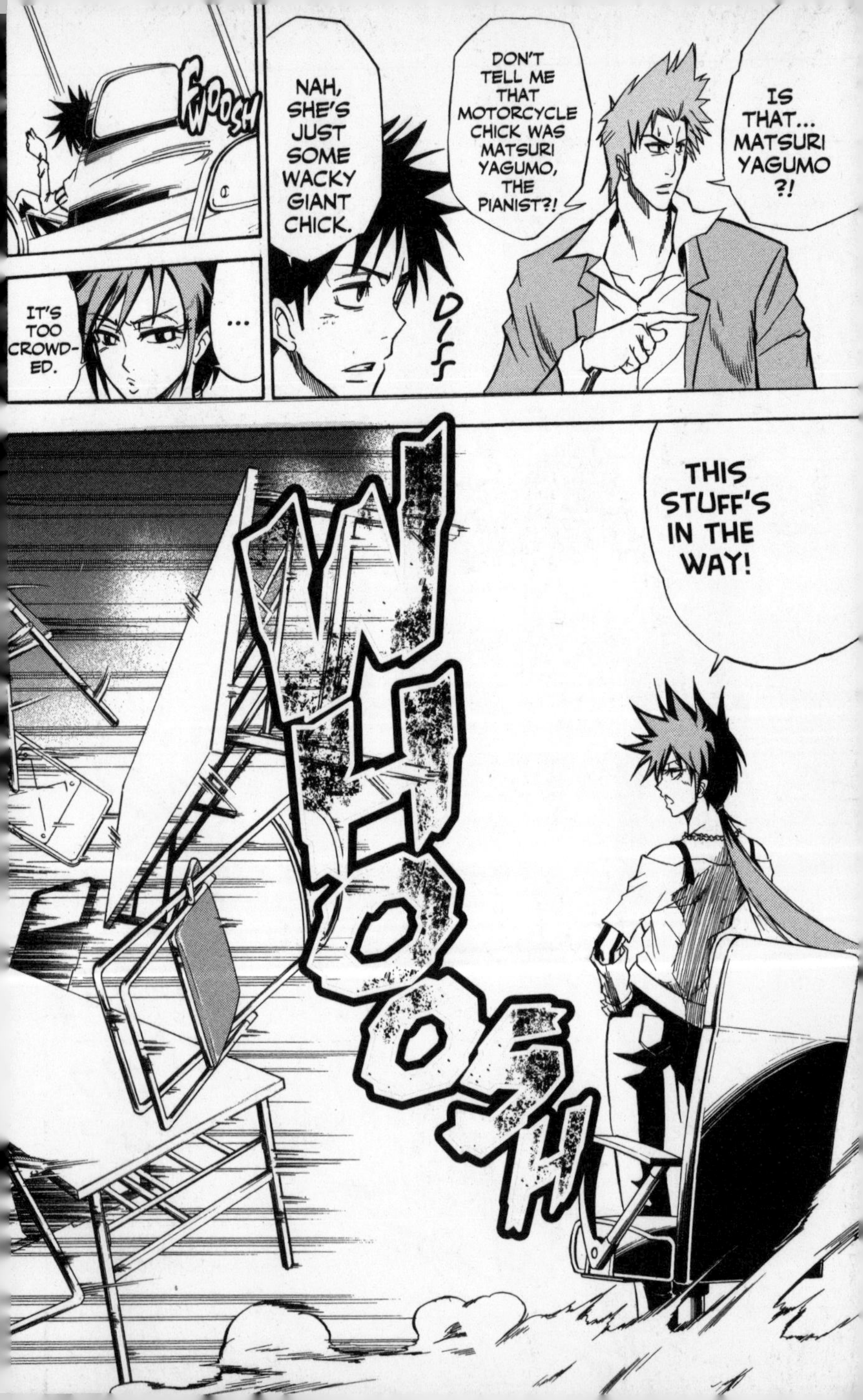
IS THAT... MATSURI YAGUMO?!
DON'T TELL ME THAT MOTORCYCLE CHICK WAS MATSURI YAGUMO, THE PIANIST?!
NAH, SHE'S JUST SOME WACKY GIANT CHICK.
FWOOSH
...
IT'S TOO CROWDED.
THIS STUFF'S IN THE WAY!
WHOOOSH

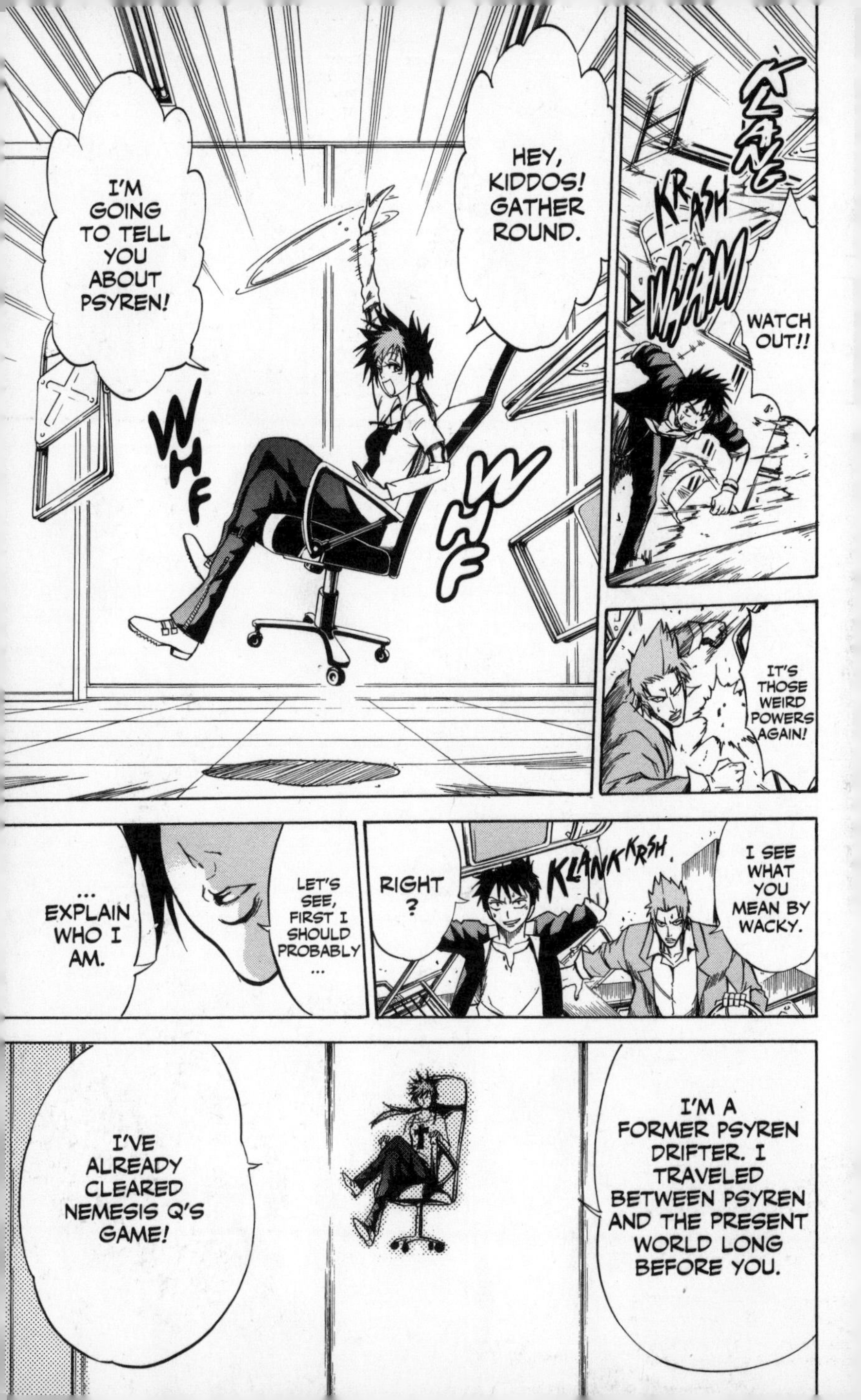
KLANG
KRASH
WHAM
WATCH OUT!!
IT'S THOSE WEIRD POWERS AGAIN!
HEY, KIDDOS! GATHER ROUND.
WHF
I'M GOING TO TELL YOU ABOUT PSYREN!
WHF
I SEE WHAT YOU MEAN BY WACKY.
KLANK KRSH
RIGHT?
LET'S SEE, FIRST I SHOULD PROBABLY ...
... EXPLAIN WHO I AM.
I'M A FORMER PSYREN DRIFTER. I TRAVELED BETWEEN PSYREN AND THE PRESENT WORLD LONG BEFORE YOU.
I'VE ALREADY CLEARED NEMESIS Q'S GAME!

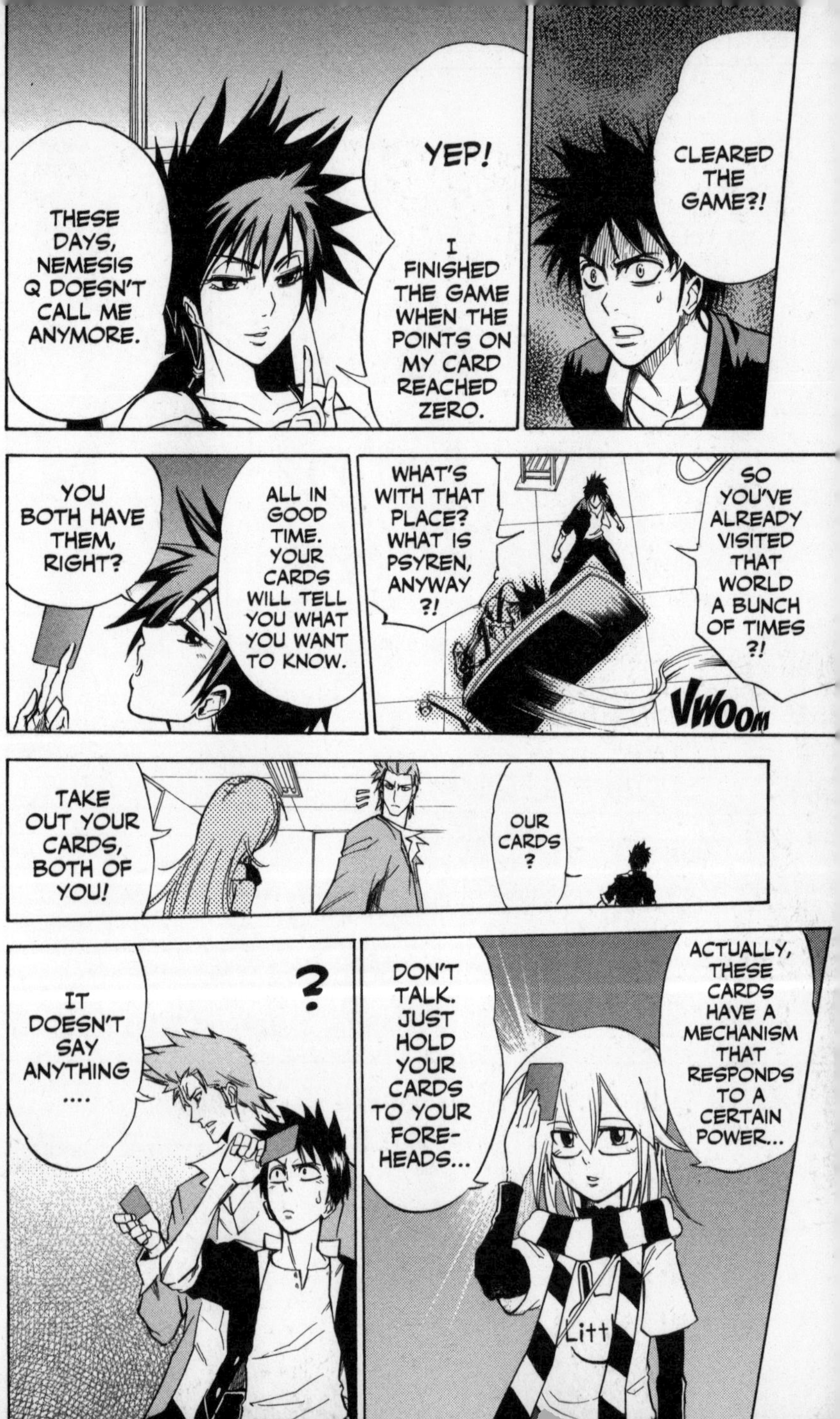
CLEARED THE GAME?!
YEP!
I FINISHED THE GAME WHEN THE POINTS ON MY CARD REACHED ZERO.
THESE DAYS, NEMESIS Q DOESN'T CALL ME ANYMORE.
SO YOU'VE ALREADY VISITED THAT WORLD A BUNCH OF TIMES?!
WHAT'S WITH THAT PLACE? WHAT IS PSYREN, ANYWAY?!
VWOOM
ALL IN GOOD TIME. YOUR CARDS WILL TELL YOU WHAT YOU WANT TO KNOW.
YOU BOTH HAVE THEM, RIGHT?
OUR CARDS?
TAKE OUT YOUR CARDS, BOTH OF YOU!
ACTUALLY, THESE CARDS HAVE A MECHANISM THAT RESPONDS TO A CERTAIN POWER...
DON'T TALK. JUST HOLD YOUR CARDS TO YOUR FOREHEADS...
Litt
?
IT DOESN'T SAY ANYTHING ....

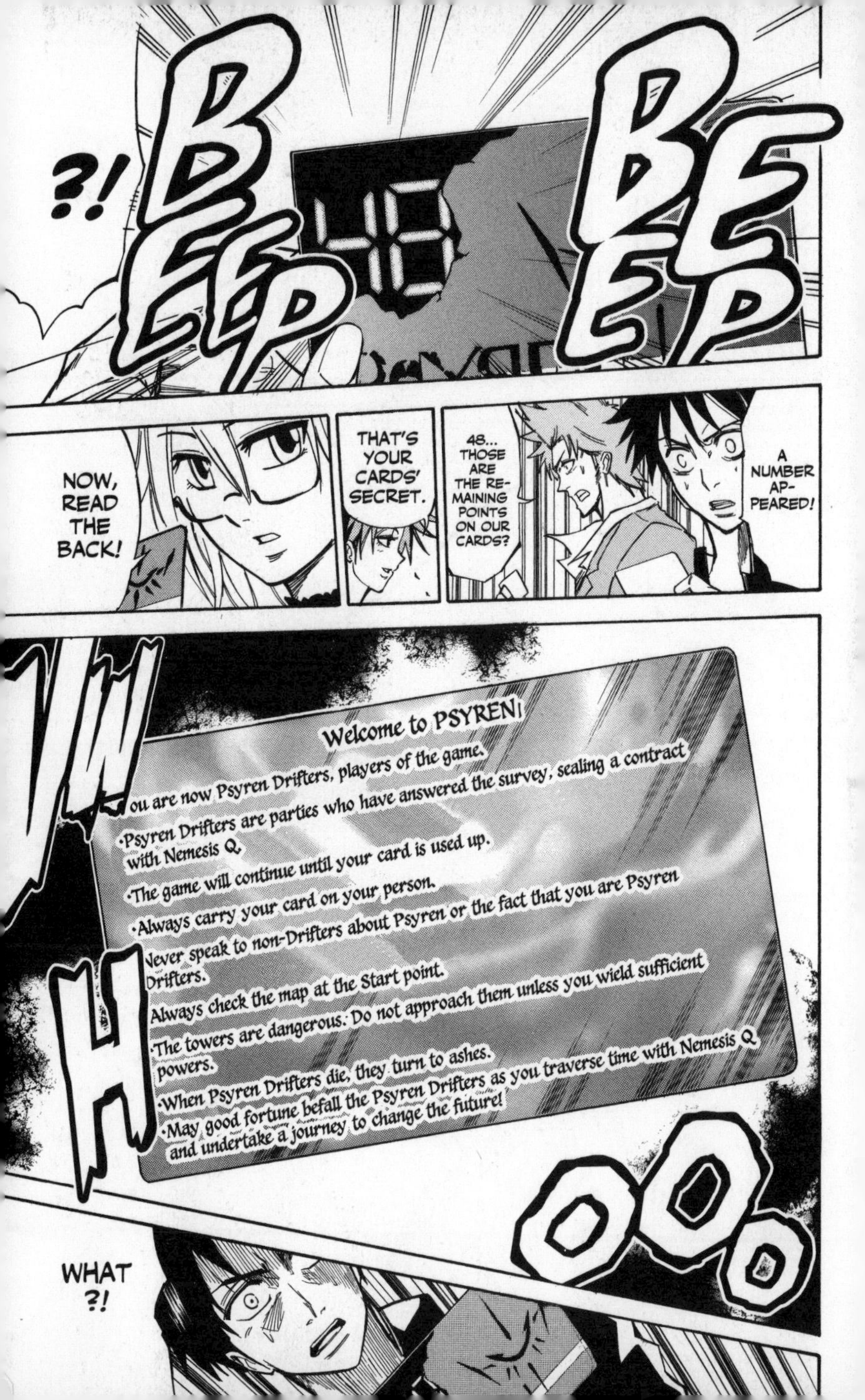
BEEP
48
BEEP
?!
A NUMBER APPEARED!
48... THOSE ARE THE REMAINING POINTS ON OUR CARDS?
THAT'S YOUR CARDS' SECRET.
NOW, READ THE BACK!
Welcome to PSYREN!
ou are now Psyren Drifters, players of the game.
·Psyren Drifters are parties who have answered the survey, sealing a contract with Nemesis Q.
·The game will continue until your card is used up.
·Always carry your card on your person.
·Never speak to non-Drifters about Psyren or the fact that you are Psyren Drifters.
·Always check the map at the Start point.
·The towers are dangerous. Do not approach them unless you wield sufficient powers.
·When Psyren Drifters die, they turn to ashes.
·May good fortune befall the Psyren Drifters as you traverse time with Nemesis Q and undertake a journey to change the future!
WHAT ?!

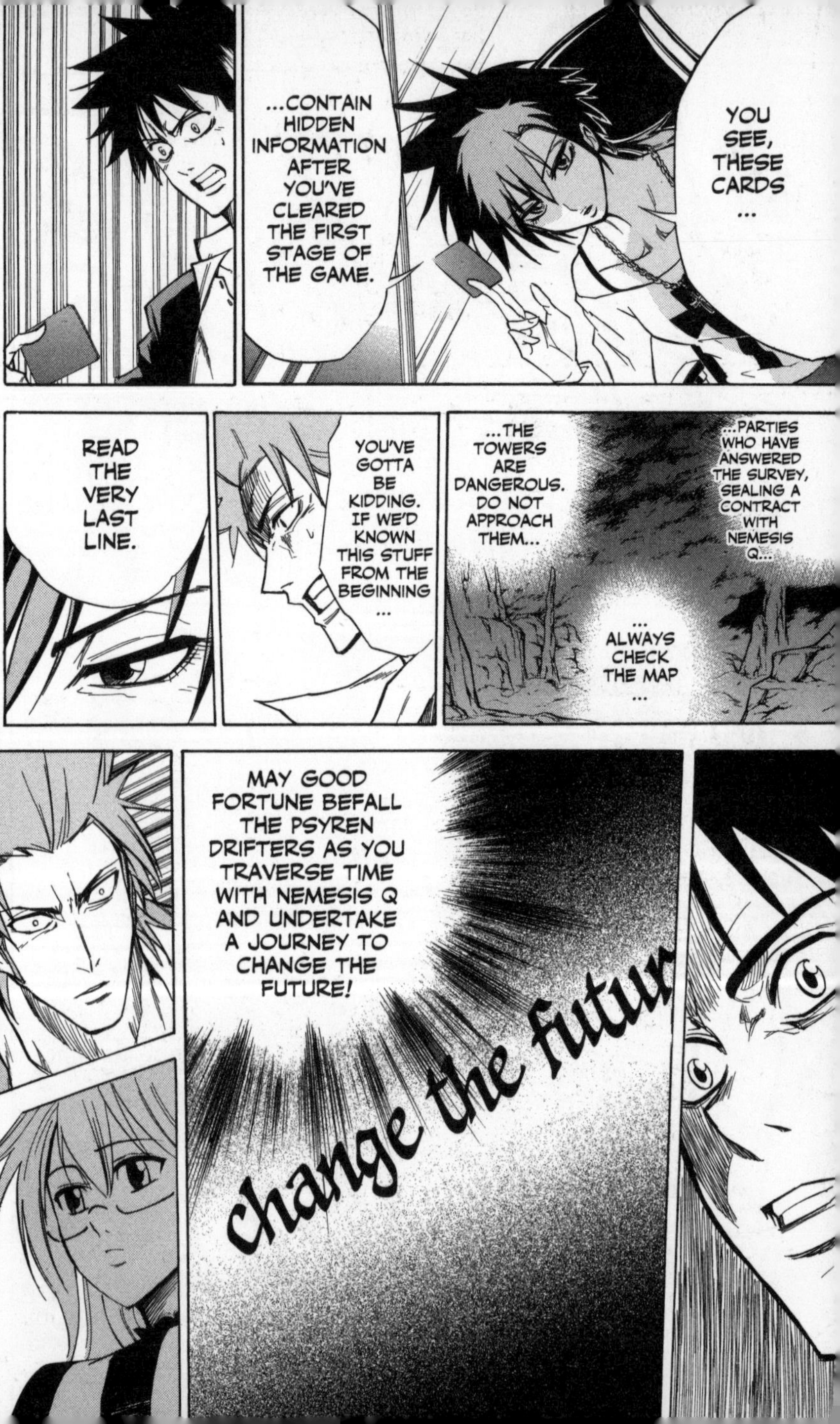
YOU SEE, THESE CARDS ...
...CONTAIN HIDDEN INFORMATION AFTER YOU'VE CLEARED THE FIRST STAGE OF THE GAME.
...PARTIES WHO HAVE ANSWERED THE SURVEY, SEALING A CONTRACT WITH NEMESIS Q...
...THE TOWERS ARE DANGEROUS. DO NOT APPROACH THEM...
... ALWAYS CHECK THE MAP ...
YOU'VE GOTTA BE KIDDING. IF WE'D KNOWN THIS STUFF FROM THE BEGINNING ...
READ THE VERY LAST LINE.
MAY GOOD FORTUNE BEFALL THE PSYREN DRIFTERS AS YOU TRAVERSE TIME WITH NEMESIS Q AND UNDERTAKE A JOURNEY TO CHANGE THE FUTURE!
change the futur

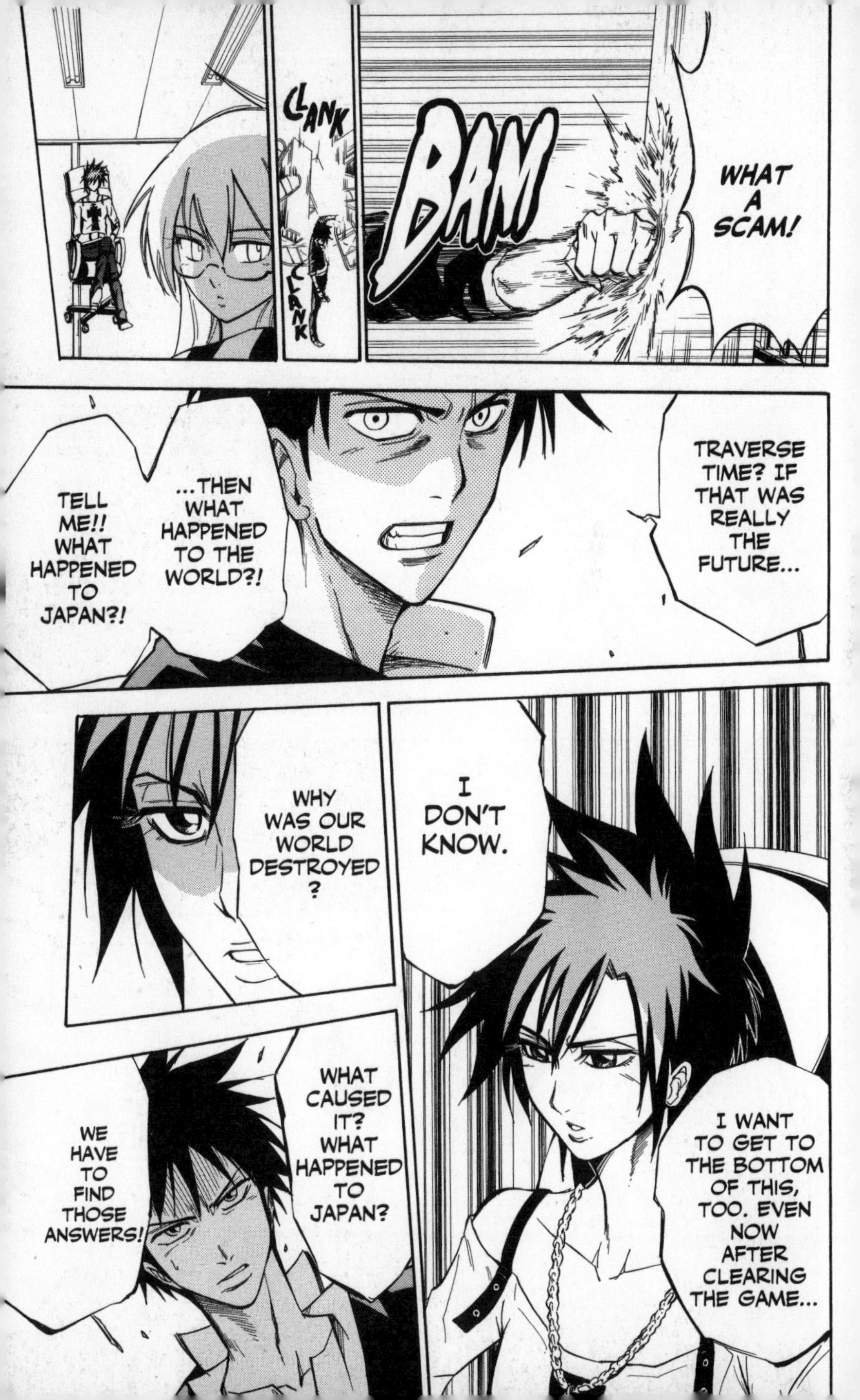
BAM
WHAT A SCAM!
CLANK
CLANK
TRAVERSE TIME? IF THAT WAS REALLY THE FUTURE...
...THEN WHAT HAPPENED TO THE WORLD?!
TELL ME!! WHAT HAPPENED TO JAPAN?!
I DON'T KNOW.
I WANT TO GET TO THE BOTTOM OF THIS, TOO. EVEN NOW AFTER CLEARING THE GAME...
WHY WAS OUR WORLD DESTROYED?
WHAT CAUSED IT? WHAT HAPPENED TO JAPAN?
WE HAVE TO FIND THOSE ANSWERS!

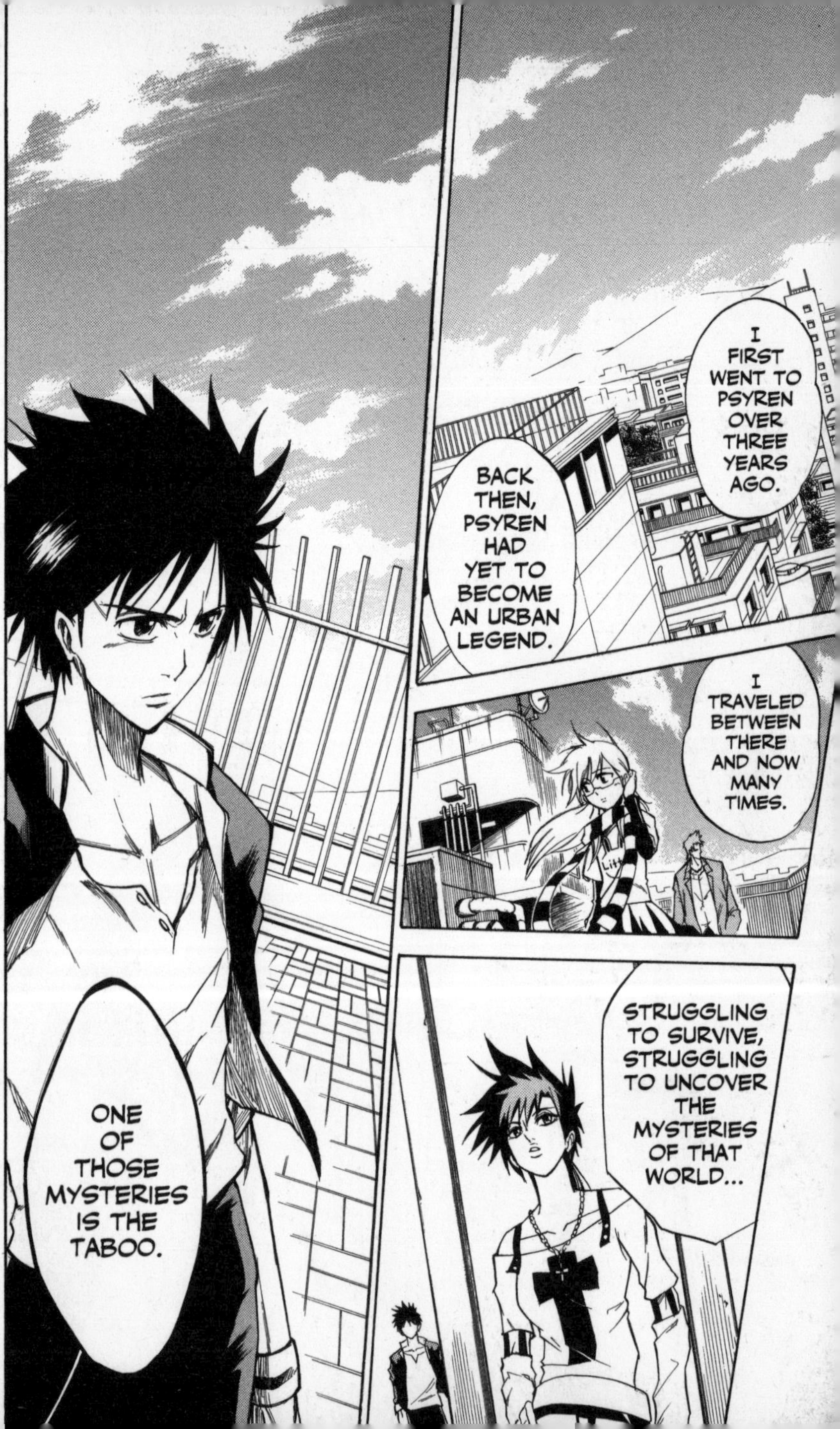
I FIRST WENT TO PSYREN OVER THREE YEARS AGO.
BACK THEN, PSYREN HAD YET TO BECOME AN URBAN LEGEND.
I TRAVELED BETWEEN THERE AND NOW MANY TIMES.
STRUGGLING TO SURVIVE, STRUGGLING TO UNCOVER THE MYSTERIES OF THAT WORLD...
ONE OF THOSE MYSTERIES IS THE TABOO.

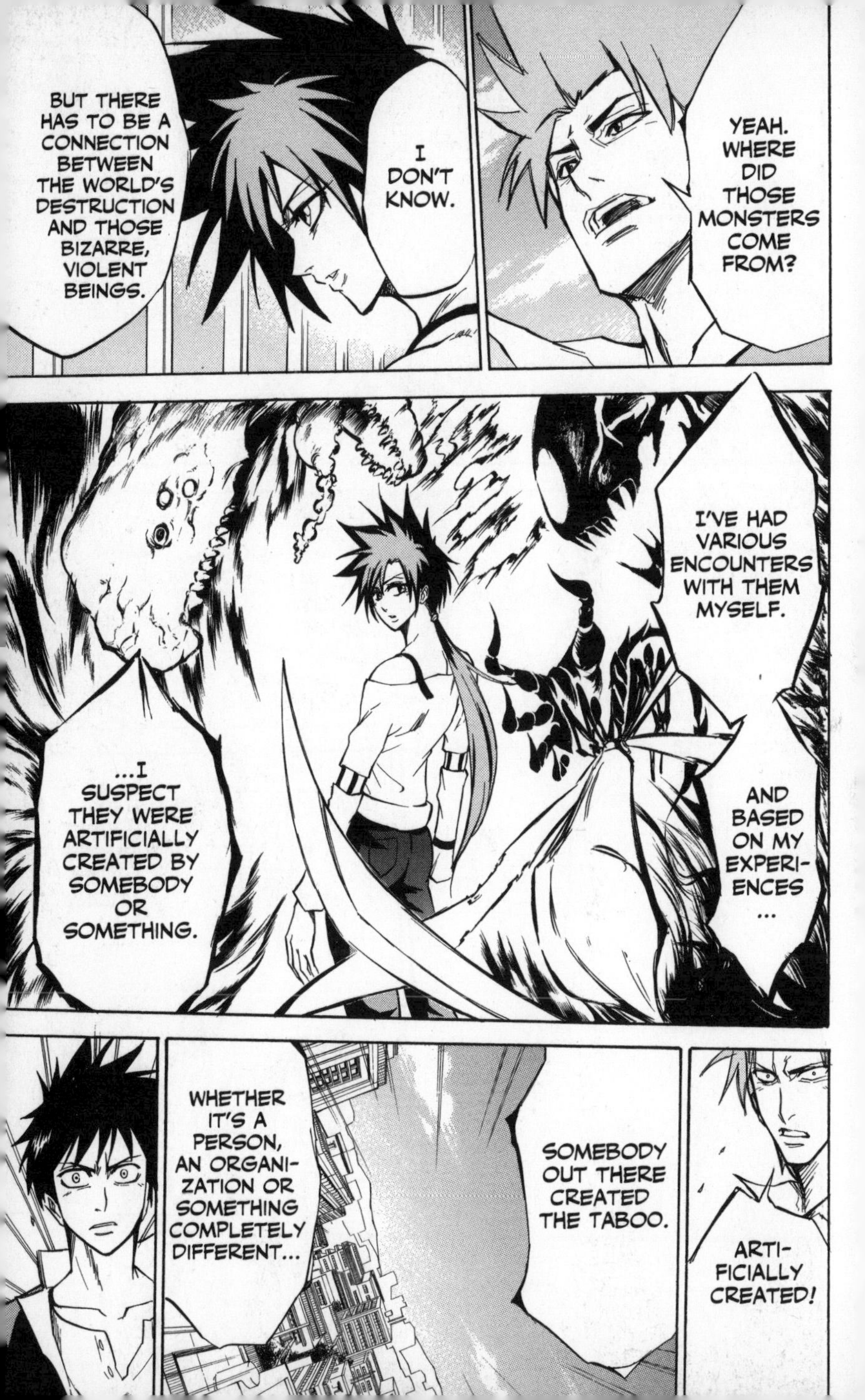
YEAH. WHERE DID THOSE MONSTERS COME FROM?
I DON'T KNOW.
BUT THERE HAS TO BE A CONNECTION BETWEEN THE WORLD'S DESTRUCTION AND THOSE BIZARRE, VIOLENT BEINGS.
I'VE HAD VARIOUS ENCOUNTERS WITH THEM MYSELF.
AND BASED ON MY EXPERI-ENCES...
...I SUSPECT THEY WERE ARTIFICIALLY CREATED BY SOMEBODY OR SOMETHING.
ARTI-FICIALLY CREATED!
SOMEBODY OUT THERE CREATED THE TABOO.
WHETHER IT'S A PERSON, AN ORGANI-ZATION OR SOMETHING COMPLETELY DIFFERENT...

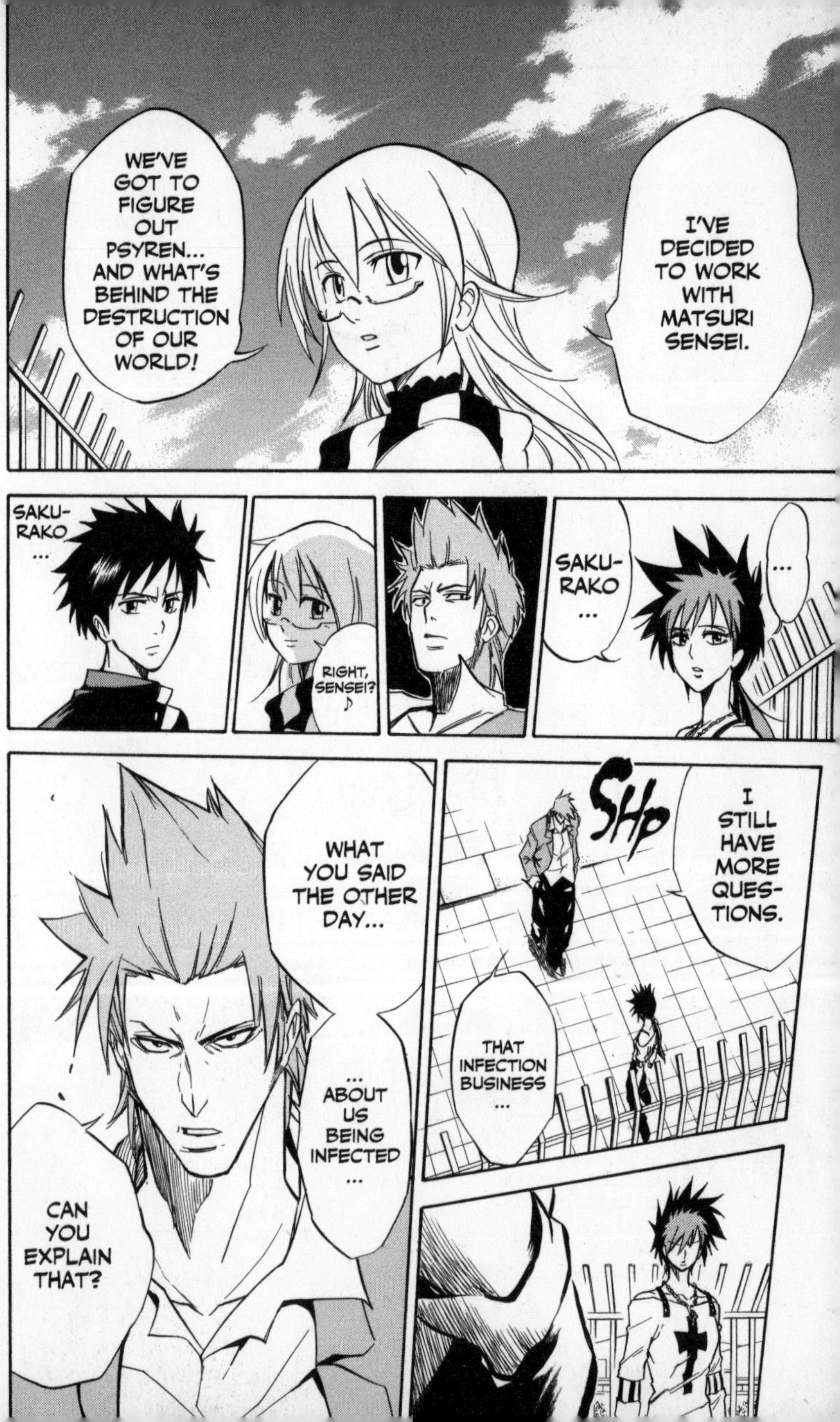
I'VE DECIDED TO WORK WITH MATSURI SENSEI.
WE'VE GOT TO FIGURE OUT PSYREN... AND WHAT'S BEHIND THE DESTRUCTION OF OUR WORLD!
...
SAKU-RAKO ...
RIGHT, SENSEI? ♪
SAKU-RAKO ...
I STILL HAVE MORE QUES-TIONS.
SHP
THAT INFECTION BUSINESS ...
WHAT YOU SAID THE OTHER DAY...
... ABOUT US BEING INFECTED ...
CAN YOU EXPLAIN THAT?

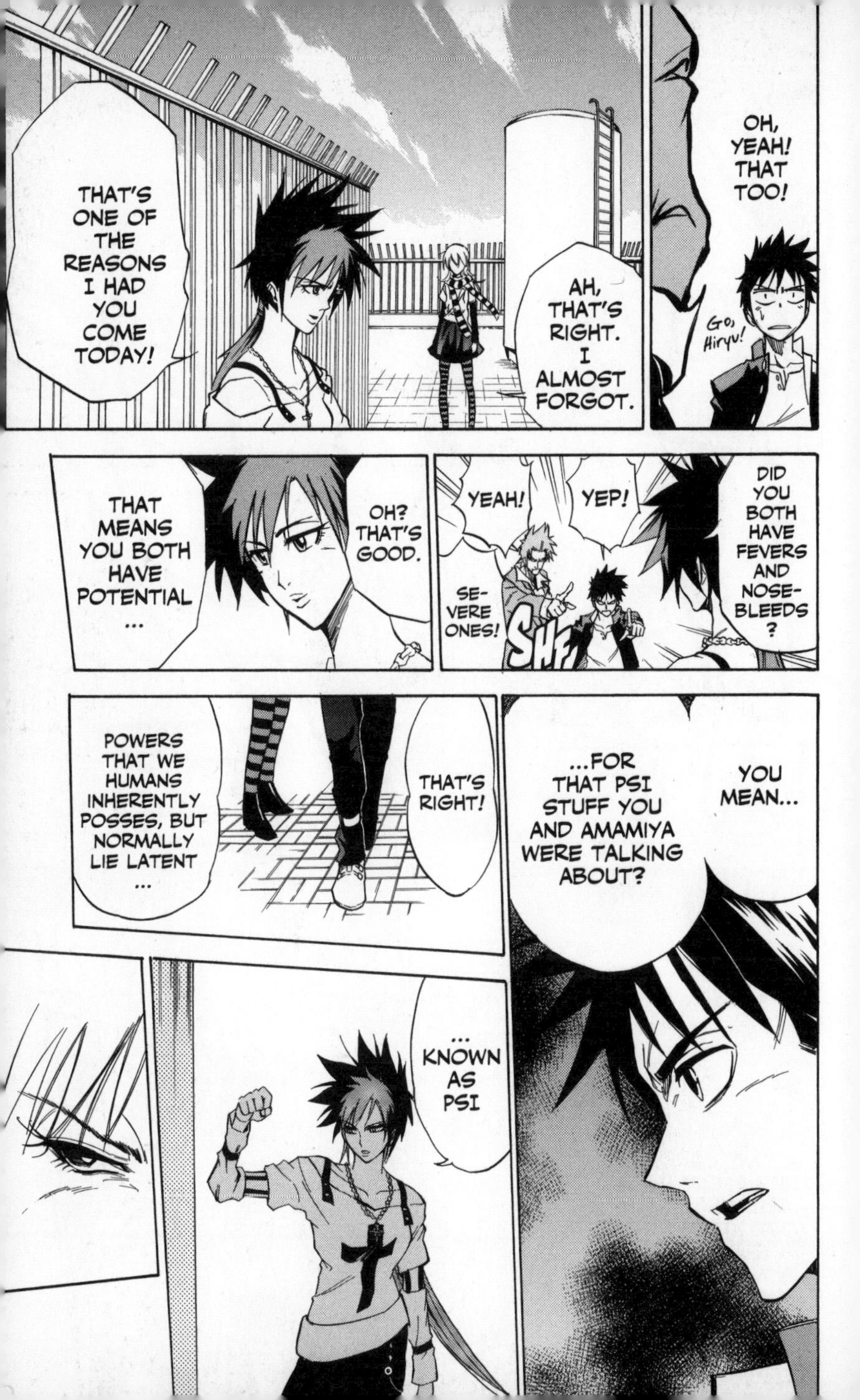
OH, YEAH! THAT TOO!
Go, Hiryu!
AH, THAT'S RIGHT. I ALMOST FORGOT.
THAT'S ONE OF THE REASONS I HAD YOU COME TODAY!
DID YOU BOTH HAVE FEVERS AND NOSE-BLEEDS?
YEP!
YEAH!
SE-VERE ONES!
SHF
OH? THAT'S GOOD.
THAT MEANS YOU BOTH HAVE POTENTIAL...
YOU MEAN...
...FOR THAT PSI STUFF YOU AND AMAMIYA WERE TALKING ABOUT?
THAT'S RIGHT!
POWERS THAT WE HUMANS INHERENTLY POSSES, BUT NORMALLY LIE LATENT...
...KNOWN AS PSI

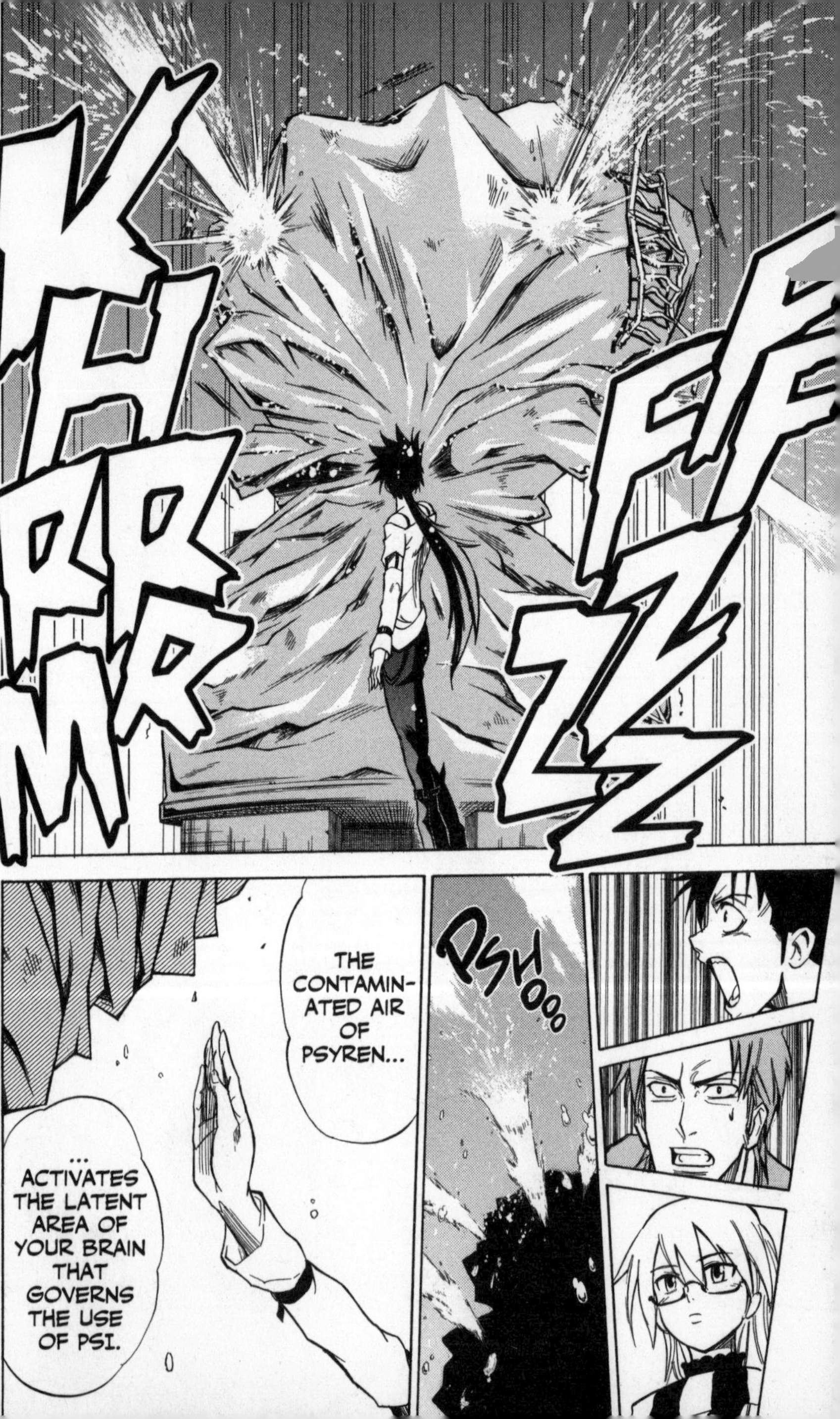
FFZZZ
KHRRMR
PSHOOO
THE CONTAMINATED AIR OF PSYREN...
... ACTIVATES THE LATENT AREA OF YOUR BRAIN THAT GOVERNS THE USE OF PSI.

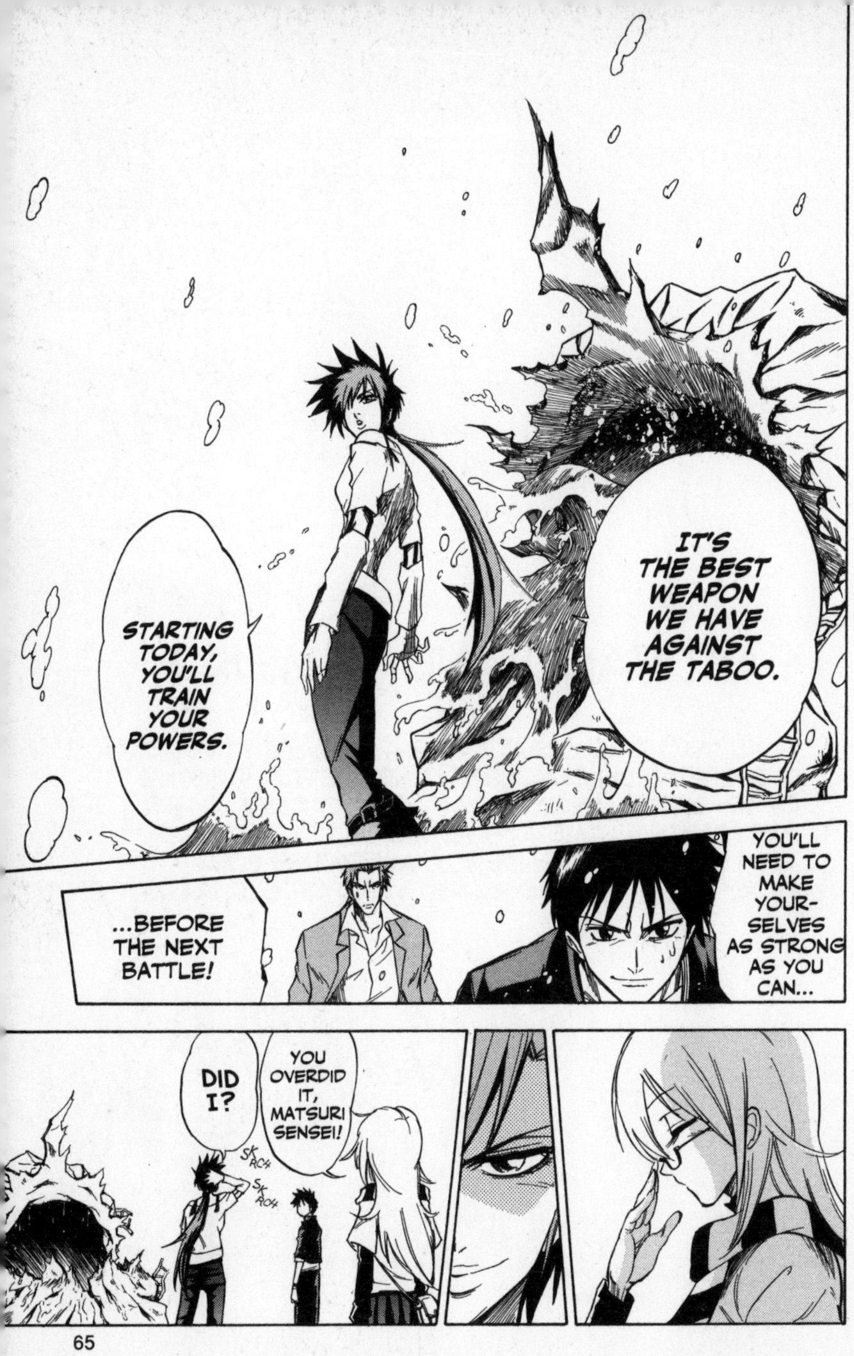
IT'S THE BEST WEAPON WE HAVE AGAINST THE TABOO.
STARTING TODAY, YOU'LL TRAIN YOUR POWERS.
YOU'LL NEED TO MAKE YOUR-SELVES AS STRONG AS YOU CAN...
...BEFORE THE NEXT BATTLE!
YOU OVERDID IT, MATSURI SENSEI!
DID I?
SKRCH
SKRCH

SAKURAKO AND HIMENO

SAKURAKO WAS CREATED AS A FOIL TO HIMENO, THE CHEERFUL, INNOCENT, ENERGETIC HEROINE OF MY LAST MANGA. I WAS VERY CAREFUL WHEN PORTRAYING HIMENO'S PERSONALITY, BUT I'VE TEMPERED THAT TENDENCY, ALLOWING FOR MORE OF A KALEIDOSCOPIC VIEW OF SAKURAKO.

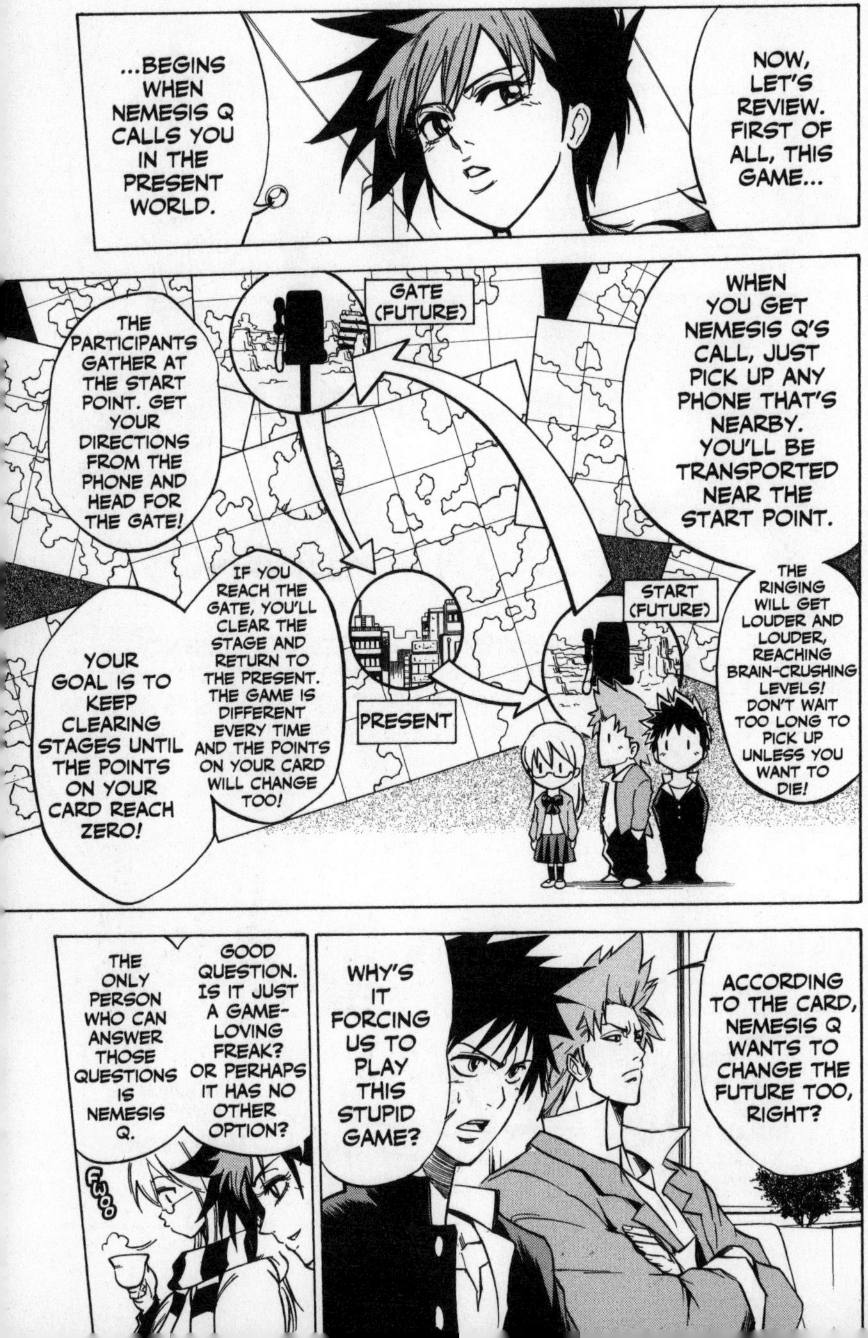
NOW, LET'S REVIEW. FIRST OF ALL, THIS GAME...
...BEGINS WHEN NEMESIS Q CALLS YOU IN THE PRESENT WORLD.
WHEN YOU GET NEMESIS Q'S CALL, JUST PICK UP ANY PHONE THAT'S NEARBY. YOU'LL BE TRANSPORTED NEAR THE START POINT.
THE RINGING WILL GET LOUDER AND LOUDER, REACHING BRAIN-CRUSHING LEVELS! DON'T WAIT TOO LONG TO PICK UP UNLESS YOU WANT TO DIE!
START (FUTURE)
GATE (FUTURE)
THE PARTICIPANTS GATHER AT THE START POINT. GET YOUR DIRECTIONS FROM THE PHONE AND HEAD FOR THE GATE!
PRESENT
IF YOU REACH THE GATE, YOU'LL CLEAR THE STAGE AND RETURN TO THE PRESENT. THE GAME IS DIFFERENT EVERY TIME AND THE POINTS ON YOUR CARD WILL CHANGE TOO!
YOUR GOAL IS TO KEEP CLEARING STAGES UNTIL THE POINTS ON YOUR CARD REACH ZERO!
ACCORDING TO THE CARD, NEMESIS Q WANTS TO CHANGE THE FUTURE TOO, RIGHT?
WHY'S IT FORCING US TO PLAY THIS STUPID GAME?
GOOD QUESTION. IS IT JUST A GAME-LOVING FREAK? OR PERHAPS IT HAS NO OTHER OPTION?
THE ONLY PERSON WHO CAN ANSWER THOSE QUESTIONS IS NEMESIS Q.
FWOO

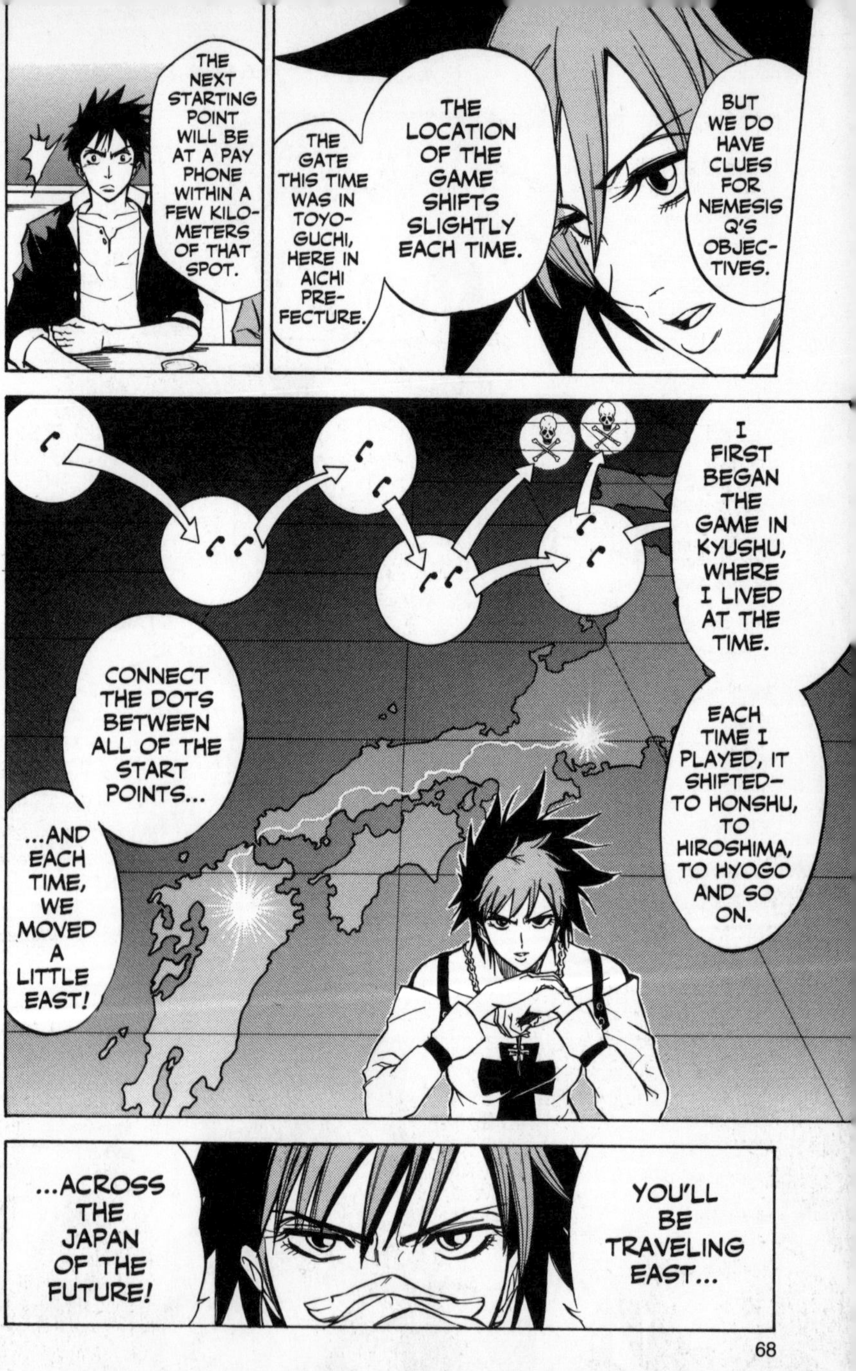
BUT WE DO HAVE CLUES FOR NEMESIS Q'S OBJECTIVES.
THE LOCATION OF THE GAME SHIFTS SLIGHTLY EACH TIME.
THE GATE THIS TIME WAS IN TOYOGUCHI, HERE IN AICHI PREFECTURE.
THE NEXT STARTING POINT WILL BE AT A PAY PHONE WITHIN A FEW KILOMETERS OF THAT SPOT.
I FIRST BEGAN THE GAME IN KYUSHU, WHERE I LIVED AT THE TIME.
EACH TIME I PLAYED, IT SHIFTED–TO HONSHU, TO HIROSHIMA, TO HYOGO AND SO ON.
CONNECT THE DOTS BETWEEN ALL OF THE START POINTS...
...AND EACH TIME, WE MOVED A LITTLE EAST!
YOU'LL BE TRAVELING EAST...
...ACROSS THE JAPAN OF THE FUTURE!

CALL.11: BABY UNIVERSE

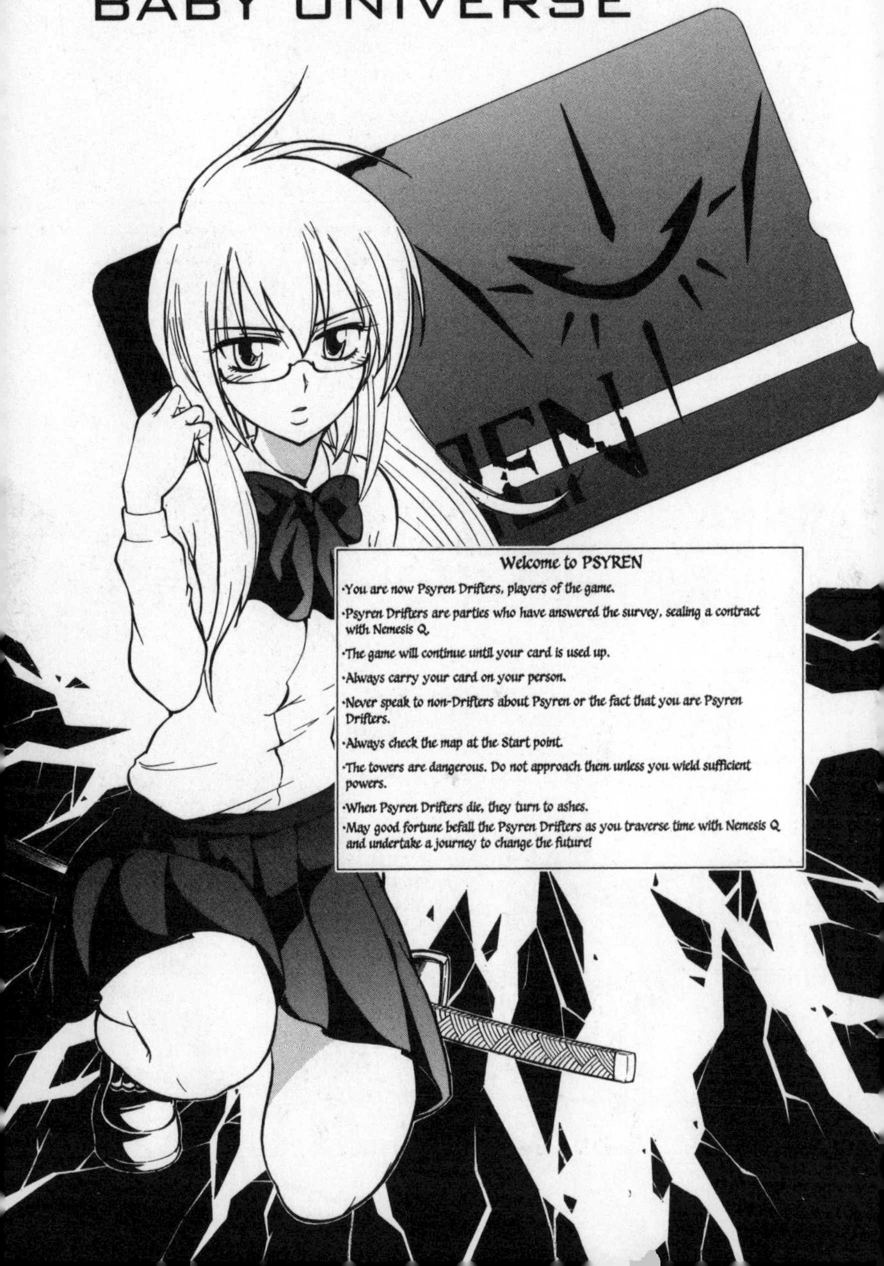
Welcome to PSYREN
•You are now Psyren Drifters, players of the game.
•Psyren Drifters are parties who have answered the survey, sealing a contract with Nemesis Q.
•The game will continue until your card is used up.
•Always carry your card on your person.
•Never speak to non-Drifters about Psyren or the fact that you are Psyren Drifters.
•Always check the map at the Start point.
•The towers are dangerous. Do not approach them unless you wield sufficient powers.
•When Psyren Drifters die, they turn to ashes.
•May good fortune befall the Psyren Drifters as you traverse time with Nemesis Q and undertake a journey to change the future!

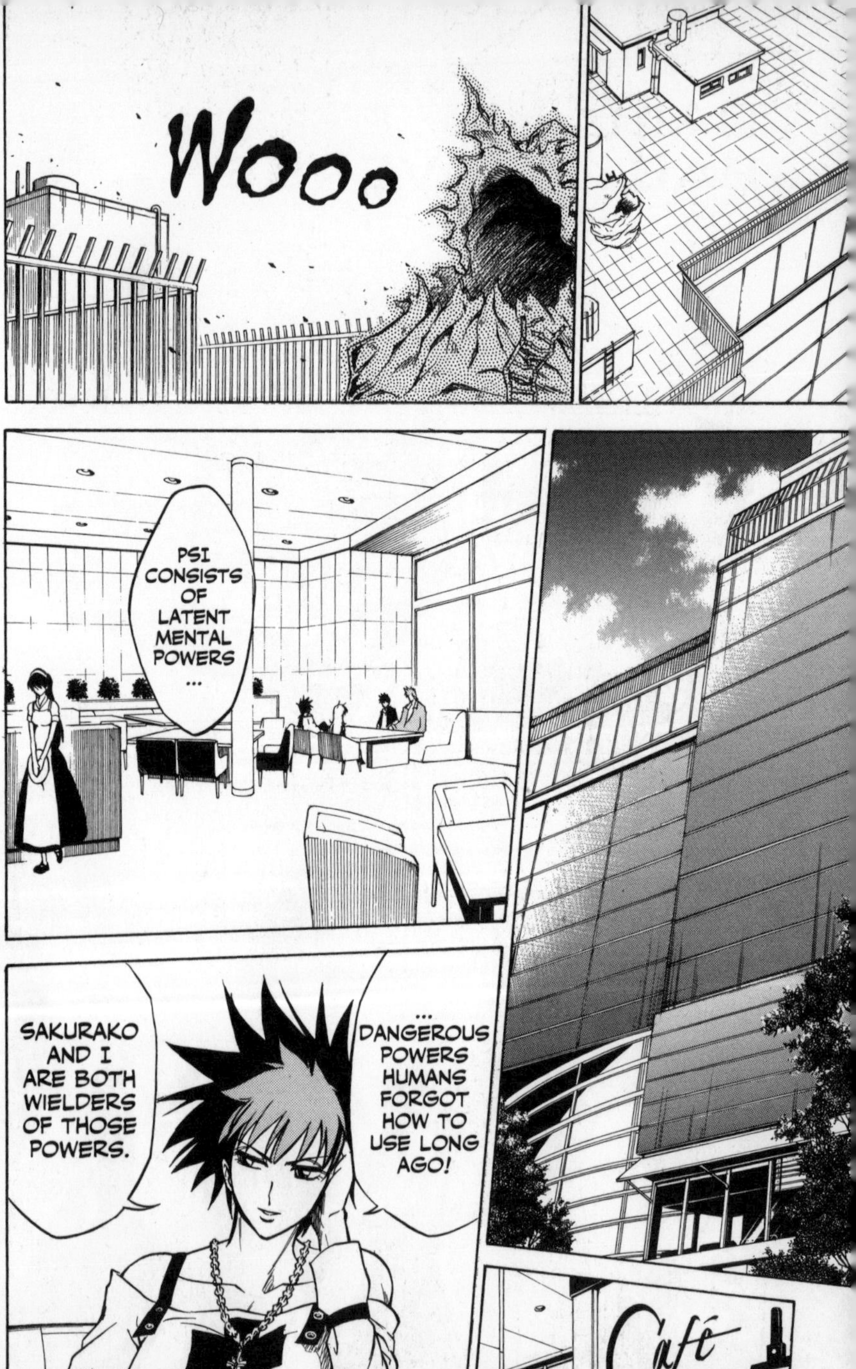
WOOO
PSI CONSISTS OF LATENT MENTAL POWERS ...
... DANGEROUS POWERS HUMANS FORGOT HOW TO USE LONG AGO!
SAKURAKO AND I ARE BOTH WIELDERS OF THOSE POWERS.
Café

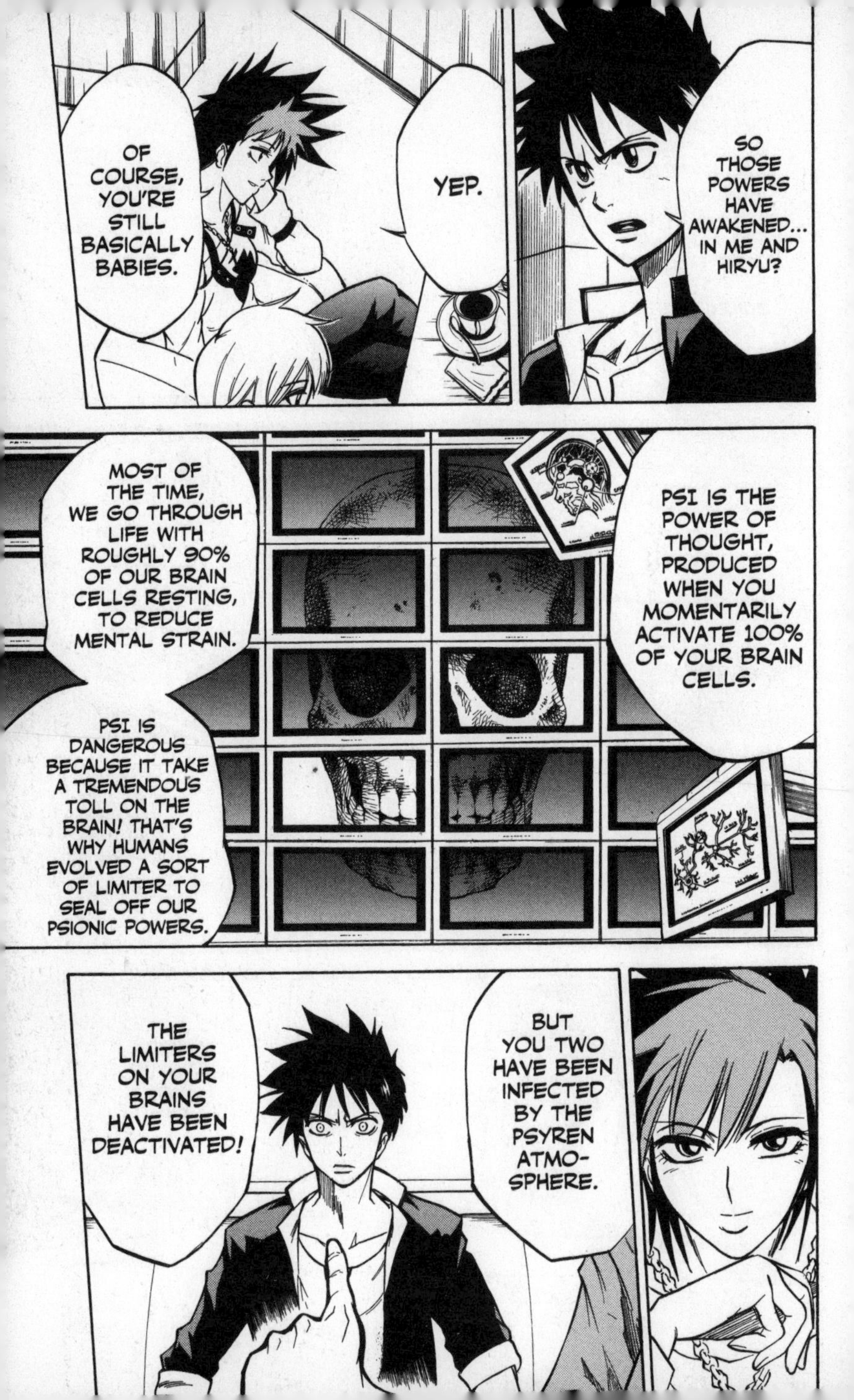
SO THOSE POWERS HAVE AWAKENED... IN ME AND HIRYU?
YEP.
OF COURSE, YOU'RE STILL BASICALLY BABIES.
PSI IS THE POWER OF THOUGHT, PRODUCED WHEN YOU MOMENTARILY ACTIVATE 100% OF YOUR BRAIN CELLS.
MOST OF THE TIME, WE GO THROUGH LIFE WITH ROUGHLY 90% OF OUR BRAIN CELLS RESTING, TO REDUCE MENTAL STRAIN.
PSI IS DANGEROUS BECAUSE IT TAKE A TREMENDOUS TOLL ON THE BRAIN! THAT'S WHY HUMANS EVOLVED A SORT OF LIMITER TO SEAL OFF OUR PSIONIC POWERS.
BUT YOU TWO HAVE BEEN INFECTED BY THE PSYREN ATMO-SPHERE.
THE LIMITERS ON YOUR BRAINS HAVE BEEN DEACTIVATED!

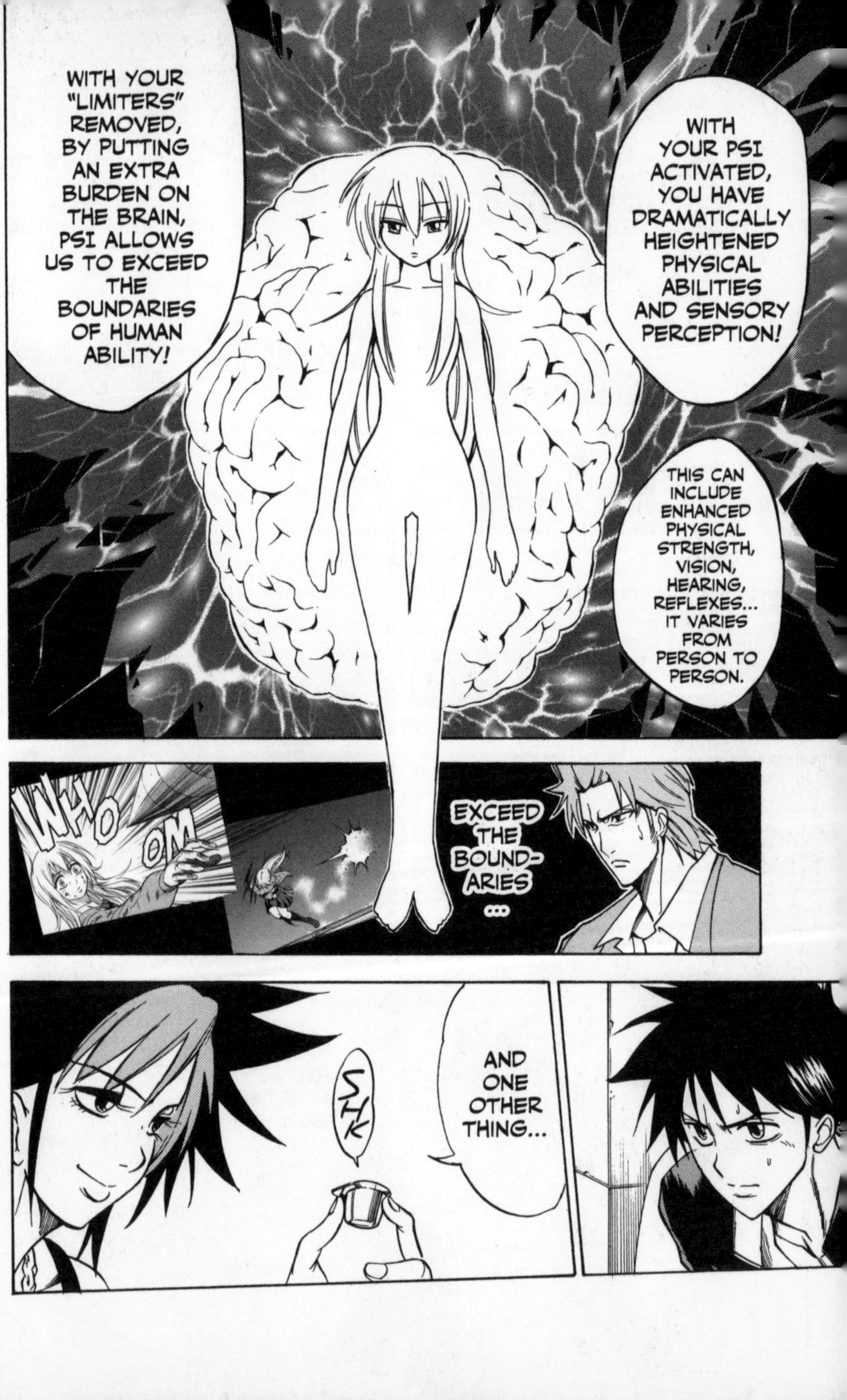
WITH YOUR PSI ACTIVATED, YOU HAVE DRAMATICALLY HEIGHTENED PHYSICAL ABILITIES AND SENSORY PERCEPTION!
WITH YOUR "LIMITERS" REMOVED, BY PUTTING AN EXTRA BURDEN ON THE BRAIN, PSI ALLOWS US TO EXCEED THE BOUNDARIES OF HUMAN ABILITY!
THIS CAN INCLUDE ENHANCED PHYSICAL STRENGTH, VISION, HEARING, REFLEXES... IT VARIES FROM PERSON TO PERSON.
EXCEED THE BOUND-ARIES ...
WHOOM
AND ONE OTHER THING...
SHK

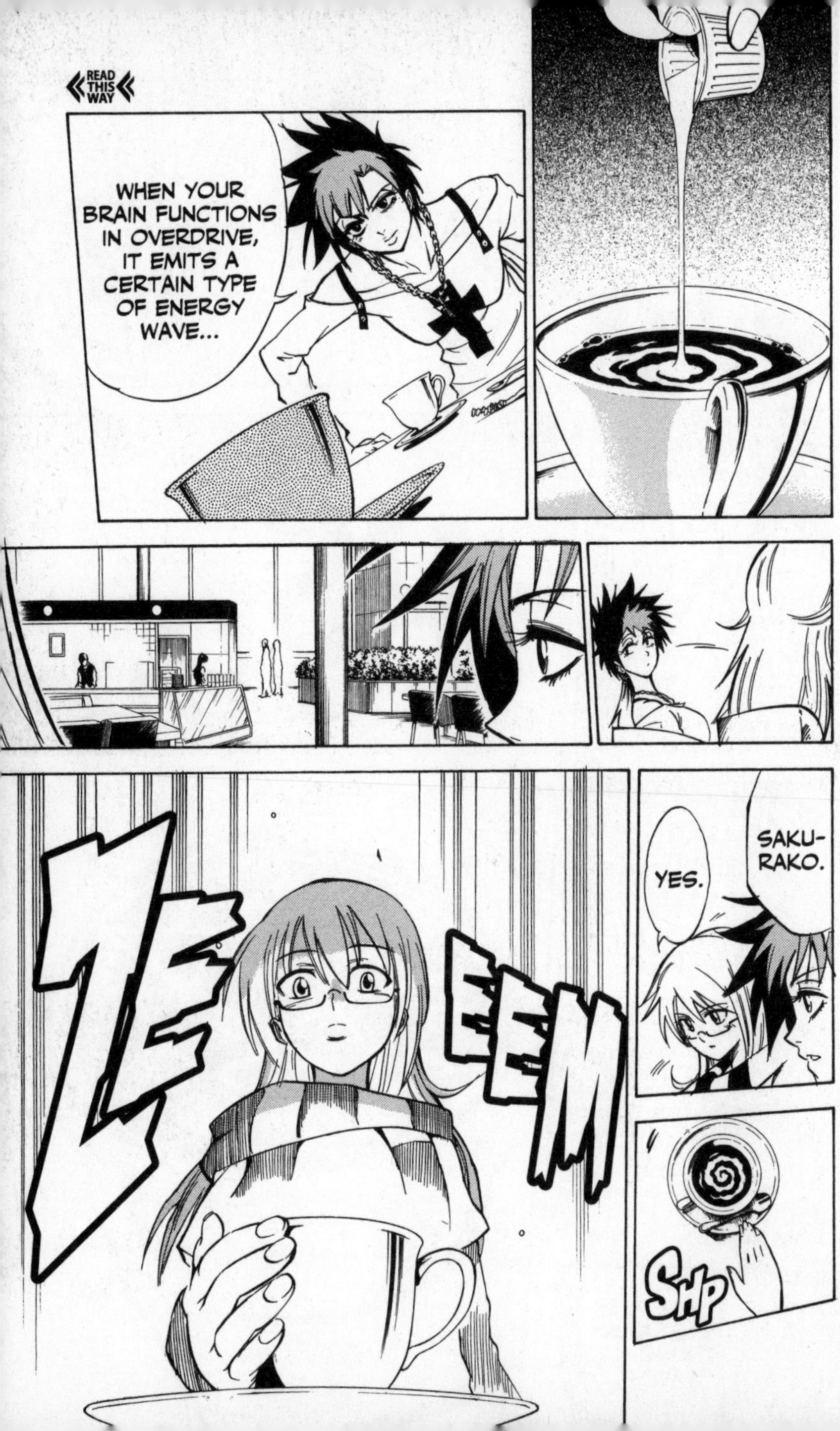
READ THIS WAY
WHEN YOUR BRAIN FUNCTIONS IN OVERDRIVE, IT EMITS A CERTAIN TYPE OF ENERGY WAVE...
SAKU-RAKO.
YES.
SHP
ZEEEM

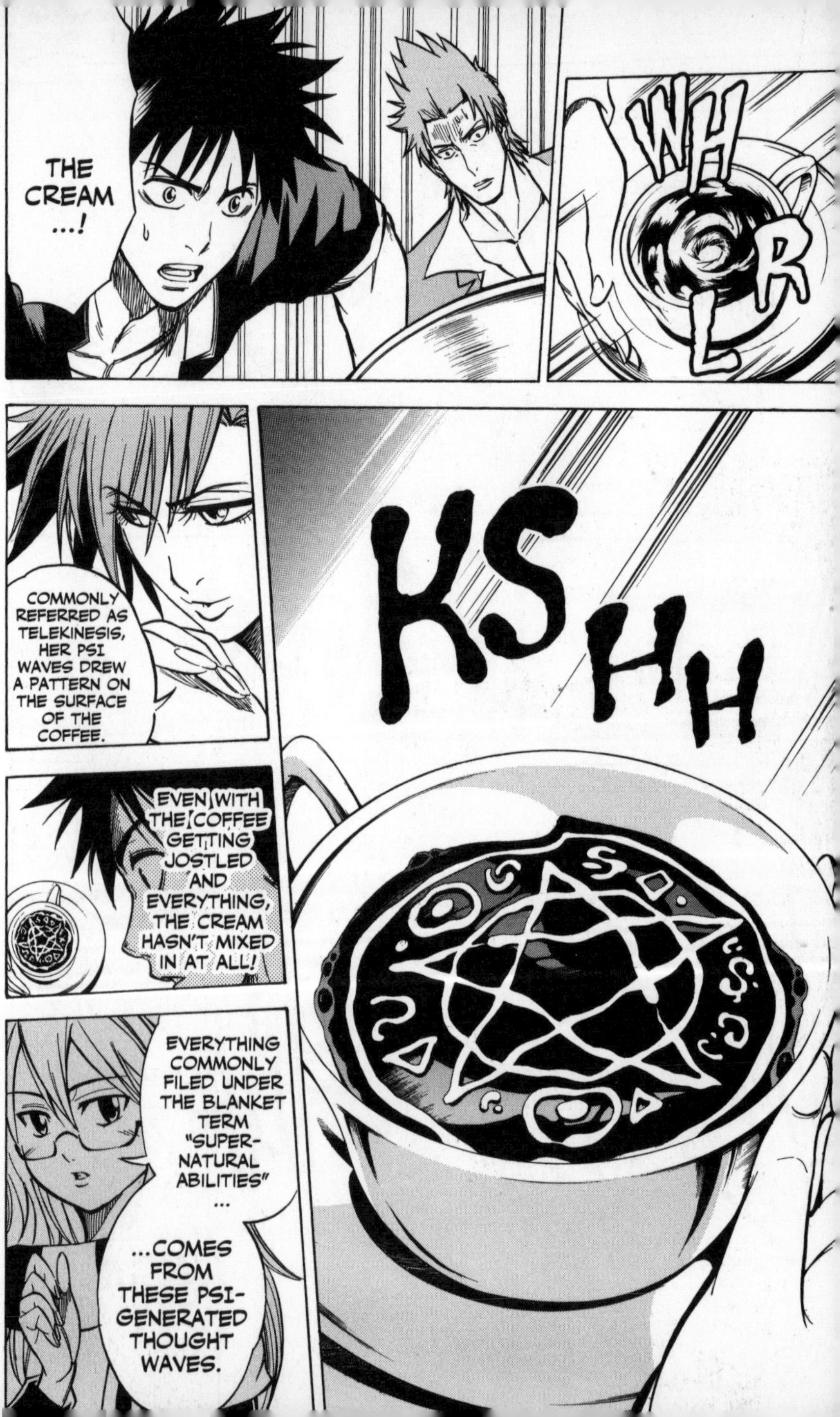
WHRL
THE CREAM ...!
KSHH
COMMONLY REFERRED AS TELEKINESIS, HER PSI WAVES DREW A PATTERN ON THE SURFACE OF THE COFFEE.
EVEN WITH THE COFFEE GETTING JOSTLED AND EVERYTHING, THE CREAM HASN'T MIXED IN AT ALL!
EVERYTHING COMMONLY FILED UNDER THE BLANKET TERM "SUPER-NATURAL ABILITIES" ...
...COMES FROM THESE PSI-GENERATED THOUGHT WAVES.

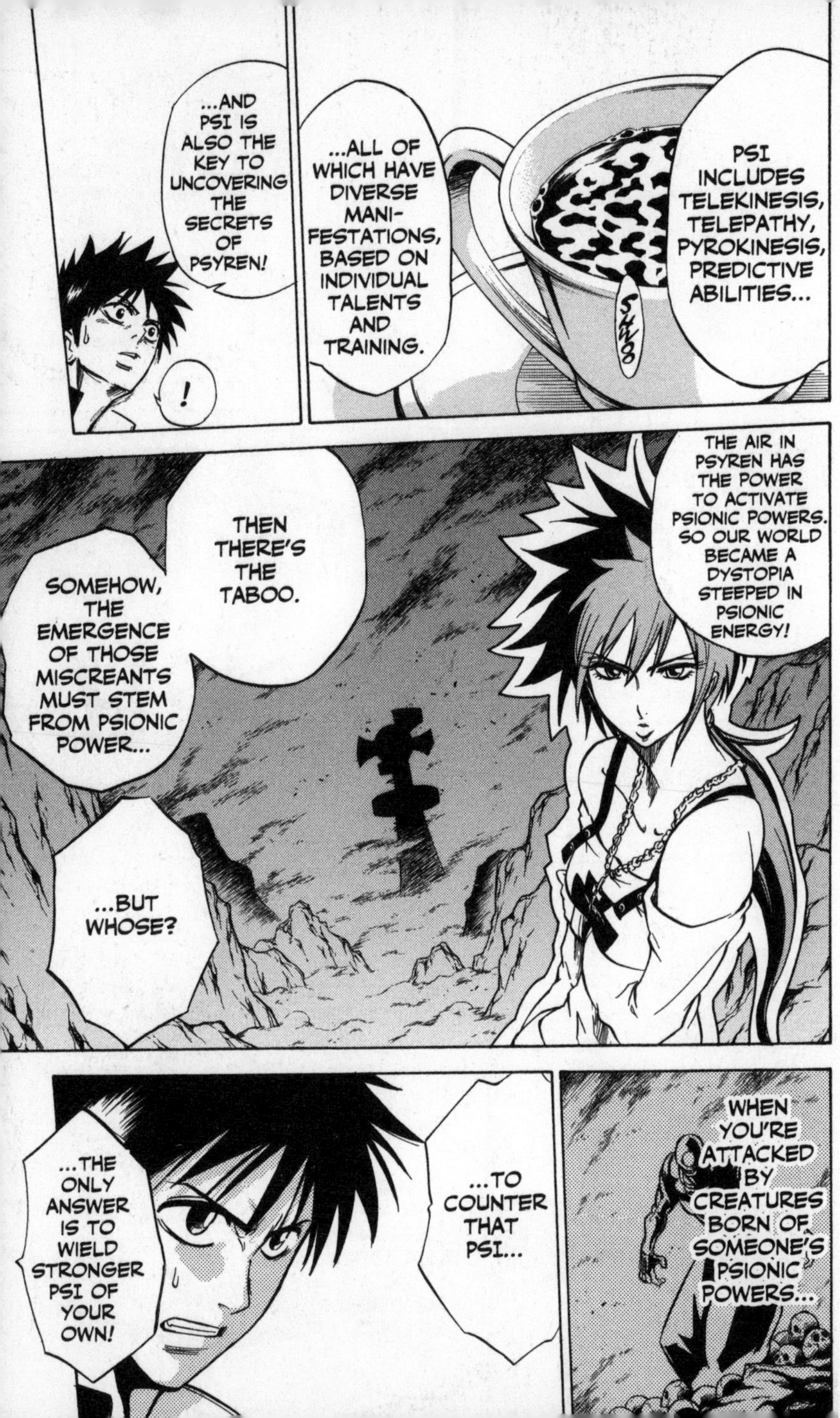
PSI INCLUDES TELEKINESIS, TELEPATHY, PYROKINESIS, PREDICTIVE ABILITIES...
...ALL OF WHICH HAVE DIVERSE MANI-FESTATIONS, BASED ON INDIVIDUAL TALENTS AND TRAINING.
...AND PSI IS ALSO THE KEY TO UNCOVERING THE SECRETS OF PSYREN!
!
THE AIR IN PSYREN HAS THE POWER TO ACTIVATE PSIONIC POWERS. SO OUR WORLD BECAME A DYSTOPIA STEEPED IN PSIONIC ENERGY!
THEN THERE'S THE TABOO.
SOMEHOW, THE EMERGENCE OF THOSE MISCREANTS MUST STEM FROM PSIONIC POWER...
...BUT WHOSE?
WHEN YOU'RE ATTACKED BY CREATURES BORN OF SOMEONE'S PSIONIC POWERS...
...TO COUNTER THAT PSI...
...THE ONLY ANSWER IS TO WIELD STRONGER PSI OF YOUR OWN!

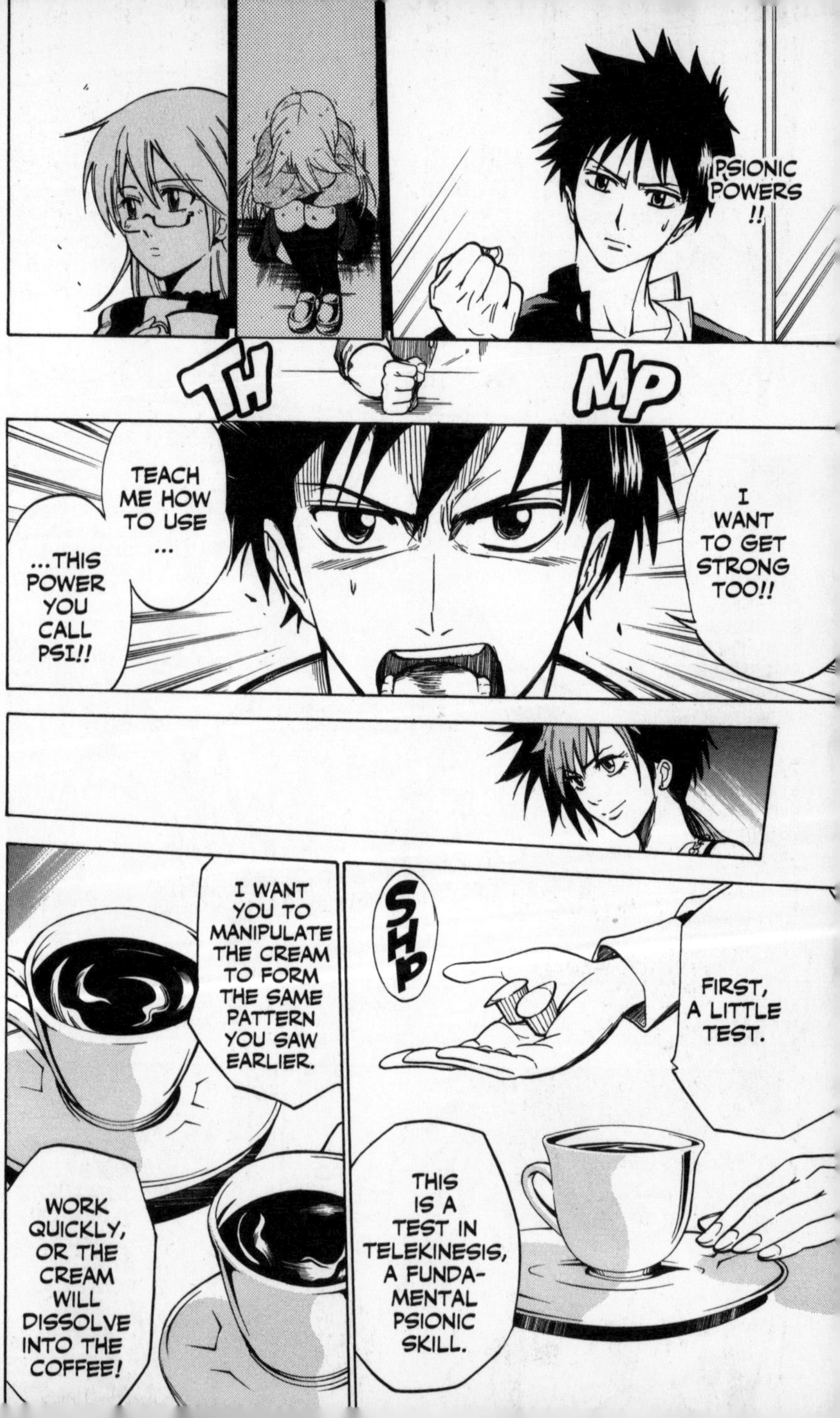
PSIONIC POWERS !!
THMP
I WANT TO GET STRONG TOO!!
TEACH ME HOW TO USE ...
...THIS POWER YOU CALL PSI!!
FIRST, A LITTLE TEST.
SHP
THIS IS A TEST IN TELEKINESIS, A FUNDA-MENTAL PSIONIC SKILL.
I WANT YOU TO MANIPULATE THE CREAM TO FORM THE SAME PATTERN YOU SAW EARLIER.
WORK QUICKLY, OR THE CREAM WILL DISSOLVE INTO THE COFFEE!

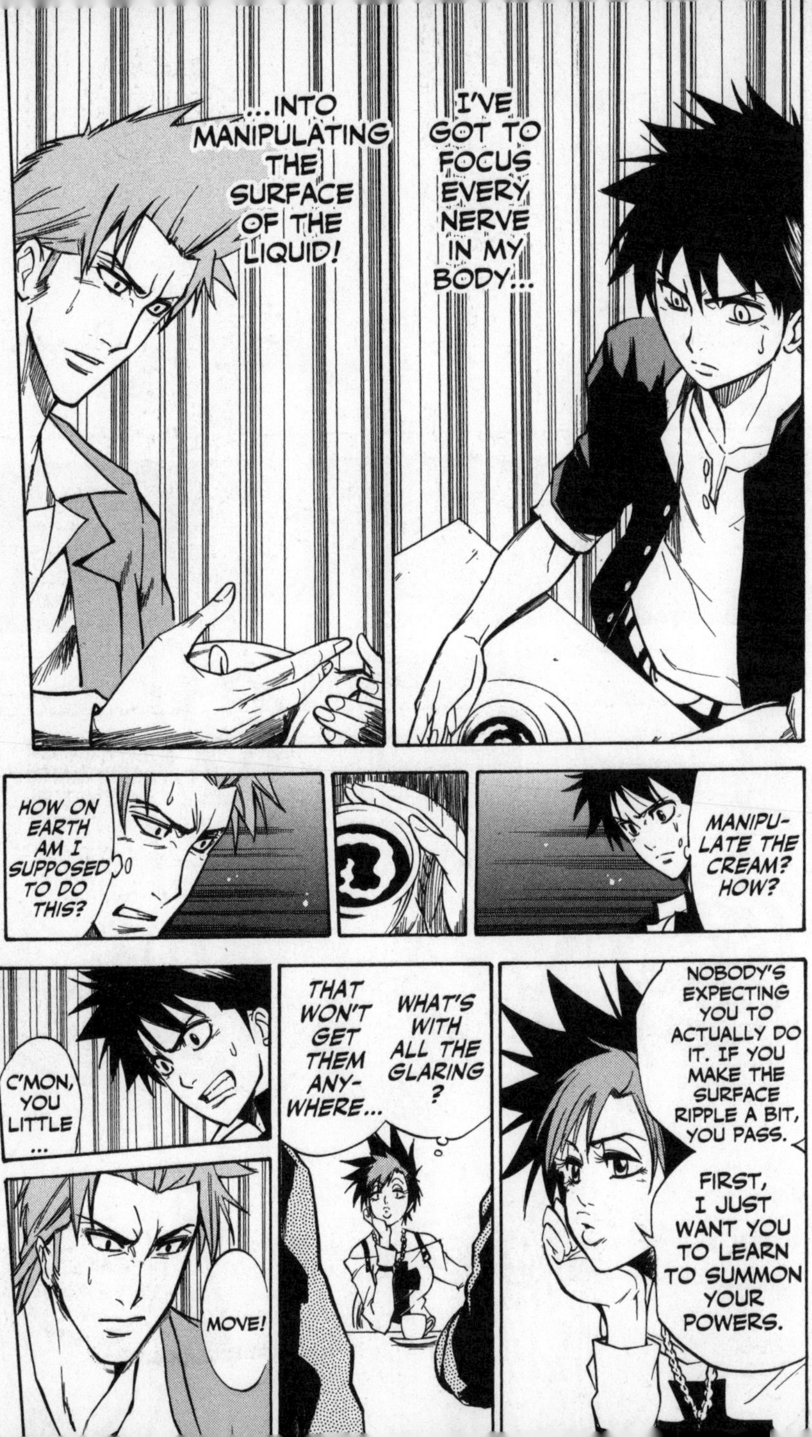
I'VE GOT TO FOCUS EVERY NERVE IN MY BODY...
...INTO MANIPULATING THE SURFACE OF THE LIQUID!
MANIPU-LATE THE CREAM? HOW?
HOW ON EARTH AM I SUPPOSED TO DO THIS?
NOBODY'S EXPECTING YOU TO ACTUALLY DO IT. IF YOU MAKE THE SURFACE RIPPLE A BIT, YOU PASS.
FIRST, I JUST WANT YOU TO LEARN TO SUMMON YOUR POWERS.
WHAT'S WITH ALL THE GLARING?
THAT WON'T GET THEM ANY-WHERE...
C'MON, YOU LITTLE...
MOVE!

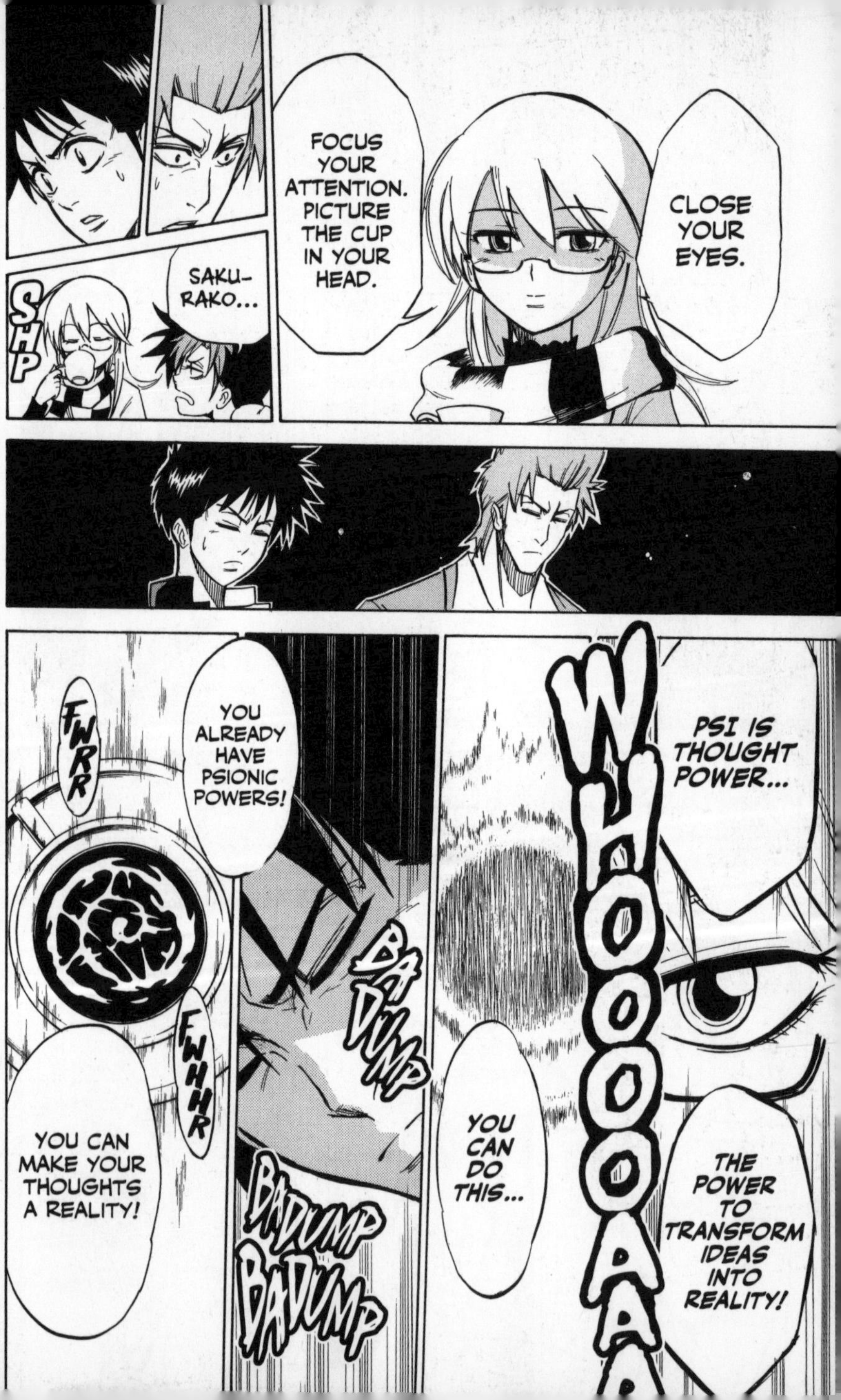
CLOSE YOUR EYES.
FOCUS YOUR ATTENTION. PICTURE THE CUP IN YOUR HEAD.
SAKU-RAKO...
SHP
PSI IS THOUGHT POWER...
WHOOOOOA
THE POWER TO TRANSFORM IDEAS INTO REALITY!
YOU CAN DO THIS...
BA DUMP
BADUMP BADUMP
YOU ALREADY HAVE PSIONIC POWERS!
FWRR
FWHHR
YOU CAN MAKE YOUR THOUGHTS A REALITY!

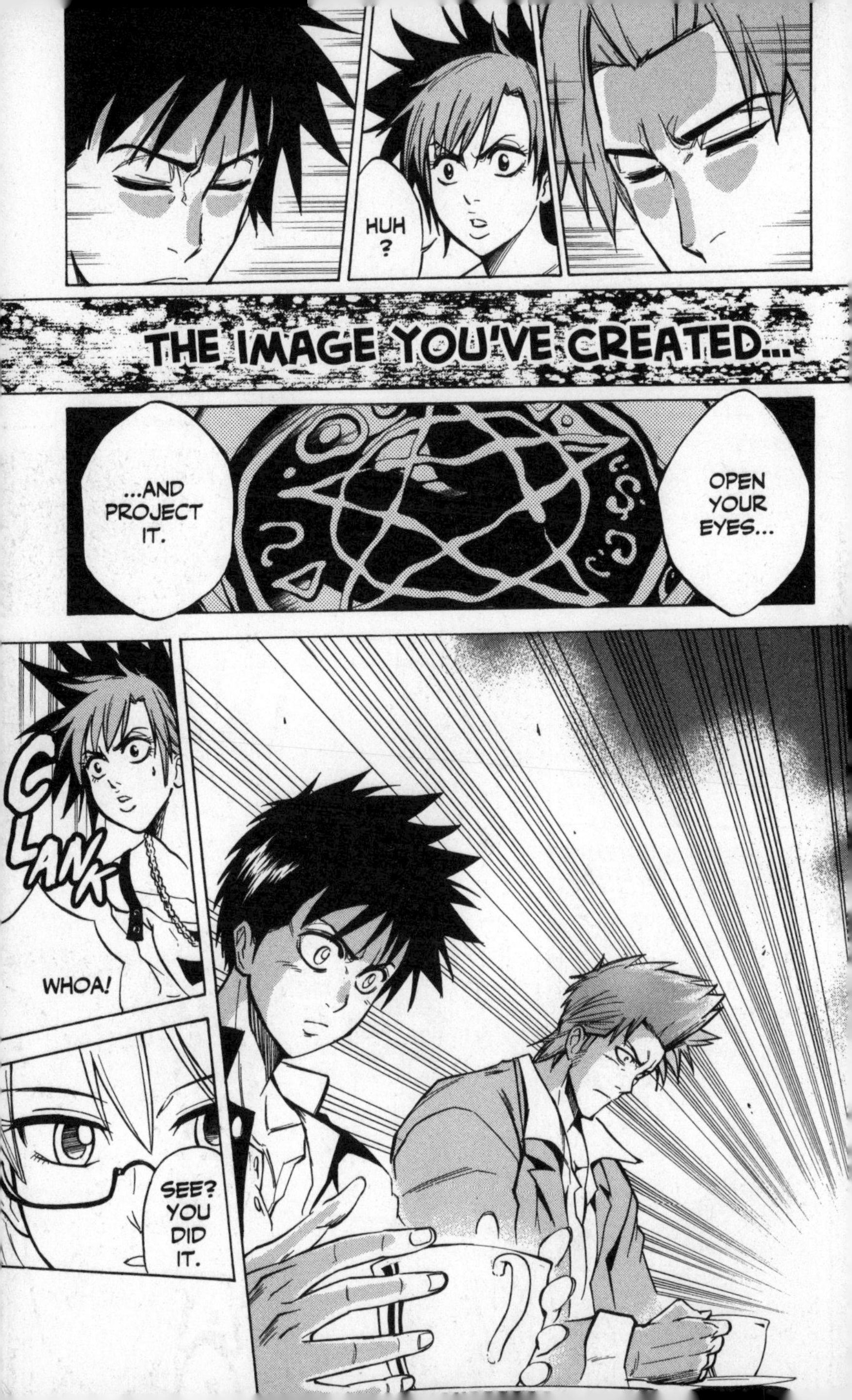
HUH?
THE IMAGE YOU'VE CREATED...
OPEN YOUR EYES...
...AND PROJECT IT.
CLANK
WHOA!
SEE? YOU DID IT.

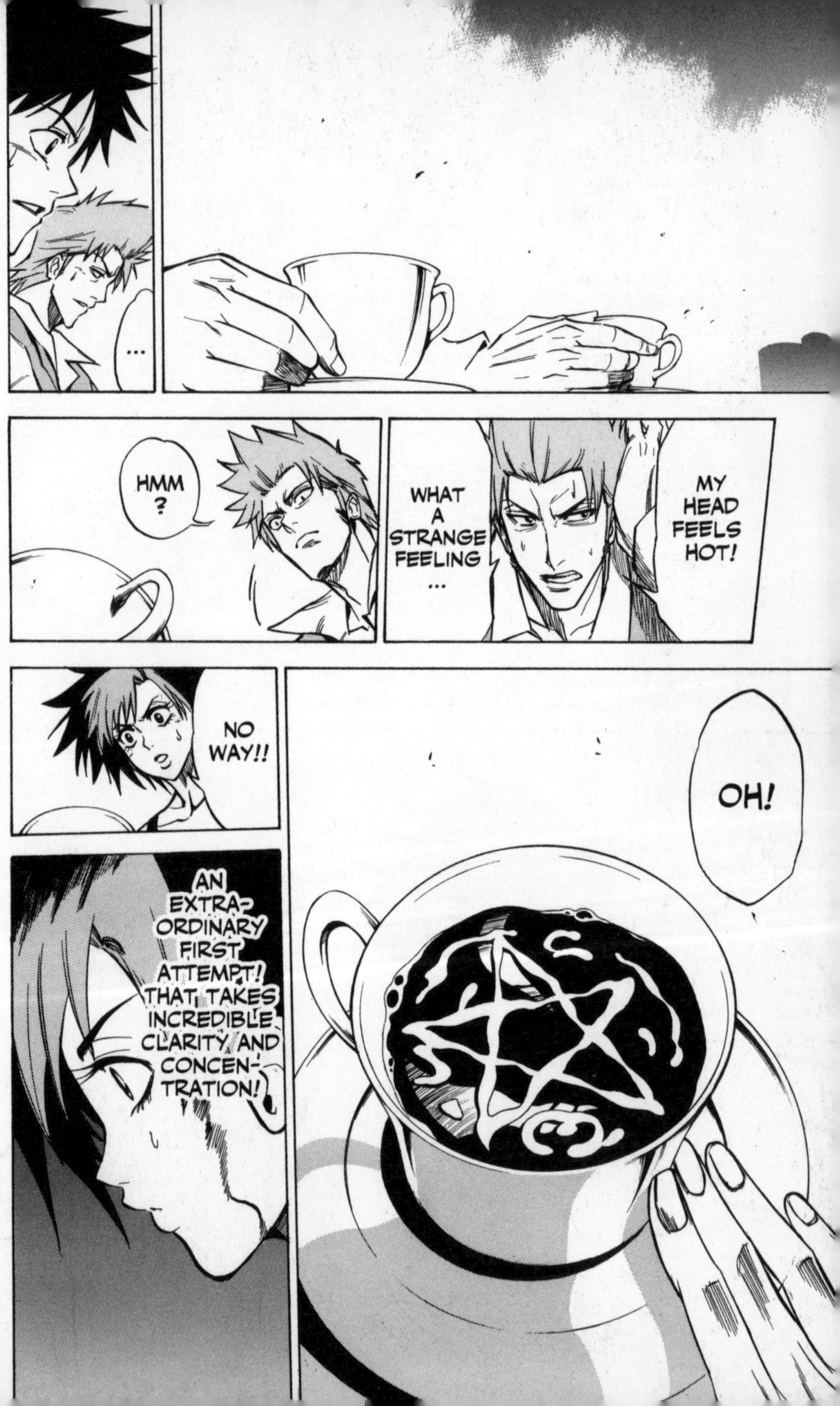
...
MY HEAD FEELS HOT!
WHAT A STRANGE FEELING ...
HMM?
OH!
NO WAY!!
AN EXTRA-ORDINARY FIRST ATTEMPT! THAT TAKES INCREDIBLE CLARITY AND CONCEN-TRATION!

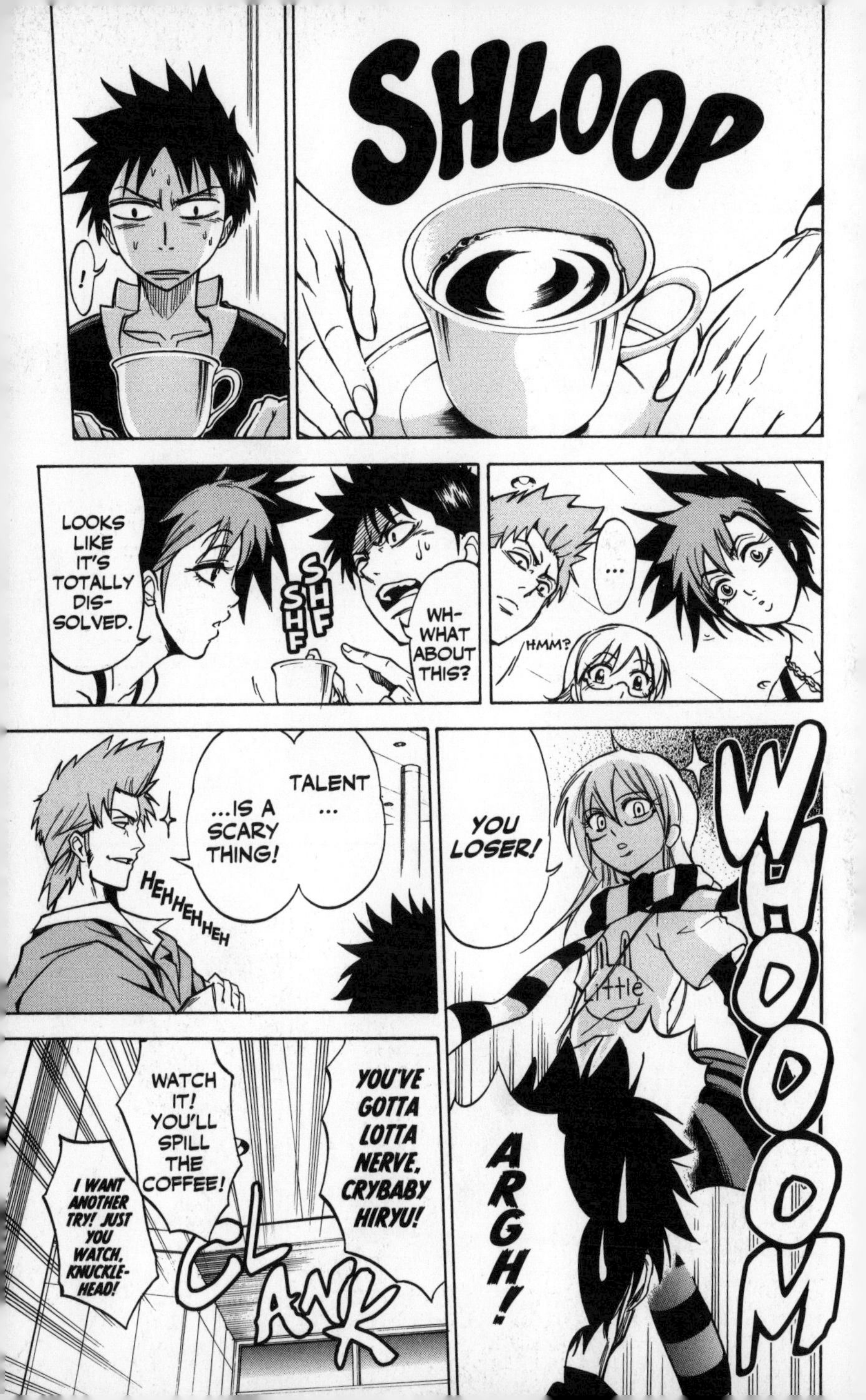
SHLOOP
!
...
HMM?
WH-WHAT ABOUT THIS?
SHF SHF
LOOKS LIKE IT'S TOTALLY DIS-SOLVED.
WHOOOOM
YOU LOSER!
little
ARGH!
TALENT ...
...IS A SCARY THING!
HEHHEHHEH
YOU'VE GOTTA LOTTA NERVE, CRYBABY HIRYU!
WATCH IT! YOU'LL SPILL THE COFFEE!
I WANT ANOTHER TRY! JUST YOU WATCH, KNUCKLE-HEAD!
CLANK

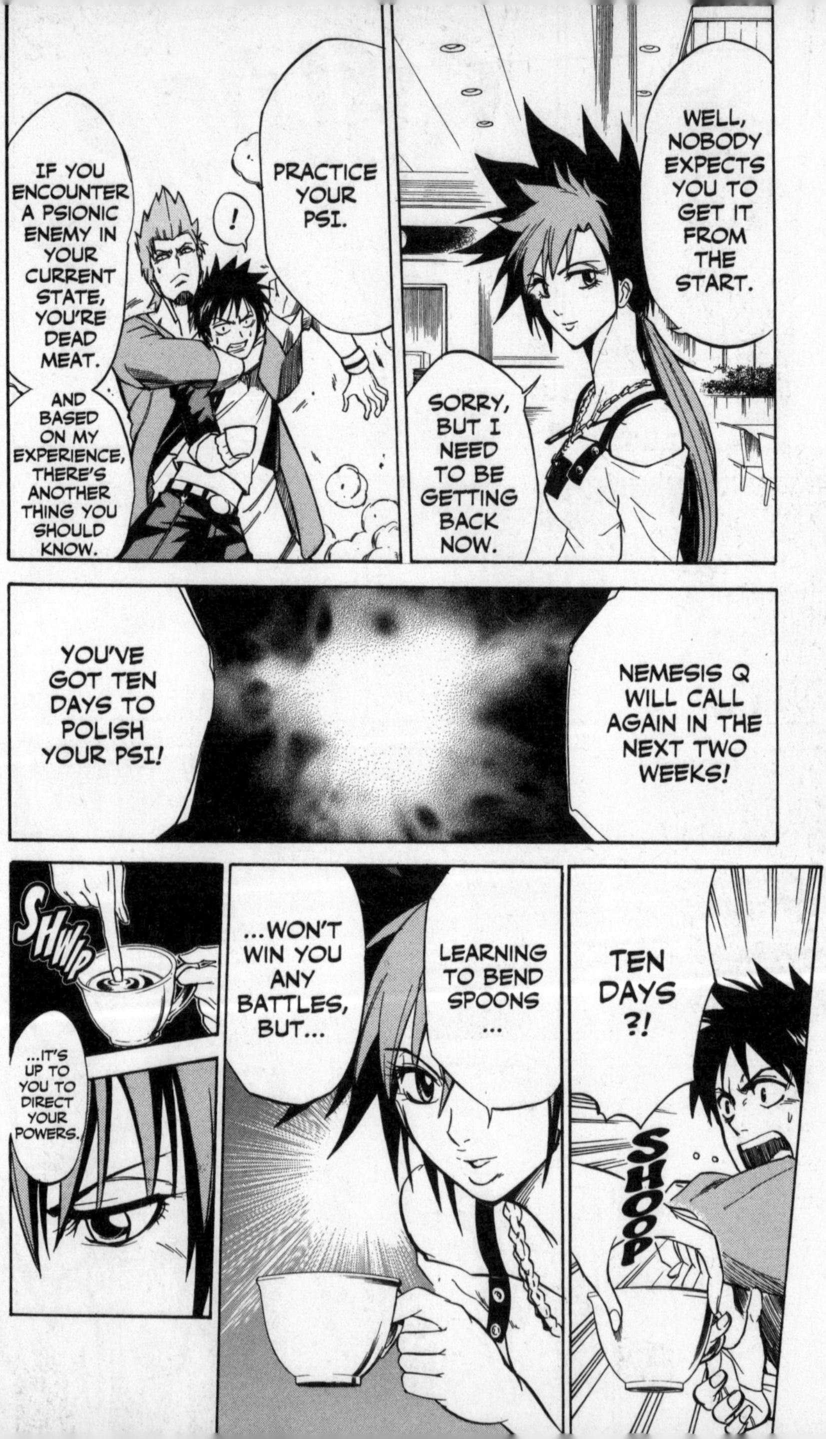
WELL, NOBODY EXPECTS YOU TO GET IT FROM THE START.
SORRY, BUT I NEED TO BE GETTING BACK NOW.
PRACTICE YOUR PSI.
!
IF YOU ENCOUNTER A PSIONIC ENEMY IN YOUR CURRENT STATE, YOU'RE DEAD MEAT.
AND BASED ON MY EXPERIENCE, THERE'S ANOTHER THING YOU SHOULD KNOW.
NEMESIS Q WILL CALL AGAIN IN THE NEXT TWO WEEKS!
YOU'VE GOT TEN DAYS TO POLISH YOUR PSI!
TEN DAYS ?!
SHOOP
LEARNING TO BEND SPOONS ...
...WON'T WIN YOU ANY BATTLES, BUT...
SHWIP
...IT'S UP TO YOU TO DIRECT YOUR POWERS.

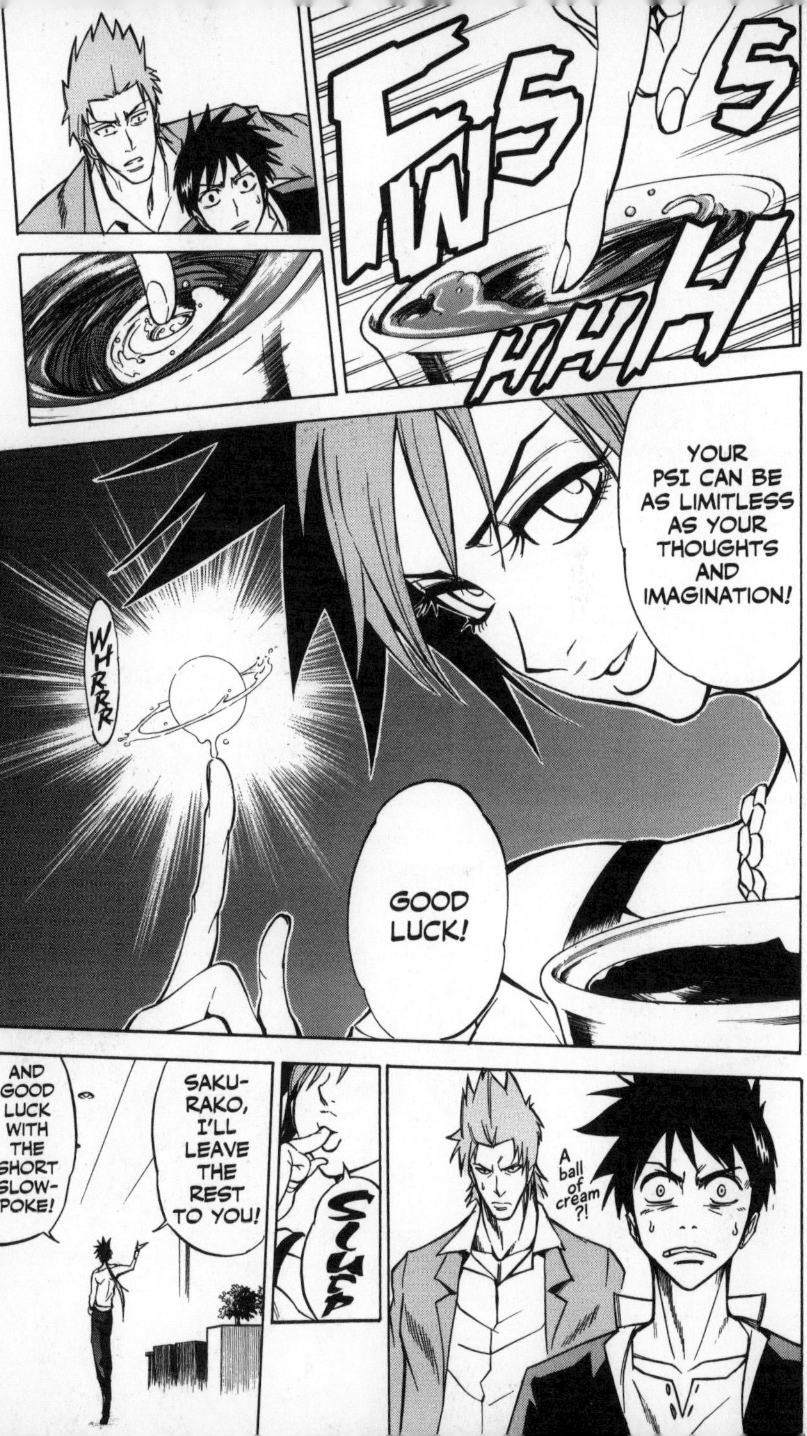
FWSSHHHH
YOUR PSI CAN BE AS LIMITLESS AS YOUR THOUGHTS AND IMAGINATION!
WHRRR
GOOD LUCK!
A ball of cream?!
SLURP
SAKU-RAKO, I'LL LEAVE THE REST TO YOU!
AND GOOD LUCK WITH THE SHORT SLOW-POKE!

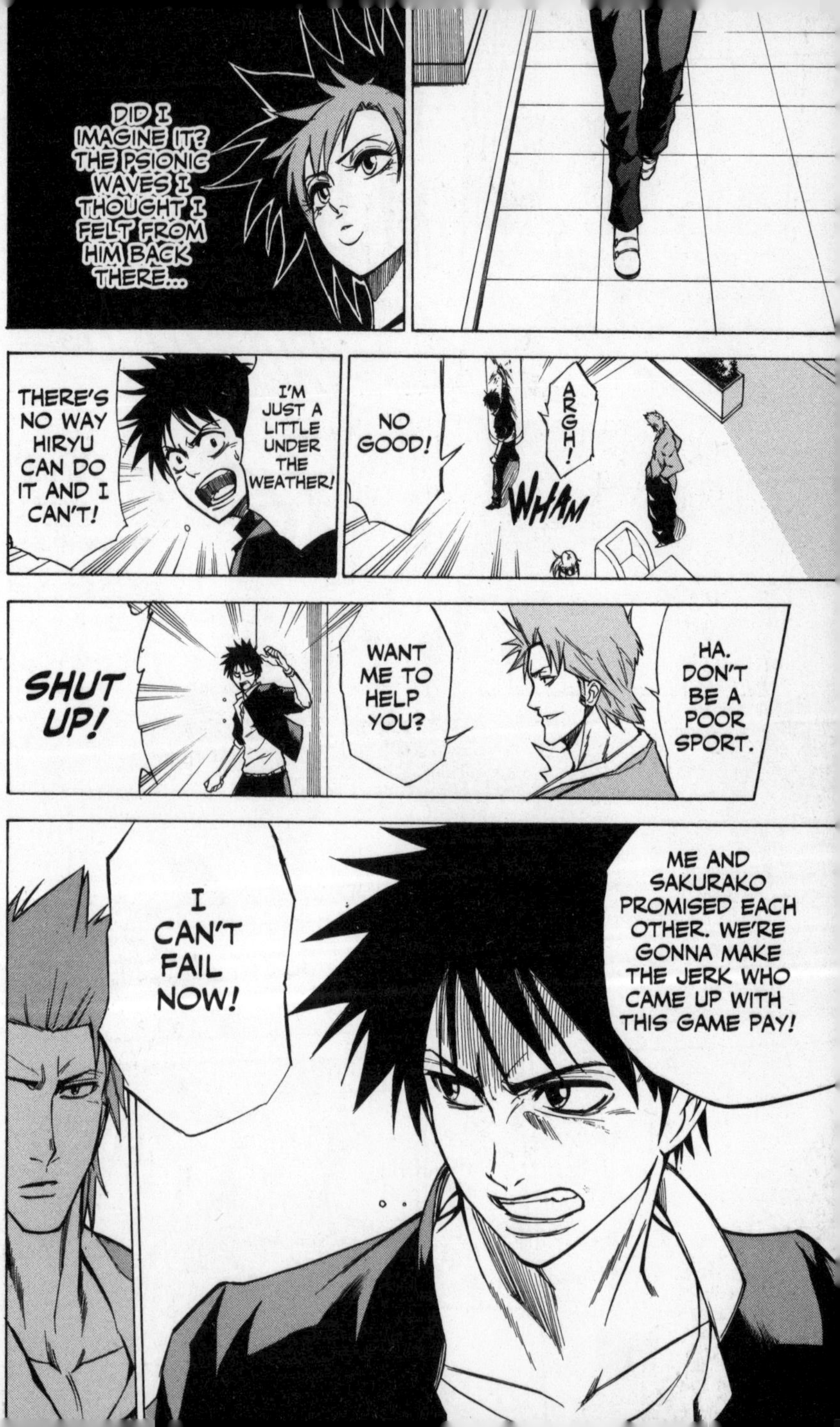
DID I IMAGINE IT? THE PSIONIC WAVES I THOUGHT I FELT FROM HIM BACK THERE...
ARGH!
WHAM
NO GOOD!
I'M JUST A LITTLE UNDER THE WEATHER!
THERE'S NO WAY HIRYU CAN DO IT AND I CAN'T!
HA. DON'T BE A POOR SPORT.
WANT ME TO HELP YOU?
SHUT UP!
ME AND SAKURAKO PROMISED EACH OTHER. WE'RE GONNA MAKE THE JERK WHO CAME UP WITH THIS GAME PAY!
I CAN'T FAIL NOW!

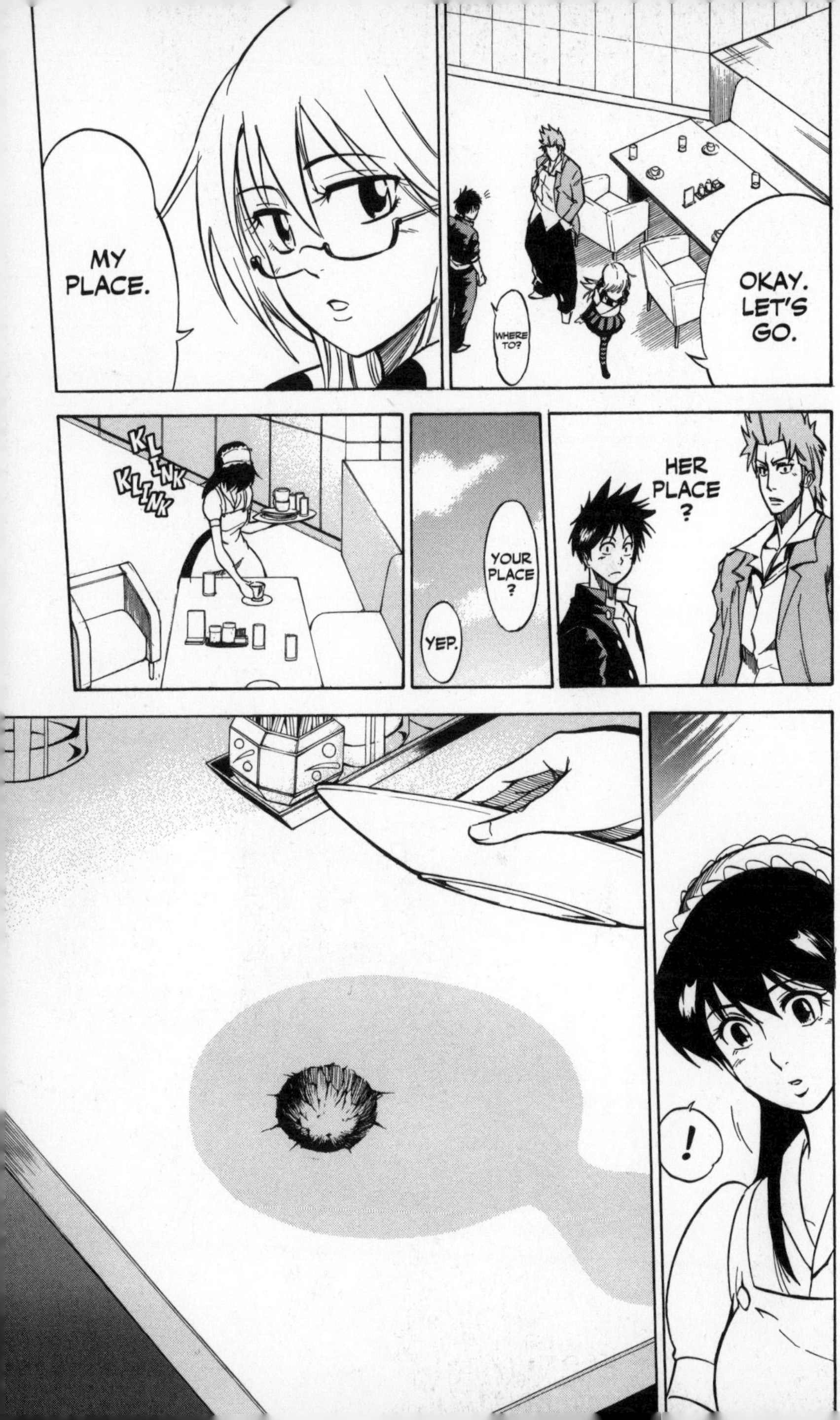
OKAY. LET'S GO.
WHERE TO?
MY PLACE.
HER PLACE?
YOUR PLACE?
YEP.
KLINK KLINK
!

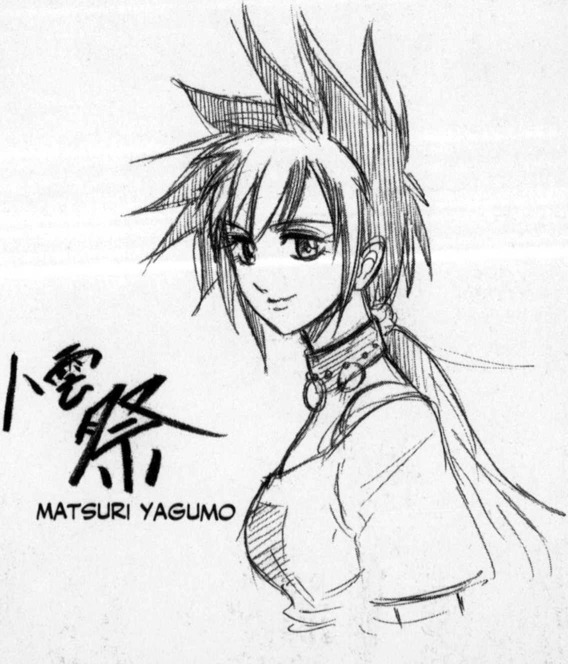
八雲祭
MATSURI YAGUMO

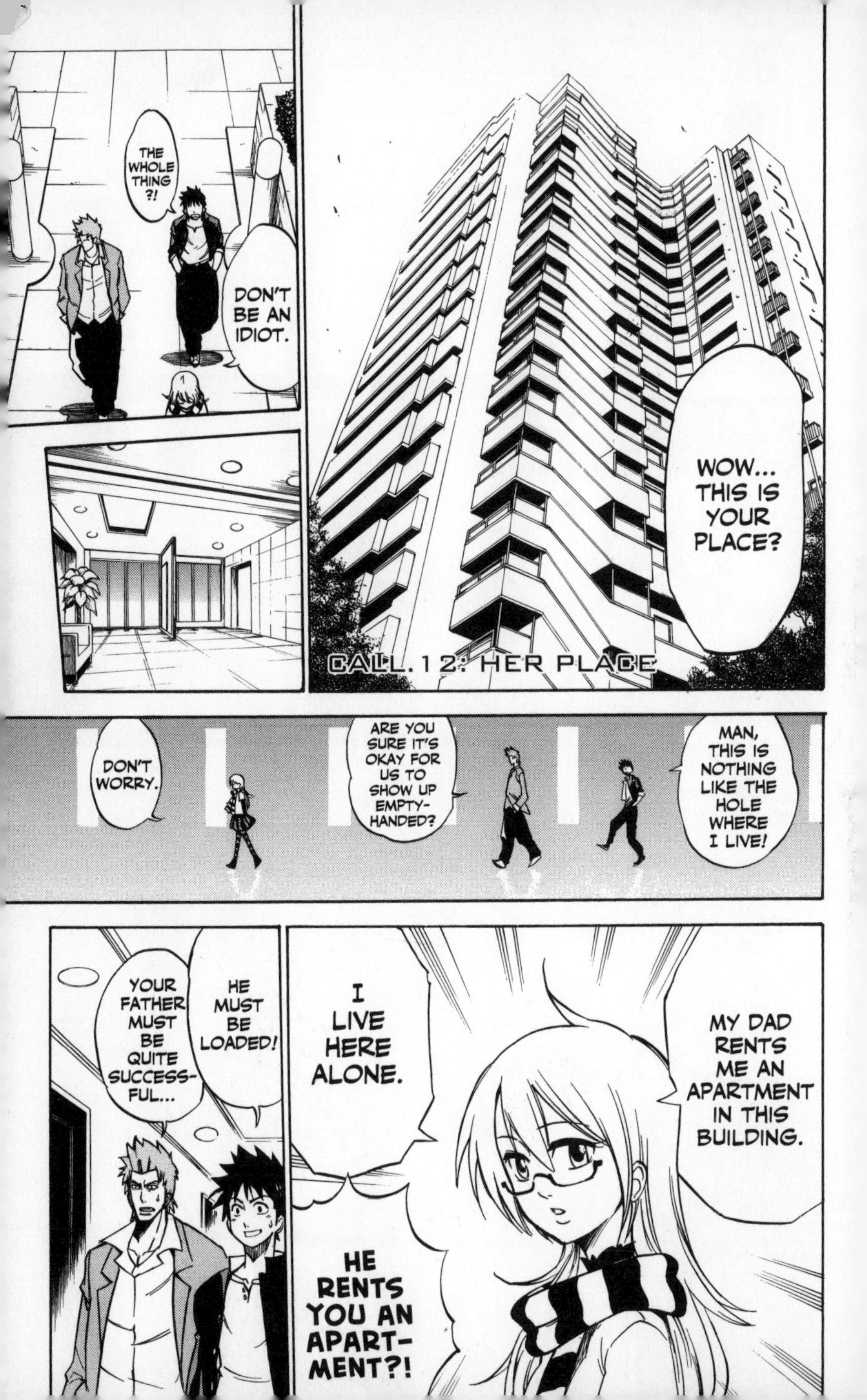
WOW... THIS IS YOUR PLACE?
CALL. 12: HER PLACE
THE WHOLE THING?!
DON'T BE AN IDIOT.
MAN, THIS IS NOTHING LIKE THE HOLE WHERE I LIVE!
ARE YOU SURE IT'S OKAY FOR US TO SHOW UP EMPTY-HANDED?
DON'T WORRY.
MY DAD RENTS ME AN APARTMENT IN THIS BUILDING.
I LIVE HERE ALONE.
HE RENTS YOU AN APART-MENT?!
HE MUST BE LOADED!
YOUR FATHER MUST BE QUITE SUCCESS-FUL...

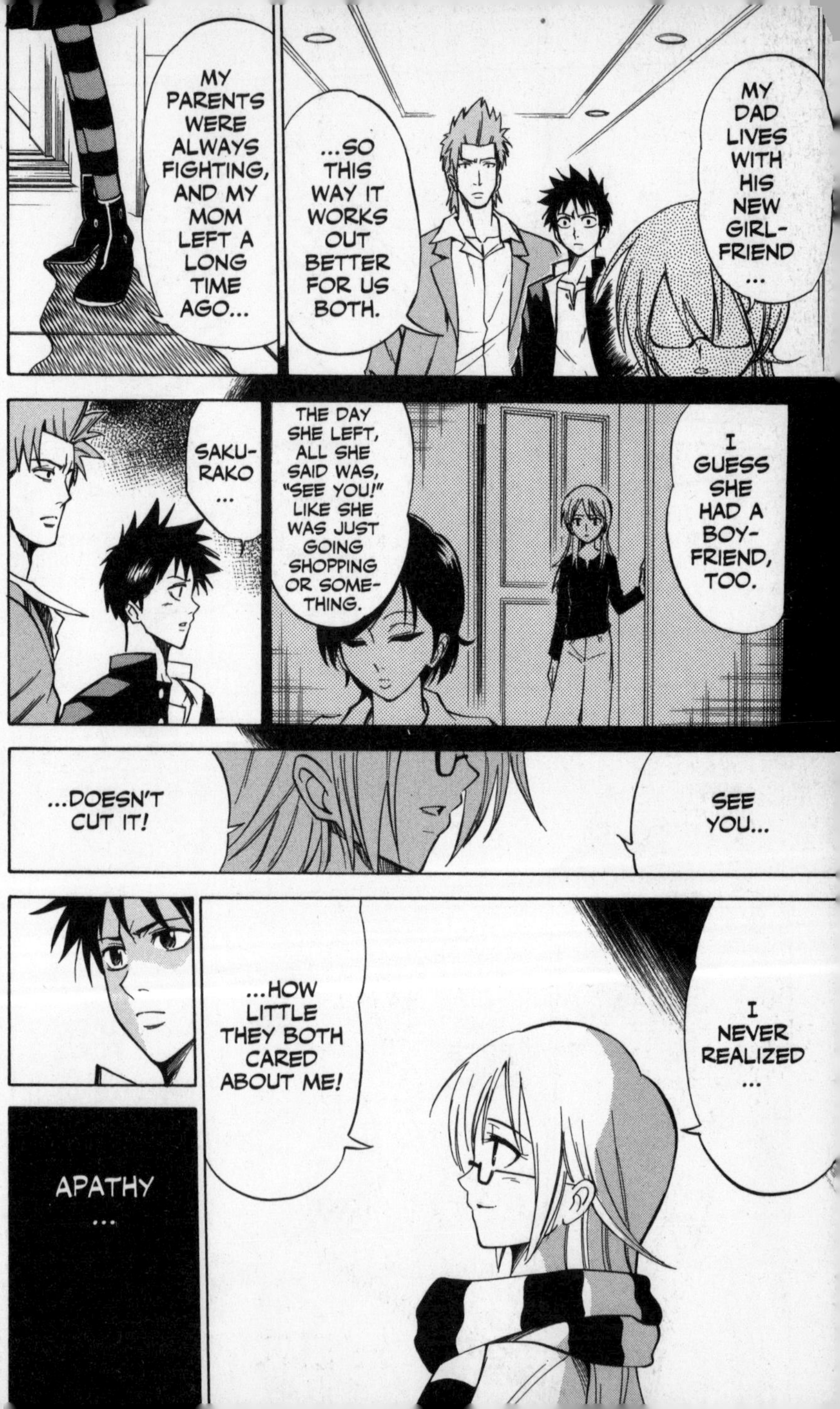
MY DAD LIVES WITH HIS NEW GIRL-FRIEND ...
...SO THIS WAY IT WORKS OUT BETTER FOR US BOTH.
MY PARENTS WERE ALWAYS FIGHTING, AND MY MOM LEFT A LONG TIME AGO...
I GUESS SHE HAD A BOY-FRIEND, TOO.
THE DAY SHE LEFT, ALL SHE SAID WAS, "SEE YOU!" LIKE SHE WAS JUST GOING SHOPPING OR SOME-THING.
SAKU-RAKO ...
SEE YOU...
...DOESN'T CUT IT!
I NEVER REALIZED ...
...HOW LITTLE THEY BOTH CARED ABOUT ME!
APATHY ...

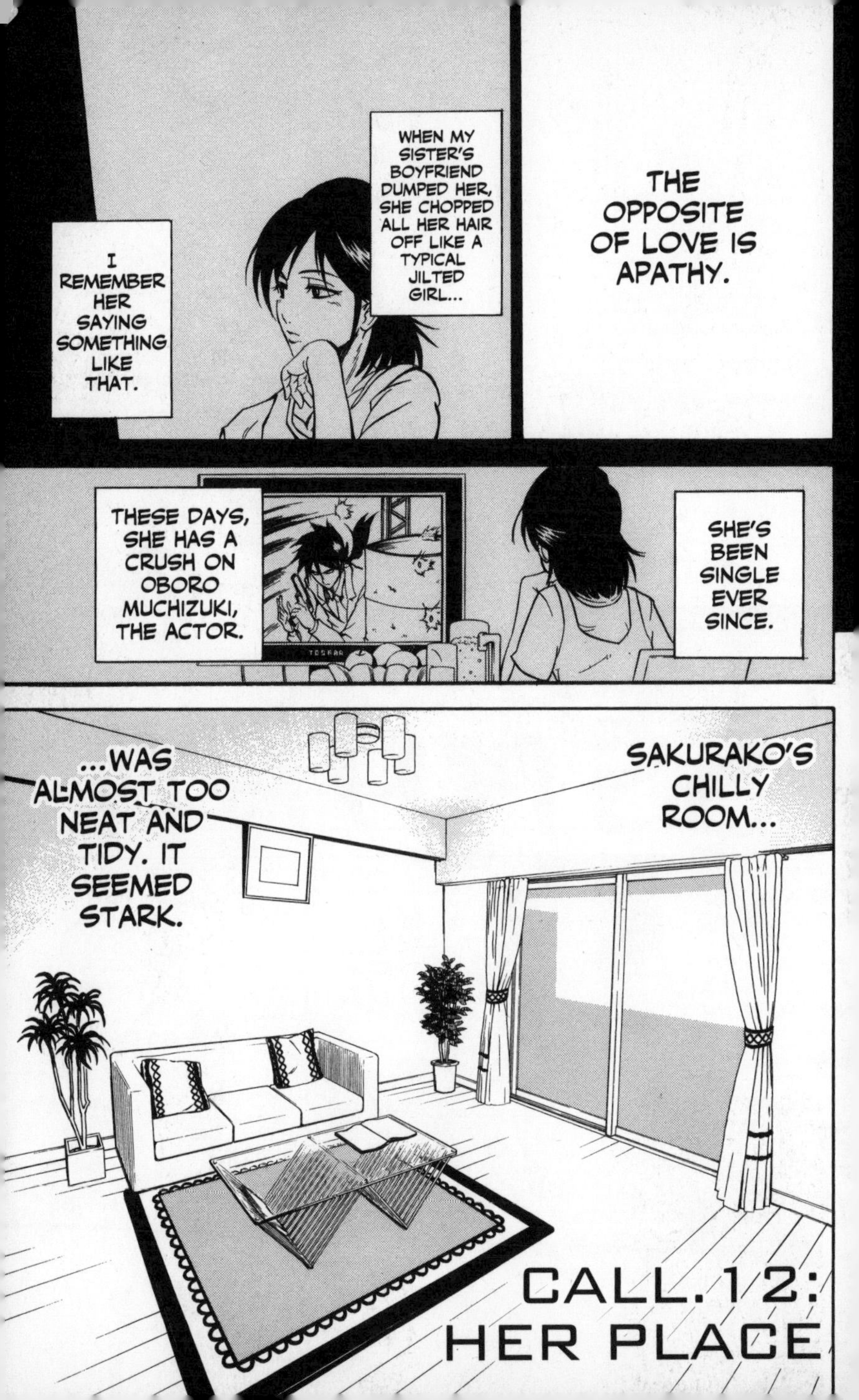
THE OPPOSITE OF LOVE IS APATHY.
WHEN MY SISTER'S BOYFRIEND DUMPED HER, SHE CHOPPED ALL HER HAIR OFF LIKE A TYPICAL JILTED GIRL...
I REMEMBER HER SAYING SOMETHING LIKE THAT.
SHE'S BEEN SINGLE EVER SINCE.
THESE DAYS, SHE HAS A CRUSH ON OBORO MUCHIZUKI, THE ACTOR.
SAKURAKO'S CHILLY ROOM...
...WAS ALMOST TOO NEAT AND TIDY. IT SEEMED STARK.
CALL.12: HER PLACE

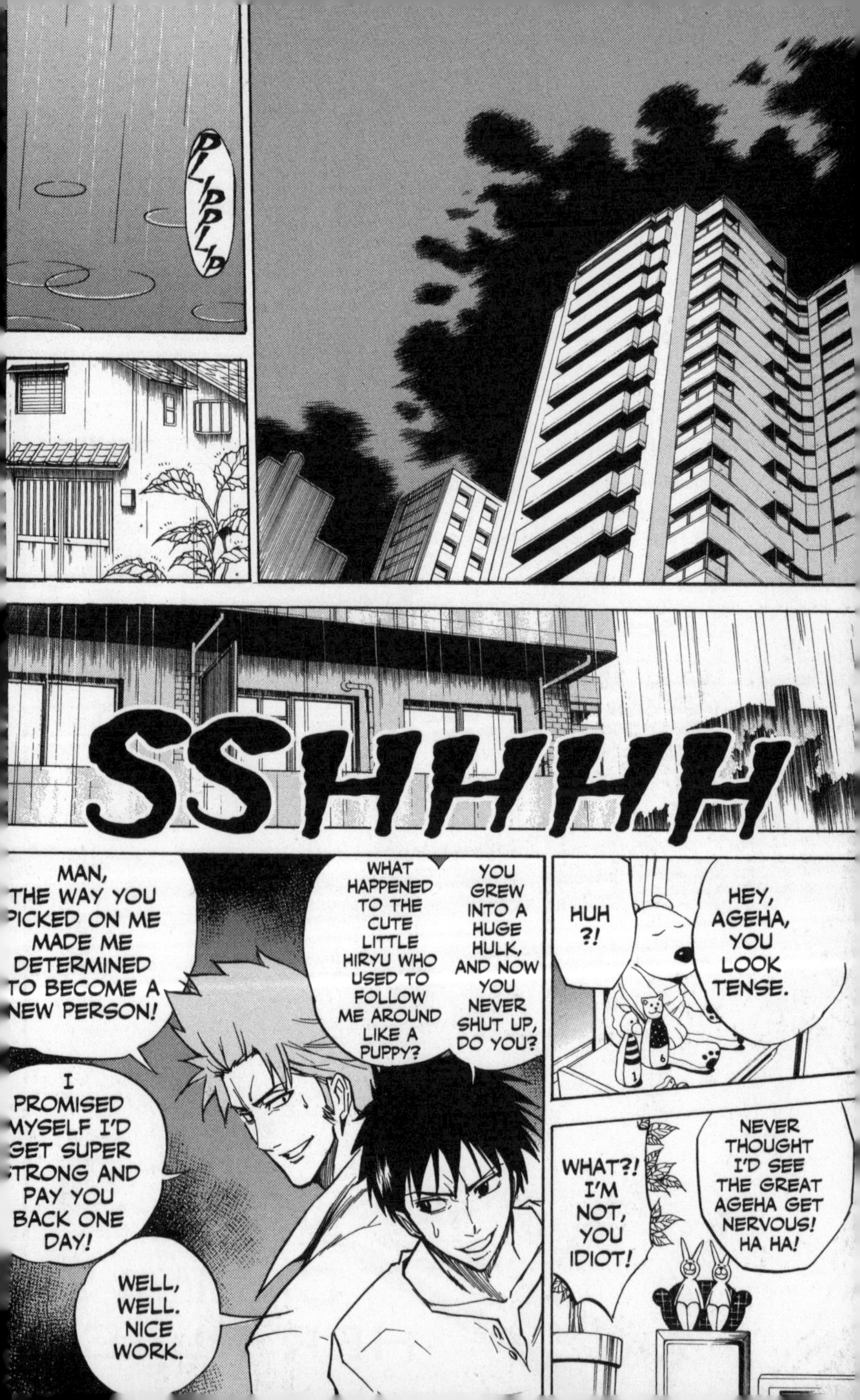
PLIPPLIP
SSHHHH
HEY, AGEHA, YOU LOOK TENSE.
HUH?!
NEVER THOUGHT I'D SEE THE GREAT AGEHA GET NERVOUS! HA HA!
WHAT?! I'M NOT, YOU IDIOT!
YOU GREW INTO A HUGE HULK, AND NOW YOU NEVER SHUT UP, DO YOU?
WHAT HAPPENED TO THE CUTE LITTLE HIRYU WHO USED TO FOLLOW ME AROUND LIKE A PUPPY?
MAN, THE WAY YOU PICKED ON ME MADE ME DETERMINED TO BECOME A NEW PERSON!
I PROMISED MYSELF I'D GET SUPER STRONG AND PAY YOU BACK ONE DAY!
WELL, WELL. NICE WORK.

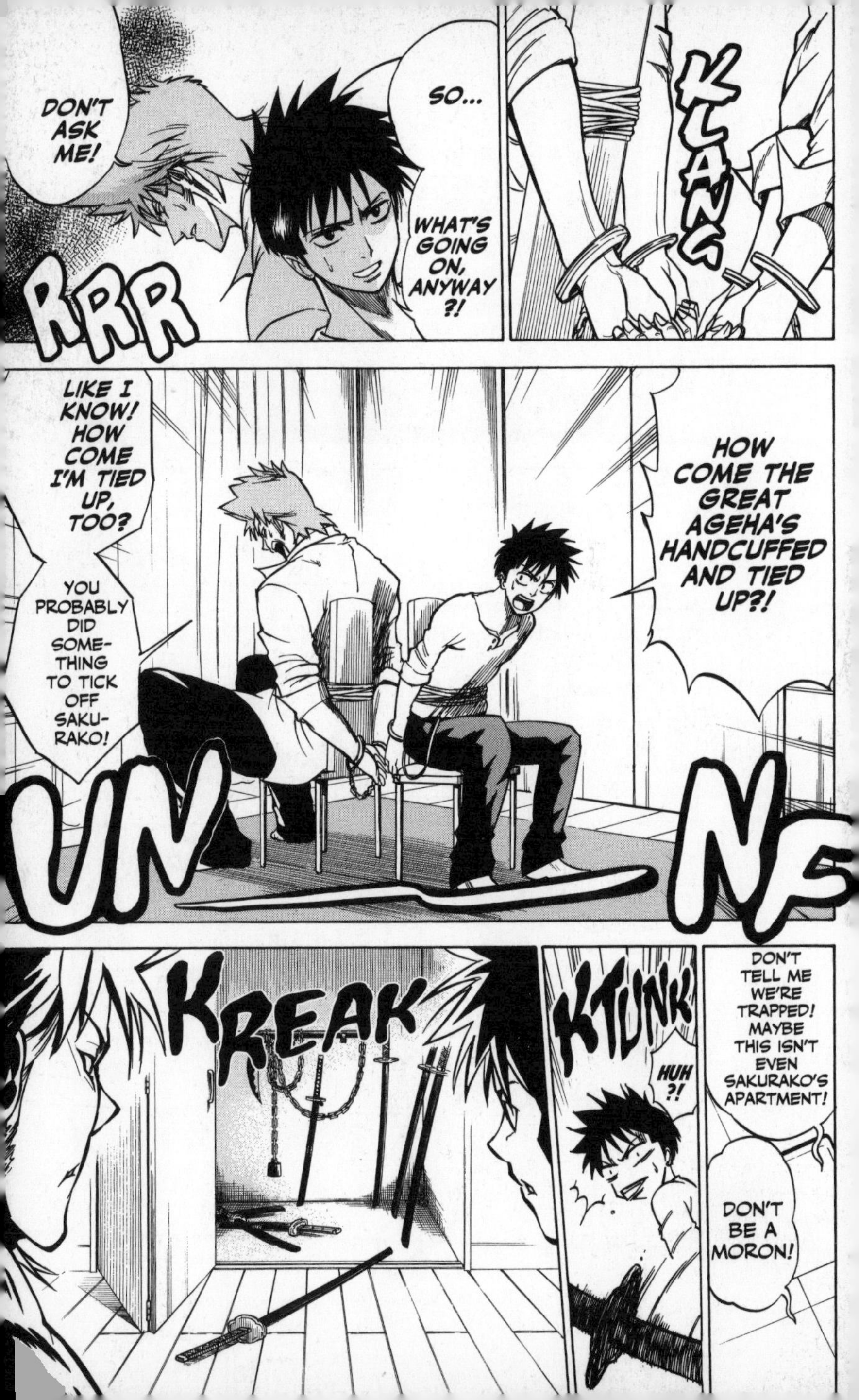
KLANG
SO...
WHAT'S GOING ON, ANYWAY?!
DON'T ASK ME!
RRR
HOW COME THE GREAT AGEHA'S HANDCUFFED AND TIED UP?!
LIKE I KNOW! HOW COME I'M TIED UP, TOO?
YOU PROBABLY DID SOME-THING TO TICK OFF SAKU-RAKO!
UNNF
DON'T TELL ME WE'RE TRAPPED! MAYBE THIS ISN'T EVEN SAKURAKO'S APARTMENT!
DON'T BE A MORON!
KTUNK
HUH?!
KREAK

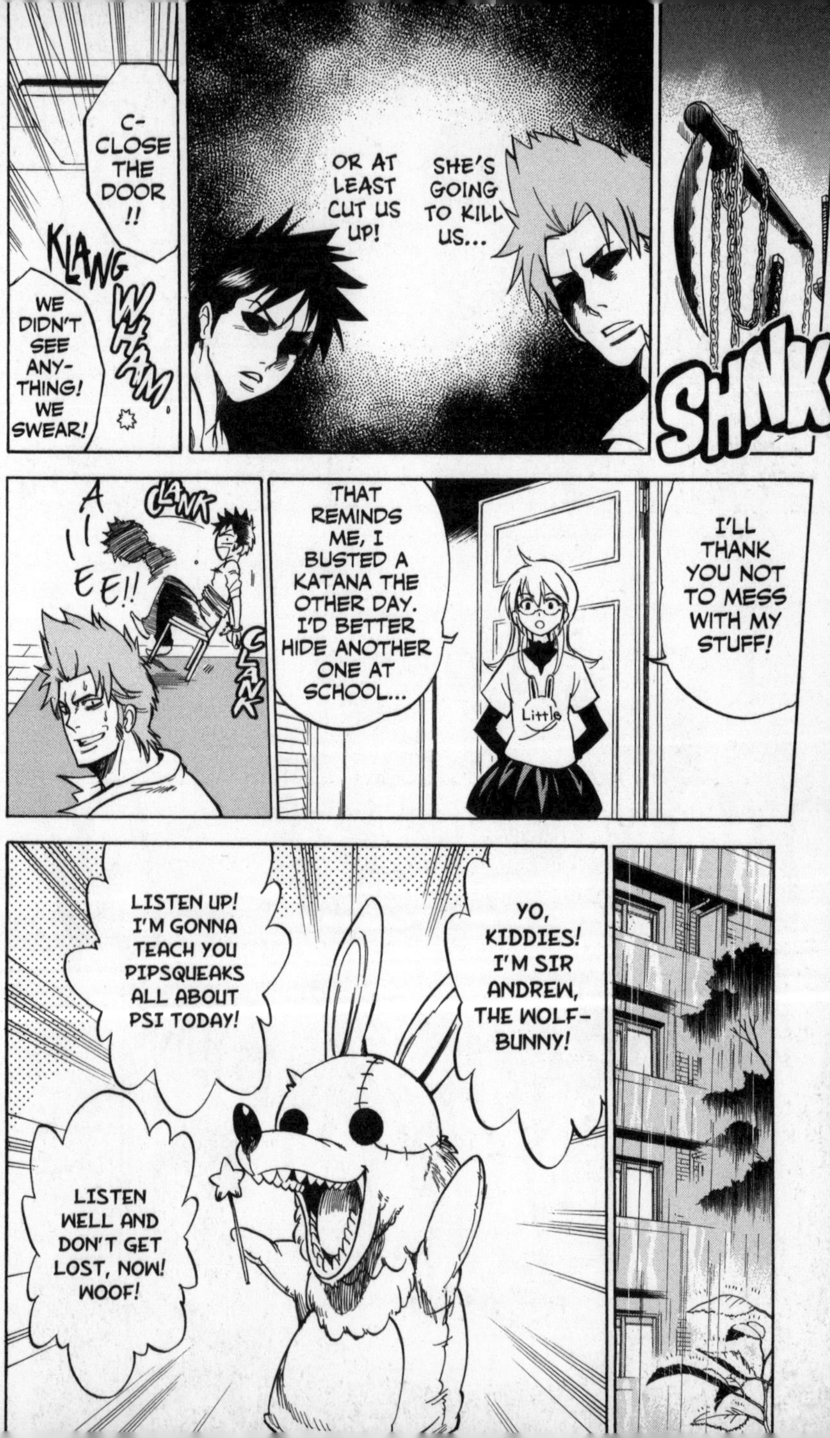
SHNK
SHE'S GOING TO KILL US...
OR AT LEAST CUT US UP!
C-CLOSE THE DOOR!!
KLANG
WHAM
WE DIDN'T SEE ANYTHING! WE SWEAR!
I'LL THANK YOU NOT TO MESS WITH MY STUFF!
Little
THAT REMINDS ME, I BUSTED A KATANA THE OTHER DAY. I'D BETTER HIDE ANOTHER ONE AT SCHOOL...
CLANK
AIIEE!!
CLANK
YO, KIDDIES! I'M SIR ANDREW, THE WOLF-BUNNY!
LISTEN UP! I'M GONNA TEACH YOU PIPSQUEAKS ALL ABOUT PSI TODAY!
LISTEN WELL AND DON'T GET LOST, NOW! WOOF!

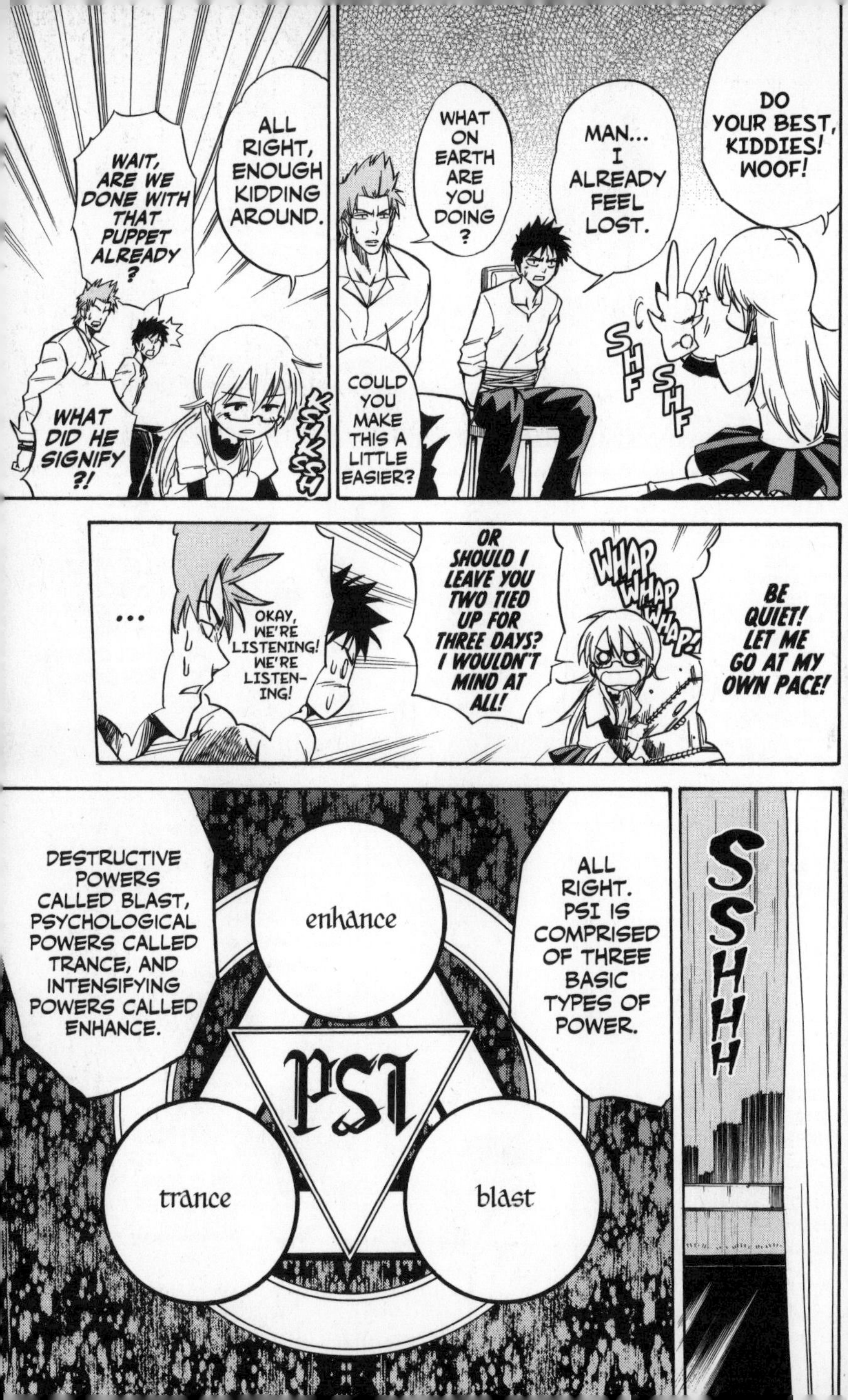
DO YOUR BEST, KIDDIES! WOOF!
SHF SHF
MAN... I ALREADY FEEL LOST.
WHAT ON EARTH ARE YOU DOING?
COULD YOU MAKE THIS A LITTLE EASIER?
ALL RIGHT, ENOUGH KIDDING AROUND.
WAIT, ARE WE DONE WITH THAT PUPPET ALREADY?
KSHKSH
WHAT DID HE SIGNIFY?!
BE QUIET! LET ME GO AT MY OWN PACE!
WHAP WHAP WHAP!
OR SHOULD I LEAVE YOU TWO TIED UP FOR THREE DAYS? I WOULDN'T MIND AT ALL!
OKAY, WE'RE LISTENING! WE'RE LISTEN-ING!
...
SSHHH
ALL RIGHT. PSI IS COMPRISED OF THREE BASIC TYPES OF POWER.
enhance
PSI
trance
blast
DESTRUCTIVE POWERS CALLED BLAST, PSYCHOLOGICAL POWERS CALLED TRANCE, AND INTENSIFYING POWERS CALLED ENHANCE.

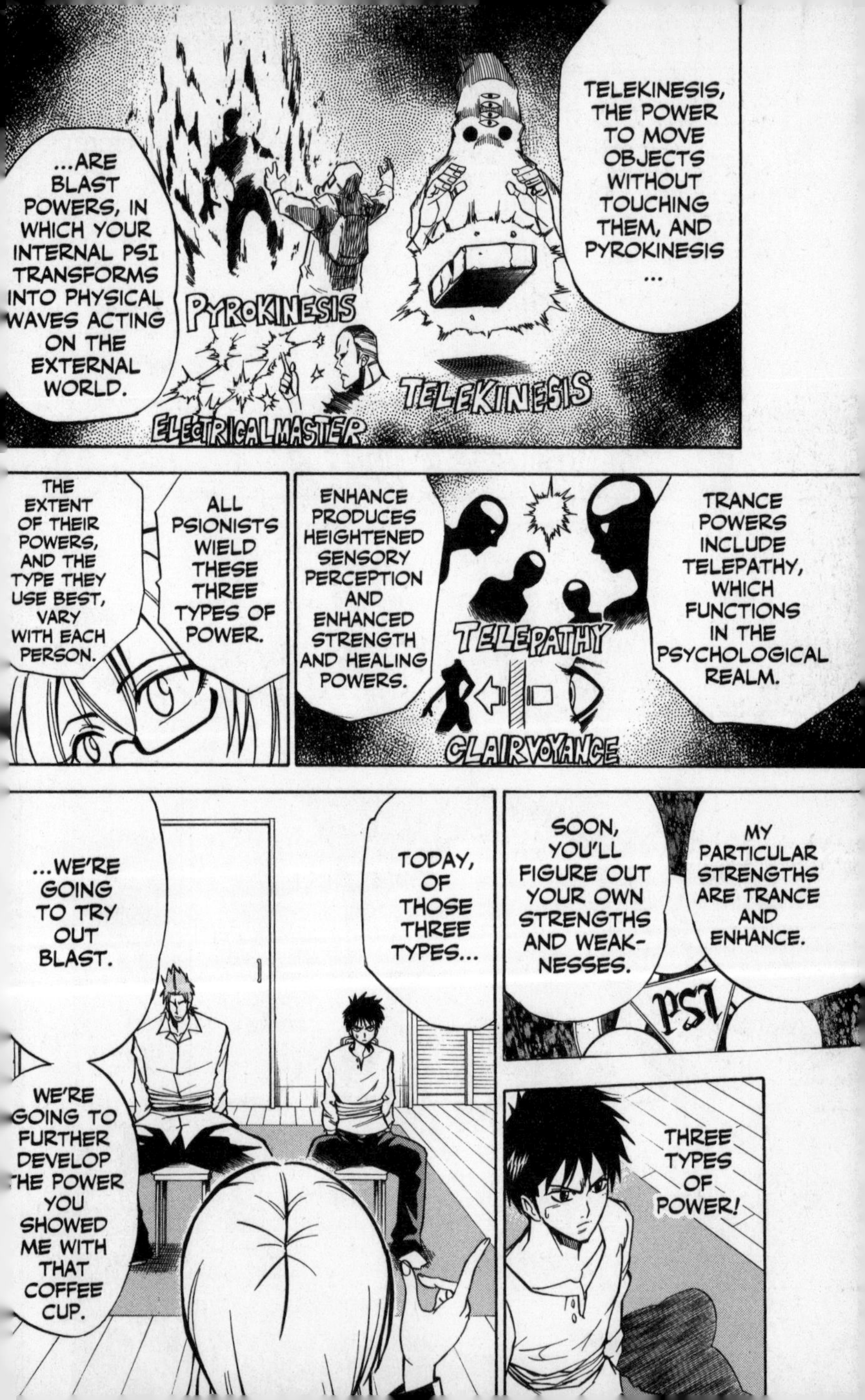

TELEKINESIS, THE POWER TO MOVE OBJECTS WITHOUT TOUCHING THEM, AND PYROKINESIS ...
...ARE BLAST POWERS, IN WHICH YOUR INTERNAL PSI TRANSFORMS INTO PHYSICAL WAVES ACTING ON THE EXTERNAL WORLD.
PYROKINESIS
TELEKINESIS
ELECTRICALMASTER
TRANCE POWERS INCLUDE TELEPATHY, WHICH FUNCTIONS IN THE PSYCHOLOGICAL REALM.
TELEPATHY
CLAIRVOYANCE
ENHANCE PRODUCES HEIGHTENED SENSORY PERCEPTION AND ENHANCED STRENGTH AND HEALING POWERS.
ALL PSIONISTS WIELD THESE THREE TYPES OF POWER.
THE EXTENT OF THEIR POWERS, AND THE TYPE THEY USE BEST, VARY WITH EACH PERSON.
MY PARTICULAR STRENGTHS ARE TRANCE AND ENHANCE.
SOON, YOU'LL FIGURE OUT YOUR OWN STRENGTHS AND WEAK-NESSES.
PSI
THREE TYPES OF POWER!
TODAY, OF THOSE THREE TYPES...
...WE'RE GOING TO TRY OUT BLAST.
WE'RE GOING TO FURTHER DEVELOP THE POWER YOU SHOWED ME WITH THAT COFFEE CUP.

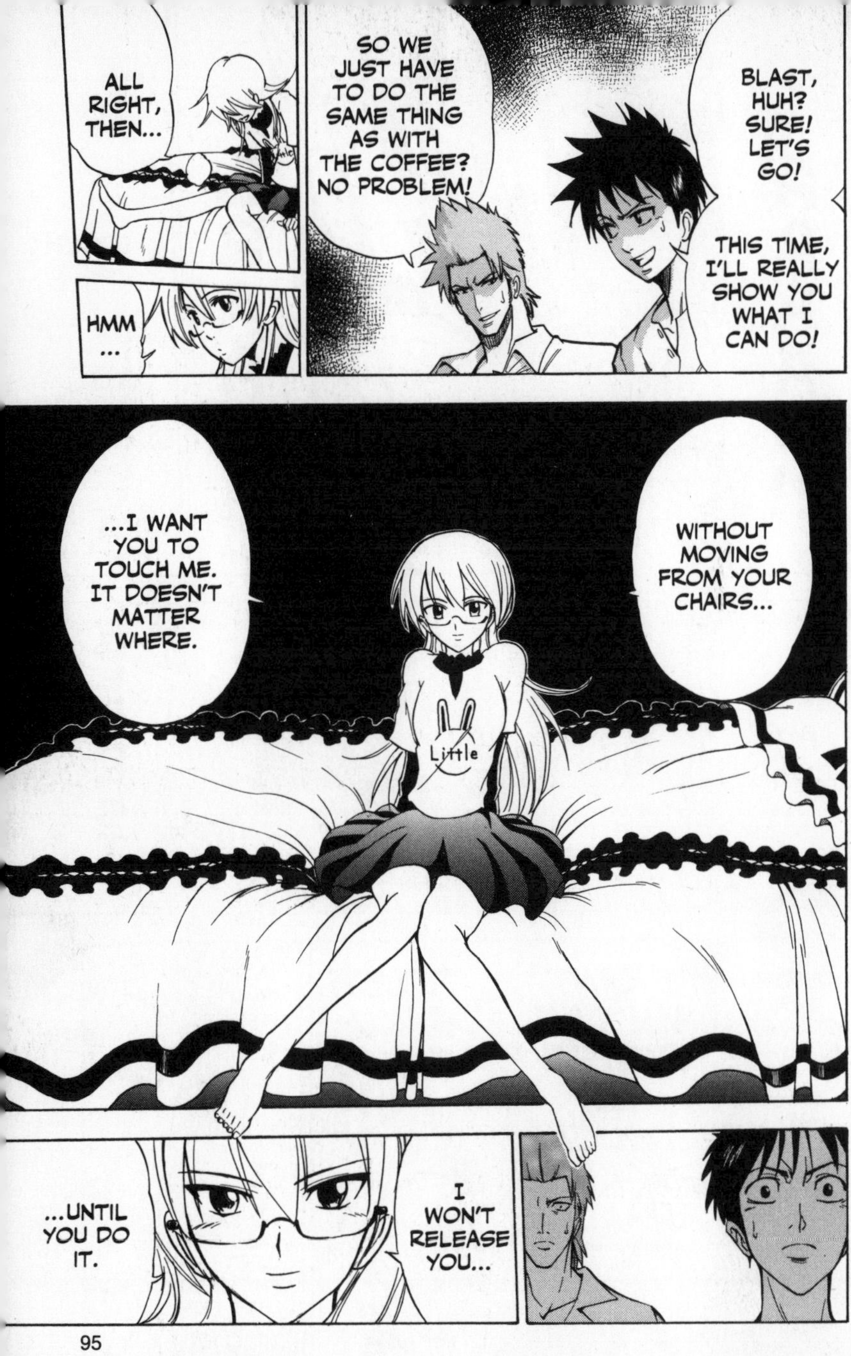
BLAST, HUH? SURE! LET'S GO!
THIS TIME, I'LL REALLY SHOW YOU WHAT I CAN DO!
SO WE JUST HAVE TO DO THE SAME THING AS WITH THE COFFEE? NO PROBLEM!
ALL RIGHT, THEN...
HMM ...
WITHOUT MOVING FROM YOUR CHAIRS...
...I WANT YOU TO TOUCH ME. IT DOESN'T MATTER WHERE.
Little
I WON'T RELEASE YOU...
...UNTIL YOU DO IT.

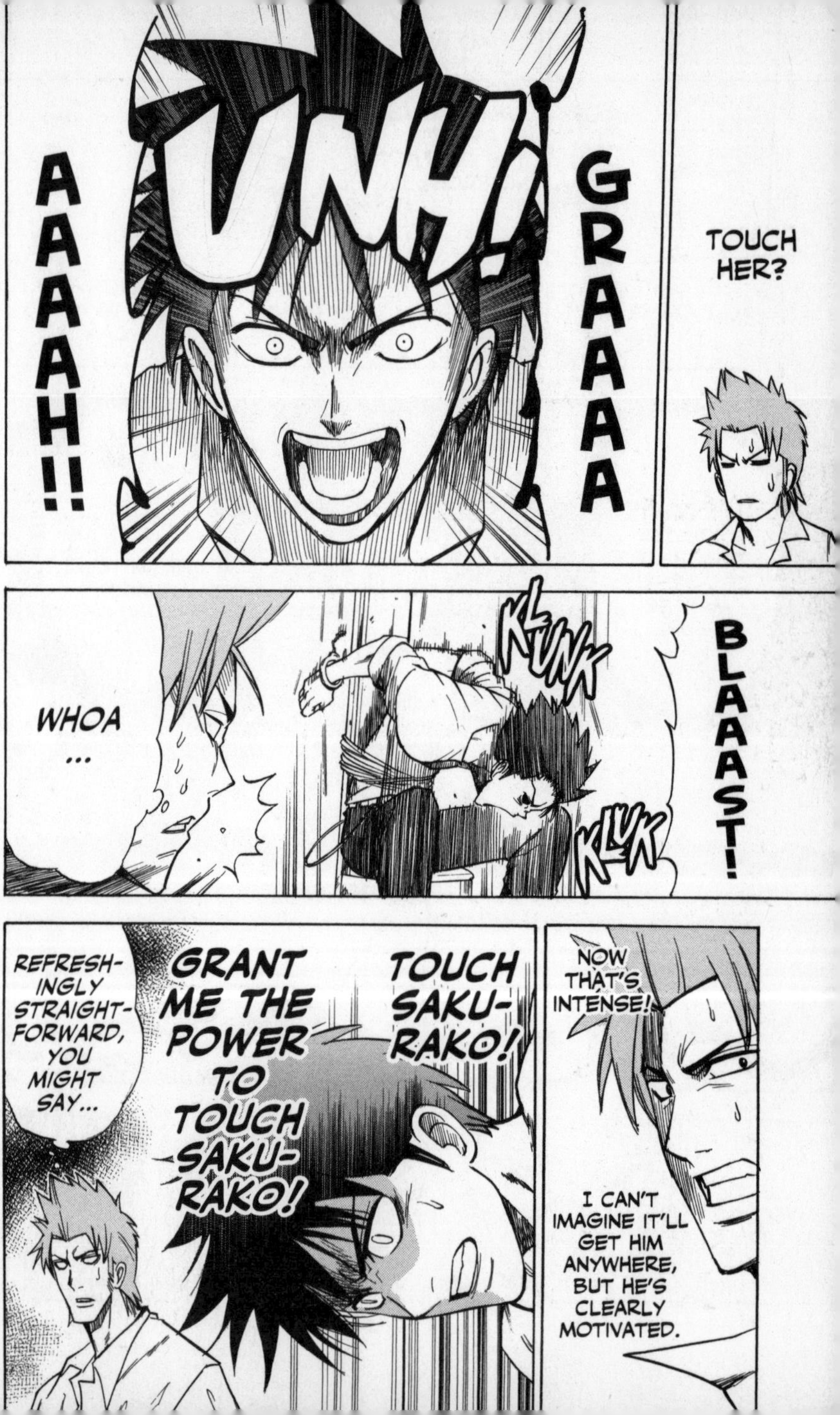
TOUCH HER?
GRAAAA
UNH!
AAAAAH!!
BLAAAST!
KLUNK
KLUK
WHOA ...
NOW THAT'S INTENSE!
I CAN'T IMAGINE IT'LL GET HIM ANYWHERE, BUT HE'S CLEARLY MOTIVATED.
TOUCH SAKU-RAKO!
GRANT ME THE POWER TO TOUCH SAKU-RAKO!
REFRESH-INGLY STRAIGHT-FORWARD, YOU MIGHT SAY...

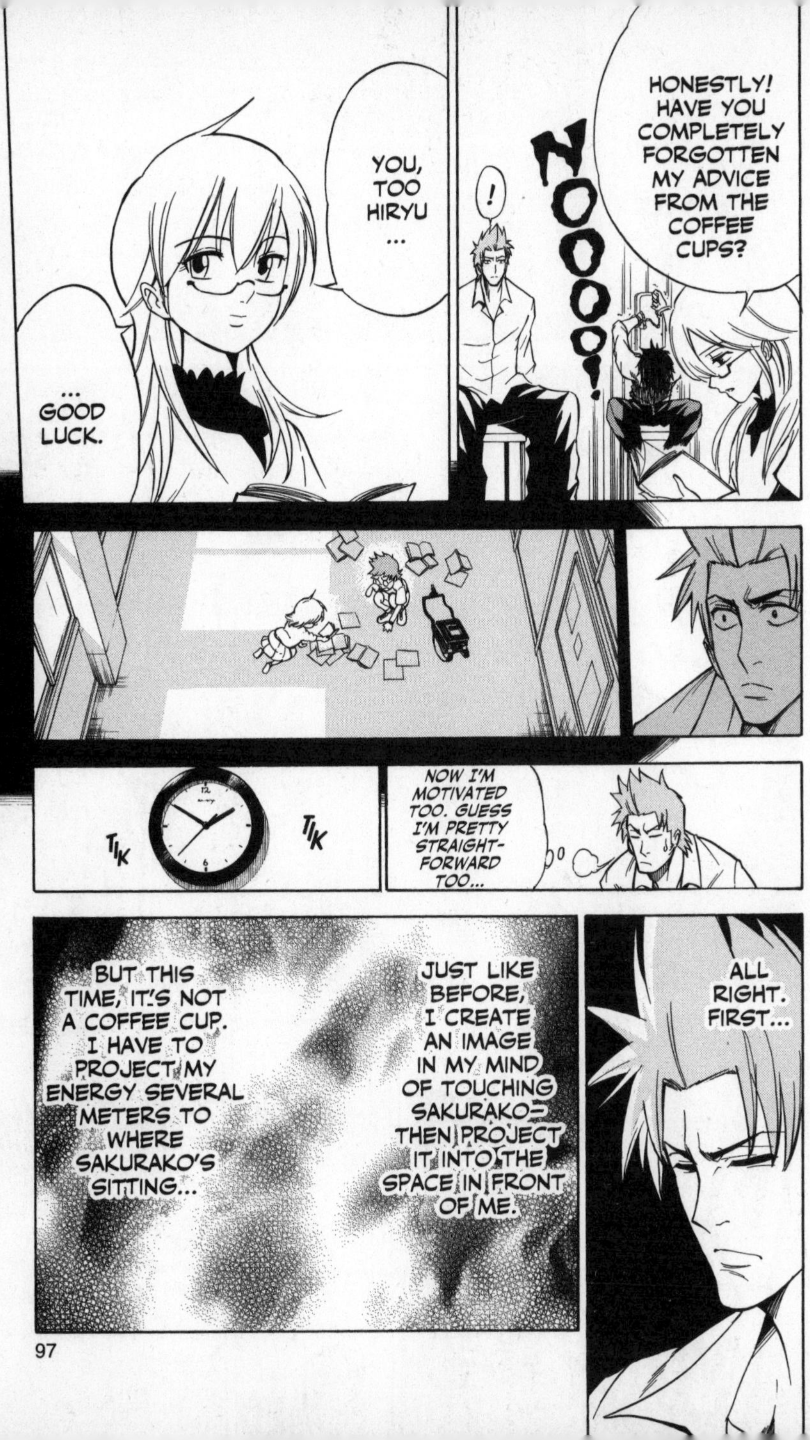
HONESTLY! HAVE YOU COMPLETELY FORGOTTEN MY ADVICE FROM THE COFFEE CUPS?
NOOOO!
!
YOU, TOO HIRYU ...
... GOOD LUCK.
NOW I'M MOTIVATED TOO. GUESS I'M PRETTY STRAIGHT-FORWARD TOO...
TIK
TIK
ALL RIGHT. FIRST...
JUST LIKE BEFORE, I CREATE AN IMAGE IN MY MIND OF TOUCHING SAKURAKO— THEN PROJECT IT INTO THE SPACE IN FRONT OF ME.
BUT THIS TIME, IT'S NOT A COFFEE CUP. I HAVE TO PROJECT MY ENERGY SEVERAL METERS TO WHERE SAKURAKO'S SITTING...

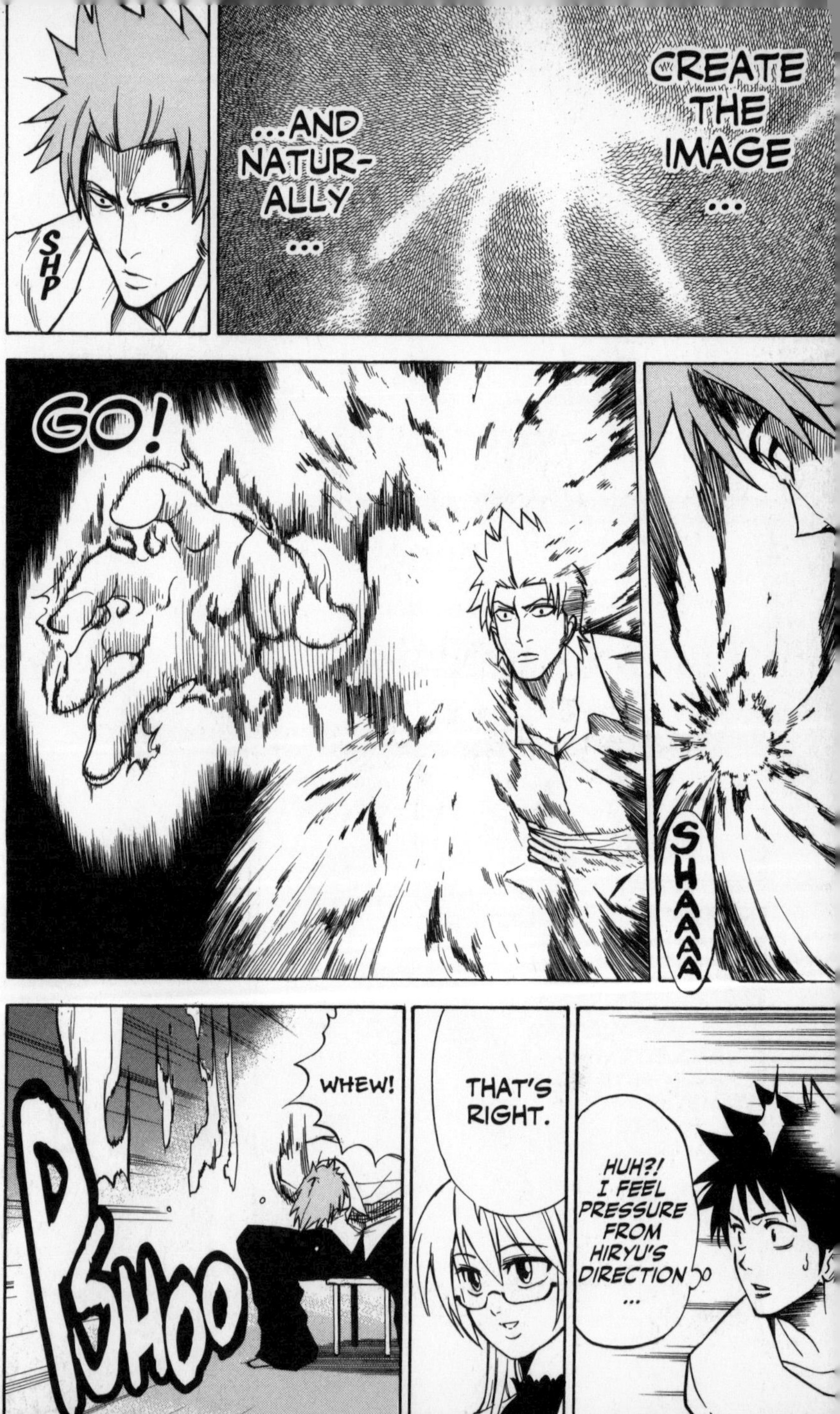
CREATE THE IMAGE...
...AND NATURALLY...
SHP
SHAAAA
GO!
HUH?! I FEEL PRESSURE FROM HIRYU'S DIRECTION...
THAT'S RIGHT.
WHEW!
PSHOO

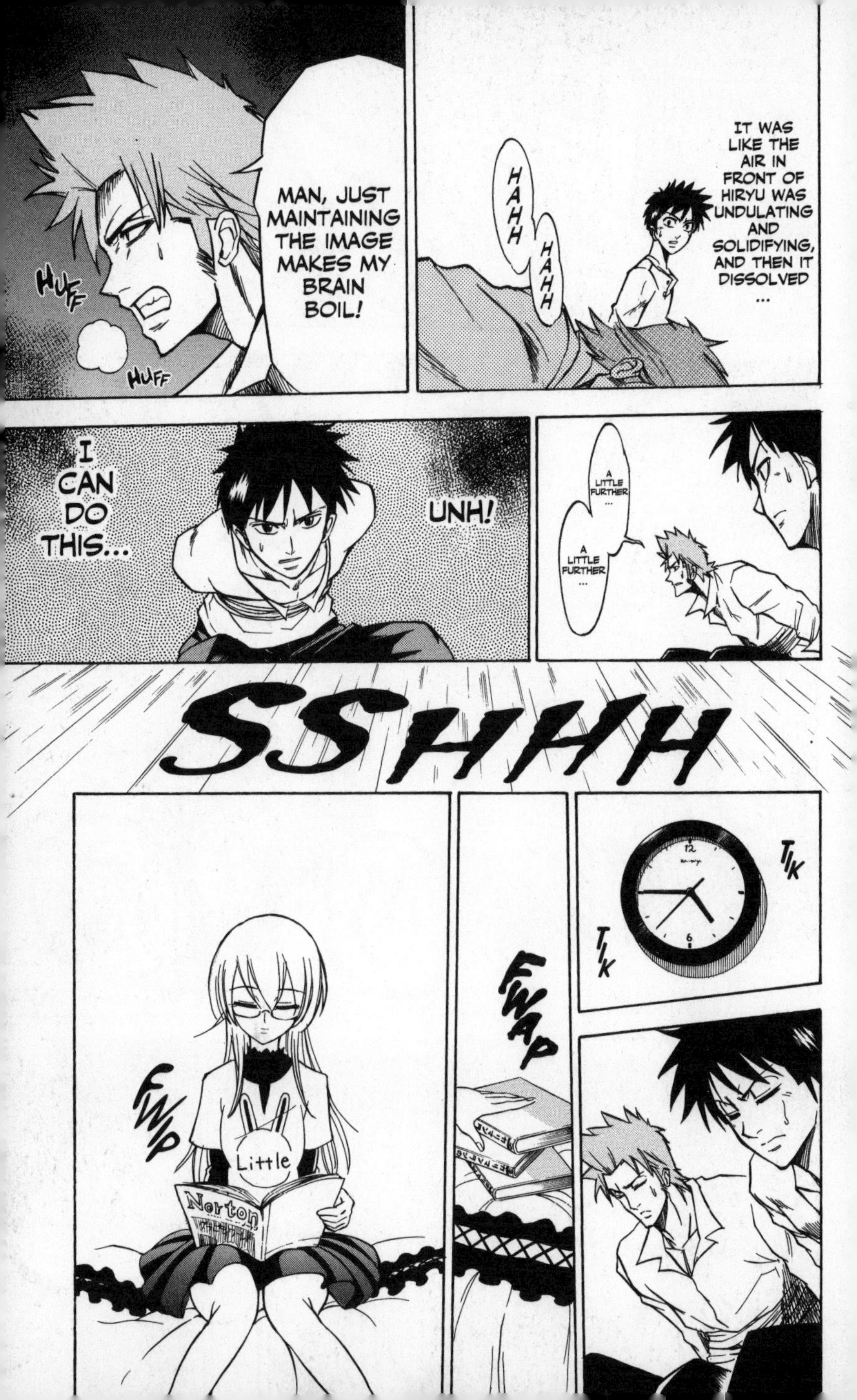
IT WAS LIKE THE AIR IN FRONT OF HIRYU WAS UNDULATING AND SOLIDIFYING, AND THEN IT DISSOLVED ...
HAHH
HAHH
MAN, JUST MAINTAINING THE IMAGE MAKES MY BRAIN BOIL!
HUFF
HUFF
A LITTLE FURTHER ...
A LITTLE FURTHER ...
UNH!
I CAN DO THIS...
SSHHH
TIK
TIK
FWAP
FWIP
Little
Norton

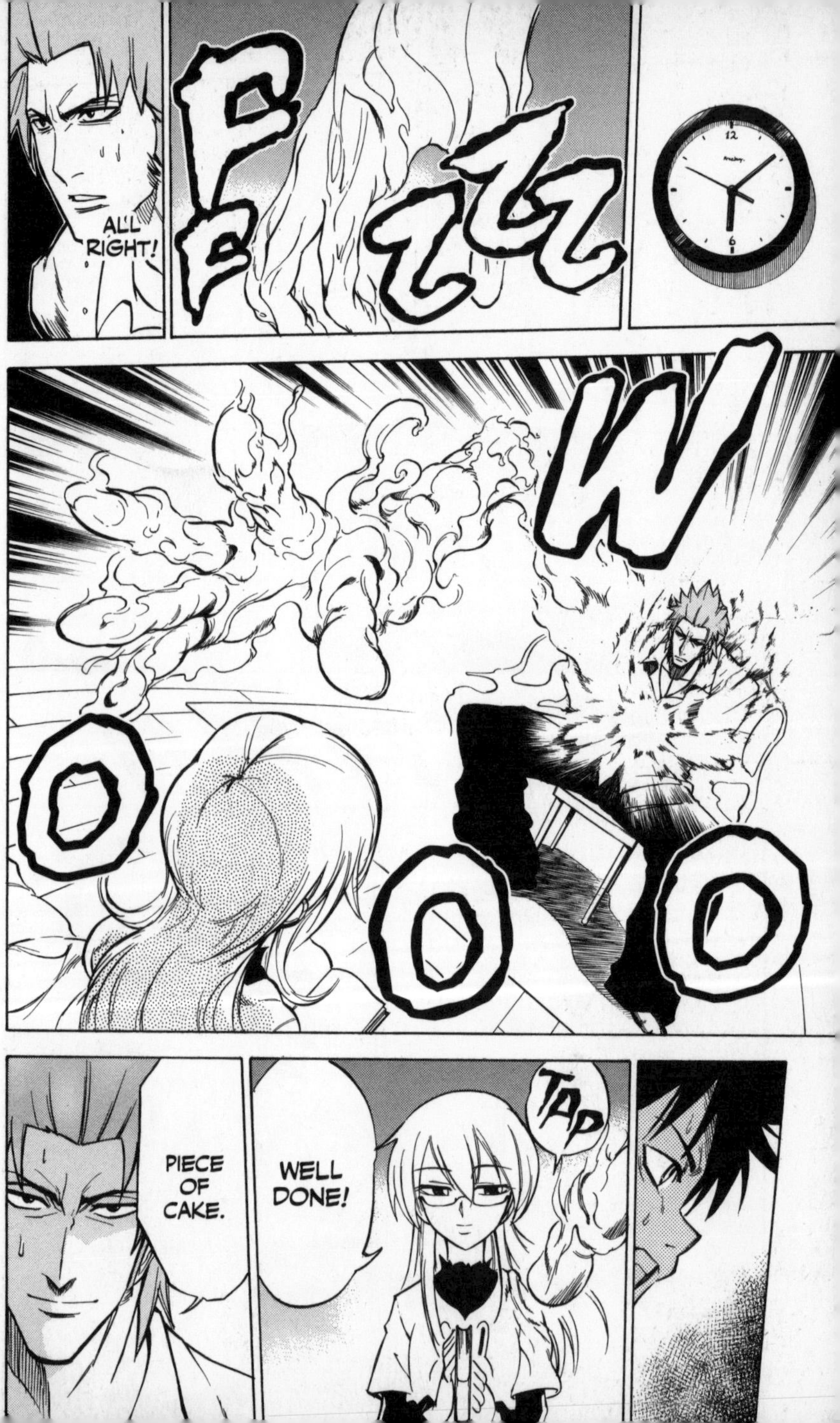
BZZZ
ALL RIGHT!
WOOO
TAP
WELL DONE!
PIECE OF CAKE.

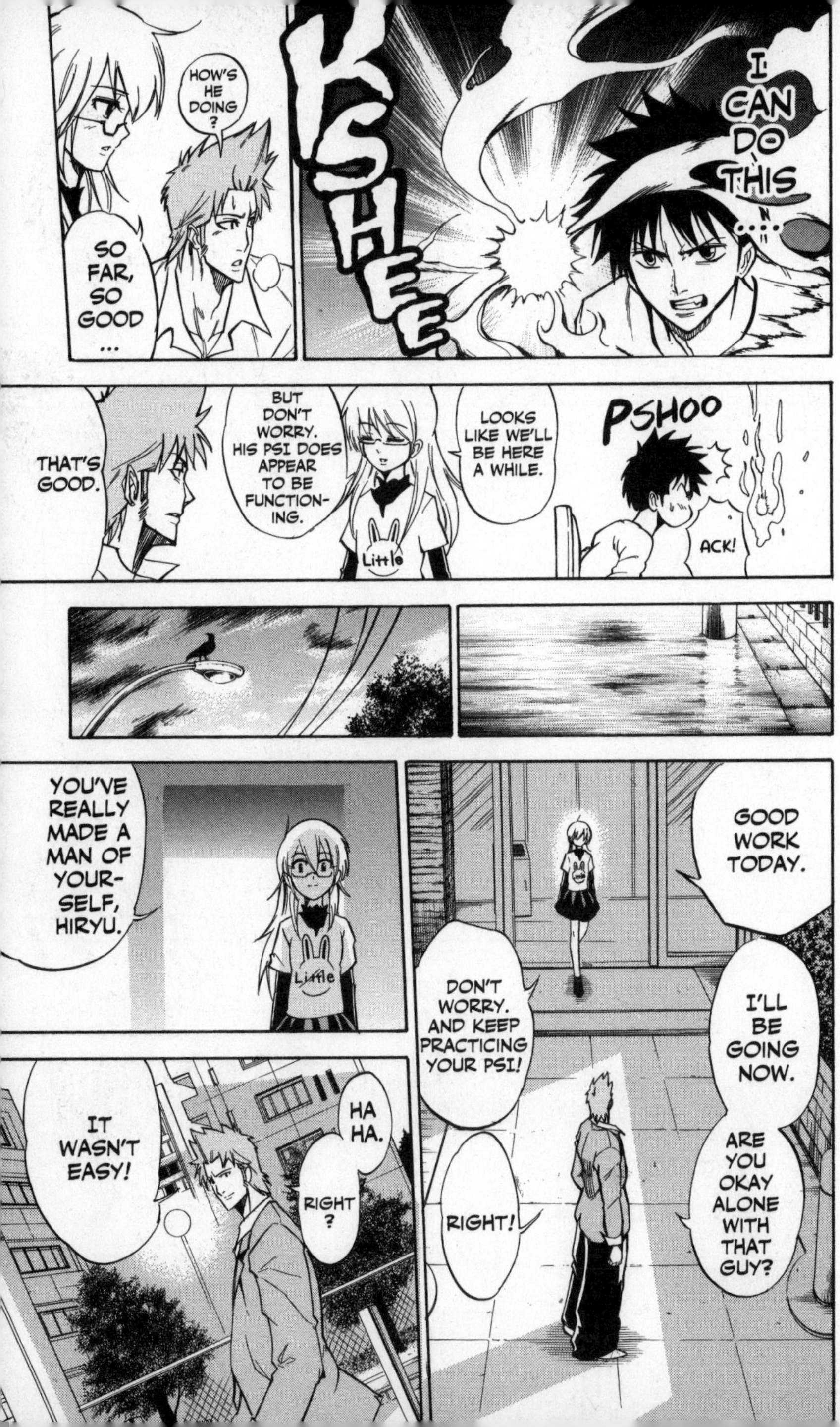

I CAN DO THIS...!!
KSHEEE
HOW'S HE DOING?
SO FAR, SO GOOD...
PSHOO
ACK!
LOOKS LIKE WE'LL BE HERE A WHILE.
BUT DON'T WORRY. HIS PSI DOES APPEAR TO BE FUNCTIONING.
THAT'S GOOD.
GOOD WORK TODAY.
I'LL BE GOING NOW.
ARE YOU OKAY ALONE WITH THAT GUY?
DON'T WORRY. AND KEEP PRACTICING YOUR PSI!
RIGHT!
YOU'VE REALLY MADE A MAN OF YOURSELF, HIRYU.
HA HA.
RIGHT?
IT WASN'T EASY!

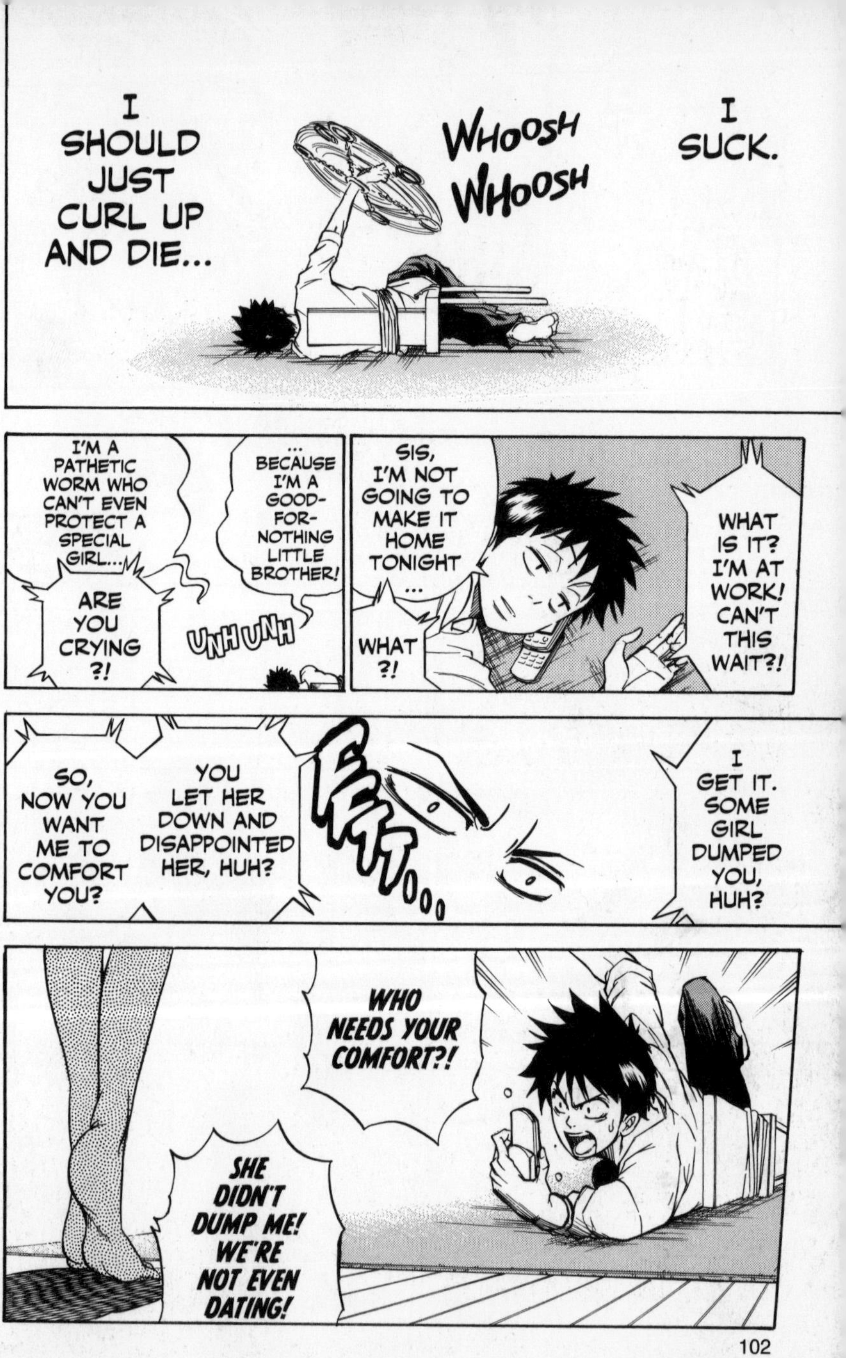
I SUCK.
WHOOSH WHOOSH
I SHOULD JUST CURL UP AND DIE...
WHAT IS IT? I'M AT WORK! CAN'T THIS WAIT?!
SIS, I'M NOT GOING TO MAKE IT HOME TONIGHT...
WHAT?!
...BECAUSE I'M A GOOD-FOR-NOTHING LITTLE BROTHER!
I'M A PATHETIC WORM WHO CAN'T EVEN PROTECT A SPECIAL GIRL...
UNH UNH
ARE YOU CRYING?!
I GET IT. SOME GIRL DUMPED YOU, HUH?
YOU LET HER DOWN AND DISAPPOINTED HER, HUH?
SO, NOW YOU WANT ME TO COMFORT YOU?
WHO NEEDS YOUR COMFORT?!
SHE DIDN'T DUMP ME! WE'RE NOT EVEN DATING!

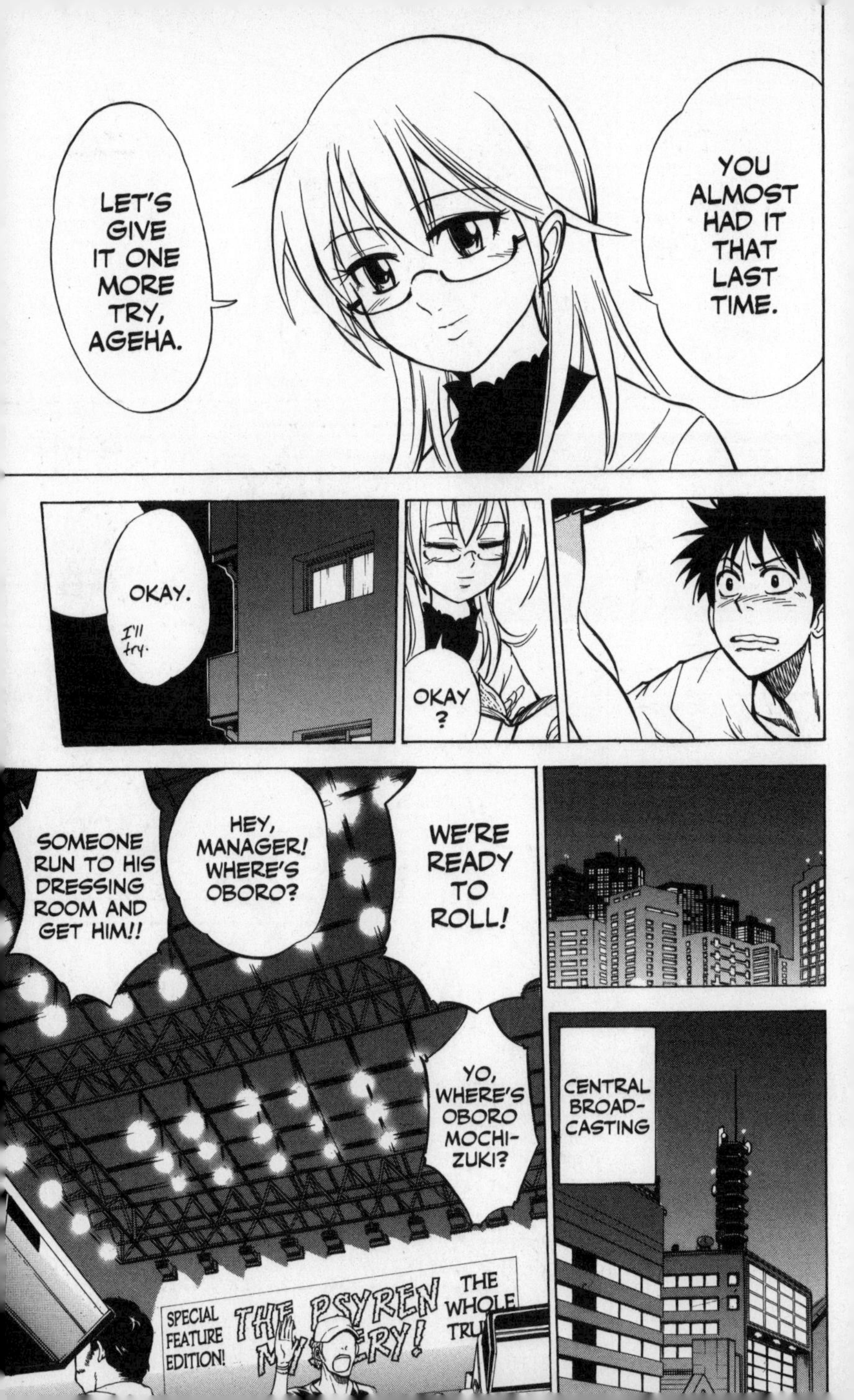
YOU ALMOST HAD IT THAT LAST TIME.
LET'S GIVE IT ONE MORE TRY, AGEHA.
OKAY?
OKAY.
I'll try.
CENTRAL BROAD-CASTING
WE'RE READY TO ROLL!
HEY, MANAGER! WHERE'S OBORO?
SOMEONE RUN TO HIS DRESSING ROOM AND GET HIM!!
YO, WHERE'S OBORO MOCHIZUKI?
SPECIAL FEATURE EDITION!
THE PSYREN
THE WHOLE

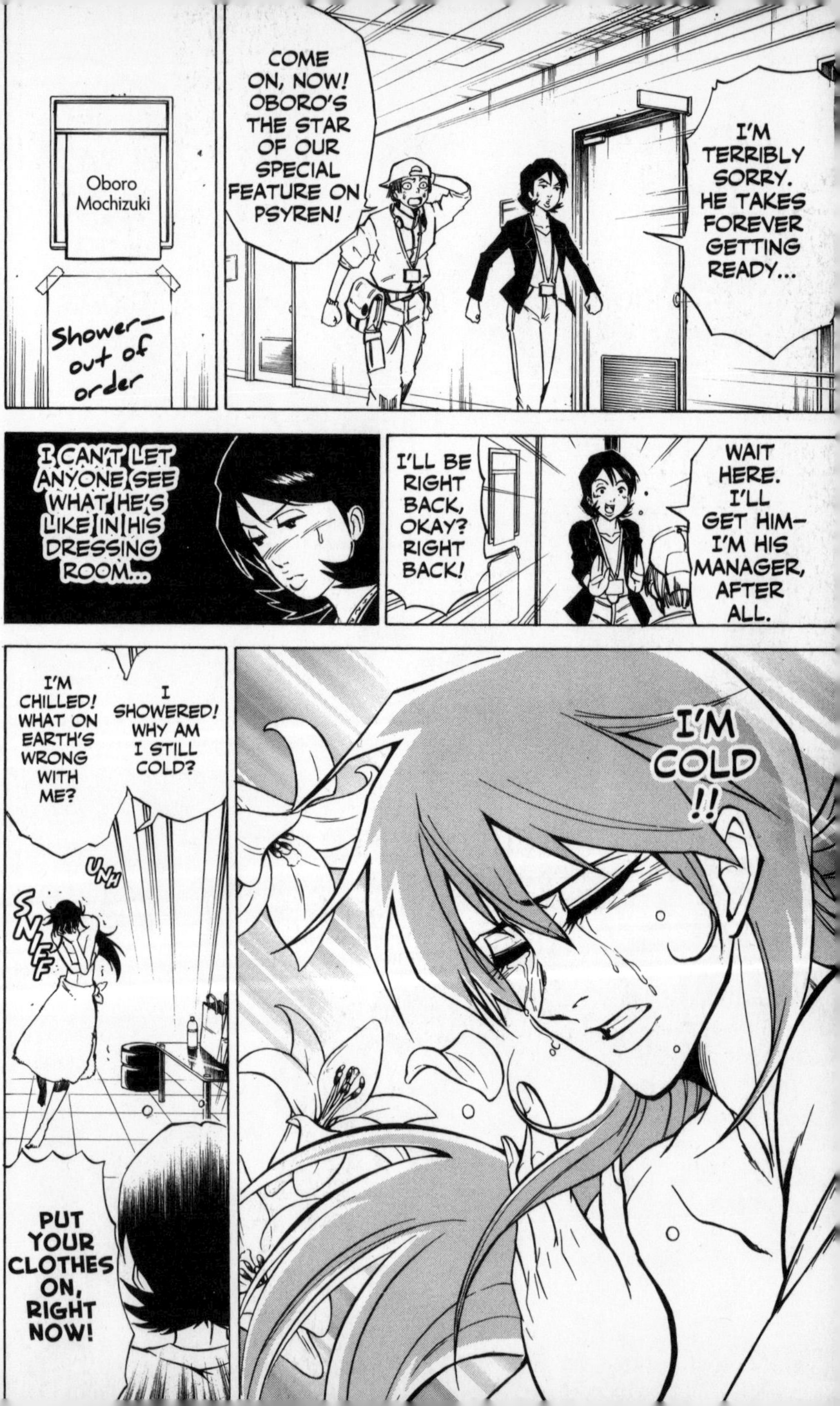

I'M TERRIBLY SORRY. HE TAKES FOREVER GETTING READY...
COME ON, NOW! OBORO'S THE STAR OF OUR SPECIAL FEATURE ON PSYREN!
Oboro Mochizuki
Shower— out of order
WAIT HERE. I'LL GET HIM— I'M HIS MANAGER, AFTER ALL.
I'LL BE RIGHT BACK, OKAY? RIGHT BACK!
I CAN'T LET ANYONE SEE WHAT HE'S LIKE IN HIS DRESSING ROOM...
I'M COLD !!
I SHOWERED! WHY AM I STILL COLD?
I'M CHILLED! WHAT ON EARTH'S WRONG WITH ME?
UNH
SNIFF
PUT YOUR CLOTHES ON, RIGHT NOW!

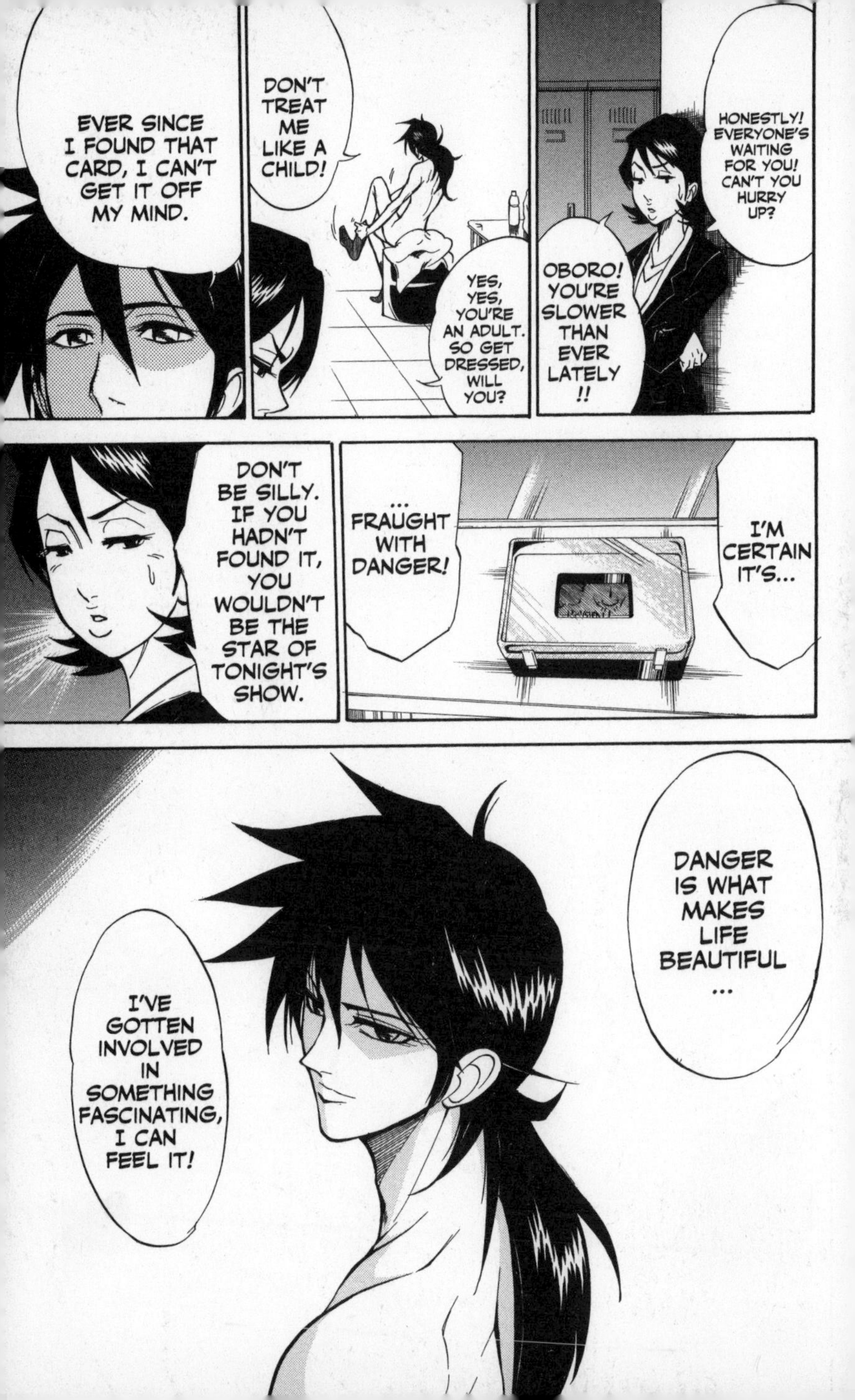
HONESTLY! EVERYONE'S WAITING FOR YOU! CAN'T YOU HURRY UP?
OBORO! YOU'RE SLOWER THAN EVER LATELY !!
DON'T TREAT ME LIKE A CHILD!
YES, YES, YOU'RE AN ADULT. SO GET DRESSED, WILL YOU?
EVER SINCE I FOUND THAT CARD, I CAN'T GET IT OFF MY MIND.
I'M CERTAIN IT'S...
... FRAUGHT WITH DANGER!
DON'T BE SILLY. IF YOU HADN'T FOUND IT, YOU WOULDN'T BE THE STAR OF TONIGHT'S SHOW.
DANGER IS WHAT MAKES LIFE BEAUTIFUL ...
I'VE GOTTEN INVOLVED IN SOMETHING FASCINATING, I CAN FEEL IT!

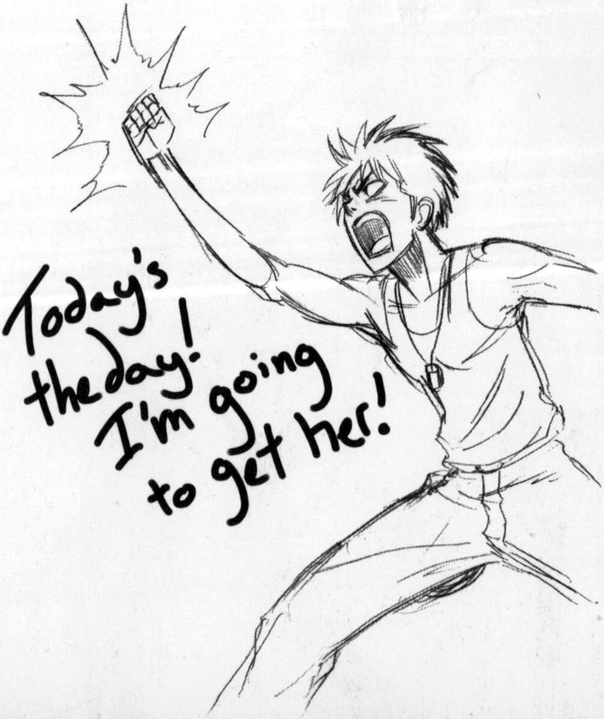
Today's the day! I'm going to get her!

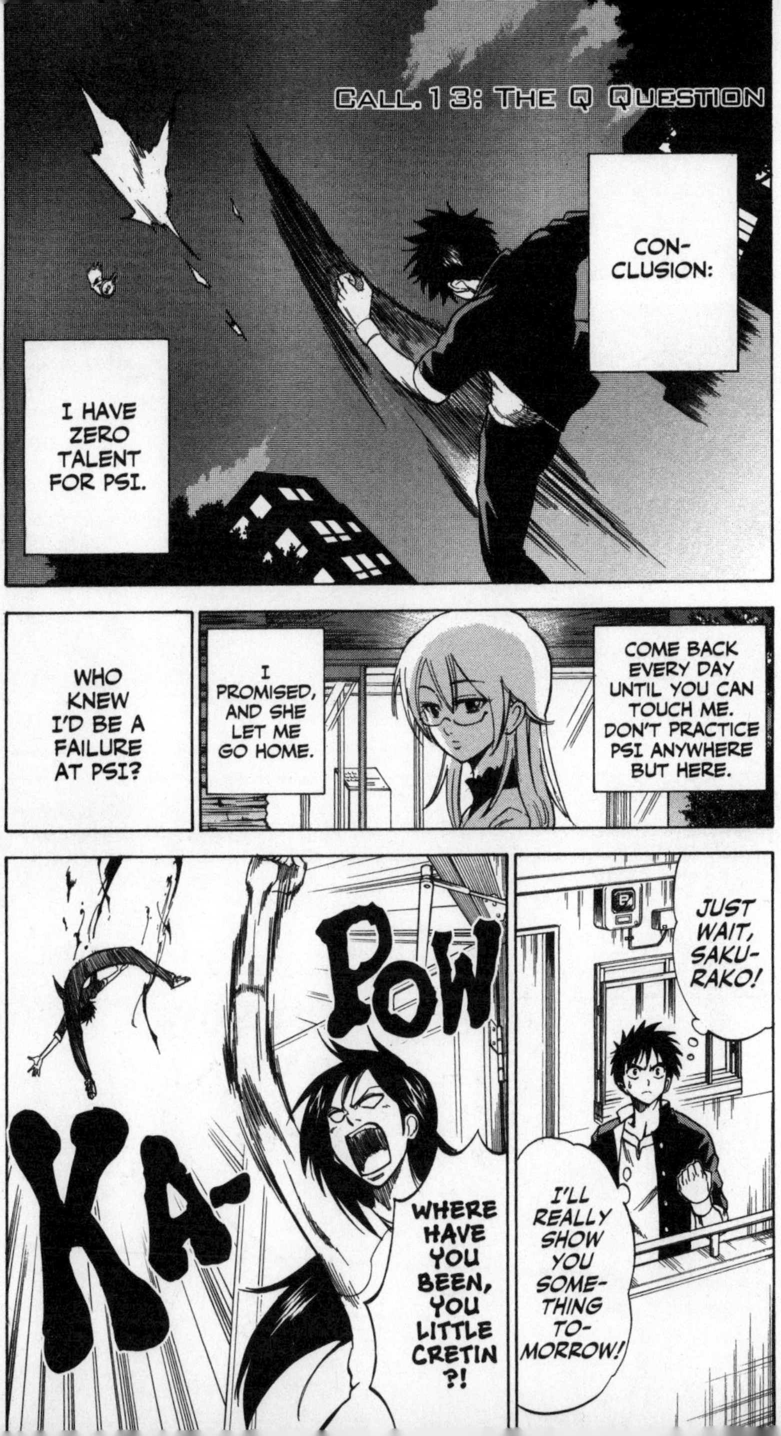
CALL. 13: THE Q QUESTION
CONCLUSION:
I HAVE ZERO TALENT FOR PSI.
COME BACK EVERY DAY UNTIL YOU CAN TOUCH ME. DON'T PRACTICE PSI ANYWHERE BUT HERE.
I PROMISED, AND SHE LET ME GO HOME.
WHO KNEW I'D BE A FAILURE AT PSI?
JUST WAIT, SAKURAKO!
I'LL REALLY SHOW YOU SOMETHING TOMORROW!
POW
WHERE HAVE YOU BEEN, YOU LITTLE CRETIN?!
KA-

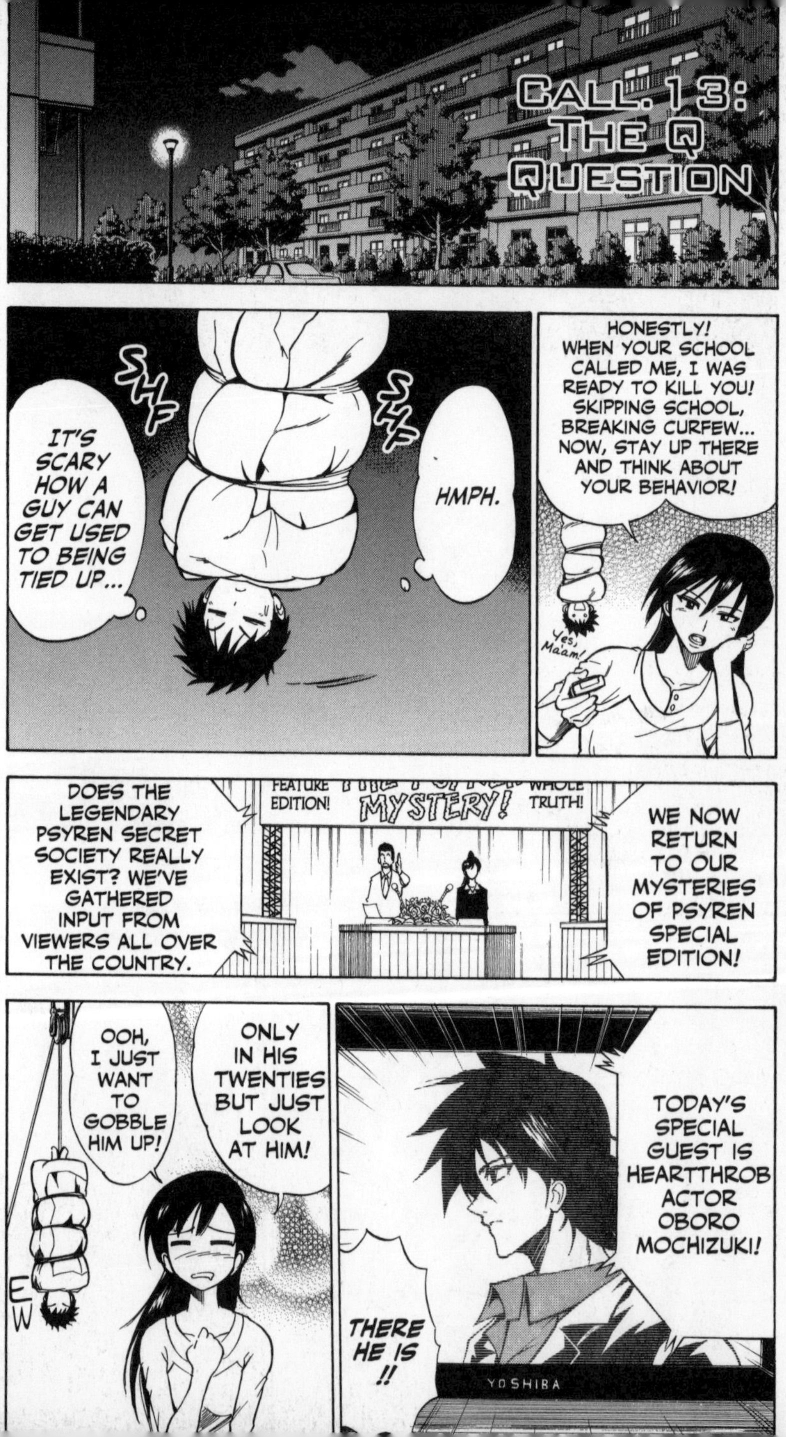

CALL. 13: THE Q QUESTION
HONESTLY! WHEN YOUR SCHOOL CALLED ME, I WAS READY TO KILL YOU! SKIPPING SCHOOL, BREAKING CURFEW... NOW, STAY UP THERE AND THINK ABOUT YOUR BEHAVIOR!
Yes, Ma'am!
SHF
HMPH.
SHF
IT'S SCARY HOW A GUY CAN GET USED TO BEING TIED UP...
FEATURE EDITION!
MYSTERY!
WHOLE TRUTH!
WE NOW RETURN TO OUR MYSTERIES OF PSYREN SPECIAL EDITION!
DOES THE LEGENDARY PSYREN SECRET SOCIETY REALLY EXIST? WE'VE GATHERED INPUT FROM VIEWERS ALL OVER THE COUNTRY.
TODAY'S SPECIAL GUEST IS HEARTTHROB ACTOR OBORO MOCHIZUKI!
THERE HE IS!!
YOSHIBA
ONLY IN HIS TWENTIES BUT JUST LOOK AT HIM!
OOH, I JUST WANT TO GOBBLE HIM UP!
EW

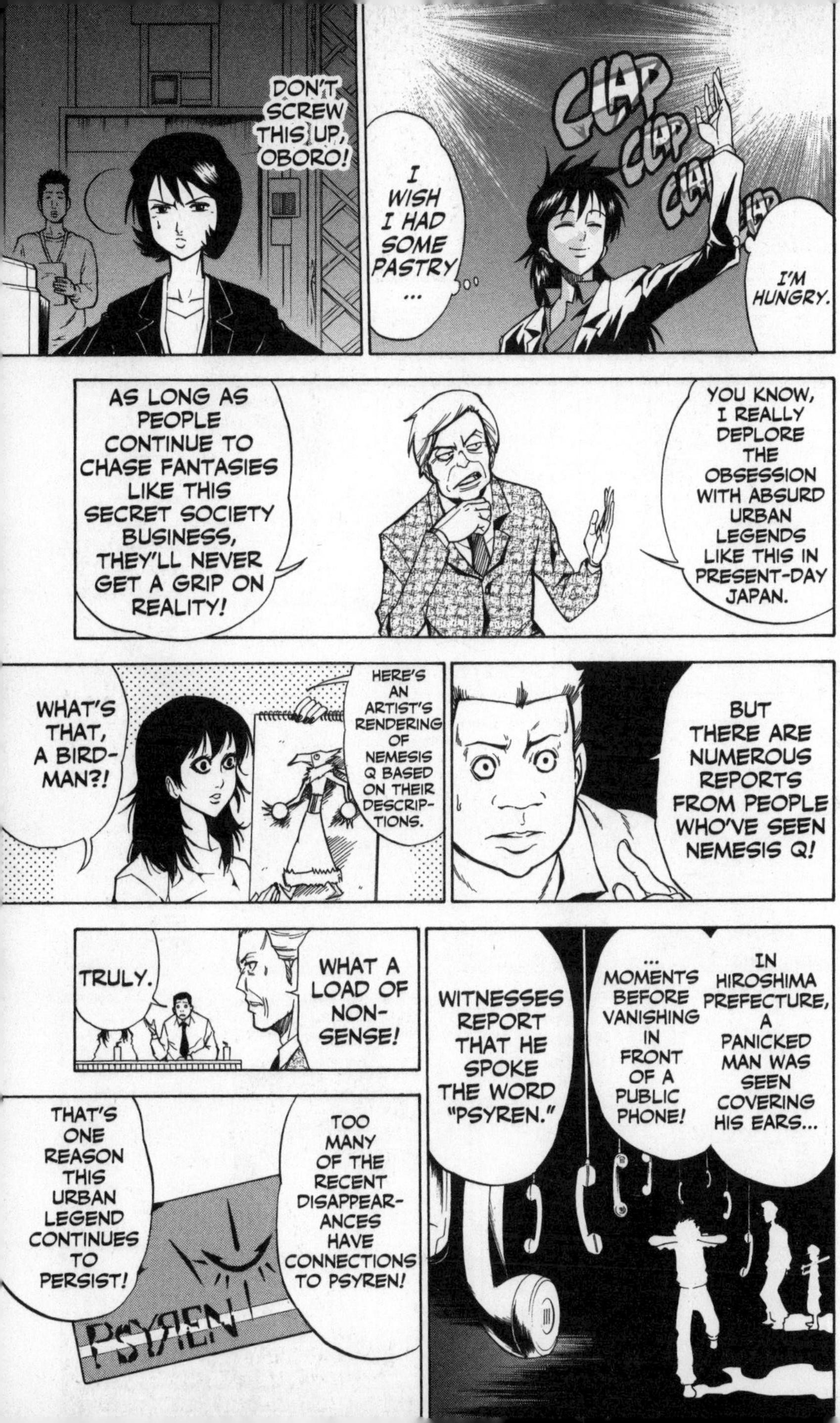
CLAP
CLAP
CLAP
I'M HUNGRY.
I WISH I HAD SOME PASTRY...
DON'T SCREW THIS UP, OBORO!
YOU KNOW, I REALLY DEPLORE THE OBSESSION WITH ABSURD URBAN LEGENDS LIKE THIS IN PRESENT-DAY JAPAN.
AS LONG AS PEOPLE CONTINUE TO CHASE FANTASIES LIKE THIS SECRET SOCIETY BUSINESS, THEY'LL NEVER GET A GRIP ON REALITY!
BUT THERE ARE NUMEROUS REPORTS FROM PEOPLE WHO'VE SEEN NEMESIS Q!
HERE'S AN ARTIST'S RENDERING OF NEMESIS Q BASED ON THEIR DESCRIPTIONS.
WHAT'S THAT, A BIRD-MAN?!
IN HIROSHIMA PREFECTURE, A PANICKED MAN WAS SEEN COVERING HIS EARS...
...MOMENTS BEFORE VANISHING IN FRONT OF A PUBLIC PHONE!
WITNESSES REPORT THAT HE SPOKE THE WORD "PSYREN."
WHAT A LOAD OF NON-SENSE!
TRULY.
TOO MANY OF THE RECENT DISAPPEAR-ANCES HAVE CONNECTIONS TO PSYREN!
THAT'S ONE REASON THIS URBAN LEGEND CONTINUES TO PERSIST!
PSYREN

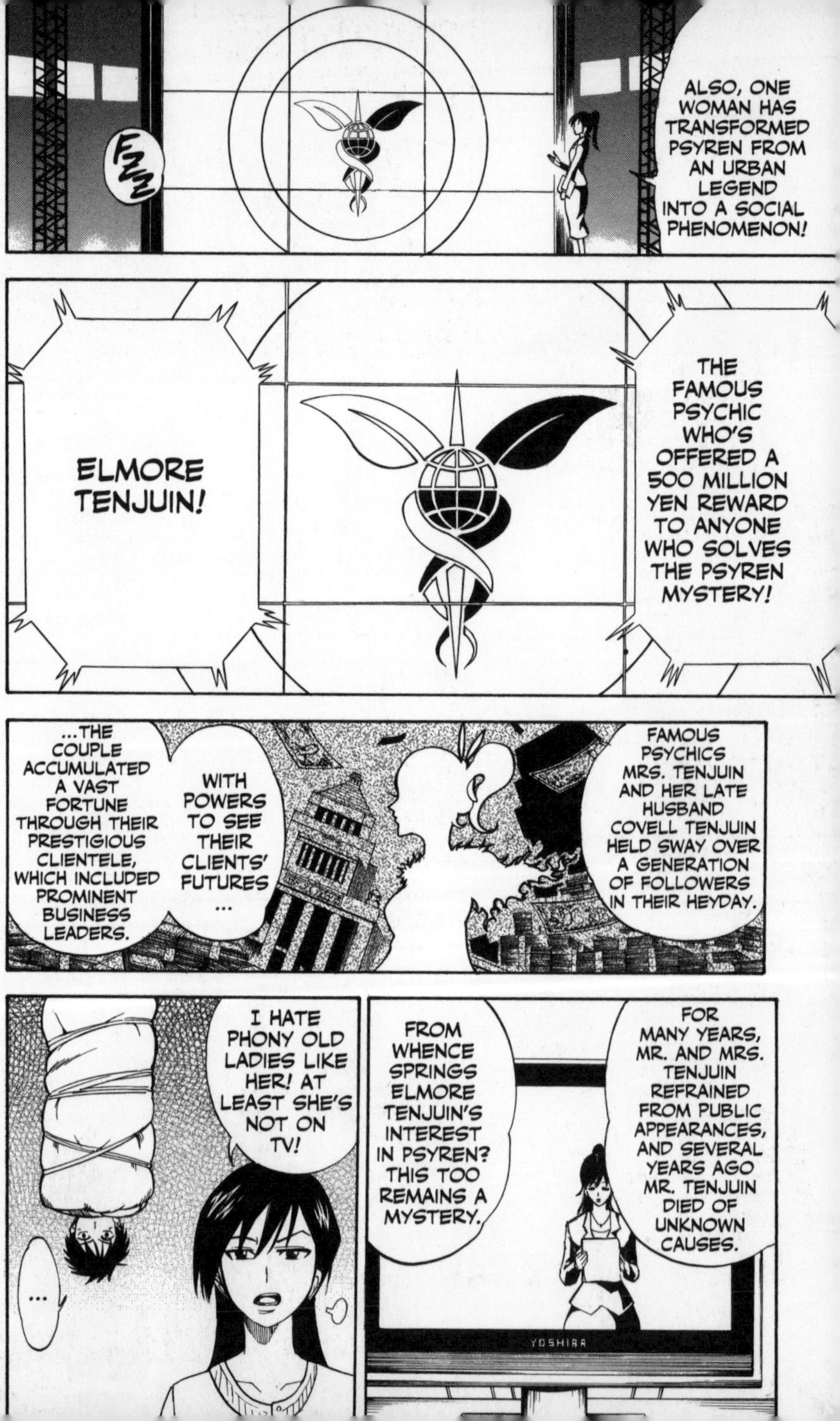
ALSO, ONE WOMAN HAS TRANSFORMED PSYREN FROM AN URBAN LEGEND INTO A SOCIAL PHENOMENON!
FZZ
THE FAMOUS PSYCHIC WHO'S OFFERED A 500 MILLION YEN REWARD TO ANYONE WHO SOLVES THE PSYREN MYSTERY!
ELMORE TENJUIN!
FAMOUS PSYCHICS MRS. TENJUIN AND HER LATE HUSBAND COVELL TENJUIN HELD SWAY OVER A GENERATION OF FOLLOWERS IN THEIR HEYDAY.
WITH POWERS TO SEE THEIR CLIENTS' FUTURES...
...THE COUPLE ACCUMULATED A VAST FORTUNE THROUGH THEIR PRESTIGIOUS CLIENTELE, WHICH INCLUDED PROMINENT BUSINESS LEADERS.
FOR MANY YEARS, MR. AND MRS. TENJUIN REFRAINED FROM PUBLIC APPEARANCES, AND SEVERAL YEARS AGO MR. TENJUIN DIED OF UNKNOWN CAUSES.
FROM WHENCE SPRINGS ELMORE TENJUIN'S INTEREST IN PSYREN? THIS TOO REMAINS A MYSTERY.
YOSHIBA
I HATE PHONY OLD LADIES LIKE HER! AT LEAST SHE'S NOT ON TV!
...

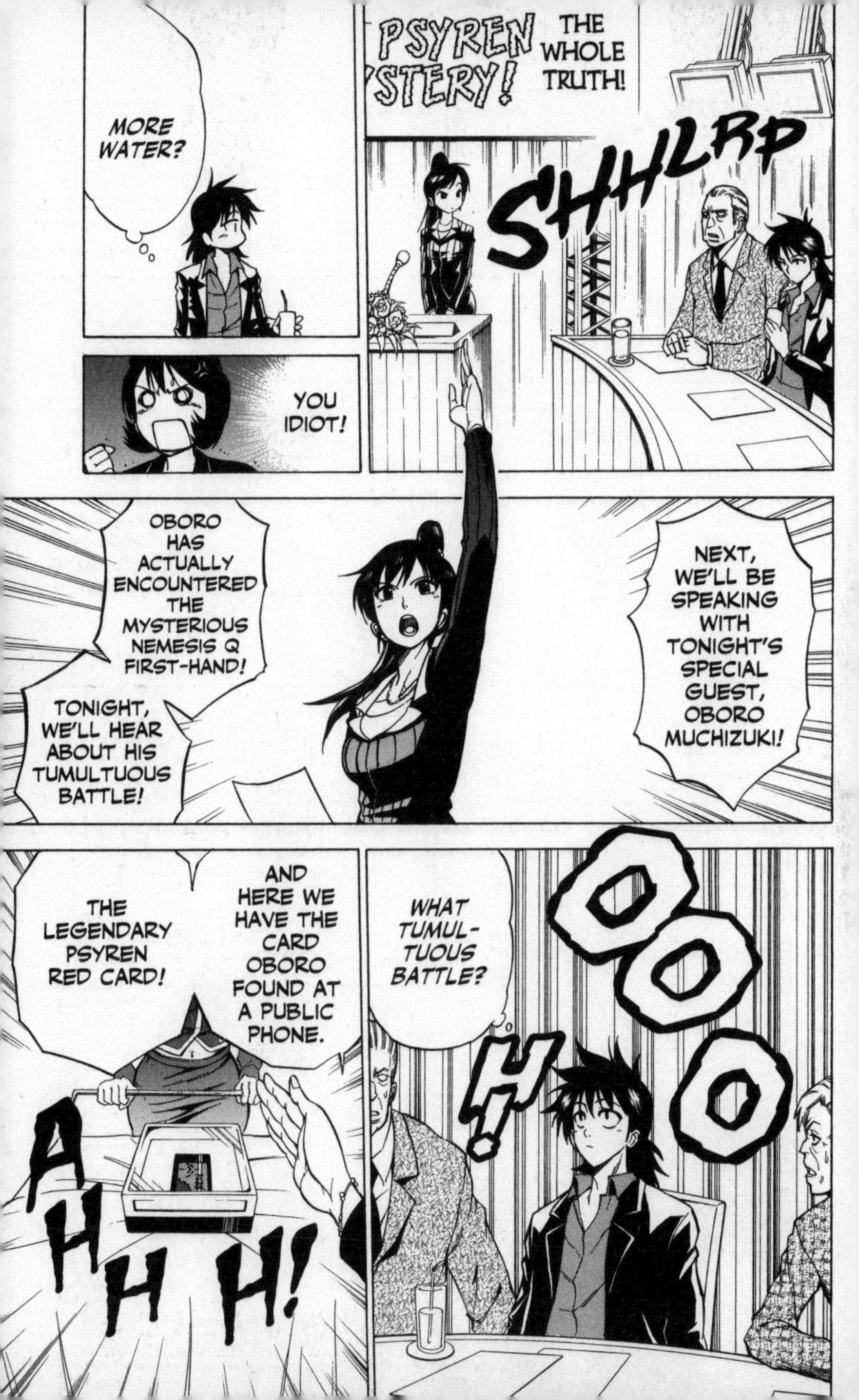
PSYREN
STERY!
THE WHOLE TRUTH!
SHHLRP
MORE WATER?
YOU IDIOT!
NEXT, WE'LL BE SPEAKING WITH TONIGHT'S SPECIAL GUEST, OBORO MUCHIZUKI!
OBORO HAS ACTUALLY ENCOUNTERED THE MYSTERIOUS NEMESIS Q FIRST-HAND!
TONIGHT, WE'LL HEAR ABOUT HIS TUMULTUOUS BATTLE!
OOOH!
WHAT TUMUL-TUOUS BATTLE?
AND HERE WE HAVE THE CARD OBORO FOUND AT A PUBLIC PHONE.
THE LEGENDARY PSYREN RED CARD!
AHHH!

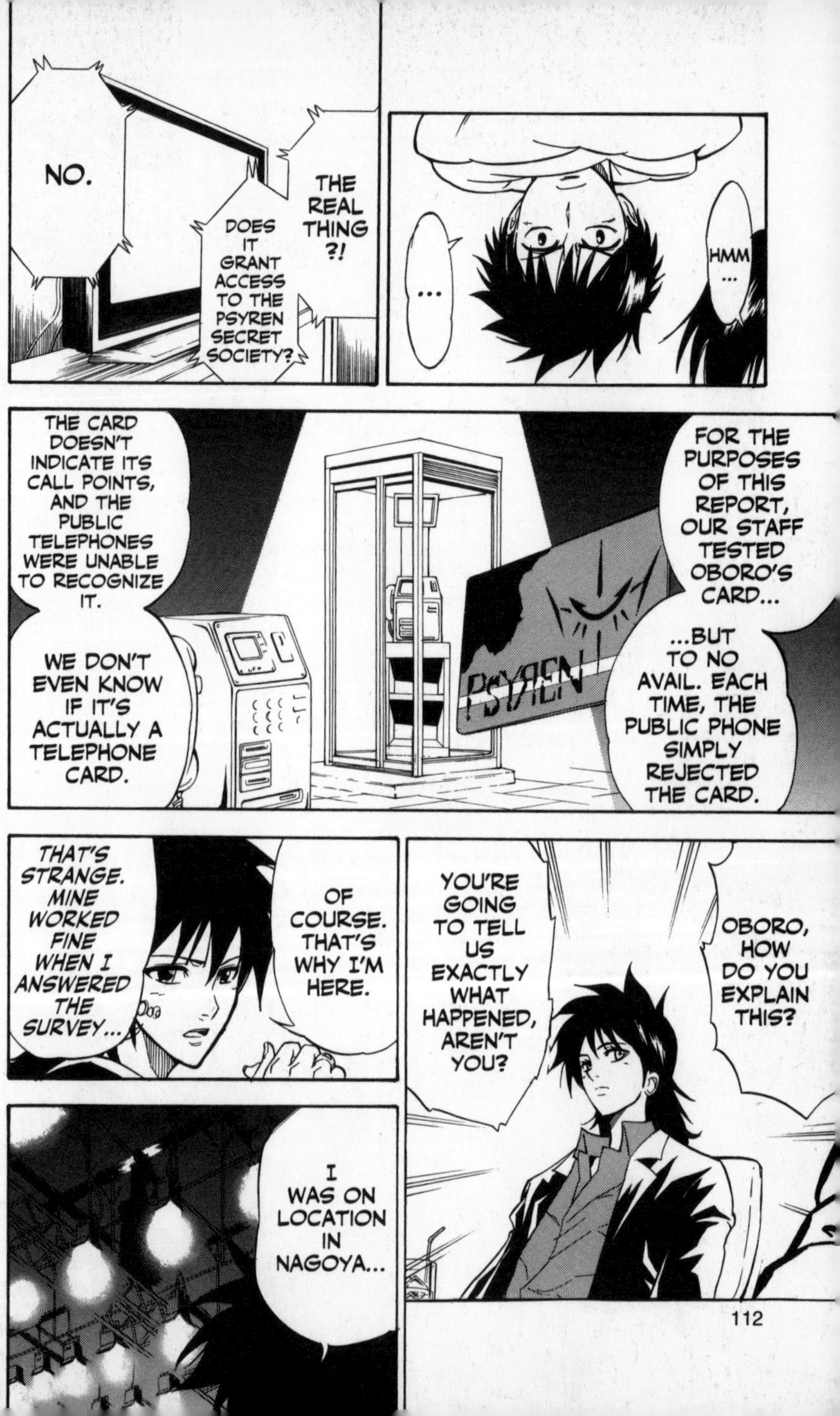
HMM...
...
THE REAL THING?!
DOES IT GRANT ACCESS TO THE PSYREN SECRET SOCIETY?
NO.
FOR THE PURPOSES OF THIS REPORT, OUR STAFF TESTED OBORO'S CARD...
...BUT TO NO AVAIL. EACH TIME, THE PUBLIC PHONE SIMPLY REJECTED THE CARD.
PSYREN
THE CARD DOESN'T INDICATE ITS CALL POINTS, AND THE PUBLIC TELEPHONES WERE UNABLE TO RECOGNIZE IT.
WE DON'T EVEN KNOW IF IT'S ACTUALLY A TELEPHONE CARD.
OBORO, HOW DO YOU EXPLAIN THIS?
YOU'RE GOING TO TELL US EXACTLY WHAT HAPPENED, AREN'T YOU?
OF COURSE. THAT'S WHY I'M HERE.
THAT'S STRANGE. MINE WORKED FINE WHEN I ANSWERED THE SURVEY...
I WAS ON LOCATION IN NAGOYA...

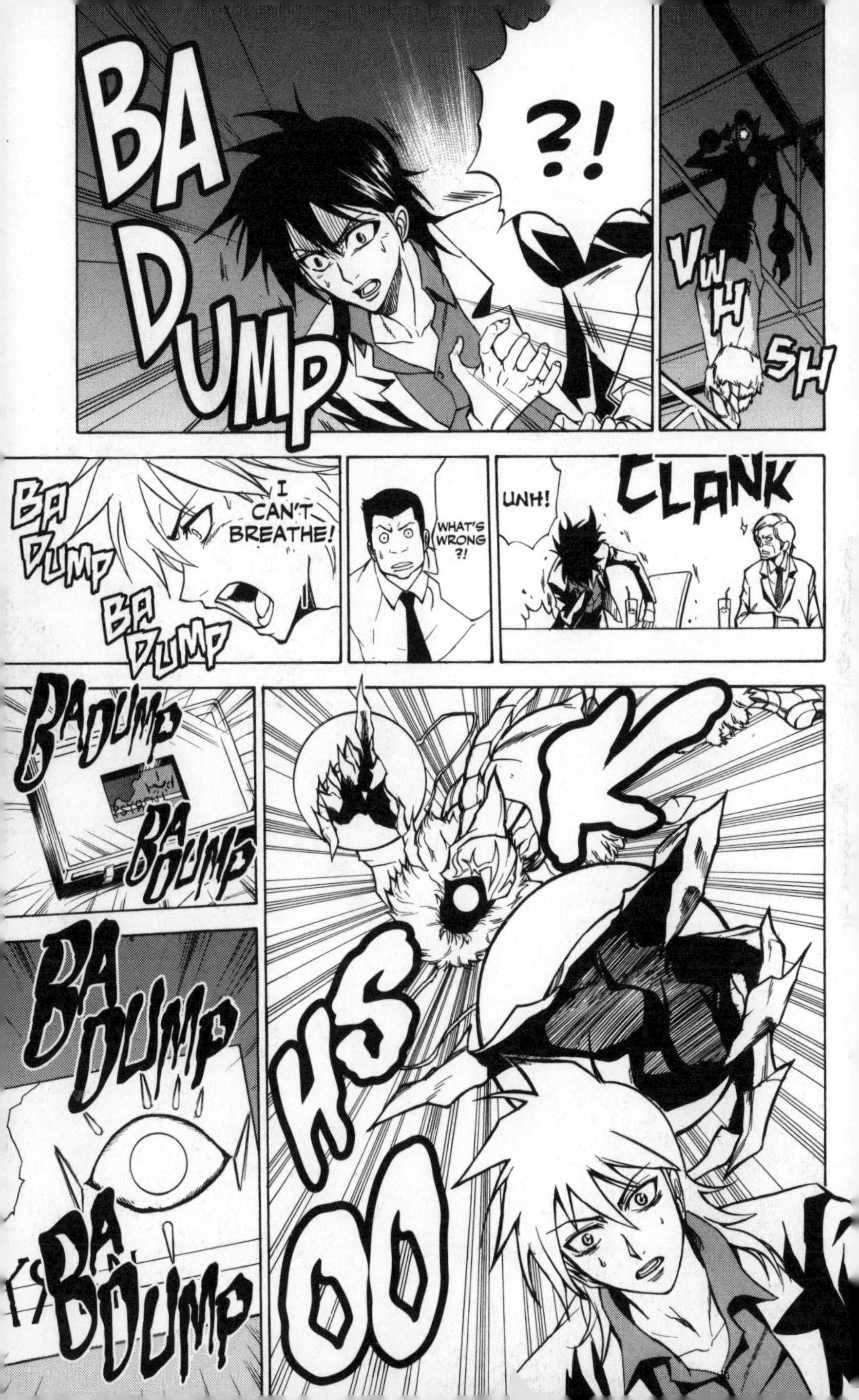
VWHSH
?!
BA DUMP
UNH!
CLANK
WHAT'S WRONG?!
I CAN'T BREATHE!
BA DUMP
BA DUMP
BADUMP
BADUMP
BA DUMP
BA DUMP

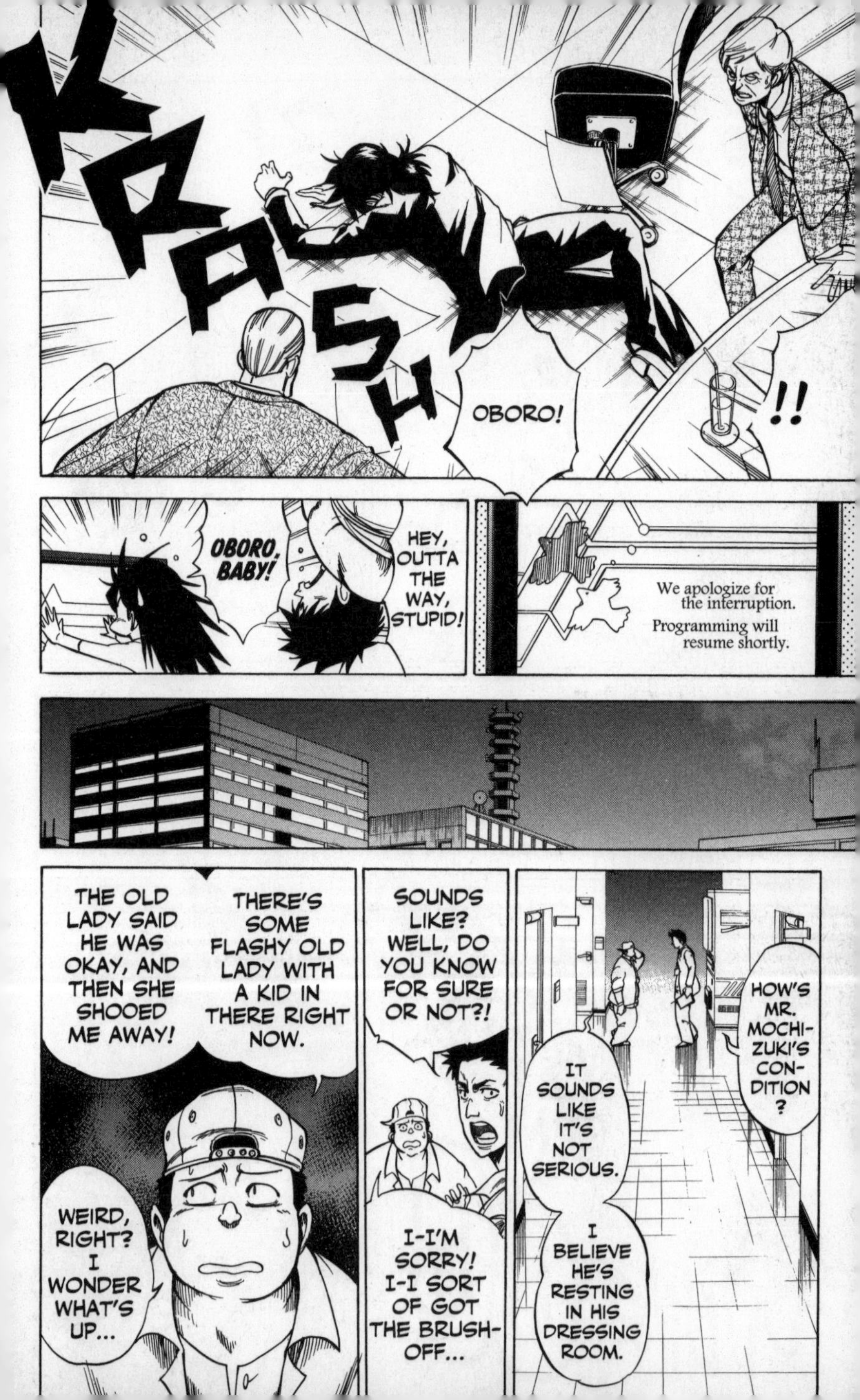
!!
OBORO!
KRASH
We apologize for the interruption.
Programming will resume shortly.
HEY, OUTTA THE WAY, STUPID!
OBORO, BABY!
HOW'S MR. MOCHIZUKI'S CONDITION?
IT SOUNDS LIKE IT'S NOT SERIOUS.
I BELIEVE HE'S RESTING IN HIS DRESSING ROOM.
SOUNDS LIKE? WELL, DO YOU KNOW FOR SURE OR NOT?!
I-I'M SORRY! I-I SORT OF GOT THE BRUSH-OFF...
THERE'S SOME FLASHY OLD LADY WITH A KID IN THERE RIGHT NOW.
THE OLD LADY SAID HE WAS OKAY, AND THEN SHE SHOOED ME AWAY!
WEIRD, RIGHT? I WONDER WHAT'S UP...

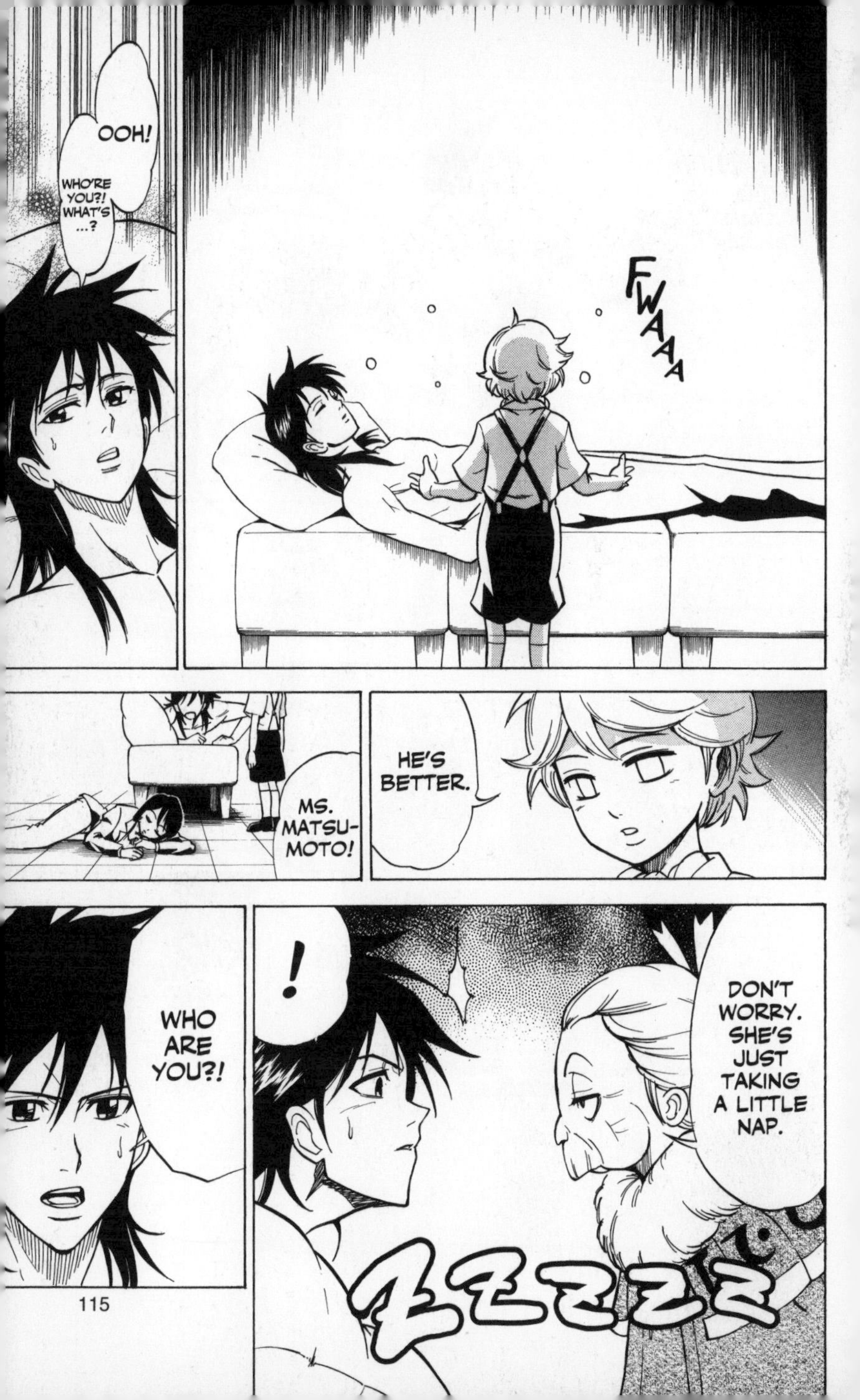
FWAAAA
OOH!
WHO'RE YOU?! WHAT'S ...?
HE'S BETTER.
MS. MATSU-MOTO!
!
DON'T WORRY. SHE'S JUST TAKING A LITTLE NAP.
ZZZZZZ
WHO ARE YOU?!

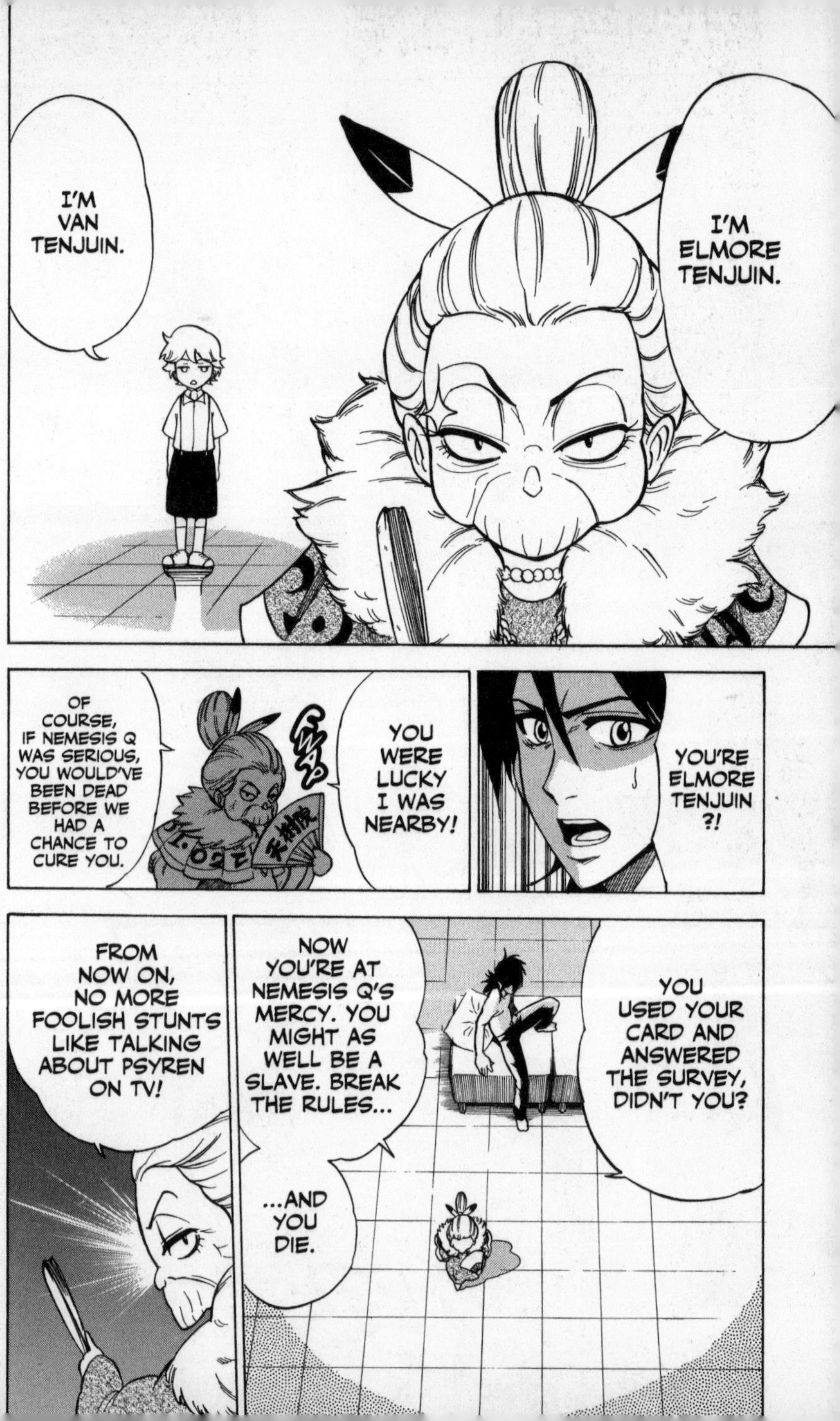
I'M ELMORE TENJUIN.
I'M VAN TENJUIN.
YOU'RE ELMORE TENJUIN ?!
YOU WERE LUCKY I WAS NEARBY!
OF COURSE, IF NEMESIS Q WAS SERIOUS, YOU WOULD'VE BEEN DEAD BEFORE WE HAD A CHANCE TO CURE YOU.
YOU USED YOUR CARD AND ANSWERED THE SURVEY, DIDN'T YOU?
NOW YOU'RE AT NEMESIS Q'S MERCY. YOU MIGHT AS WELL BE A SLAVE. BREAK THE RULES...
...AND YOU DIE.
FROM NOW ON, NO MORE FOOLISH STUNTS LIKE TALKING ABOUT PSYREN ON TV!

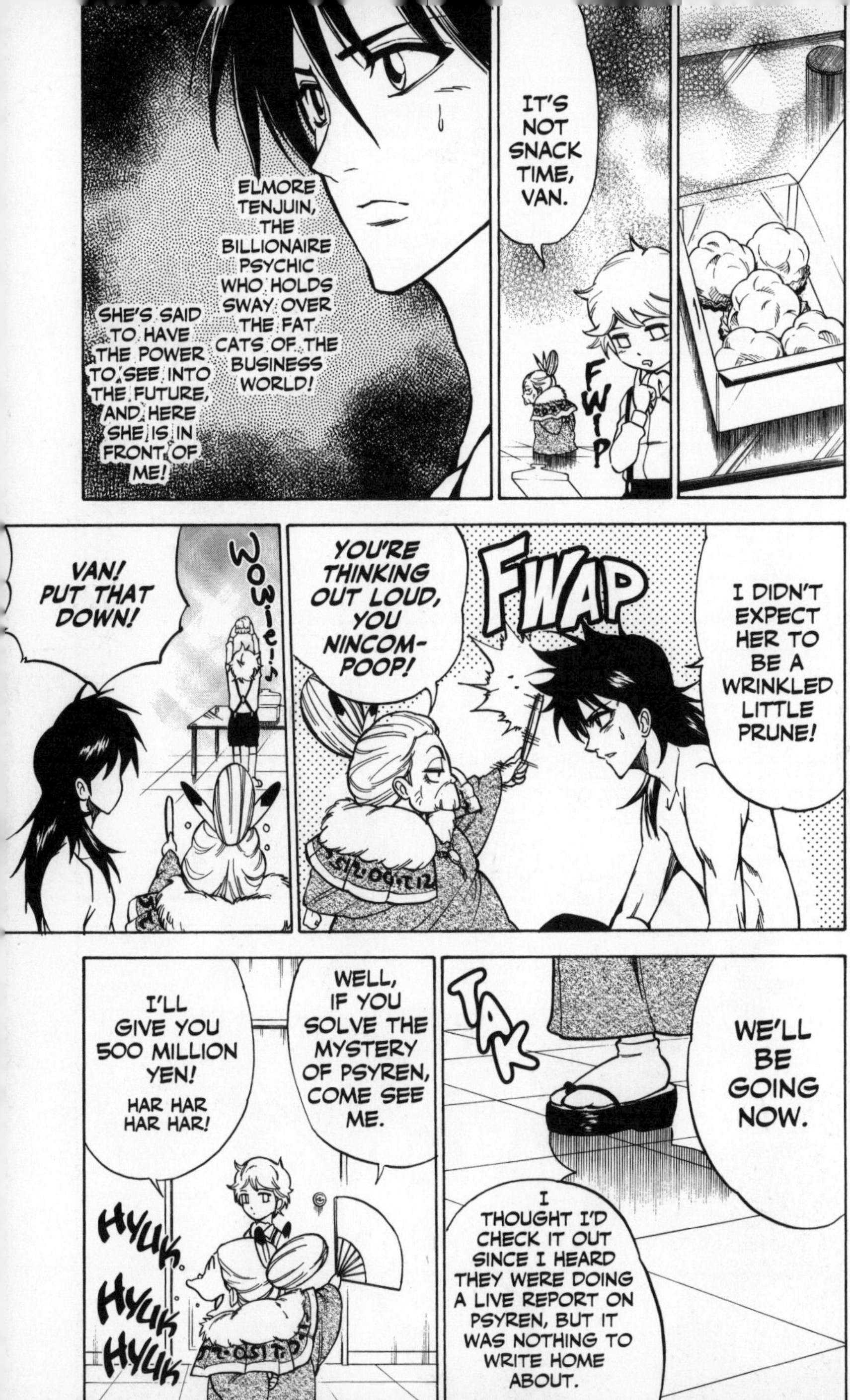
IT'S NOT SNACK TIME, VAN.
FWIP
ELMORE TENJUIN, THE BILLIONAIRE PSYCHIC WHO HOLDS SWAY OVER THE FAT CATS OF THE BUSINESS WORLD!
SHE'S SAID TO HAVE THE POWER TO SEE INTO THE FUTURE, AND HERE SHE IS IN FRONT OF ME!
I DIDN'T EXPECT HER TO BE A WRINKLED LITTLE PRUNE!
FWAP
YOU'RE THINKING OUT LOUD, YOU NINCOMPOOP!
WOWie!!
VAN! PUT THAT DOWN!
WE'LL BE GOING NOW.
TAK
I THOUGHT I'D CHECK IT OUT SINCE I HEARD THEY WERE DOING A LIVE REPORT ON PSYREN, BUT IT WAS NOTHING TO WRITE HOME ABOUT.
WELL, IF YOU SOLVE THE MYSTERY OF PSYREN, COME SEE ME.
I'LL GIVE YOU 500 MILLION YEN!
HAR HAR HAR HAR!
HYUK HYUK HYUK

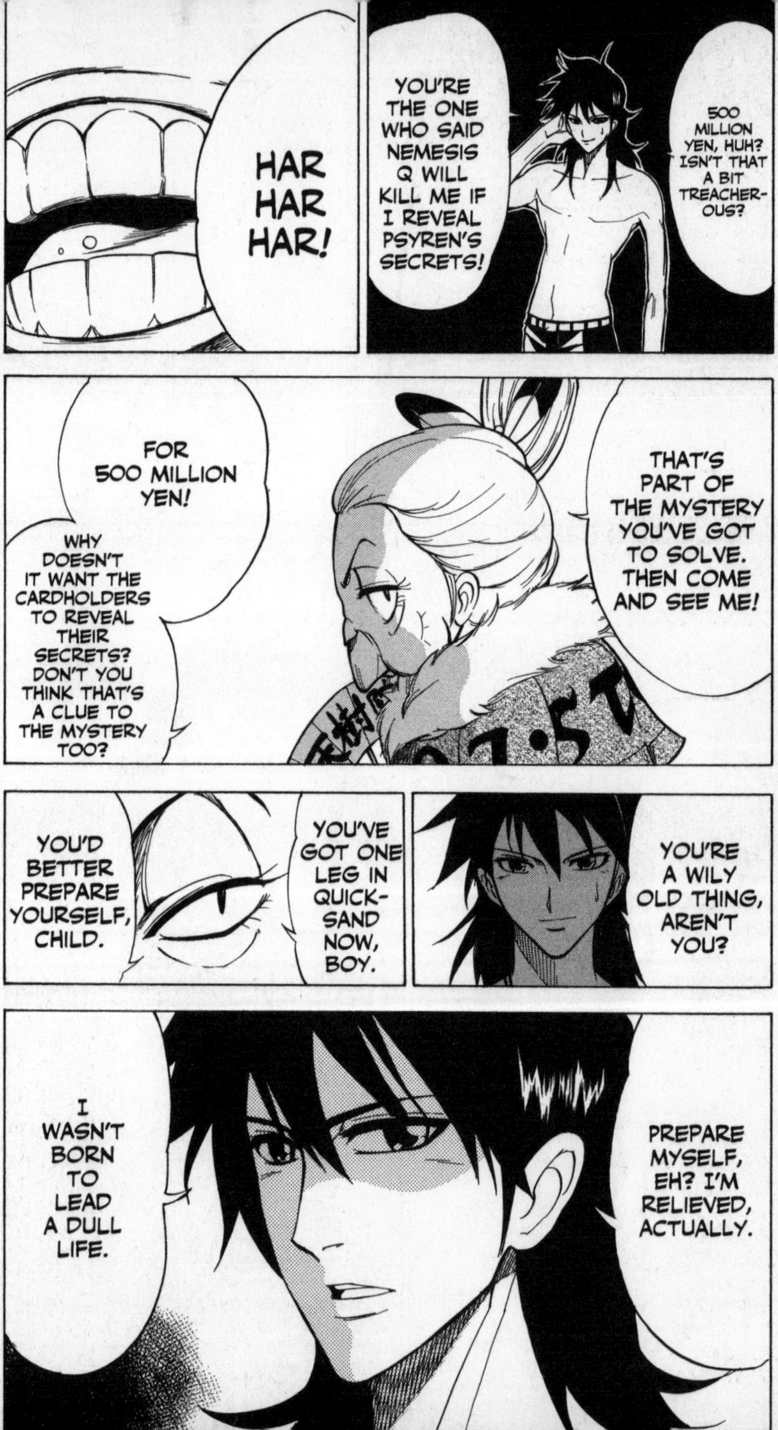
500 MILLION YEN, HUH? ISN'T THAT A BIT TREACHER-OUS?
YOU'RE THE ONE WHO SAID NEMESIS Q WILL KILL ME IF I REVEAL PSYREN'S SECRETS!
HAR HAR HAR!
THAT'S PART OF THE MYSTERY YOU'VE GOT TO SOLVE. THEN COME AND SEE ME!
FOR 500 MILLION YEN!
WHY DOESN'T IT WANT THE CARDHOLDERS TO REVEAL THEIR SECRETS? DON'T YOU THINK THAT'S A CLUE TO THE MYSTERY TOO?
YOU'RE A WILY OLD THING, AREN'T YOU?
YOU'VE GOT ONE LEG IN QUICK-SAND NOW, BOY.
YOU'D BETTER PREPARE YOURSELF, CHILD.
PREPARE MYSELF, EH? I'M RELIEVED, ACTUALLY.
I WASN'T BORN TO LEAD A DULL LIFE.

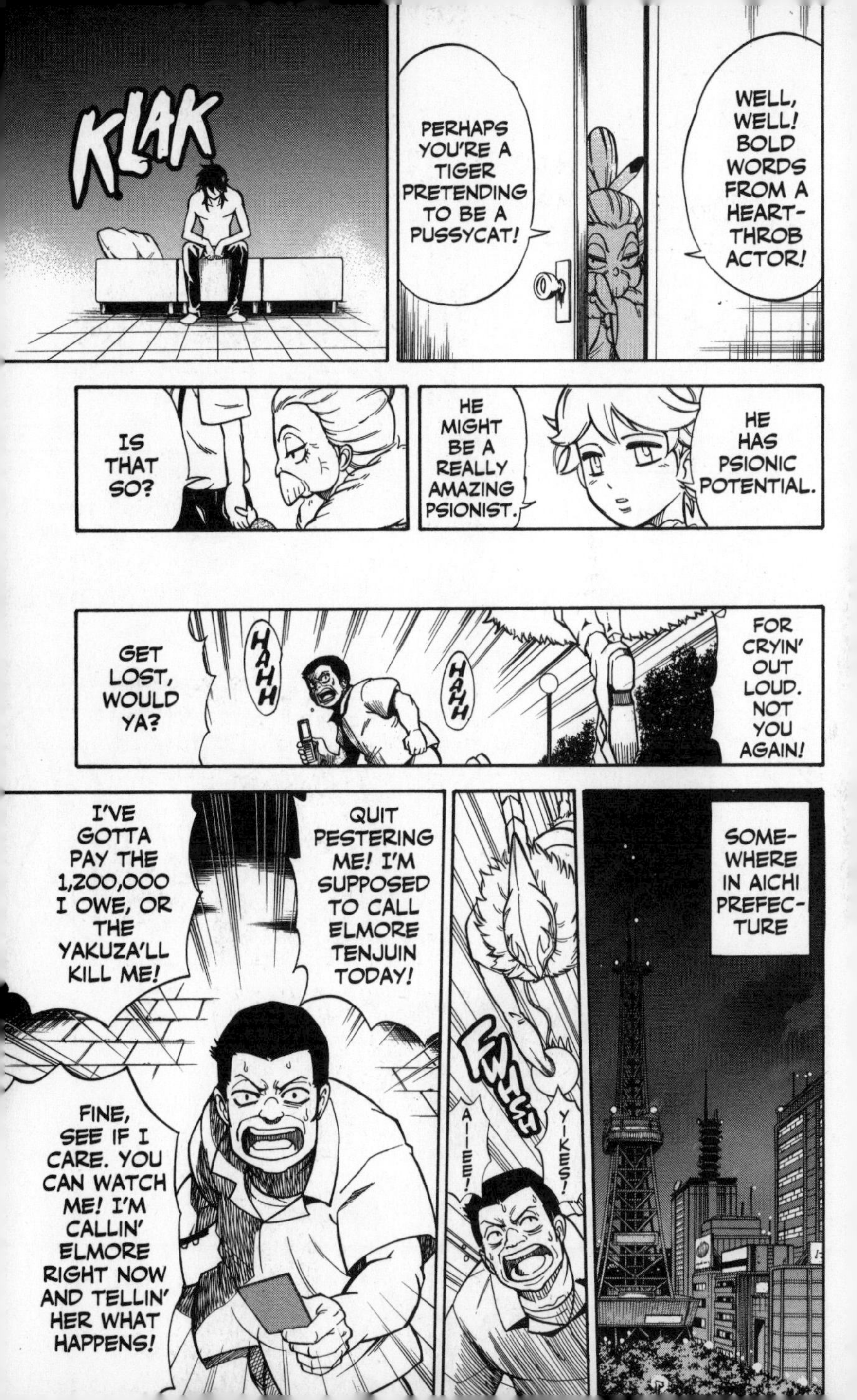
WELL, WELL! BOLD WORDS FROM A HEART-THROB ACTOR!
PERHAPS YOU'RE A TIGER PRETENDING TO BE A PUSSYCAT!
KLAK
HE HAS PSIONIC POTENTIAL.
HE MIGHT BE A REALLY AMAZING PSIONIST.
IS THAT SO?
FOR CRYIN' OUT LOUD. NOT YOU AGAIN!
HAHH
HAHH
GET LOST, WOULD YA?
SOME-WHERE IN AICHI PREFEC-TURE
FWHSH
YIKES!
AIIEE!
QUIT PESTERING ME! I'M SUPPOSED TO CALL ELMORE TENJUIN TODAY!
I'VE GOTTA PAY THE 1,200,000 I OWE, OR THE YAKUZA'LL KILL ME!
FINE, SEE IF I CARE. YOU CAN WATCH ME! I'M CALLIN' ELMORE RIGHT NOW AND TELLIN' HER WHAT HAPPENS!

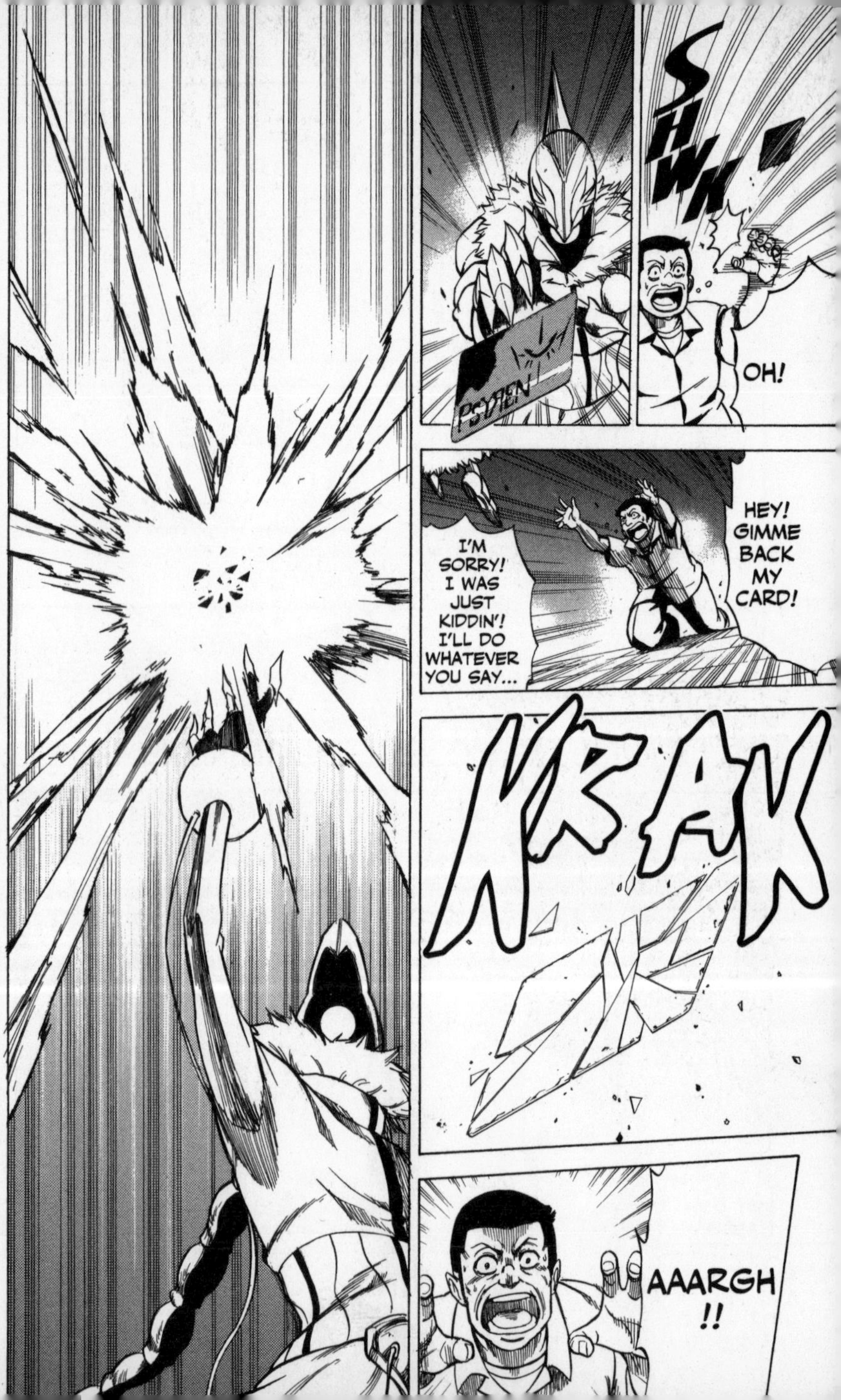
SHWK
OH!
PSYREN
HEY! GIMME BACK MY CARD!
I'M SORRY! I WAS JUST KIDDIN'! I'LL DO WHATEVER YOU SAY...
KRAK
AAARGH !!

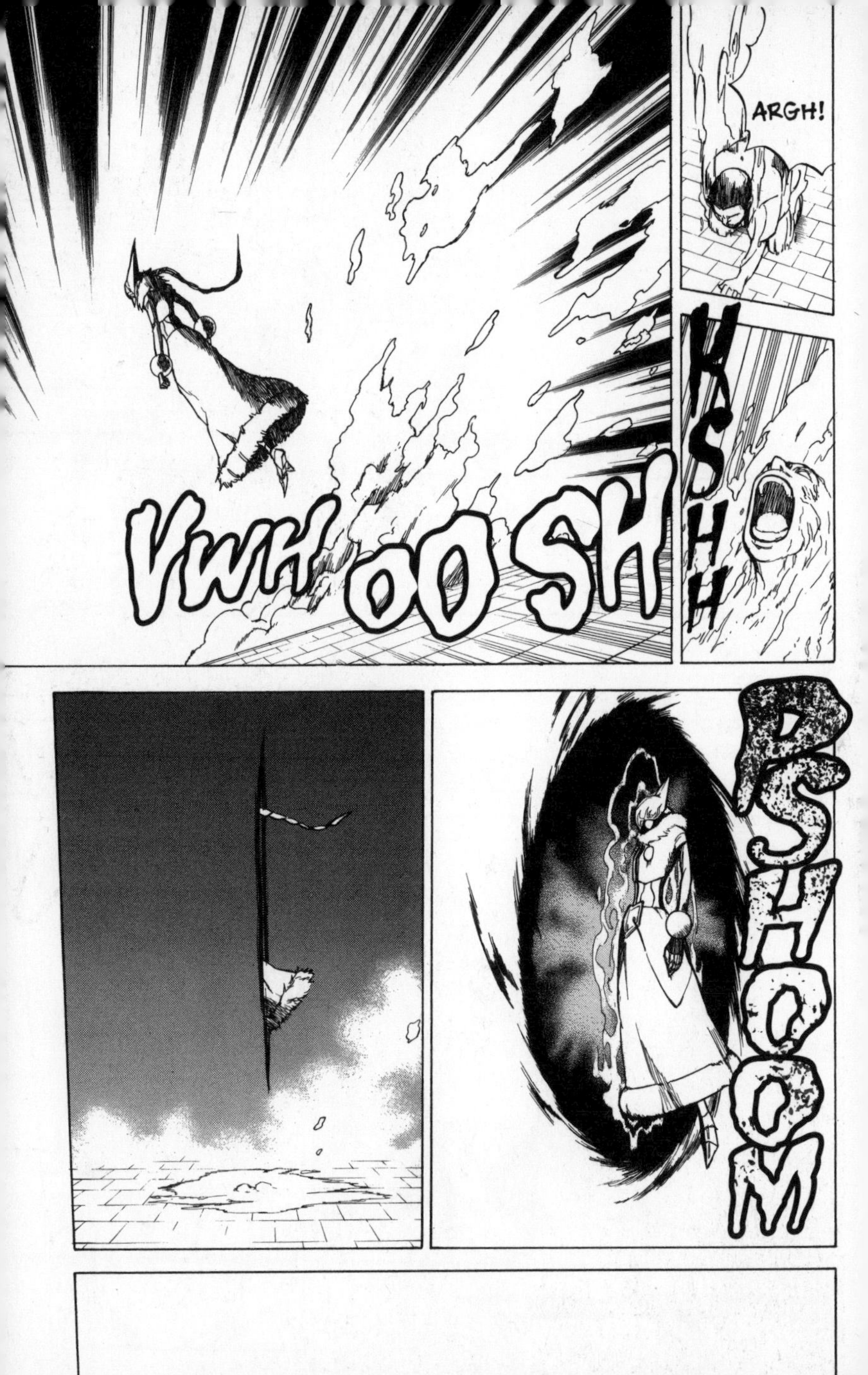

ARGH!
KASHHH
VWHOOSH
PSHOOM

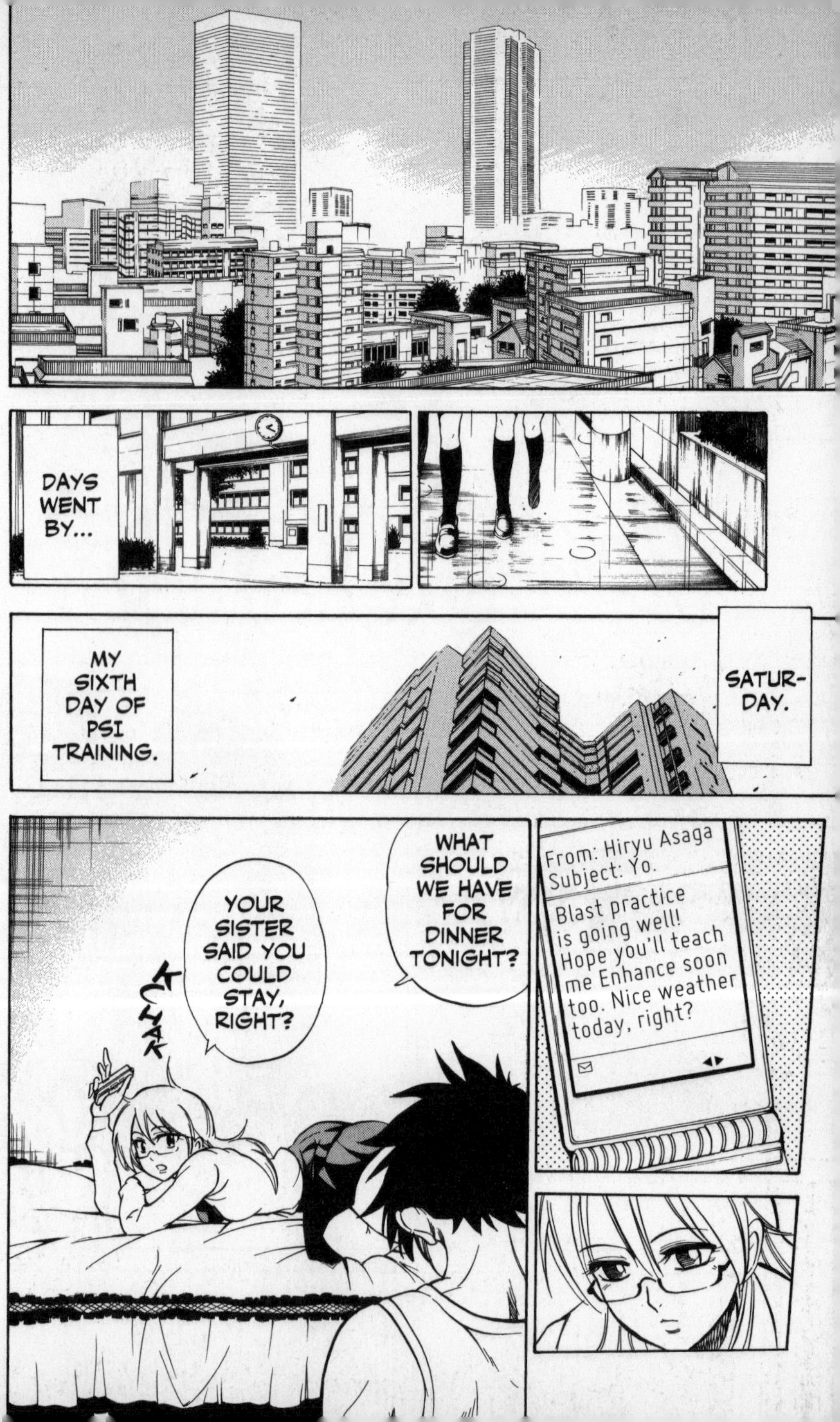
DAYS WENT BY...
SATUR-DAY.
MY SIXTH DAY OF PSI TRAINING.
From: Hiryu Asaga
Subject: Yo.
Blast practice is going well! Hope you'll teach me Enhance soon too. Nice weather today, right?
WHAT SHOULD WE HAVE FOR DINNER TONIGHT?
YOUR SISTER SAID YOU COULD STAY, RIGHT?
KCHAK

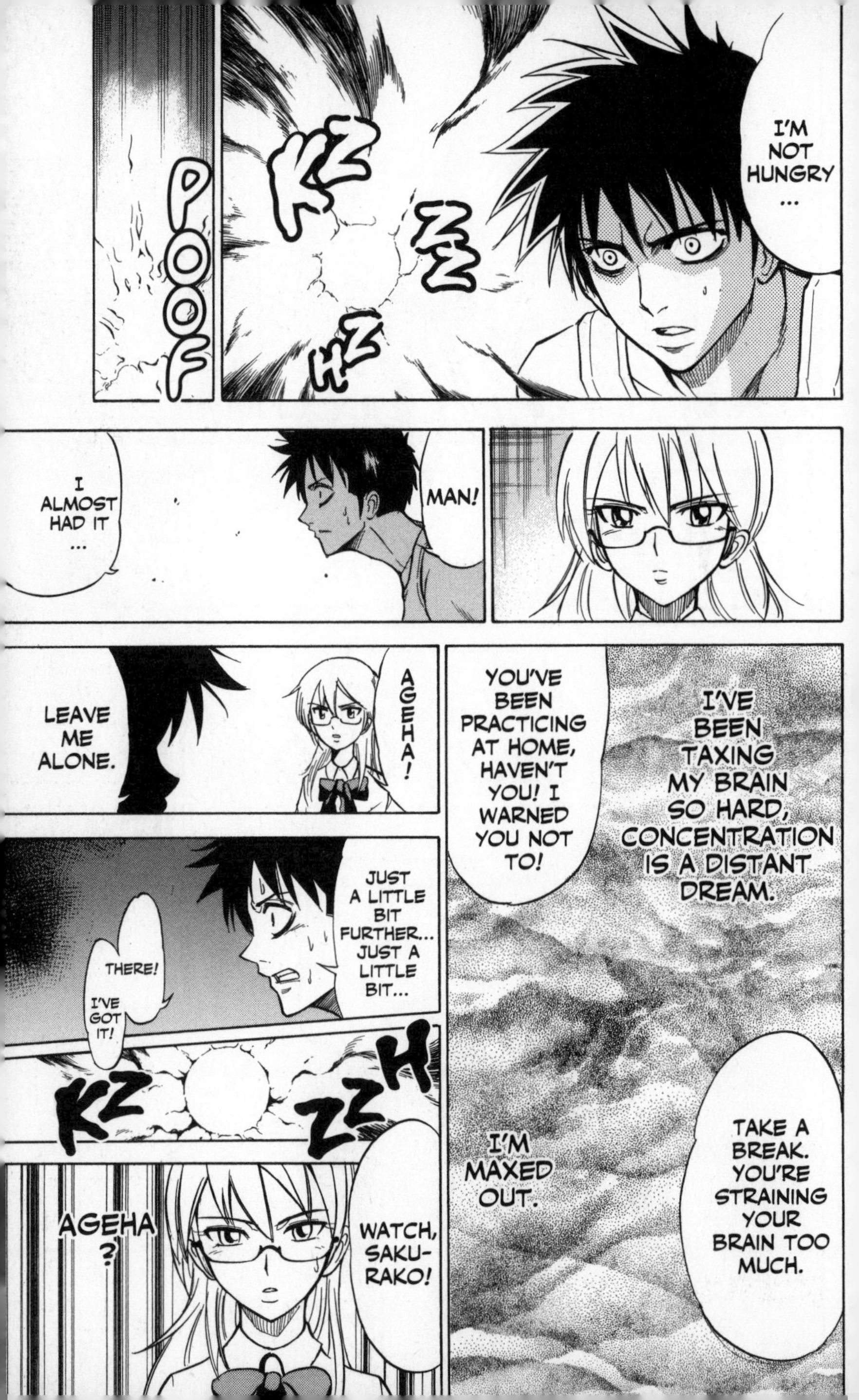
I'M NOT HUNGRY...
KZZZH
POOF
MAN!
I ALMOST HAD IT...
I'VE BEEN TAXING MY BRAIN SO HARD, CONCENTRATION IS A DISTANT DREAM.
YOU'VE BEEN PRACTICING AT HOME, HAVEN'T YOU! I WARNED YOU NOT TO!
TAKE A BREAK. YOU'RE STRAINING YOUR BRAIN TOO MUCH.
I'M MAXED OUT.
AGEHA!
LEAVE ME ALONE.
JUST A LITTLE BIT FURTHER... JUST A LITTLE BIT...
THERE!
I'VE GOT IT!
KZZZH
WATCH, SAKU-RAKO!
AGEHA?

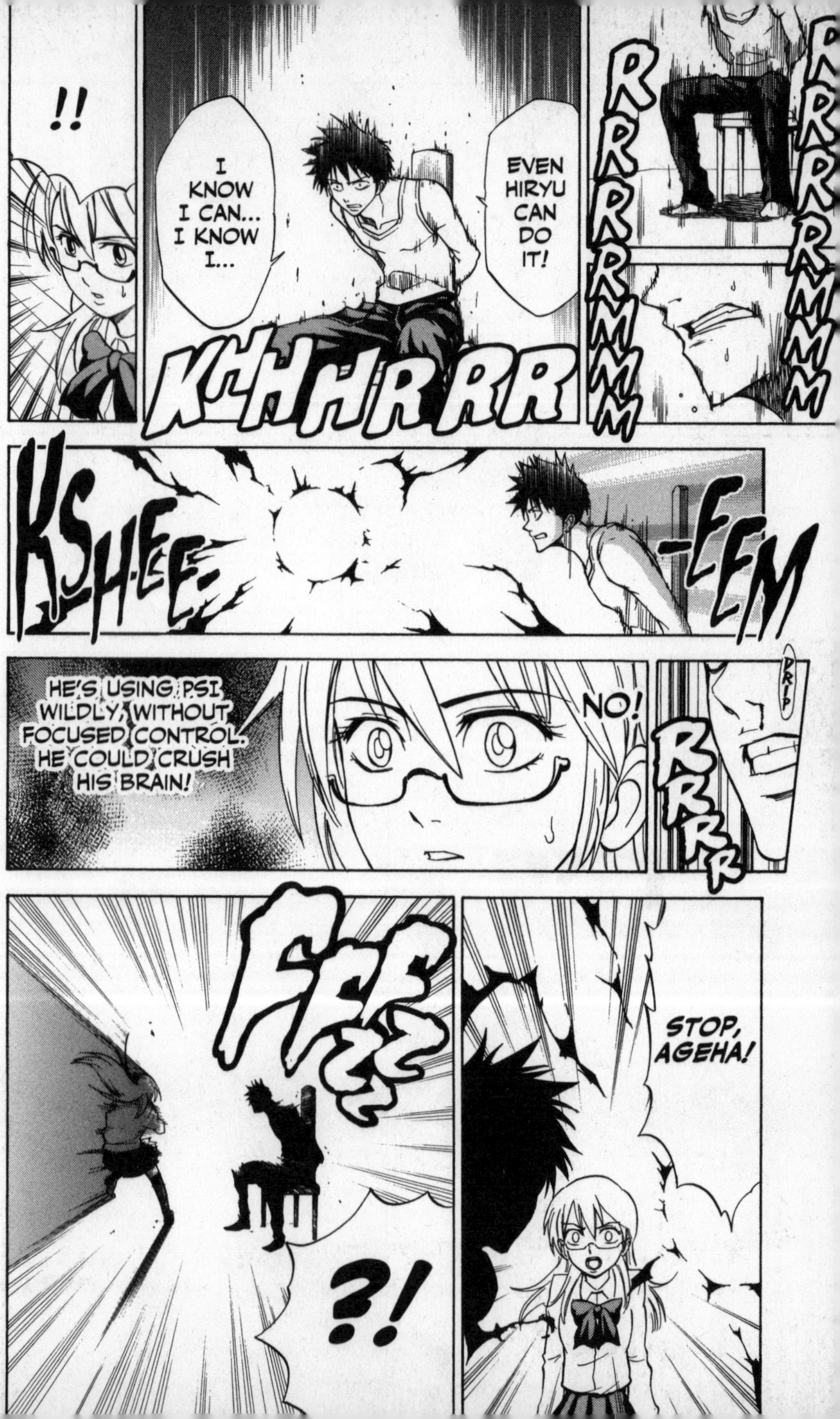
RRRRRMMMM
RRRRRRMMMM
EVEN HIRYU CAN DO IT!
I KNOW I CAN... I KNOW I...
K-HHRRRR
!!
KSHEE-EEM
DRIP
RRRR
NO!
HE'S USING PSI WILDLY, WITHOUT FOCUSED CONTROL. HE COULD CRUSH HIS BRAIN!
STOP, AGEHA!
FFF
?!

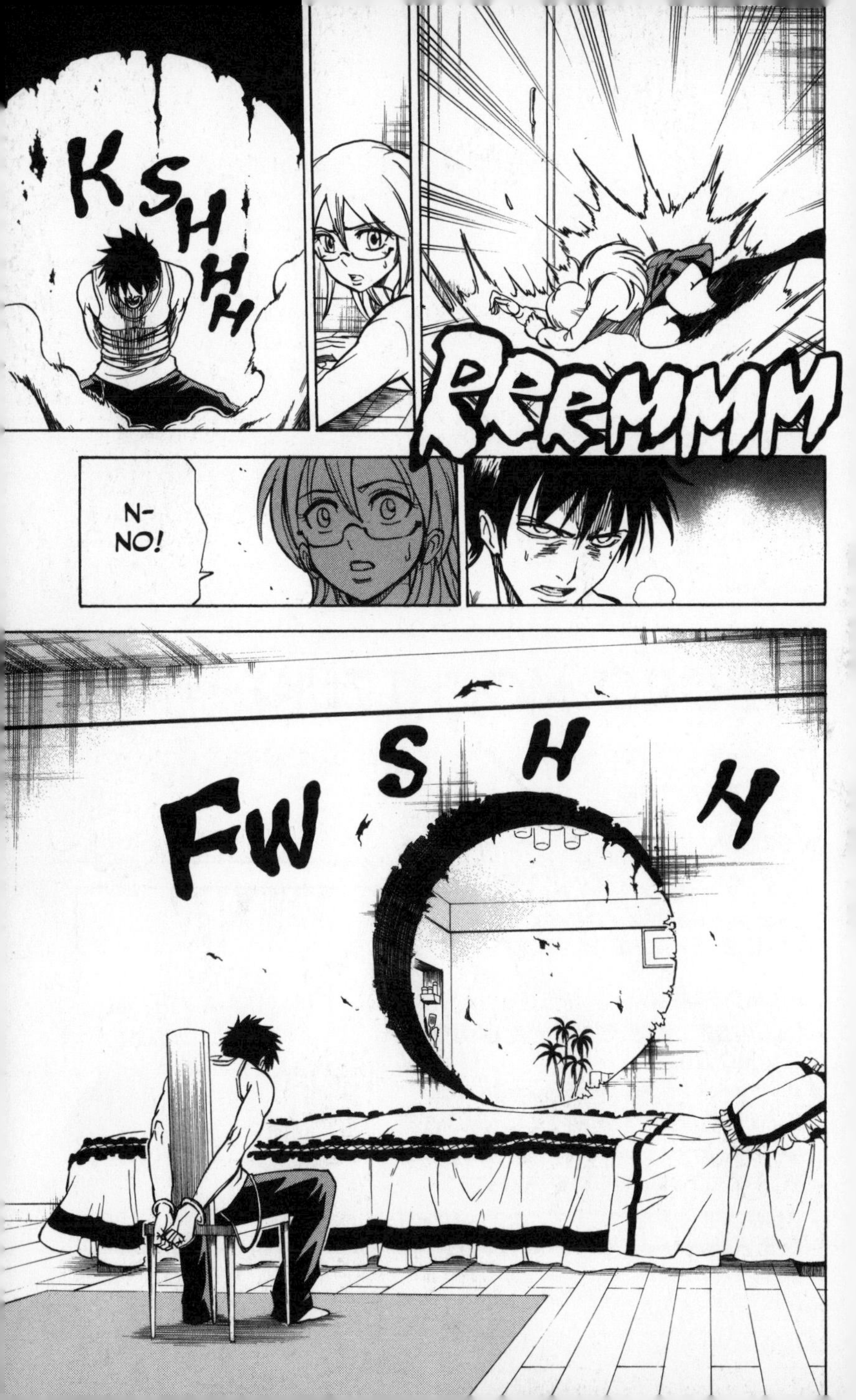
PRRMMM
KSHHH
N-NO!
FWSHH

OBORO MOCHIZUKI

AGE 21. ACTOR.
OBORO DOESN'T SHOW HIS TRUE
PERSONALITY ON TV. HE HAS HIS
OWN IDEAS ABOUT MORALITY. OBORO
LOVES STEAK AND MELON PASTRIES,
AND HE HATES COCKROACHES, JUST
LIKE EVERYONE ELSE.

FILMOGRAPHY:

VAMPIRE DETECTIVE CROSSEYES
(TV MOVIE)

HOT BOY CLUB (TV DRAMA)
BLOODCURDLING SPIRAL (MOVIE)

VAMPIRE DETECTIVE CROSSEYES
GOES TO NEW YORK (MOVIE)

VAMPIRE DETECTIVE CROSSEYES:
THE FINAL BATTLE (MOVIE)

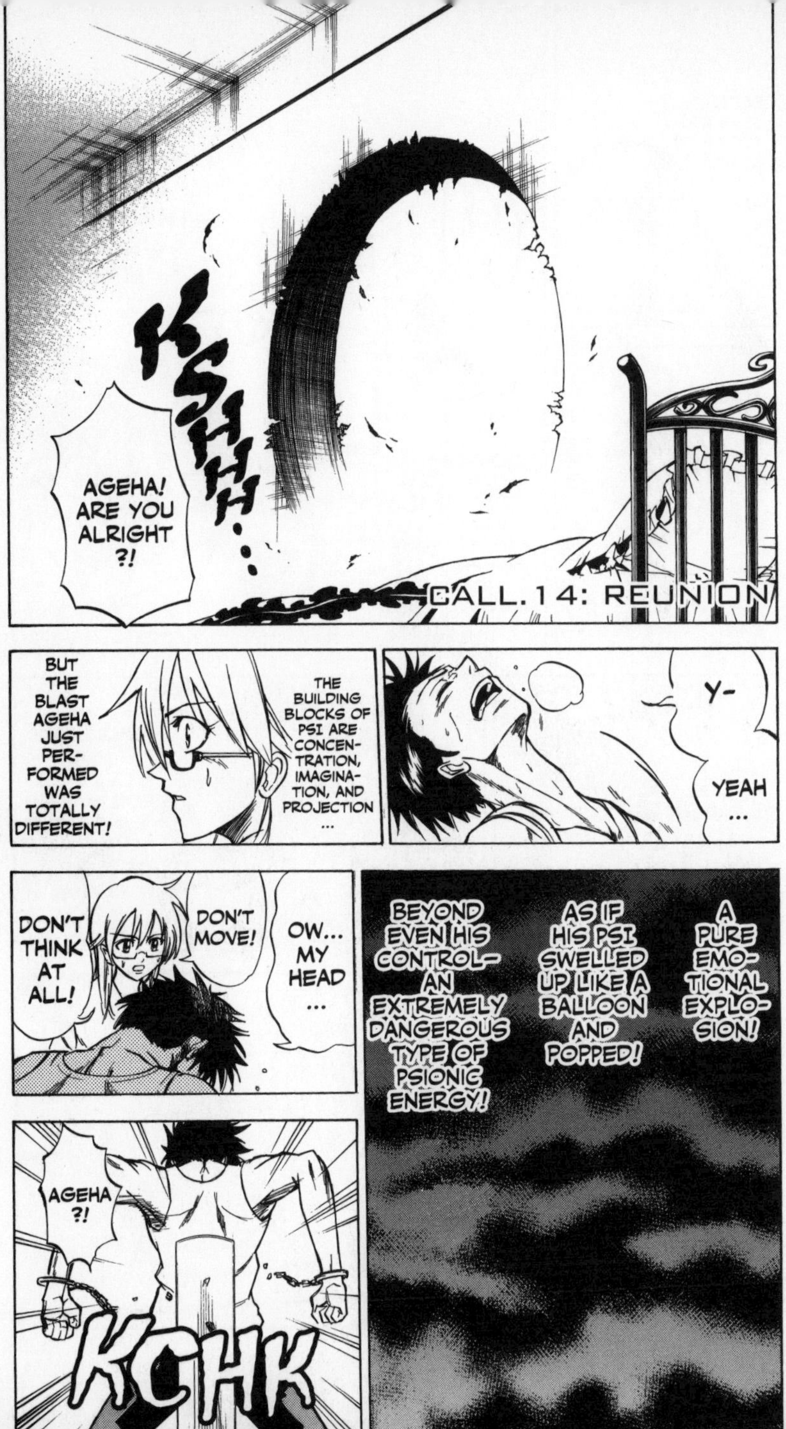
KSHHH...
AGEHA! ARE YOU ALRIGHT?!
CALL.14: REUNION
Y-
YEAH...
THE BUILDING BLOCKS OF PSI ARE CONCENTRATION, IMAGINATION, AND PROJECTION...
BUT THE BLAST AGEHA JUST PERFORMED WAS TOTALLY DIFFERENT!
A PURE EMOTIONAL EXPLOSION!
AS IF HIS PSI SWELLED UP LIKE A BALLOON AND POPPED!
BEYOND EVEN HIS CONTROL— AN EXTREMELY DANGEROUS TYPE OF PSIONIC ENERGY!
OW... MY HEAD...
DON'T MOVE!
DON'T THINK AT ALL!
AGEHA?!
KCHK

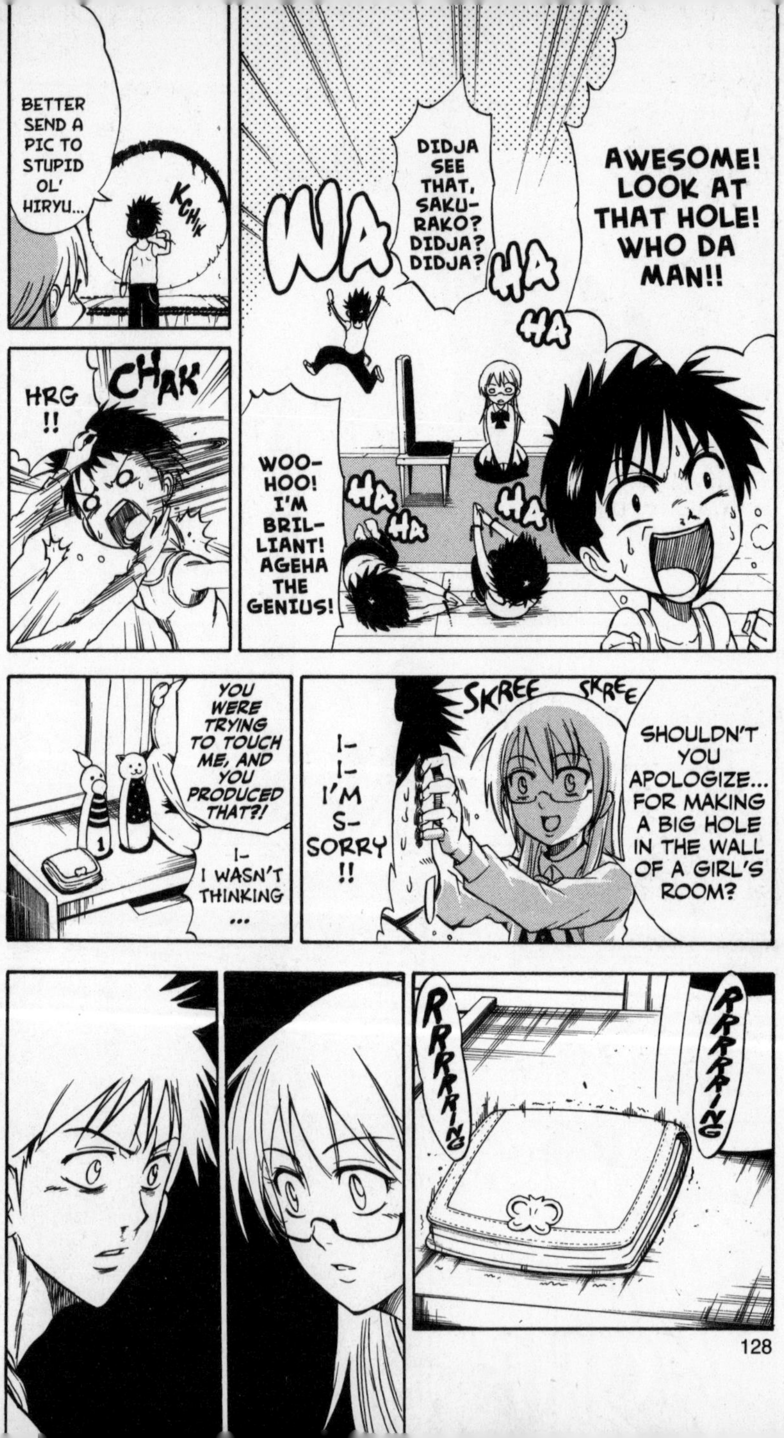
AWESOME! LOOK AT THAT HOLE! WHO DA MAN!!
DIDJA SEE THAT, SAKU-RAKO? DIDJA? DIDJA?
WA
HA
HA
HA
HA
HA
WOO-HOO! I'M BRIL-LIANT! AGEHA THE GENIUS!
BETTER SEND A PIC TO STUPID OL' HIRYU...
KCHIK
CHAK
HRG!!
SKREE
SKREE
SHOULDN'T YOU APOLOGIZE... FOR MAKING A BIG HOLE IN THE WALL OF A GIRL'S ROOM?
I- I- I'M S-SORRY!!
YOU WERE TRYING TO TOUCH ME, AND YOU PRODUCED THAT?!
I- I WASN'T THINKING...
RRRRRING
RRRRRING

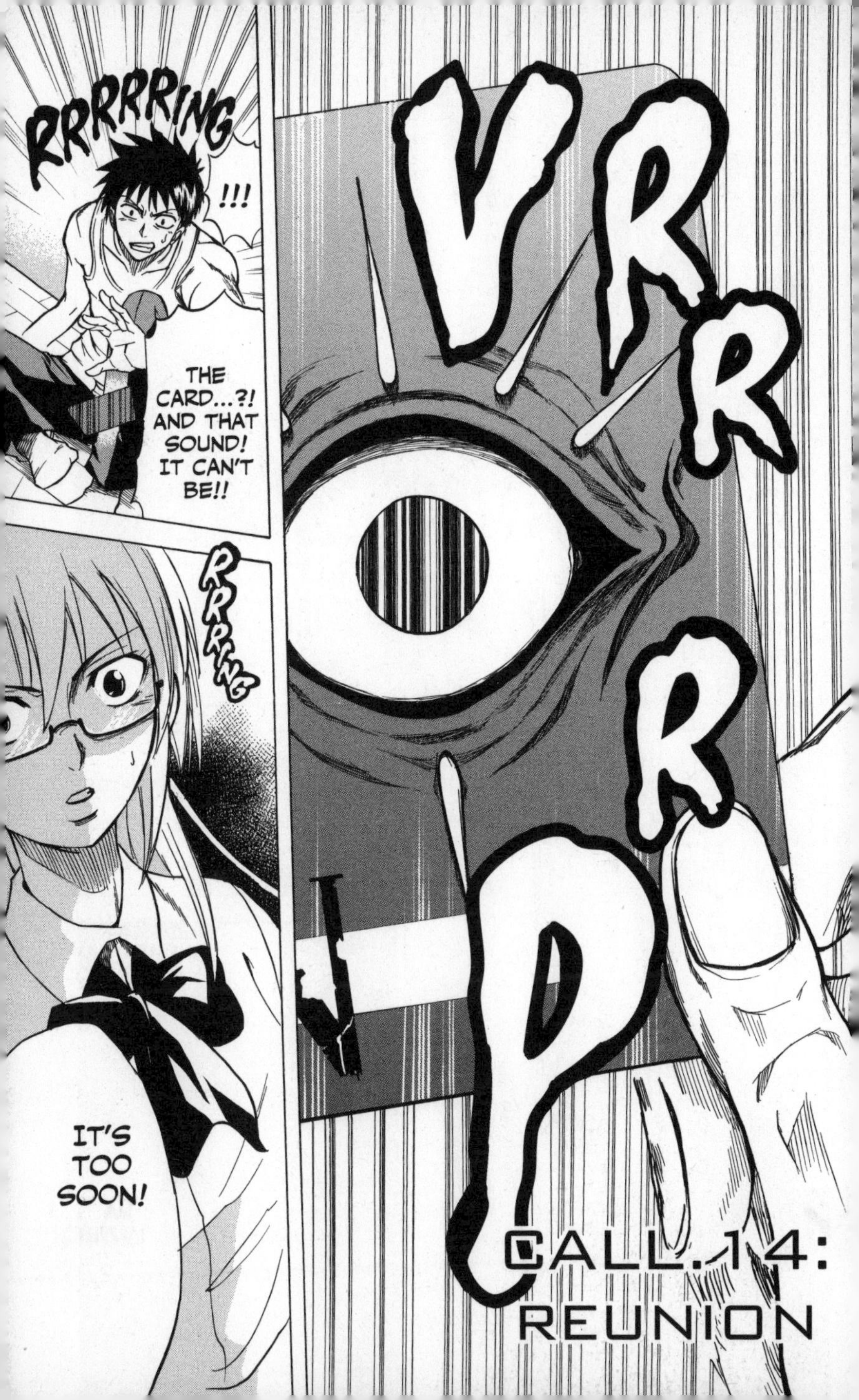
VRRRP
CALL.14: REUNION
RRRRRING
!!!
THE CARD...?! AND THAT SOUND! IT CAN'T BE!!
RRRRING
IT'S TOO SOON!

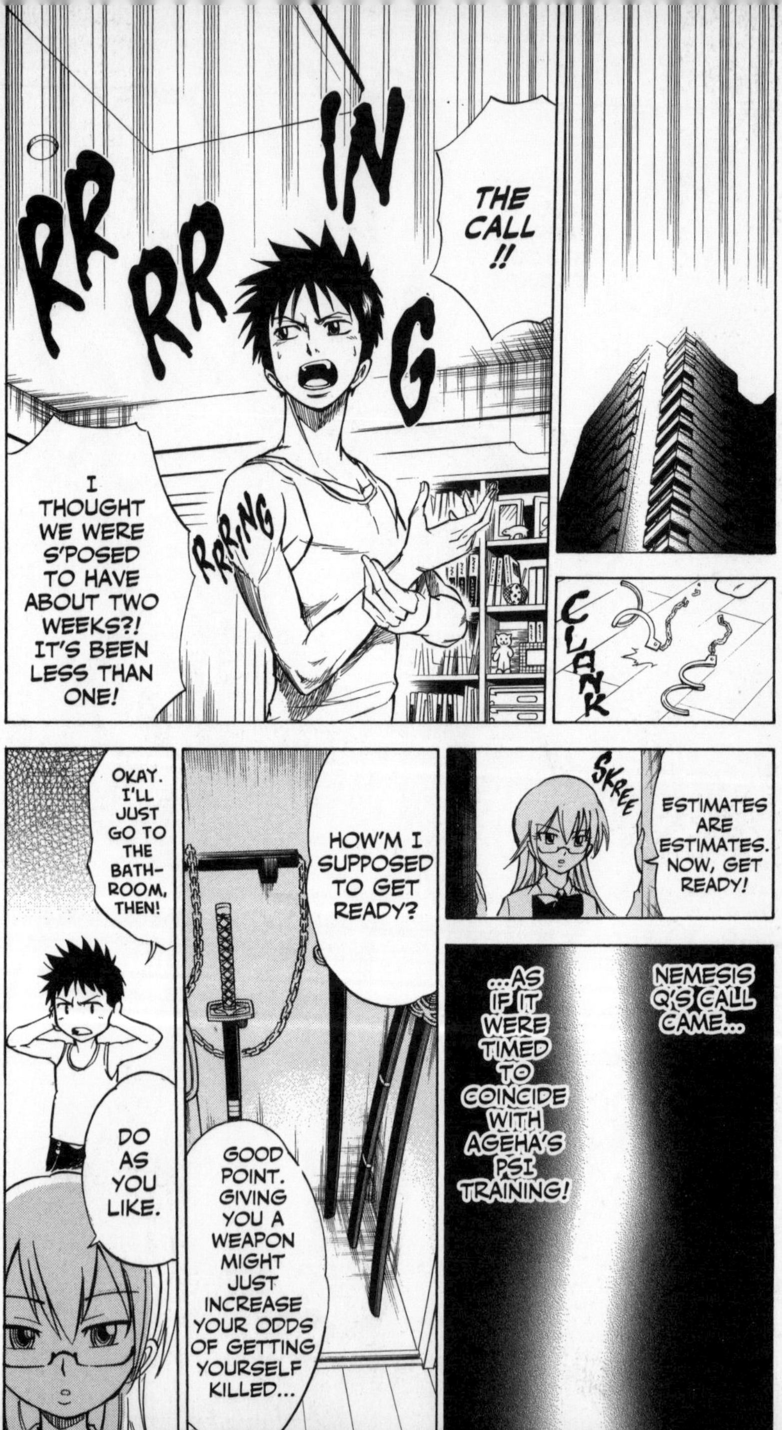
CLANK
RRRR
IN
G
THE CALL!!
I THOUGHT WE WERE S'POSED TO HAVE ABOUT TWO WEEKS?! IT'S BEEN LESS THAN ONE!
RRRING
SKREE
ESTIMATES ARE ESTIMATES. NOW, GET READY!
NEMESIS Q'S CALL CAME...
...AS IF IT WERE TIMED TO COINCIDE WITH AGEHA'S PSI TRAINING!
HOW'M I SUPPOSED TO GET READY?
GOOD POINT. GIVING YOU A WEAPON MIGHT JUST INCREASE YOUR ODDS OF GETTING YOURSELF KILLED...
OKAY. I'LL JUST GO TO THE BATH-ROOM, THEN!
DO AS YOU LIKE.

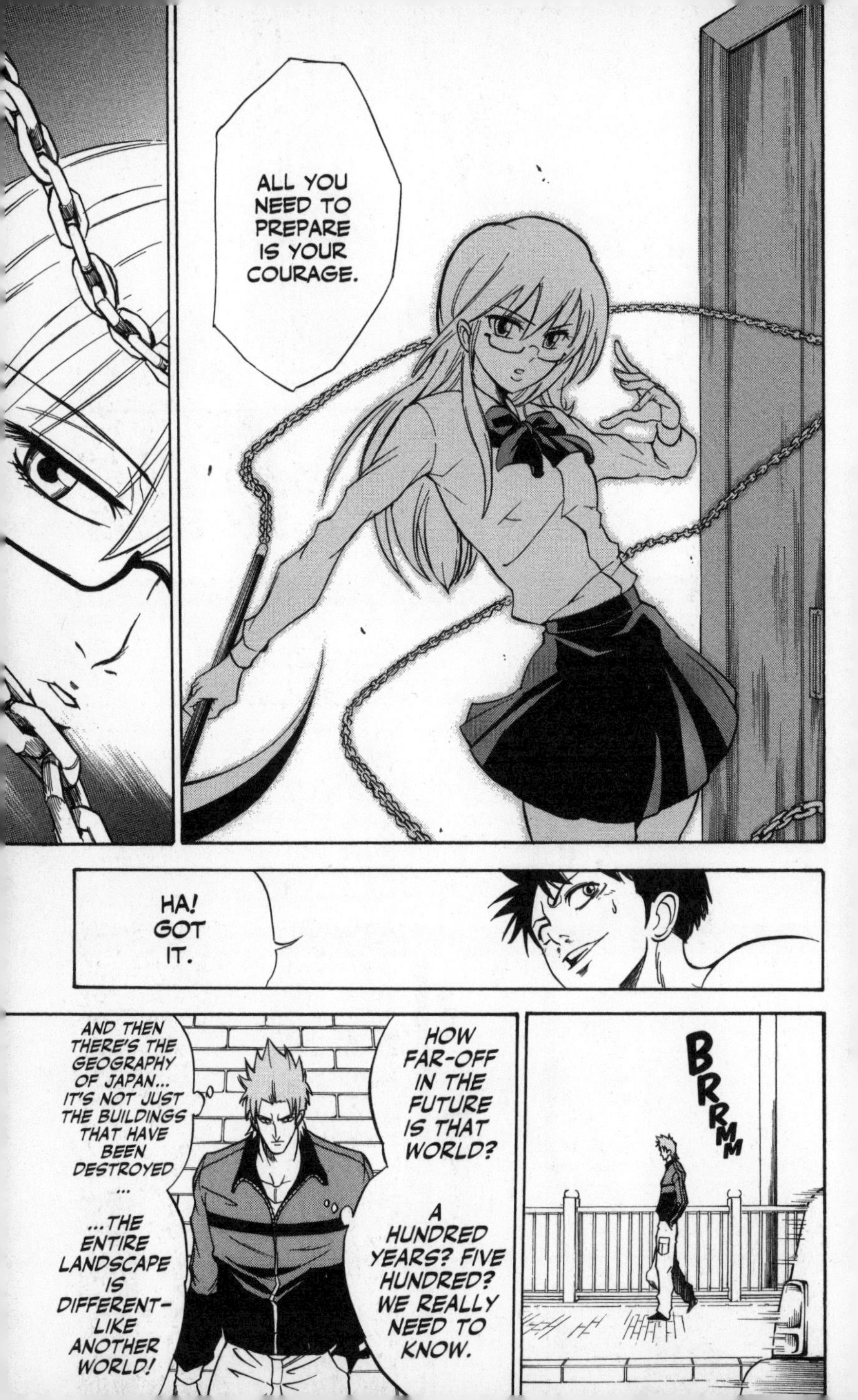
ALL YOU NEED TO PREPARE IS YOUR COURAGE.
HA! GOT IT.
BRRMM
HOW FAR-OFF IN THE FUTURE IS THAT WORLD?
A HUNDRED YEARS? FIVE HUNDRED? WE REALLY NEED TO KNOW.
AND THEN THERE'S THE GEOGRAPHY OF JAPAN... IT'S NOT JUST THE BUILDINGS THAT HAVE BEEN DESTROYED...
...THE ENTIRE LANDSCAPE IS DIFFERENT—LIKE ANOTHER WORLD!

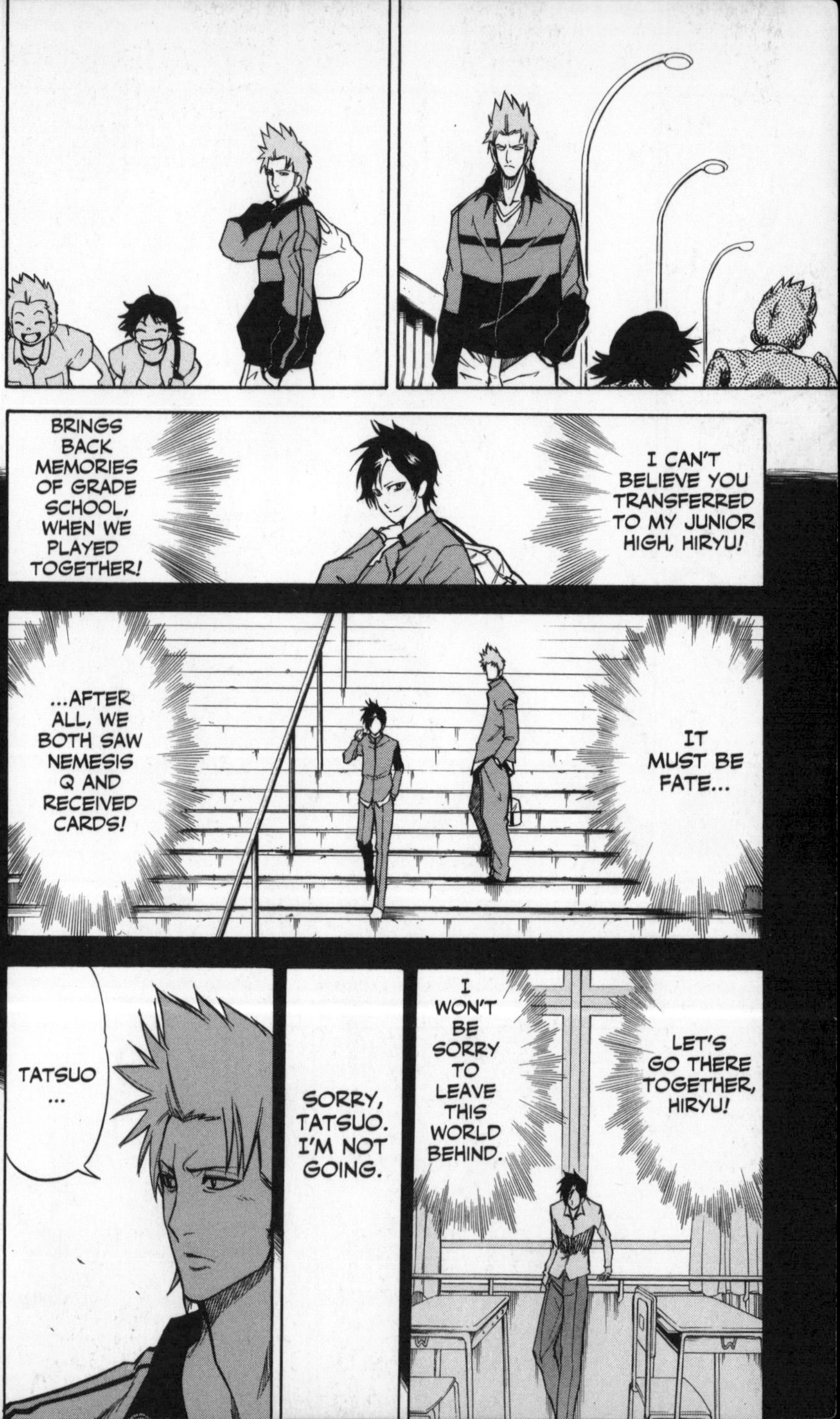
I CAN'T BELIEVE YOU TRANSFERRED TO MY JUNIOR HIGH, HIRYU!
BRINGS BACK MEMORIES OF GRADE SCHOOL, WHEN WE PLAYED TOGETHER!
IT MUST BE FATE...
...AFTER ALL, WE BOTH SAW NEMESIS Q AND RECEIVED CARDS!
LET'S GO THERE TOGETHER, HIRYU!
I WON'T BE SORRY TO LEAVE THIS WORLD BEHIND.
SORRY, TATSUO. I'M NOT GOING.
TATSUO ...

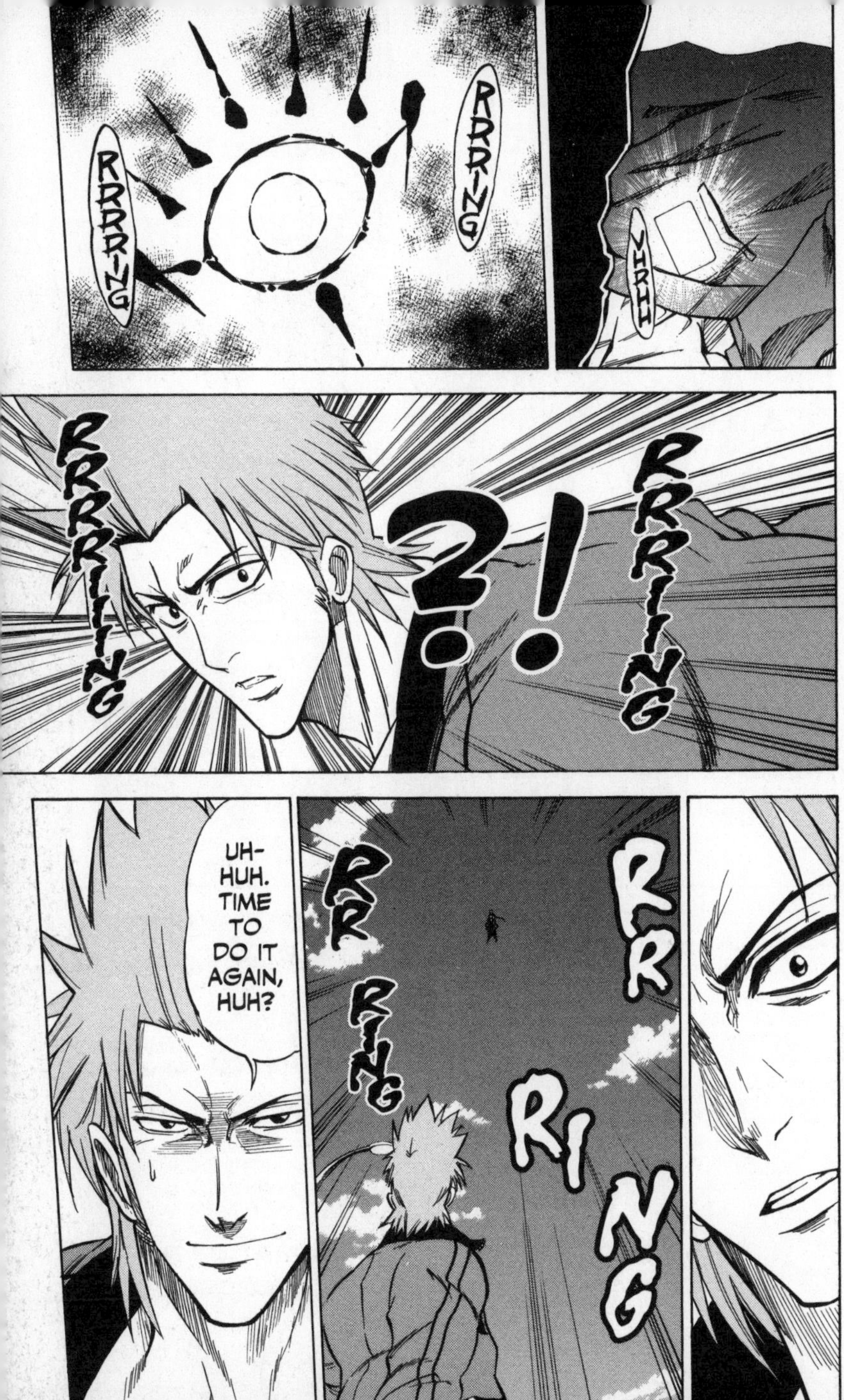
VHRH
RRRING
RRRRING
RRRIING
?!
RRRRIIING
RRRRING
RRRING
UH-HUH. TIME TO DO IT AGAIN, HUH?

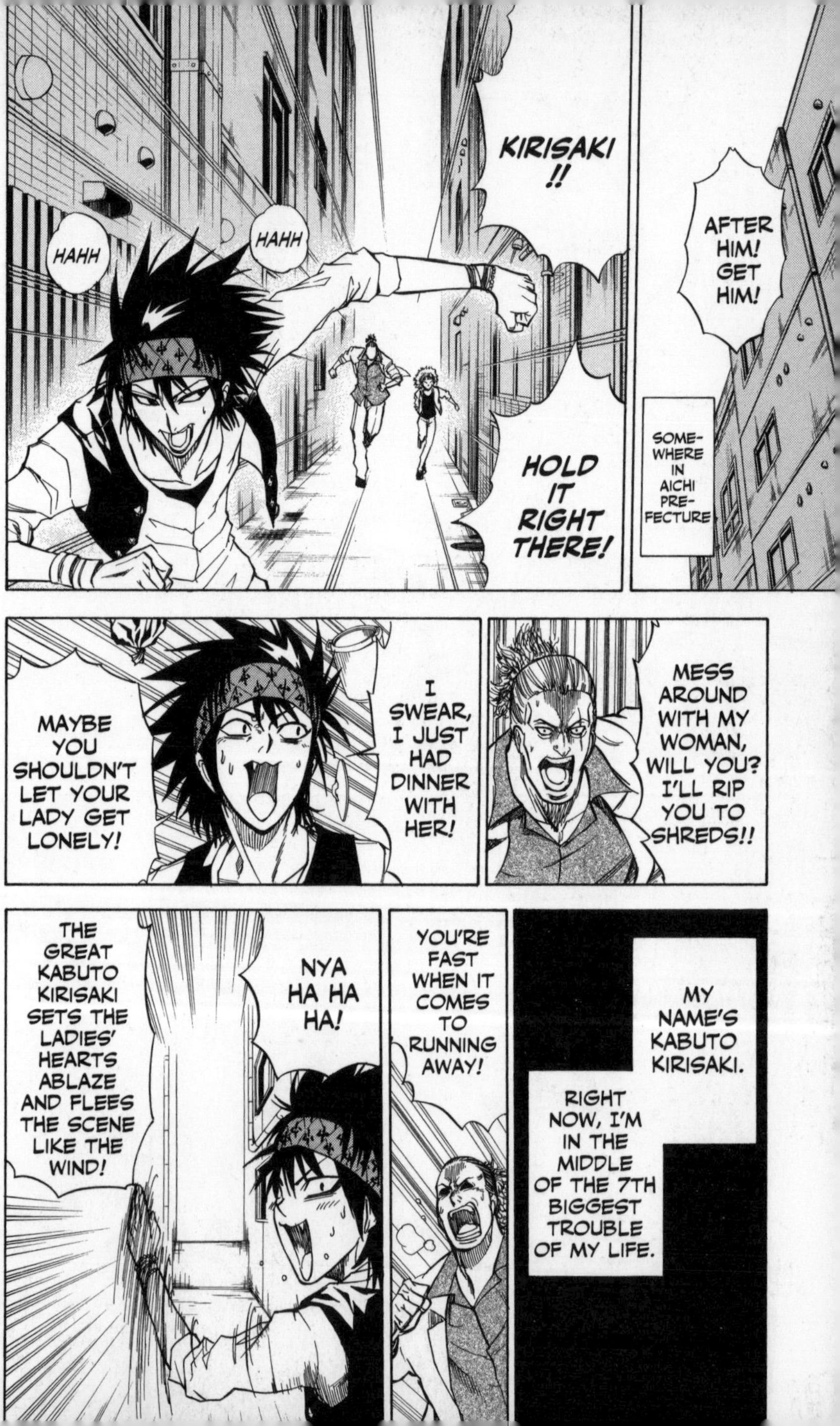
AFTER HIM! GET HIM!
SOMEWHERE IN AICHI PREFECTURE
KIRISAKI!!
HAHH
HAHH
HOLD IT RIGHT THERE!
MESS AROUND WITH MY WOMAN, WILL YOU? I'LL RIP YOU TO SHREDS!!
I SWEAR, I JUST HAD DINNER WITH HER!
MAYBE YOU SHOULDN'T LET YOUR LADY GET LONELY!
MY NAME'S KABUTO KIRISAKI.
RIGHT NOW, I'M IN THE MIDDLE OF THE 7TH BIGGEST TROUBLE OF MY LIFE.
YOU'RE FAST WHEN IT COMES TO RUNNING AWAY!
NYA HA HA HA!
THE GREAT KABUTO KIRISAKI SETS THE LADIES' HEARTS ABLAZE AND FLEES THE SCENE LIKE THE WIND!

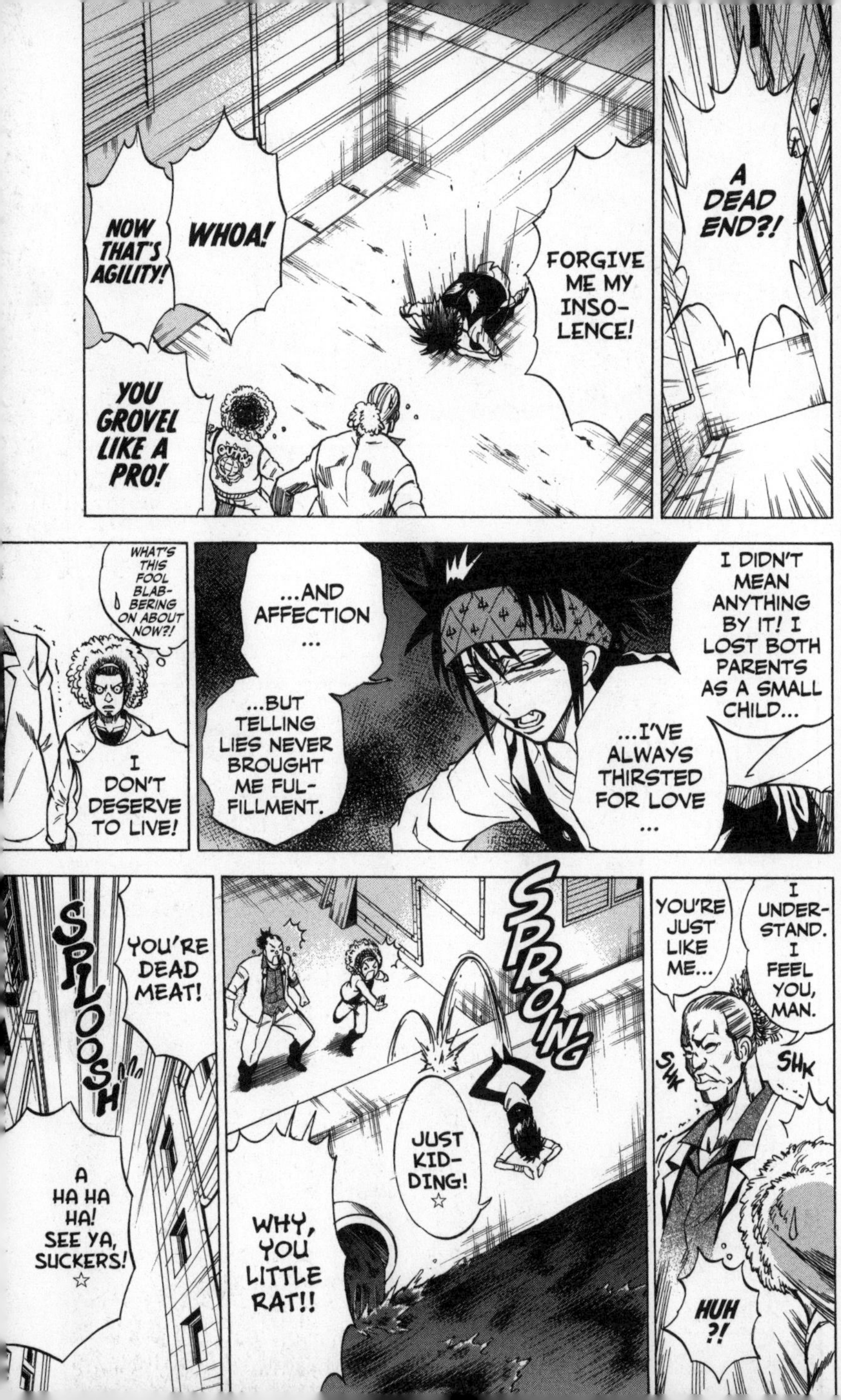
A DEAD END?!
FORGIVE ME MY INSOLENCE!
WHOA!
NOW THAT'S AGILITY!
YOU GROVEL LIKE A PRO!
I DIDN'T MEAN ANYTHING BY IT! I LOST BOTH PARENTS AS A SMALL CHILD...
...I'VE ALWAYS THIRSTED FOR LOVE ...
...AND AFFECTION ...
...BUT TELLING LIES NEVER BROUGHT ME FULFILLMENT.
WHAT'S THIS FOOL BLABBERING ON ABOUT NOW?!
I DON'T DESERVE TO LIVE!
I UNDERSTAND. I FEEL YOU, MAN.
YOU'RE JUST LIKE ME...
SHK
SHK
HUH ?!
SPROING
JUST KIDDING! ☆
WHY, YOU LITTLE RAT!!
YOU'RE DEAD MEAT!
SPLOOSH
A HA HA HA! SEE YA, SUCKERS! ☆

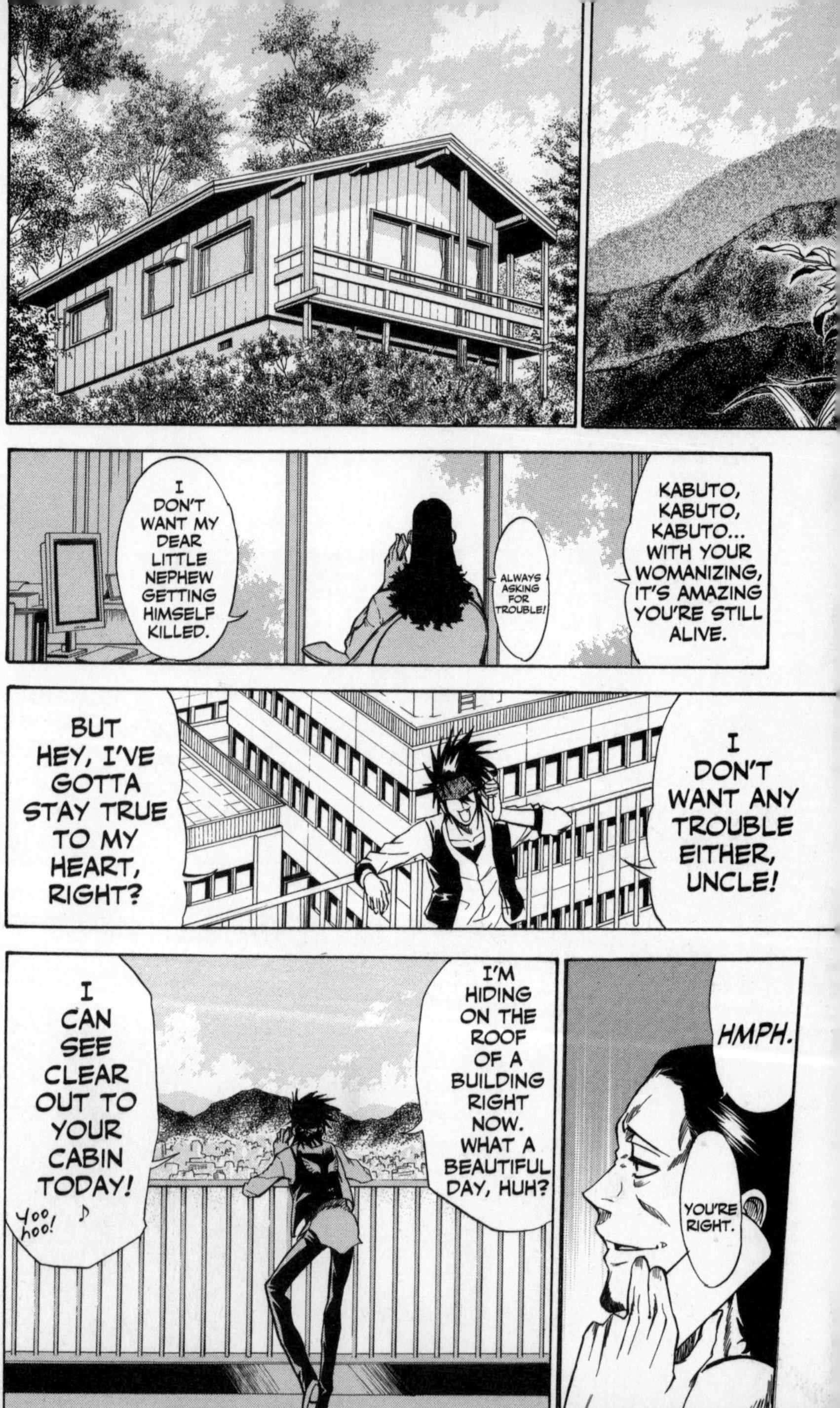
KABUTO, KABUTO, KABUTO... WITH YOUR WOMANIZING, IT'S AMAZING YOU'RE STILL ALIVE.
ALWAYS ASKING FOR TROUBLE!
I DON'T WANT MY DEAR LITTLE NEPHEW GETTING HIMSELF KILLED.
I DON'T WANT ANY TROUBLE EITHER, UNCLE!
BUT HEY, I'VE GOTTA STAY TRUE TO MY HEART, RIGHT?
HMPH.
YOU'RE RIGHT.
I'M HIDING ON THE ROOF OF A BUILDING RIGHT NOW. WHAT A BEAUTIFUL DAY, HUH?
I CAN SEE CLEAR OUT TO YOUR CABIN TODAY!
Yoo hoo! ♪

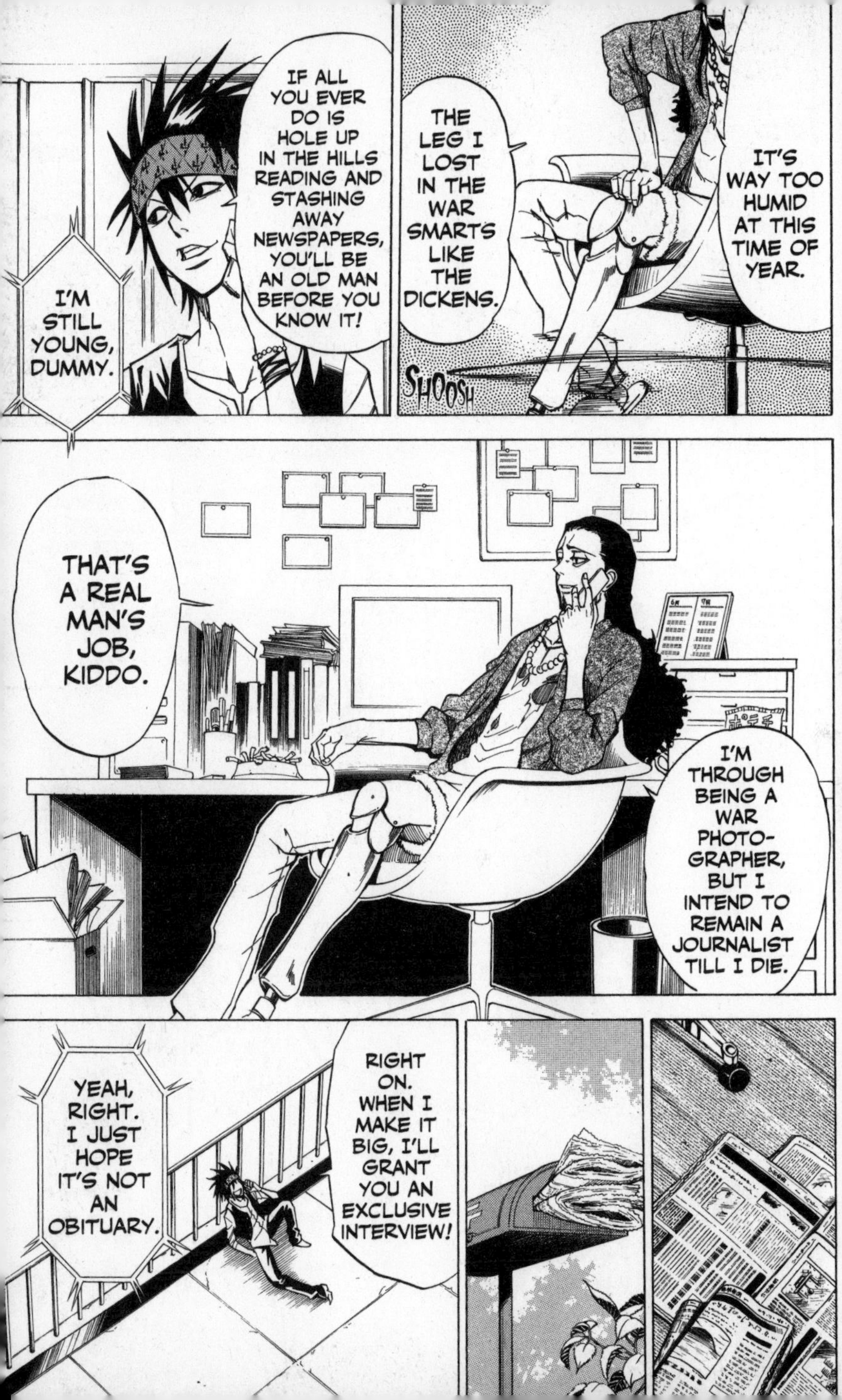
IT'S WAY TOO HUMID AT THIS TIME OF YEAR.
THE LEG I LOST IN THE WAR SMARTS LIKE THE DICKENS.
SHOOSH
IF ALL YOU EVER DO IS HOLE UP IN THE HILLS READING AND STASHING AWAY NEWSPAPERS, YOU'LL BE AN OLD MAN BEFORE YOU KNOW IT!
I'M STILL YOUNG, DUMMY.
I'M THROUGH BEING A WAR PHOTOGRAPHER, BUT I INTEND TO REMAIN A JOURNALIST TILL I DIE.
THAT'S A REAL MAN'S JOB, KIDDO.
RIGHT ON. WHEN I MAKE IT BIG, I'LL GRANT YOU AN EXCLUSIVE INTERVIEW!
YEAH, RIGHT. I JUST HOPE IT'S NOT AN OBITUARY.

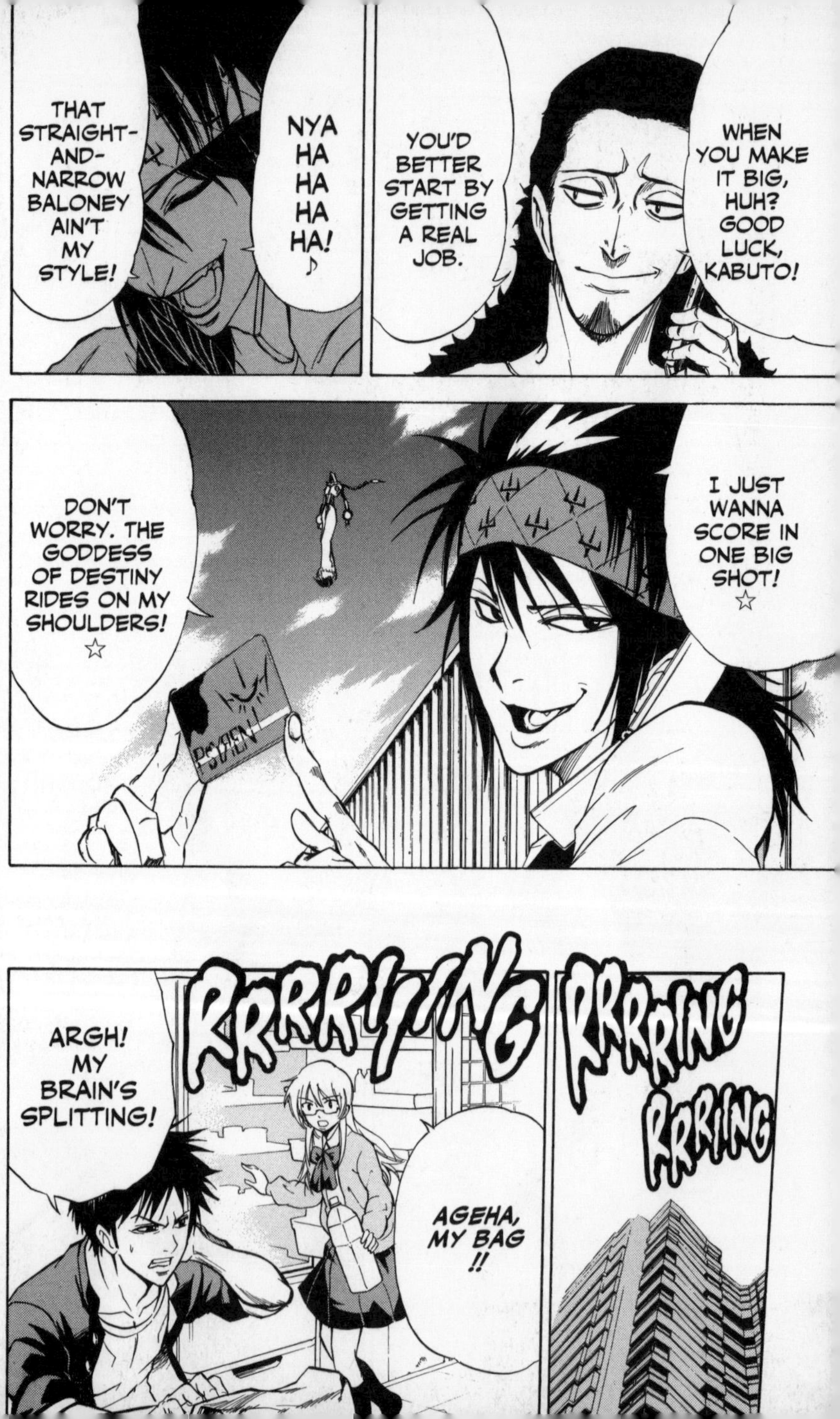
WHEN YOU MAKE IT BIG, HUH? GOOD LUCK, KABUTO!
YOU'D BETTER START BY GETTING A REAL JOB.
NYA HA HA HA HA! ♪
THAT STRAIGHT-AND-NARROW BALONEY AIN'T MY STYLE!
I JUST WANNA SCORE IN ONE BIG SHOT! ☆
DON'T WORRY. THE GODDESS OF DESTINY RIDES ON MY SHOULDERS! ☆
PSYREN
RRRRING
RRRING
RRRRIIING
AGEHA, MY BAG!!
ARGH! MY BRAIN'S SPLITTING!

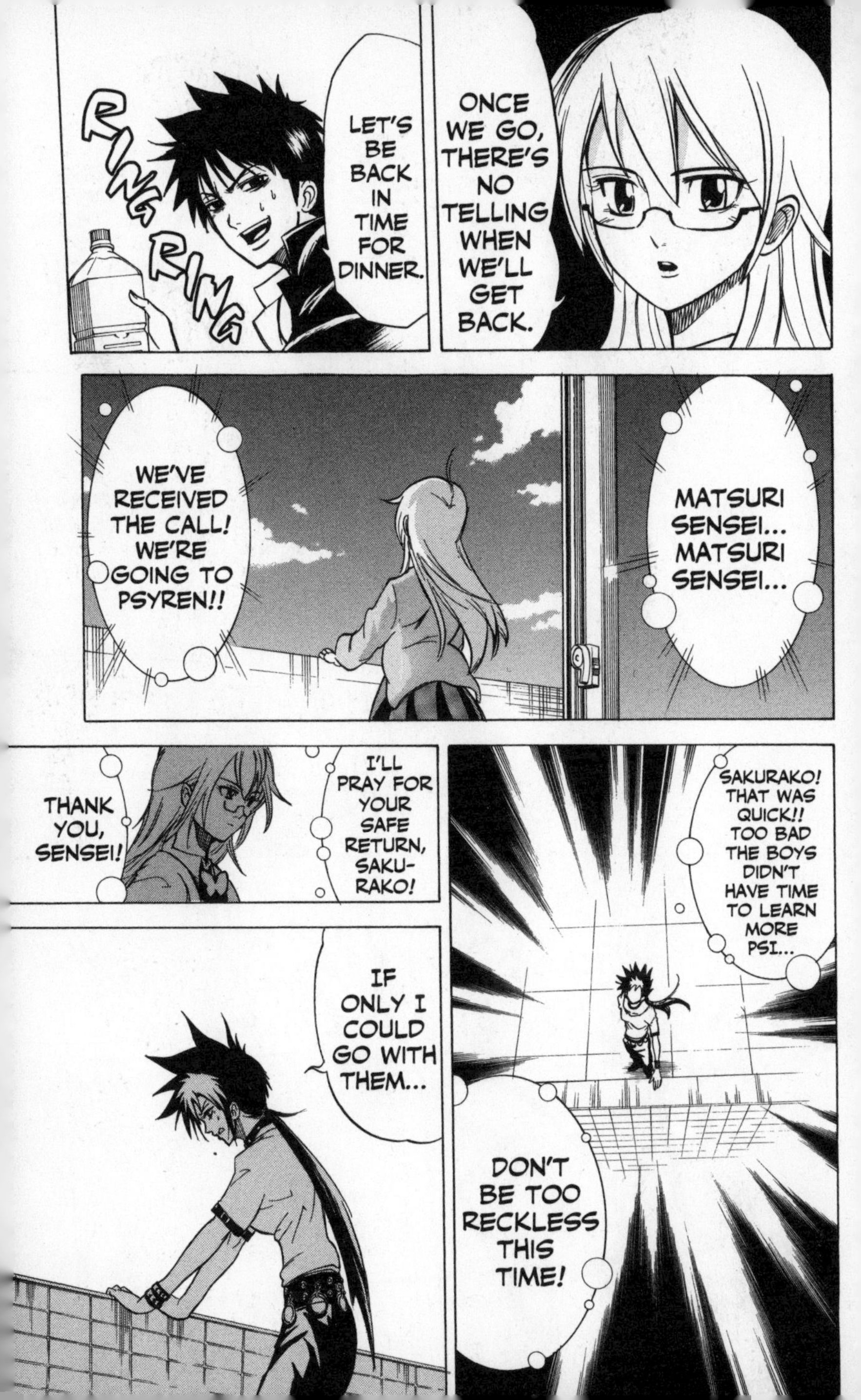
ONCE WE GO, THERE'S NO TELLING WHEN WE'LL GET BACK.
LET'S BE BACK IN TIME FOR DINNER.
RING RING
MATSURI SENSEI... MATSURI SENSEI...
WE'VE RECEIVED THE CALL! WE'RE GOING TO PSYREN!!
SAKURAKO! THAT WAS QUICK!! TOO BAD THE BOYS DIDN'T HAVE TIME TO LEARN MORE PSI...
DON'T BE TOO RECKLESS THIS TIME!
I'LL PRAY FOR YOUR SAFE RETURN, SAKURAKO!
THANK YOU, SENSEI!
IF ONLY I COULD GO WITH THEM...

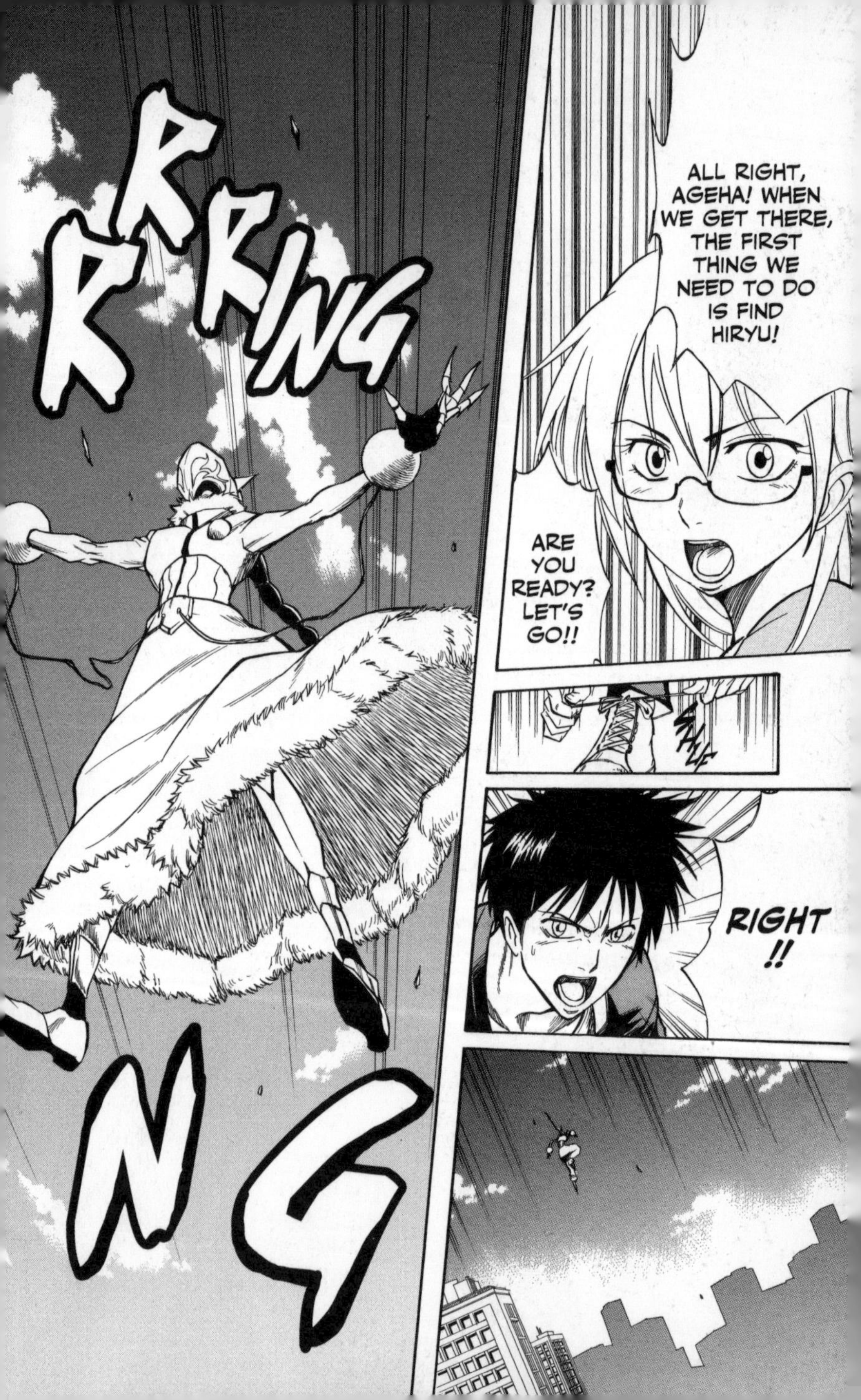
ALL RIGHT, AGEHA! WHEN WE GET THERE, THE FIRST THING WE NEED TO DO IS FIND HIRYU!
ARE YOU READY? LET'S GO!!
RIGHT!!
RRRING
NG

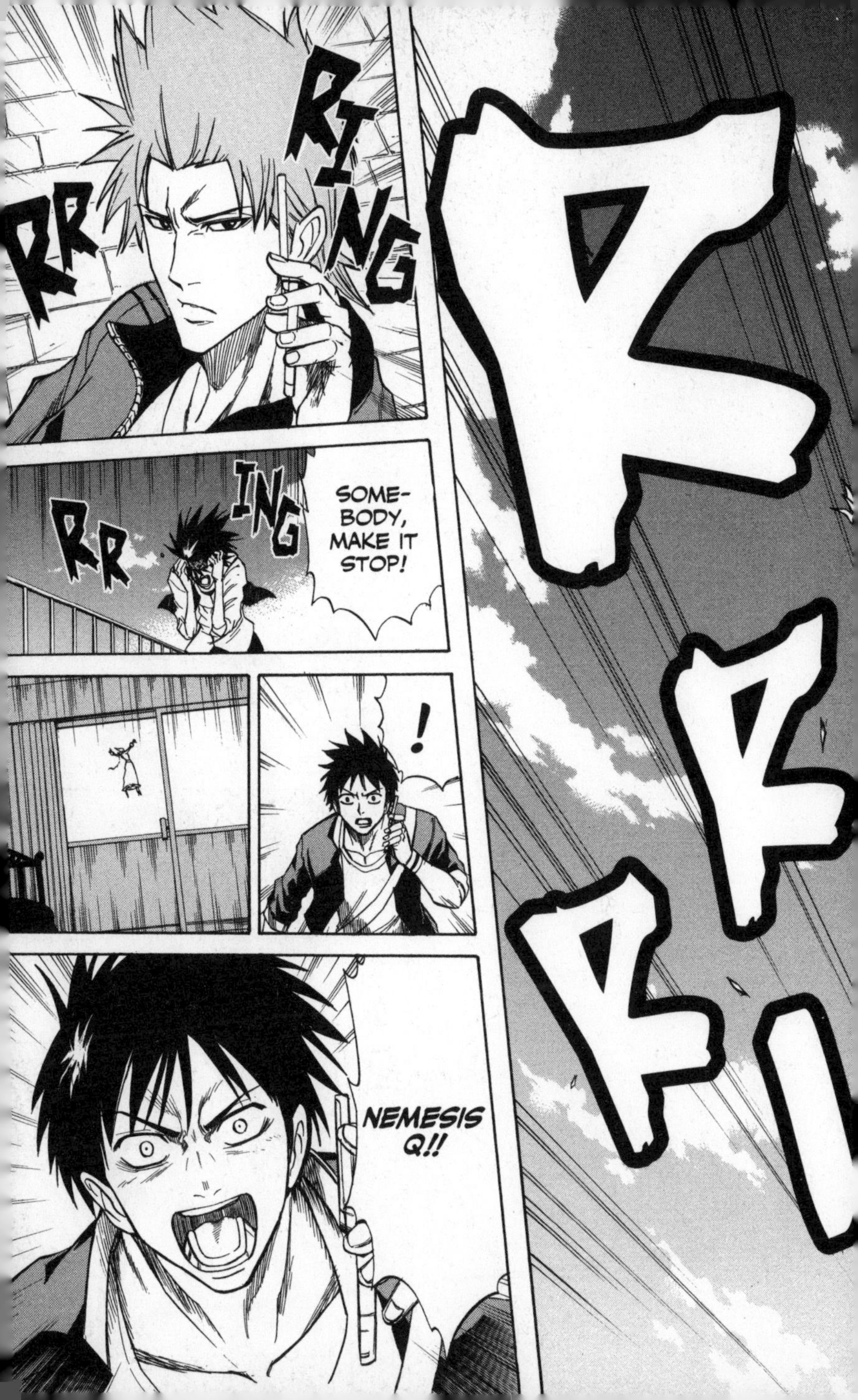
RRRI
RR
RING
RR
ING
SOME-BODY, MAKE IT STOP!
!
NEMESIS Q!!

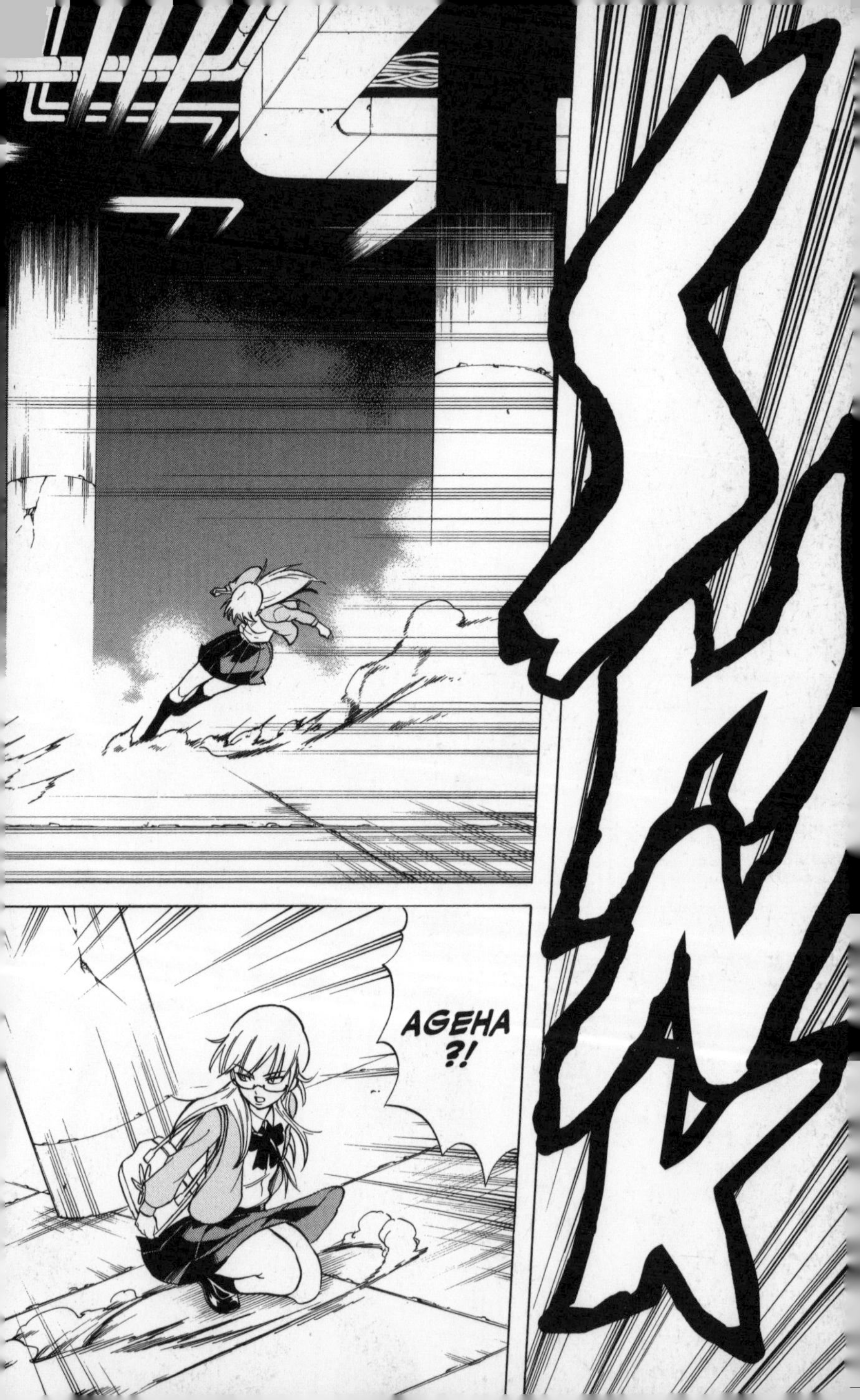
AGEHA ?!

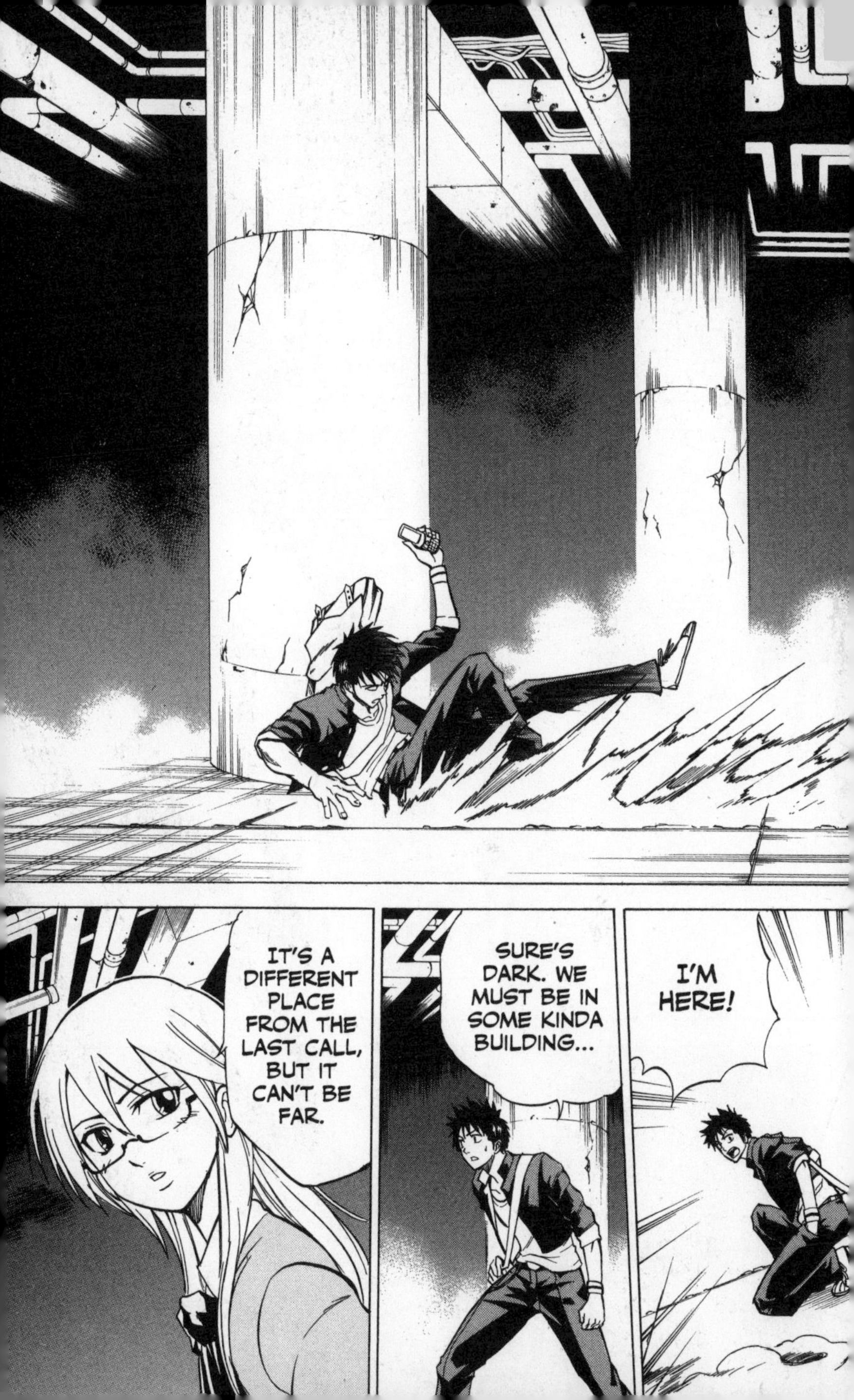
I'M HERE!
SURE'S DARK. WE MUST BE IN SOME KINDA BUILDING...
IT'S A DIFFERENT PLACE FROM THE LAST CALL, BUT IT CAN'T BE FAR.

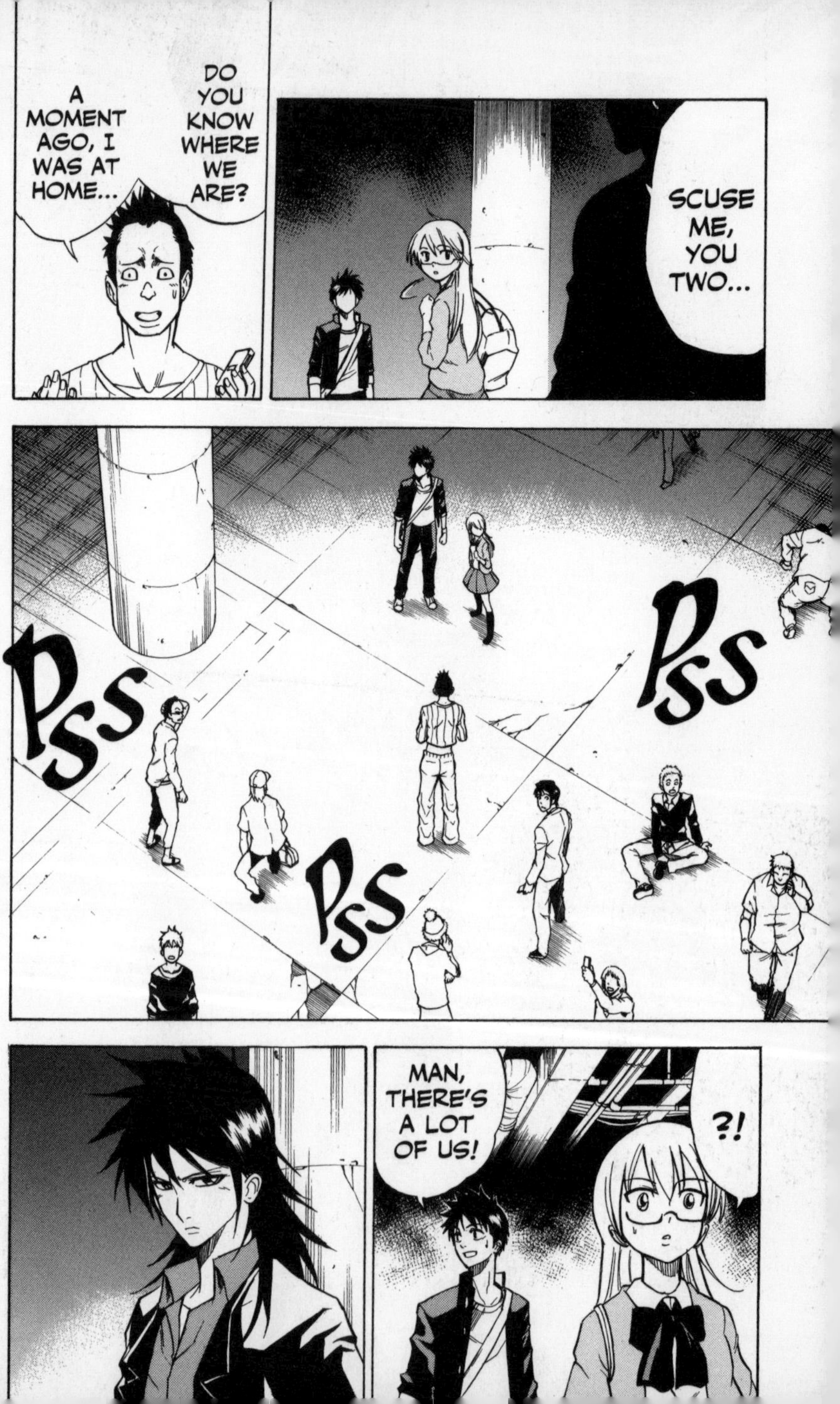
SCUSE ME, YOU TWO...
DO YOU KNOW WHERE WE ARE?
A MOMENT AGO, I WAS AT HOME...
PSS
PSS
PSS
?!
MAN, THERE'S A LOT OF US!

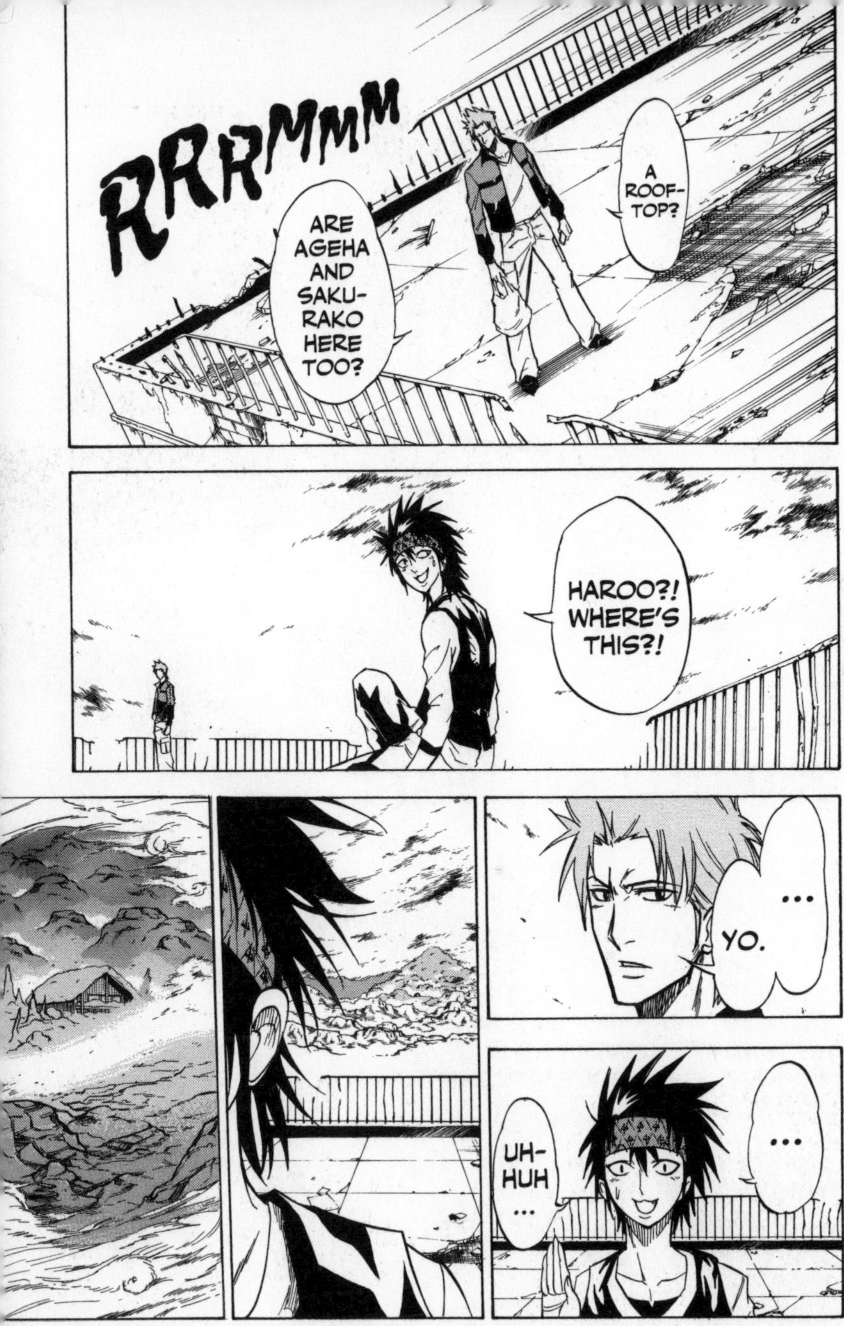
A ROOF-TOP?
ARE AGEHA AND SAKU-RAKO HERE TOO?
RRRMMMM
HAROO?! WHERE'S THIS?!
... YO.
...
UH-HUH ...

KABUTO KIRISAKI

AGE 19.
KABUTO LIVES ALONE AND
DOESN'T HAVE A GIRLFRIEND.
HE OFTEN ENDS UP DOING
THINGS THE HARD WAY IN AN
ATTEMPT TO LIVE A LIFE OF
EASE, BUT HE DOESN'T LIKE TO
FIGHT.

LIKES: MONEY AND GIRLS, AND
NOT MUCH ELSE.
DISLIKES: A LOT OF THINGS.

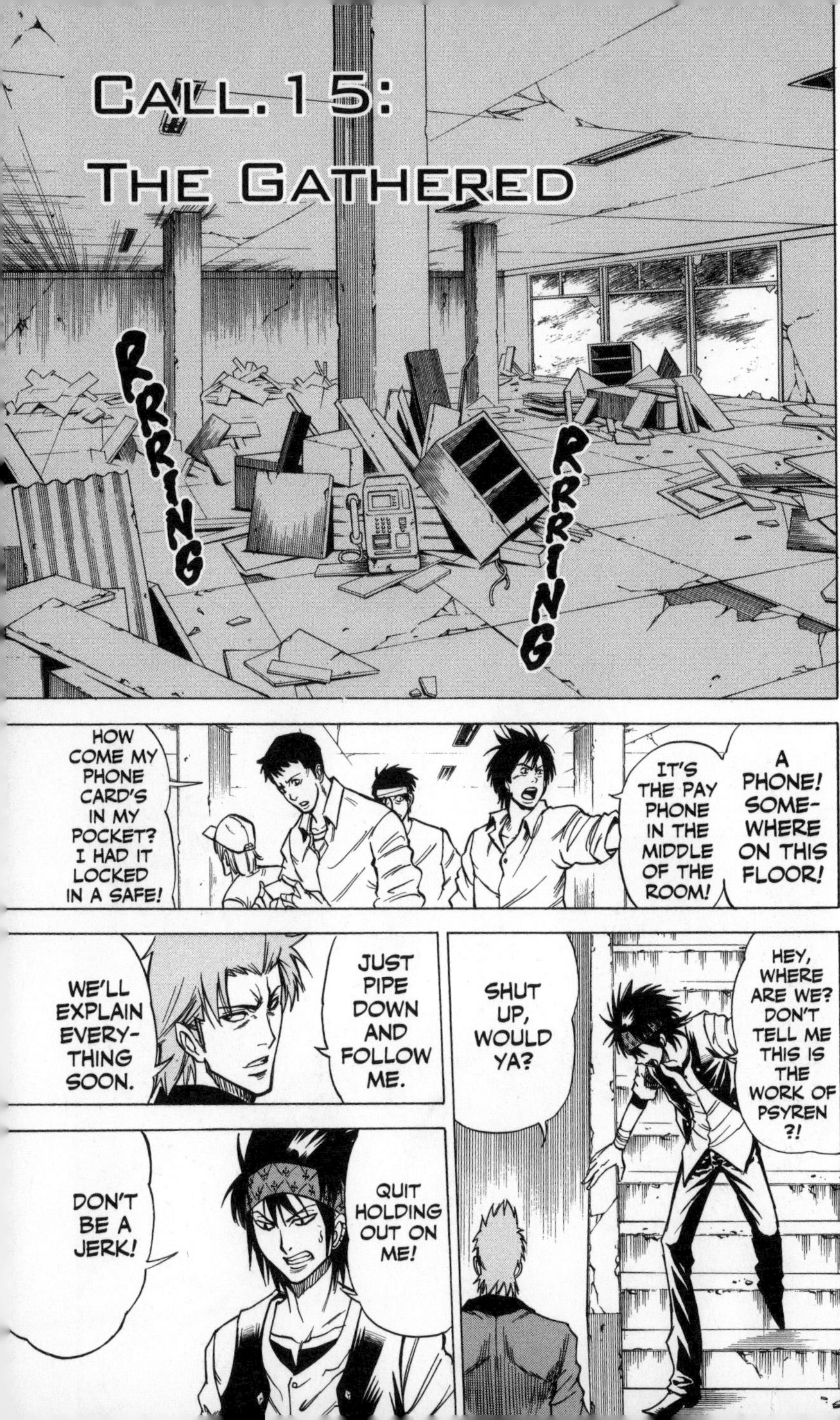
CALL. 15:
THE GATHERED
RRRING
RRRING
A PHONE! SOMEWHERE ON THIS FLOOR!
IT'S THE PAY PHONE IN THE MIDDLE OF THE ROOM!
HOW COME MY PHONE CARD'S IN MY POCKET? I HAD IT LOCKED IN A SAFE!
HEY, WHERE ARE WE? DON'T TELL ME THIS IS THE WORK OF PSYREN?!
SHUT UP, WOULD YA?
JUST PIPE DOWN AND FOLLOW ME.
WE'LL EXPLAIN EVERYTHING SOON.
QUIT HOLDING OUT ON ME!
DON'T BE A JERK!

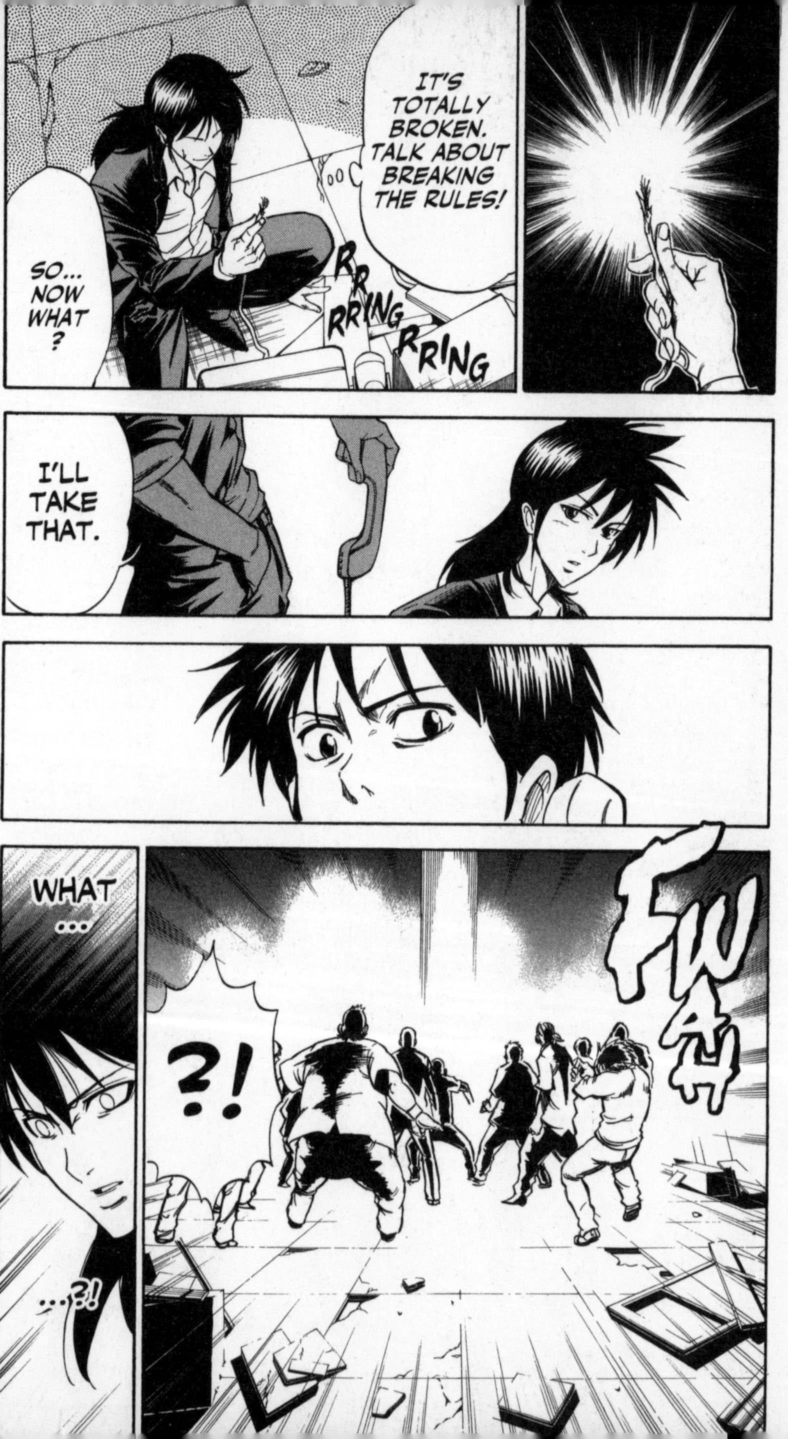
IT'S TOTALLY BROKEN. TALK ABOUT BREAKING THE RULES!
RRRING RRRING
SO... NOW WHAT?
I'LL TAKE THAT.
FWAH
?!
WHAT...
...?!

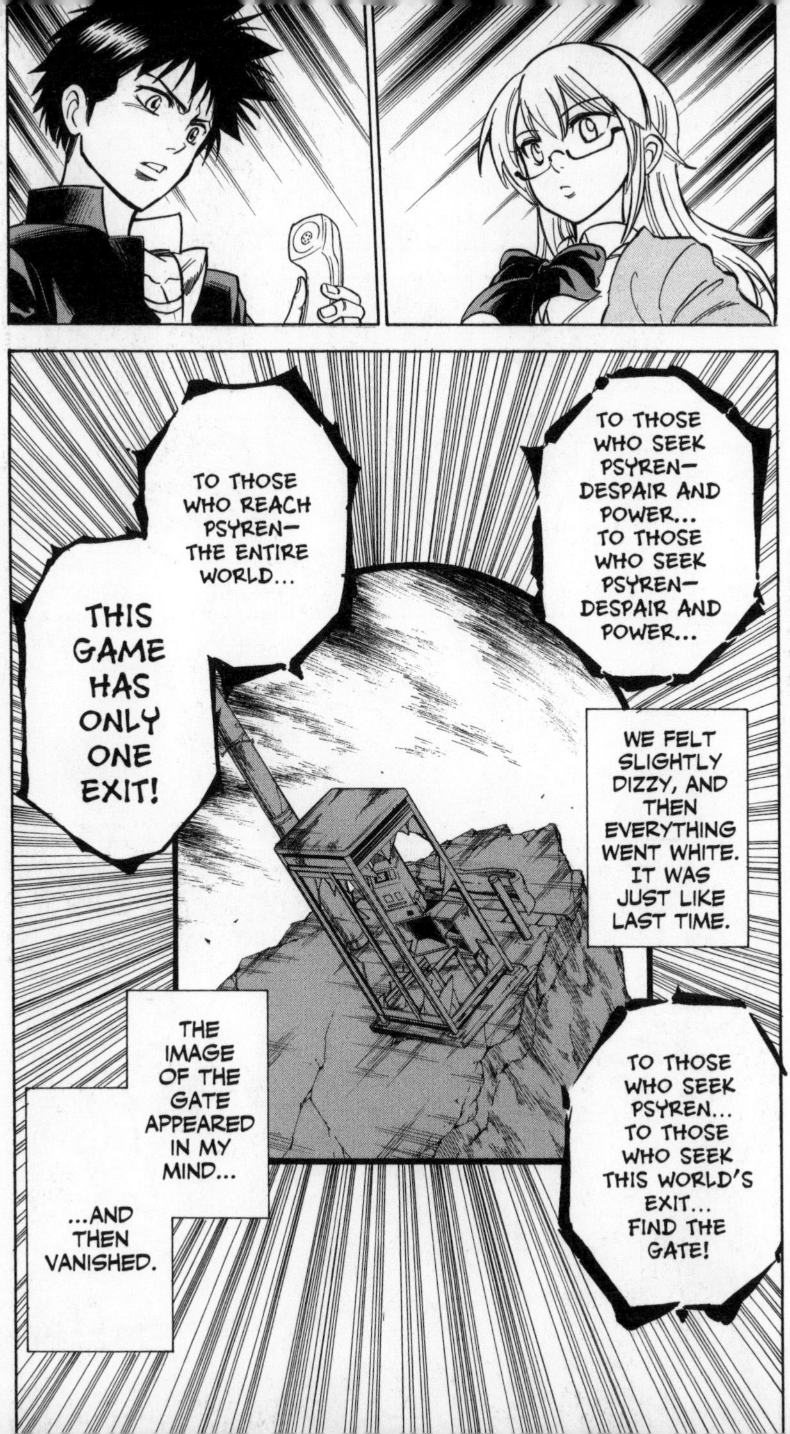
TO THOSE WHO SEEK PSYREN— DESPAIR AND POWER... TO THOSE WHO SEEK PSYREN— DESPAIR AND POWER...
TO THOSE WHO REACH PSYREN— THE ENTIRE WORLD...
THIS GAME HAS ONLY ONE EXIT!
WE FELT SLIGHTLY DIZZY, AND THEN EVERYTHING WENT WHITE. IT WAS JUST LIKE LAST TIME.
TO THOSE WHO SEEK PSYREN... TO THOSE WHO SEEK THIS WORLD'S EXIT... FIND THE GATE!
THE IMAGE OF THE GATE APPEARED IN MY MIND...
...AND THEN VANISHED.

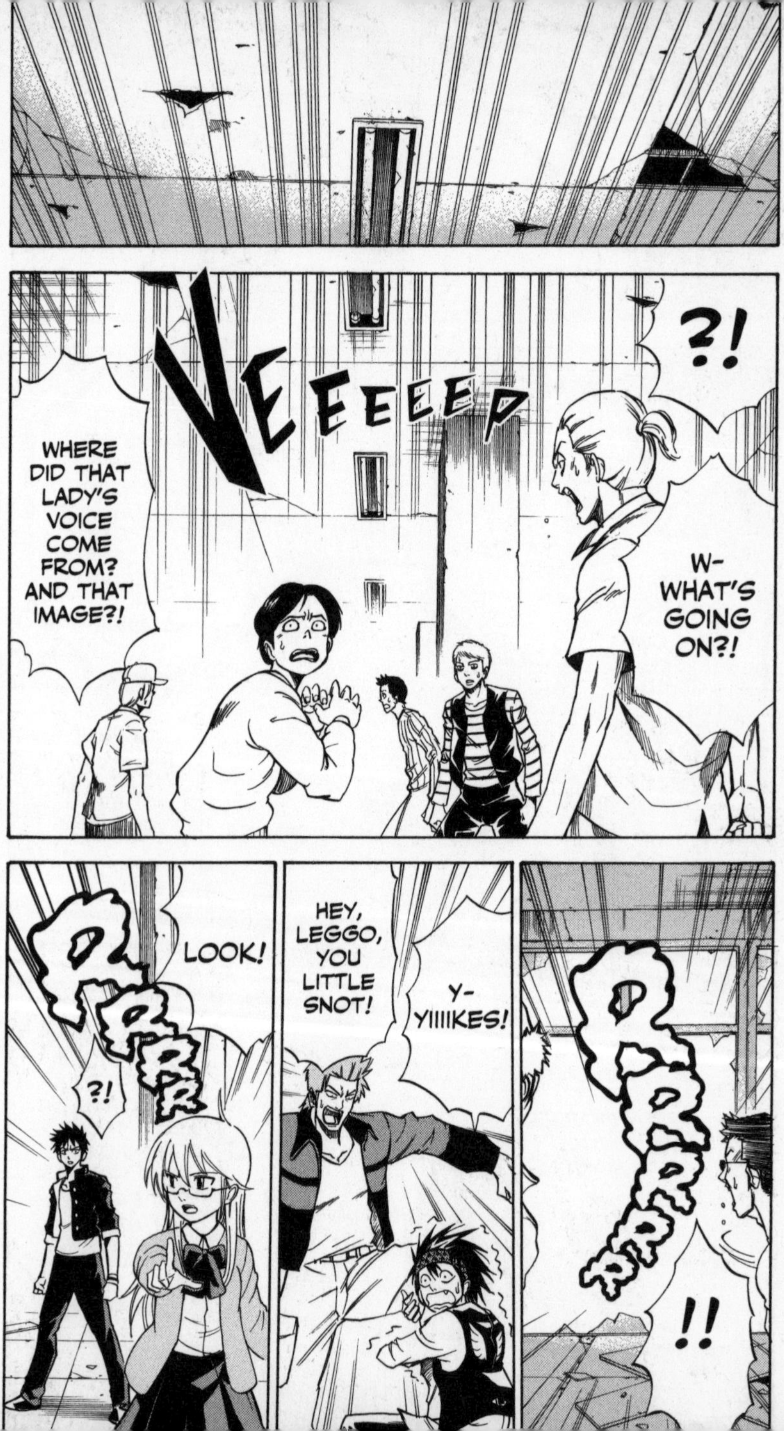
?!
VEEEEEP
W- WHAT'S GOING ON?!
WHERE DID THAT LADY'S VOICE COME FROM? AND THAT IMAGE?!
!!
Y- YIIIIKES!
HEY, LEGGO, YOU LITTLE SNOT!
LOOK!
?!

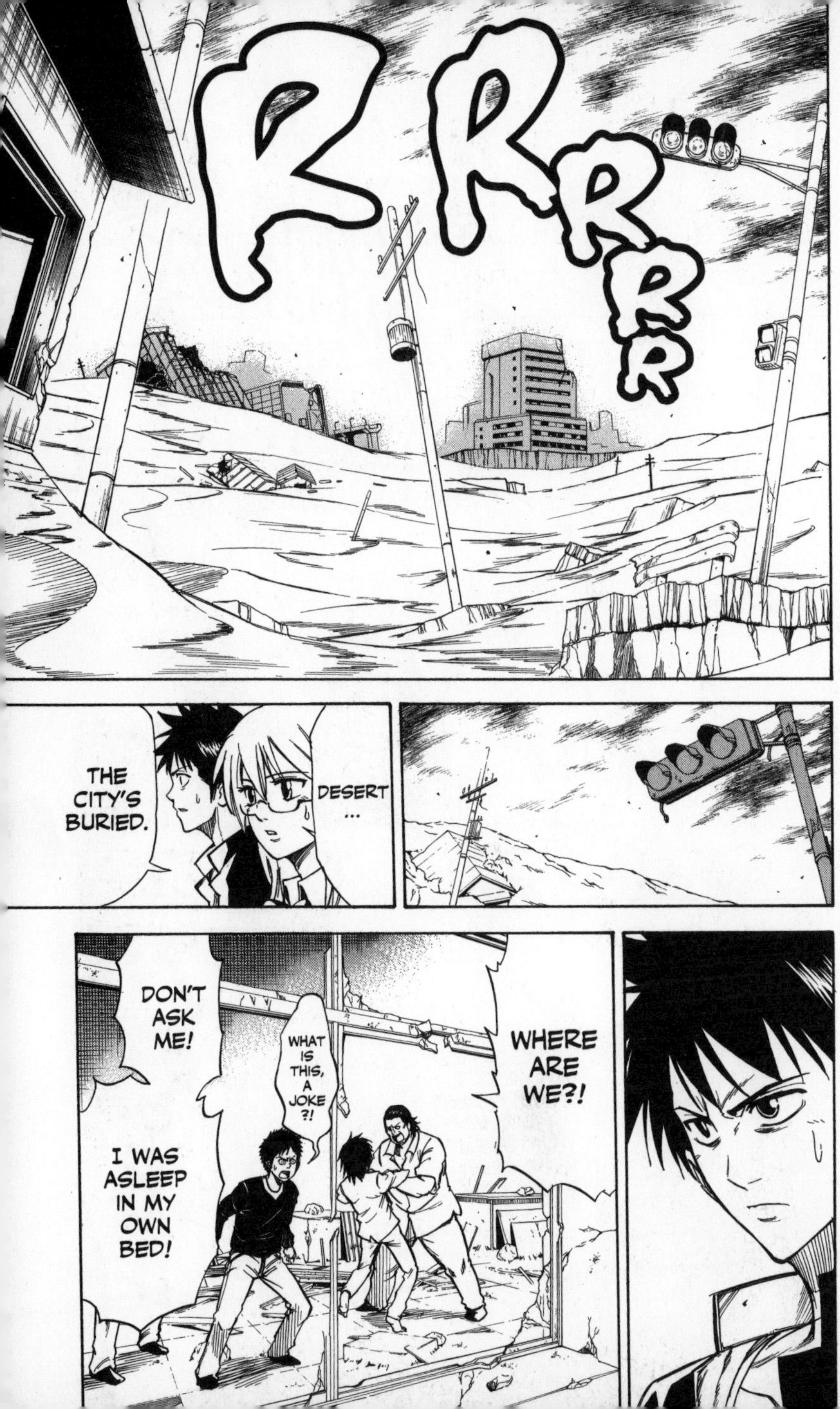
RRRRRR
DESERT...
THE CITY'S BURIED.
WHERE ARE WE?!
WHAT IS THIS, A JOKE?!
DON'T ASK ME!
I WAS ASLEEP IN MY OWN BED!

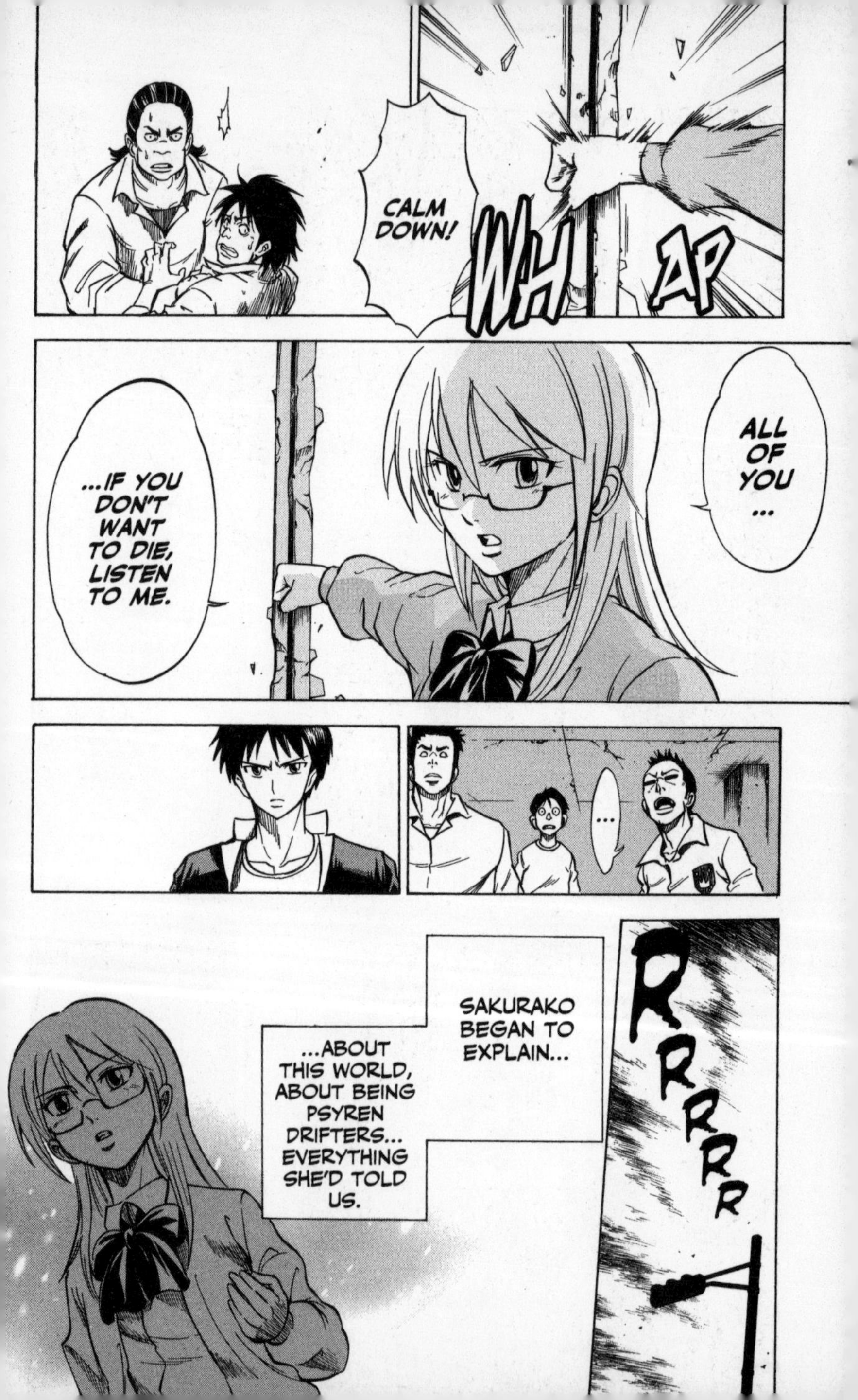
CALM DOWN!
WHAP
ALL OF YOU ...
...IF YOU DON'T WANT TO DIE, LISTEN TO ME.
...
RRRRR
SAKURAKO BEGAN TO EXPLAIN...
...ABOUT THIS WORLD, ABOUT BEING PSYREN DRIFTERS... EVERYTHING SHE'D TOLD US.

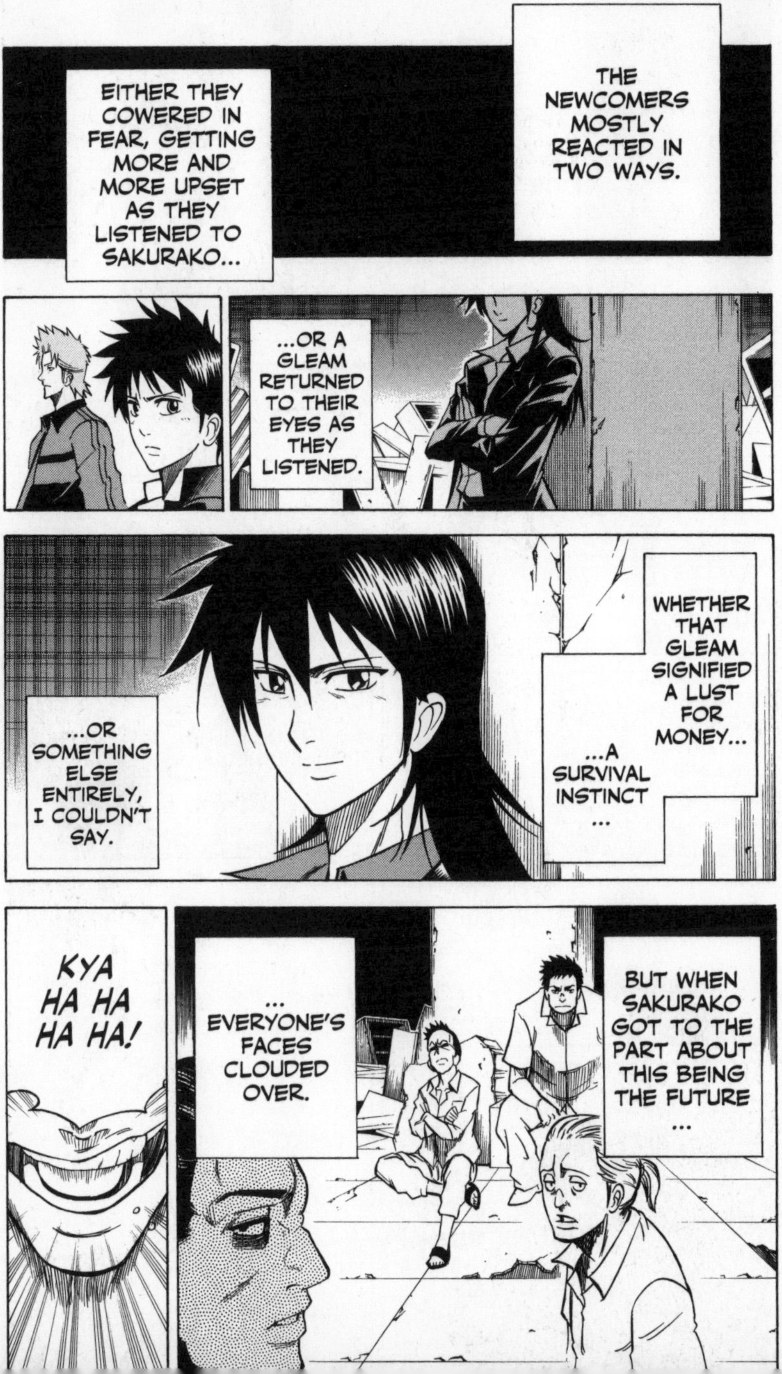
THE NEWCOMERS MOSTLY REACTED IN TWO WAYS.
EITHER THEY COWERED IN FEAR, GETTING MORE AND MORE UPSET AS THEY LISTENED TO SAKURAKO...
...OR A GLEAM RETURNED TO THEIR EYES AS THEY LISTENED.
WHETHER THAT GLEAM SIGNIFIED A LUST FOR MONEY...
...A SURVIVAL INSTINCT ...
...OR SOMETHING ELSE ENTIRELY, I COULDN'T SAY.
BUT WHEN SAKURAKO GOT TO THE PART ABOUT THIS BEING THE FUTURE ...
... EVERYONE'S FACES CLOUDED OVER.
KYA HA HA HA HA!

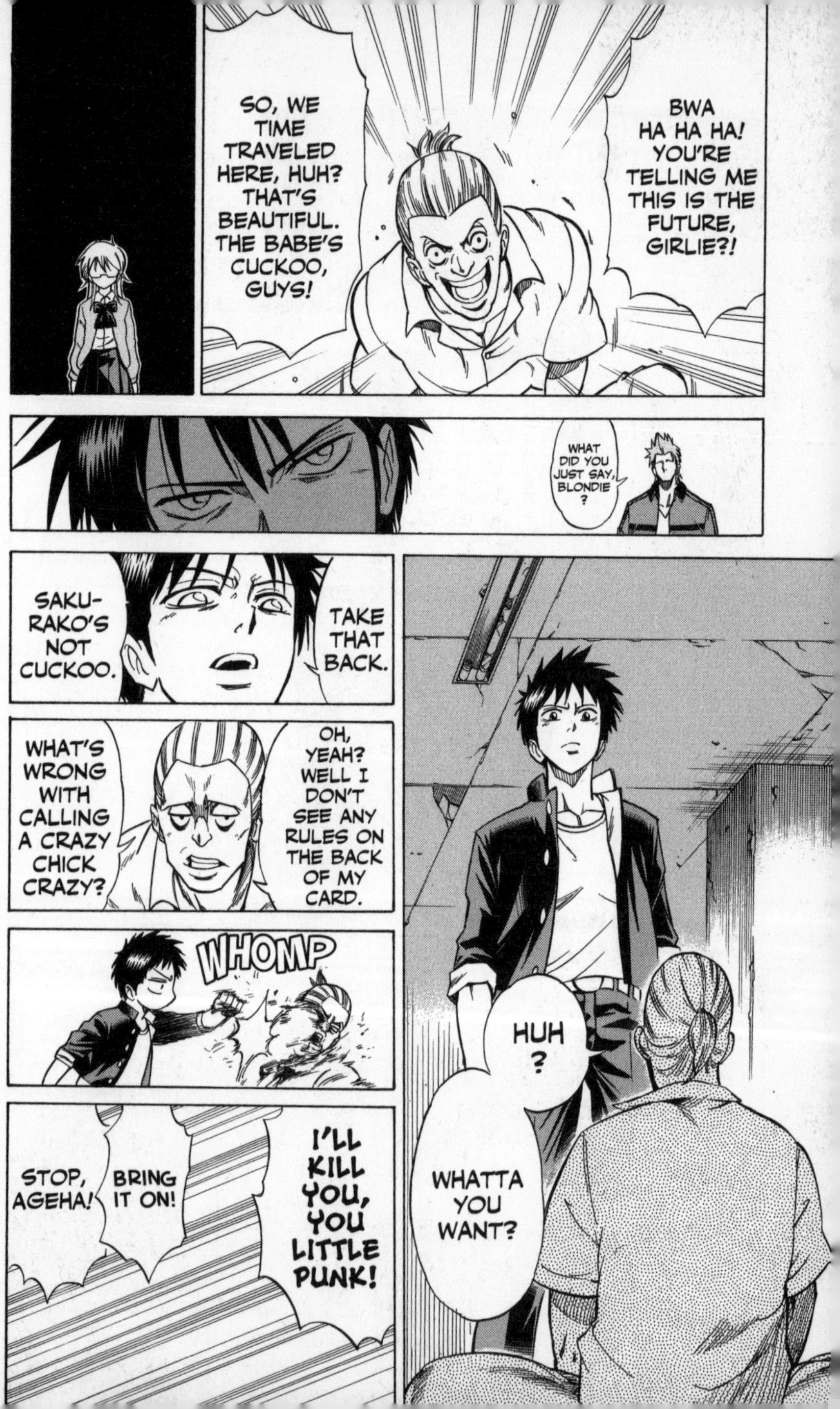
BWA HA HA HA! YOU'RE TELLING ME THIS IS THE FUTURE, GIRLIE?!
SO, WE TIME TRAVELED HERE, HUH? THAT'S BEAUTIFUL. THE BABE'S CUCKOO, GUYS!
WHAT DID YOU JUST SAY, BLONDIE?
HUH?
WHATTA YOU WANT?
TAKE THAT BACK.
SAKURAKO'S NOT CUCKOO.
OH, YEAH? WELL I DON'T SEE ANY RULES ON THE BACK OF MY CARD.
WHAT'S WRONG WITH CALLING A CRAZY CHICK CRAZY?
WHOMP
I'LL KILL YOU, YOU LITTLE PUNK!
BRING IT ON!
STOP, AGEHA!

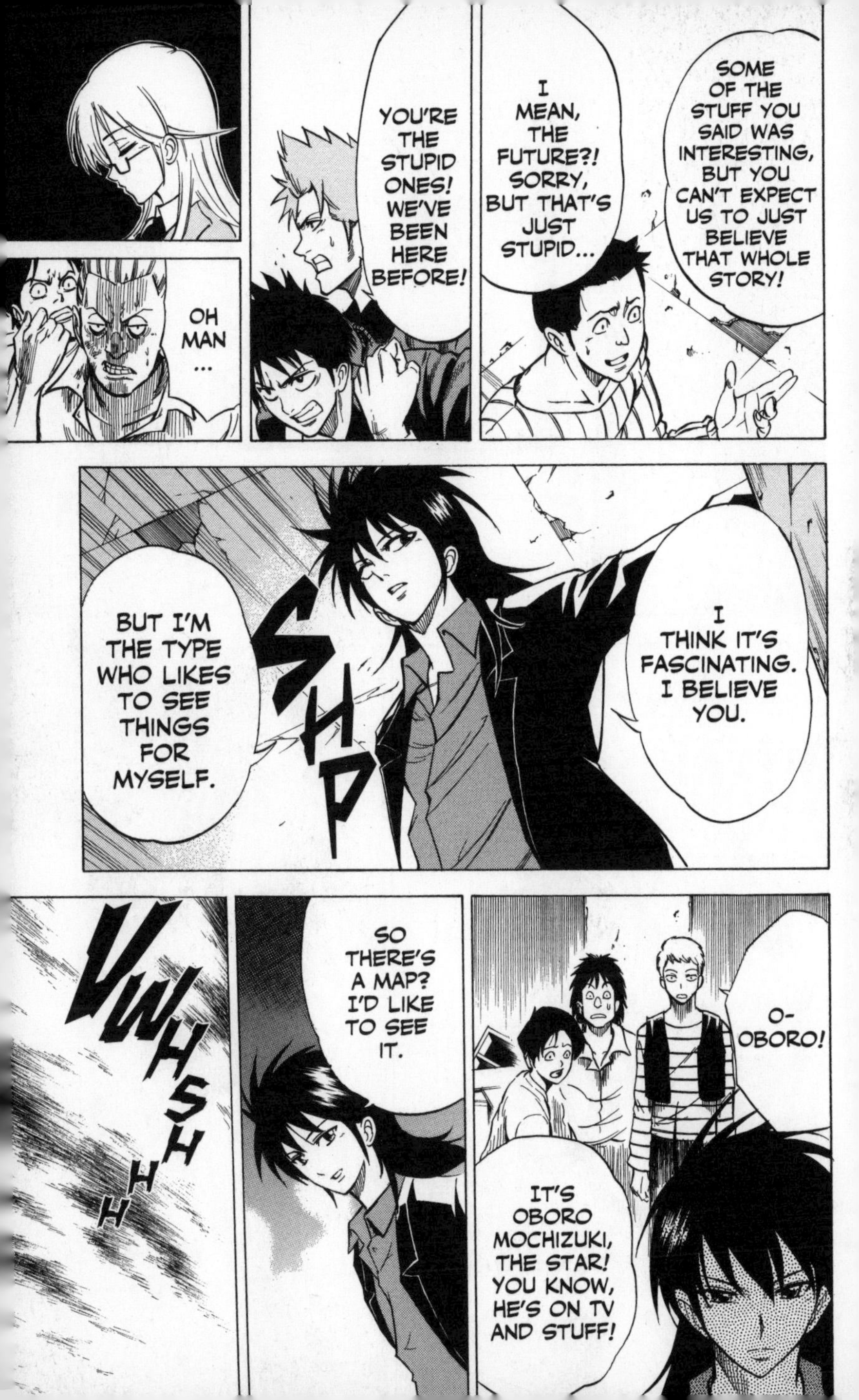
SOME OF THE STUFF YOU SAID WAS INTERESTING, BUT YOU CAN'T EXPECT US TO JUST BELIEVE THAT WHOLE STORY!
I MEAN, THE FUTURE?! SORRY, BUT THAT'S JUST STUPID...
YOU'RE THE STUPID ONES! WE'VE BEEN HERE BEFORE!
OH MAN ...
I THINK IT'S FASCINATING. I BELIEVE YOU.
SHP
BUT I'M THE TYPE WHO LIKES TO SEE THINGS FOR MYSELF.
O-OBORO!
IT'S OBORO MOCHIZUKI, THE STAR! YOU KNOW, HE'S ON TV AND STUFF!
SO THERE'S A MAP? I'D LIKE TO SEE IT.
VWHSHHHH

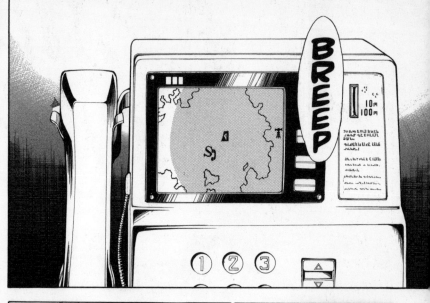

BREEP

WHOA!

THE ENTIRE THING'S IN THE DANGER ZONE?!

!!

Haroo?

SO, IF WE SO MUCH AS SET FOOT OUTSIDE WE'RE IN DANGER?

WHAT ?!

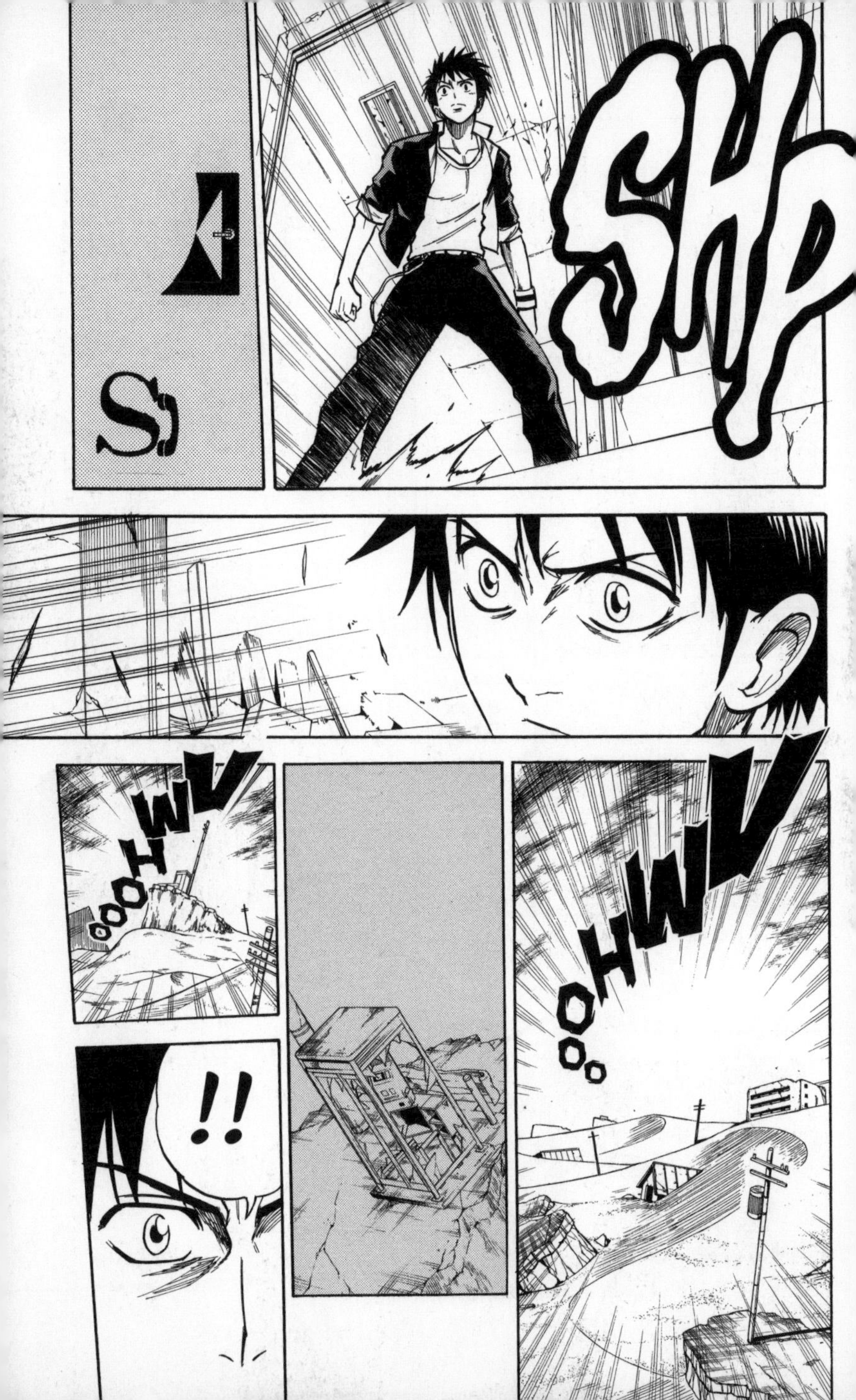
SHP
S
VWHOOOO
VWHOOO
!!

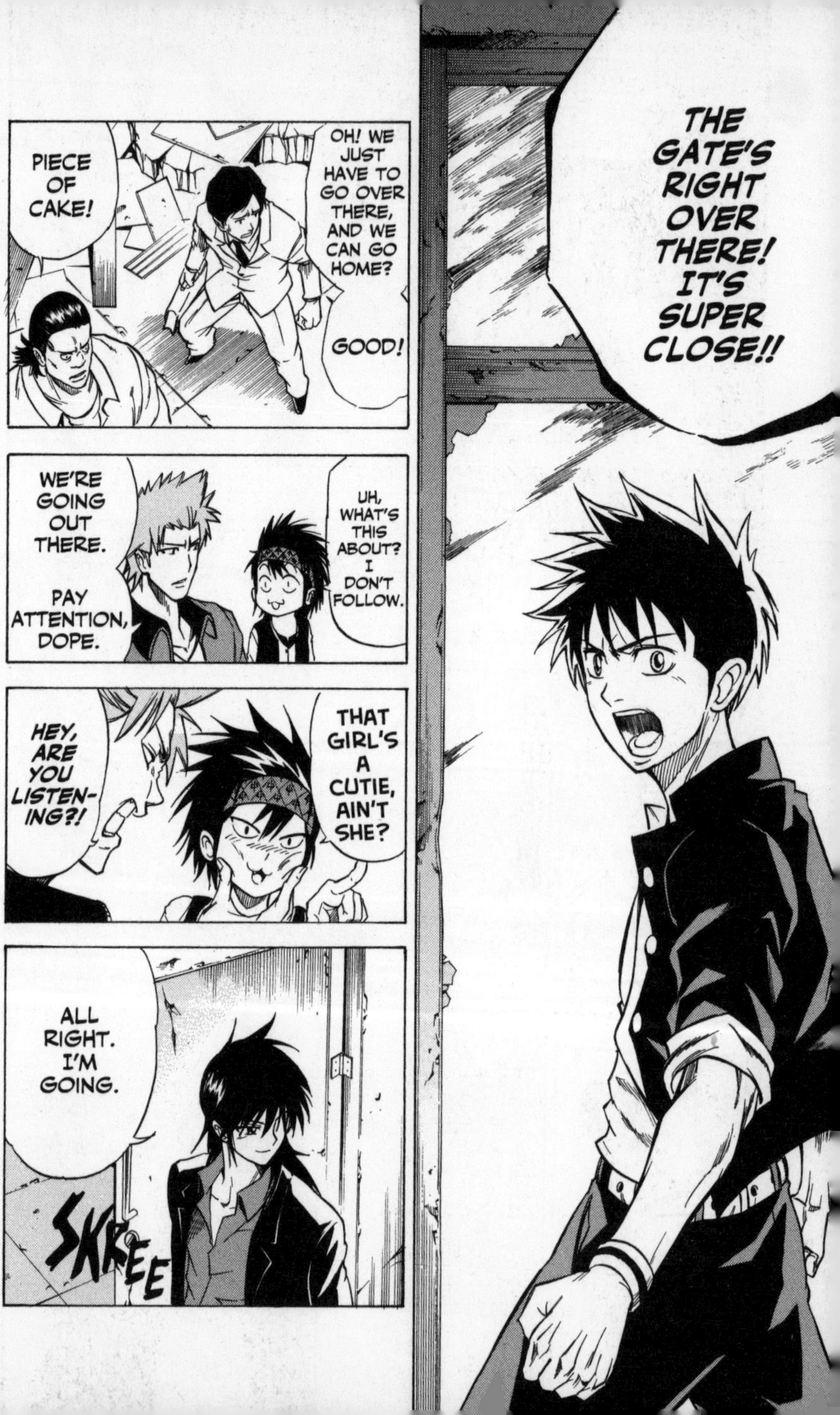
THE GATE'S RIGHT OVER THERE! IT'S SUPER CLOSE!!
OH! WE JUST HAVE TO GO OVER THERE, AND WE CAN GO HOME?
GOOD!
PIECE OF CAKE!
UH, WHAT'S THIS ABOUT? I DON'T FOLLOW.
WE'RE GOING OUT THERE.
PAY ATTENTION, DOPE.
THAT GIRL'S A CUTIE, AIN'T SHE?
HEY, ARE YOU LISTENING?!
ALL RIGHT. I'M GOING.
SKREEE

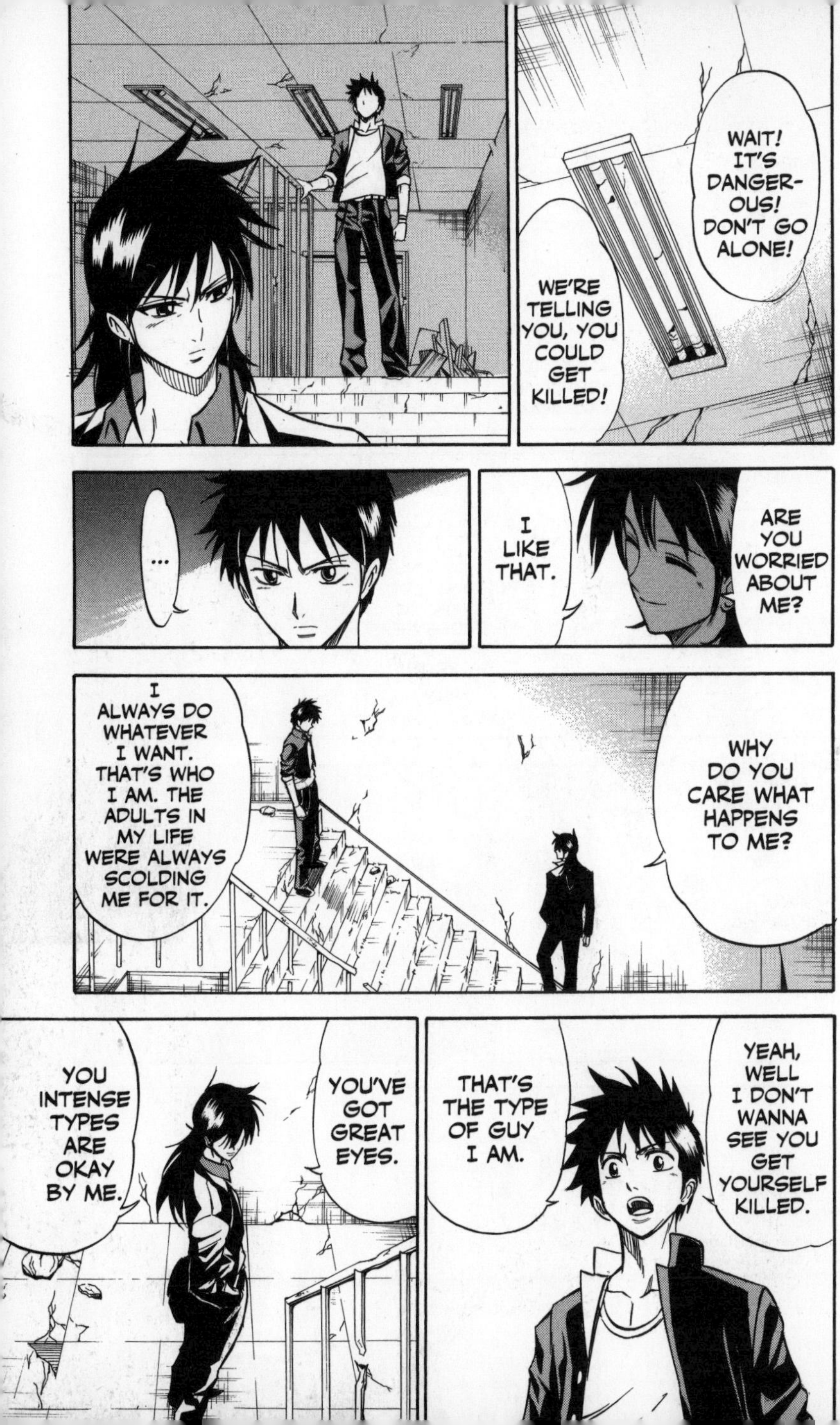
WAIT! IT'S DANGER-OUS! DON'T GO ALONE!
WE'RE TELLING YOU, YOU COULD GET KILLED!
ARE YOU WORRIED ABOUT ME?
I LIKE THAT.
...
WHY DO YOU CARE WHAT HAPPENS TO ME?
I ALWAYS DO WHATEVER I WANT. THAT'S WHO I AM. THE ADULTS IN MY LIFE WERE ALWAYS SCOLDING ME FOR IT.
YEAH, WELL I DON'T WANNA SEE YOU GET YOURSELF KILLED.
THAT'S THE TYPE OF GUY I AM.
YOU'VE GOT GREAT EYES.
YOU INTENSE TYPES ARE OKAY BY ME.

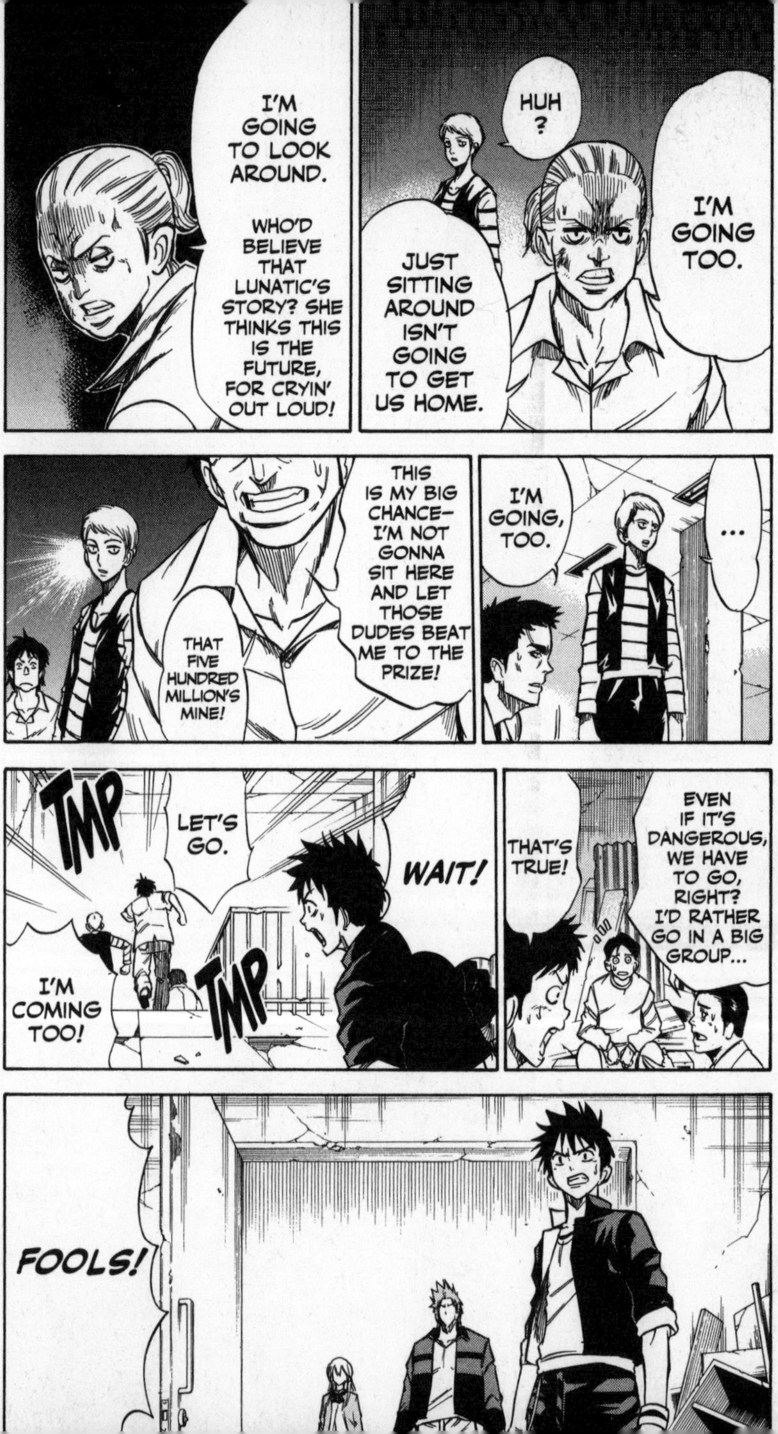
I'M GOING TOO.
HUH ?
JUST SITTING AROUND ISN'T GOING TO GET US HOME.
I'M GOING TO LOOK AROUND.
WHO'D BELIEVE THAT LUNATIC'S STORY? SHE THINKS THIS IS THE FUTURE, FOR CRYIN' OUT LOUD!
...
I'M GOING, TOO.
THIS IS MY BIG CHANCE— I'M NOT GONNA SIT HERE AND LET THOSE DUDES BEAT ME TO THE PRIZE!
THAT FIVE HUNDRED MILLION'S MINE!
EVEN IF IT'S DANGEROUS, WE HAVE TO GO, RIGHT? I'D RATHER GO IN A BIG GROUP...
THAT'S TRUE!
WAIT!
LET'S GO.
TMP
TMP
I'M COMING TOO!
FOOLS!

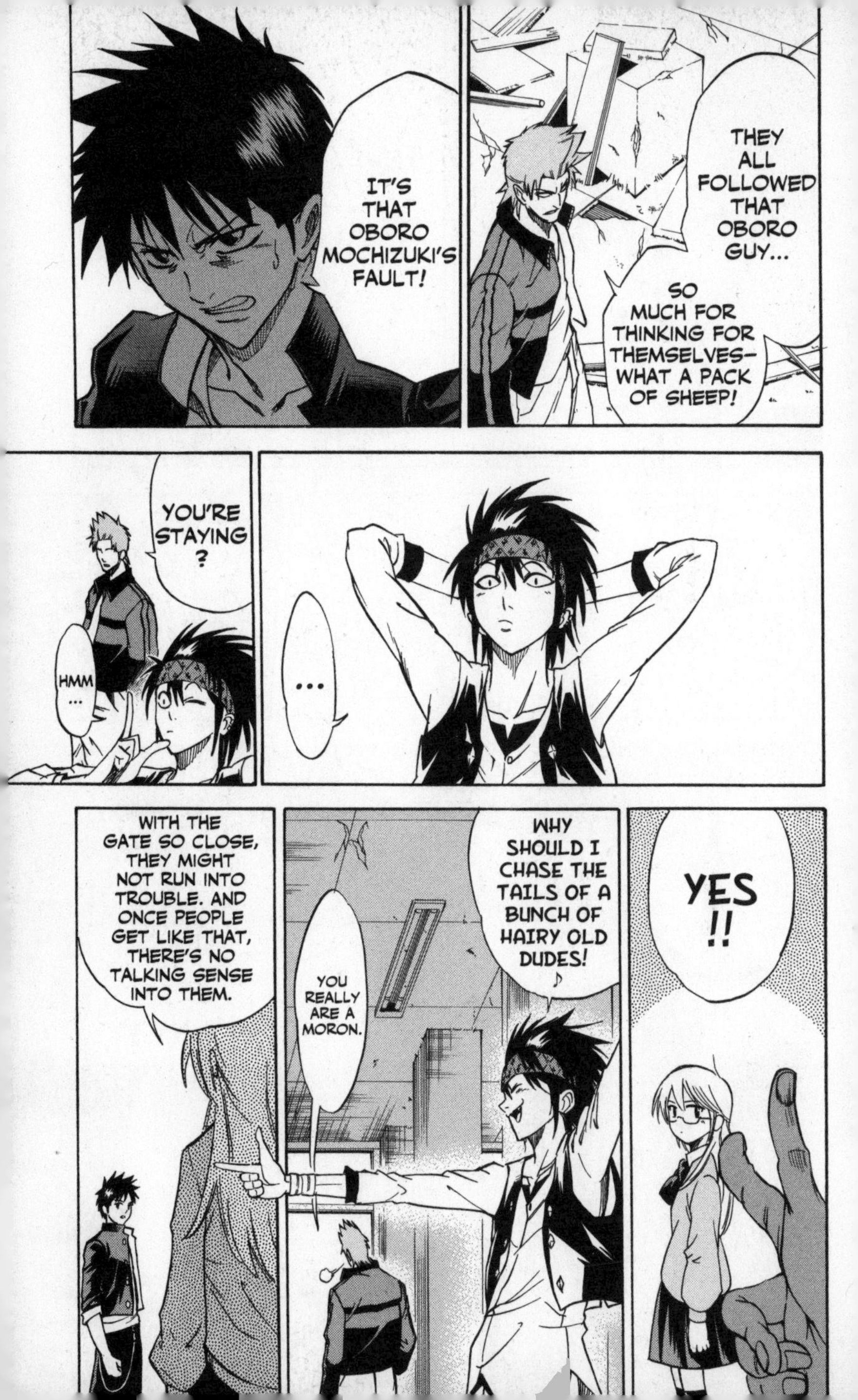
THEY ALL FOLLOWED THAT OBORO GUY...
SO MUCH FOR THINKING FOR THEMSELVES—WHAT A PACK OF SHEEP!
IT'S THAT OBORO MOCHIZUKI'S FAULT!
...
YOU'RE STAYING?
HMM...
YES!!
WHY SHOULD I CHASE THE TAILS OF A BUNCH OF HAIRY OLD DUDES! ♪
YOU REALLY ARE A MORON.
WITH THE GATE SO CLOSE, THEY MIGHT NOT RUN INTO TROUBLE. AND ONCE PEOPLE GET LIKE THAT, THERE'S NO TALKING SENSE INTO THEM.

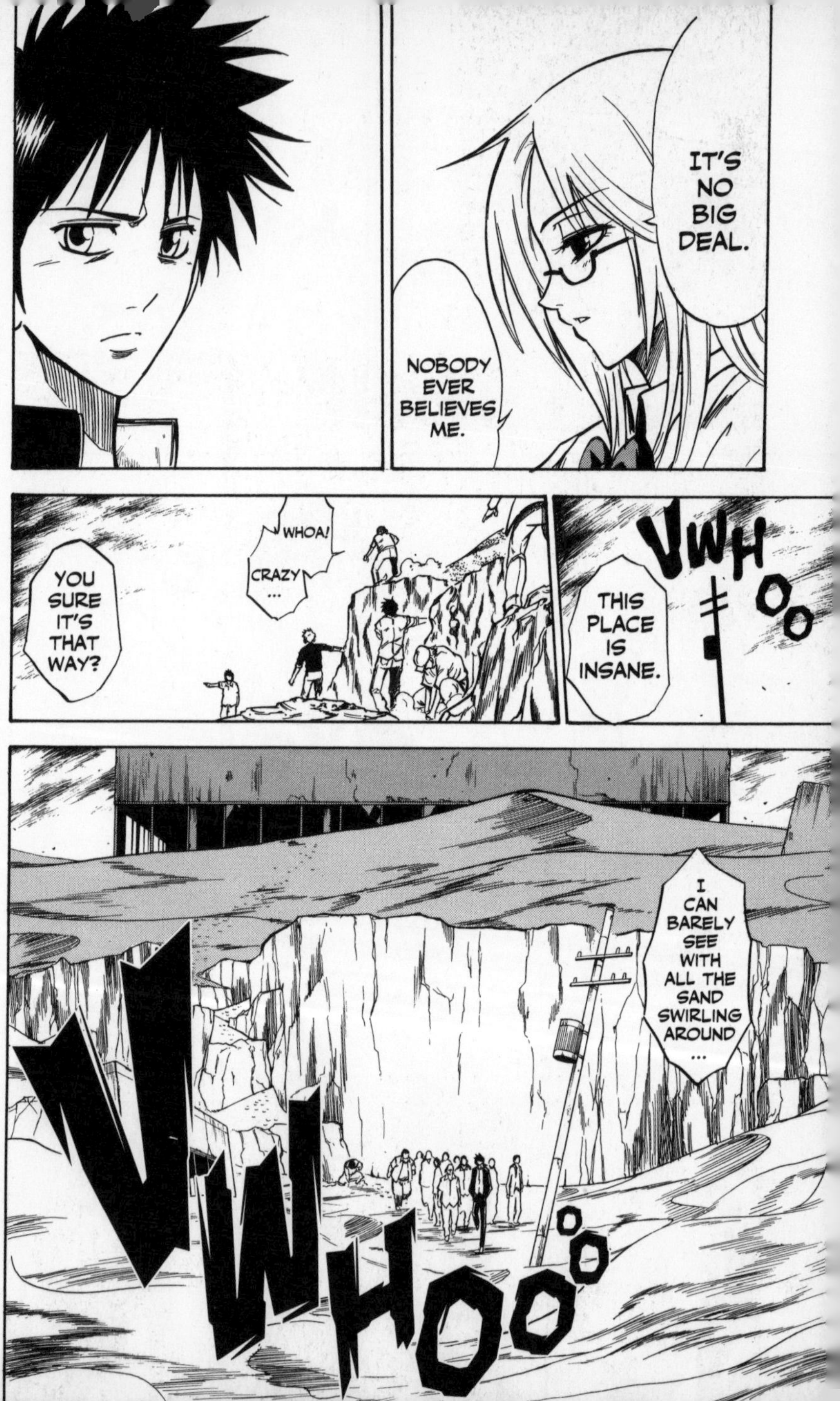
IT'S NO BIG DEAL.
NOBODY EVER BELIEVES ME.
VWHOO
THIS PLACE IS INSANE.
WHOA!
CRAZY...
YOU SURE IT'S THAT WAY?
I CAN BARELY SEE WITH ALL THE SAND SWIRLING AROUND...
VWHOOOO

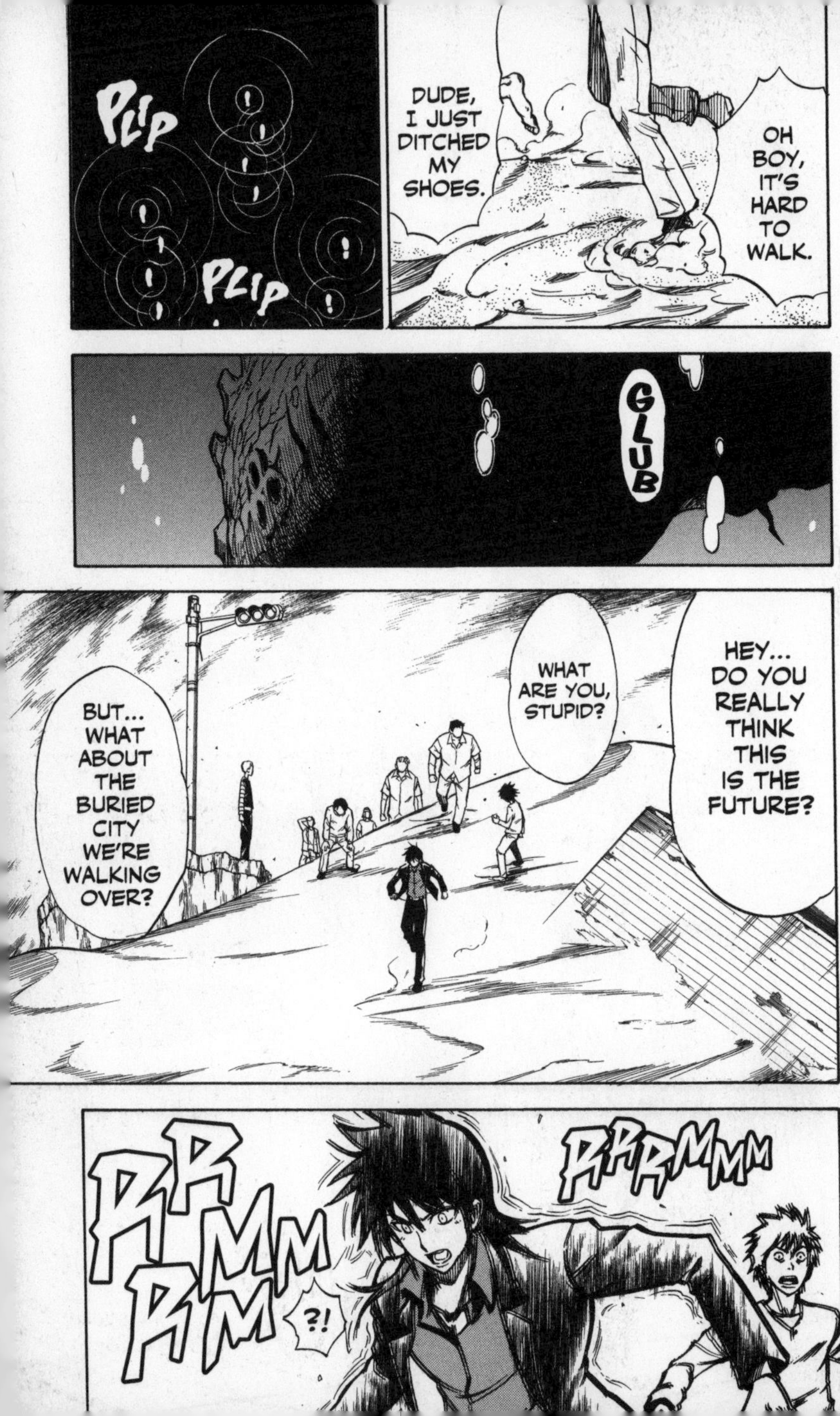
OH BOY, IT'S HARD TO WALK.
DUDE, I JUST DITCHED MY SHOES.
PLIP
PLIP
GLUB
HEY... DO YOU REALLY THINK THIS IS THE FUTURE?
WHAT ARE YOU, STUPID?
BUT... WHAT ABOUT THE BURIED CITY WE'RE WALKING OVER?
RRRMMM
RRMMM RM
?!

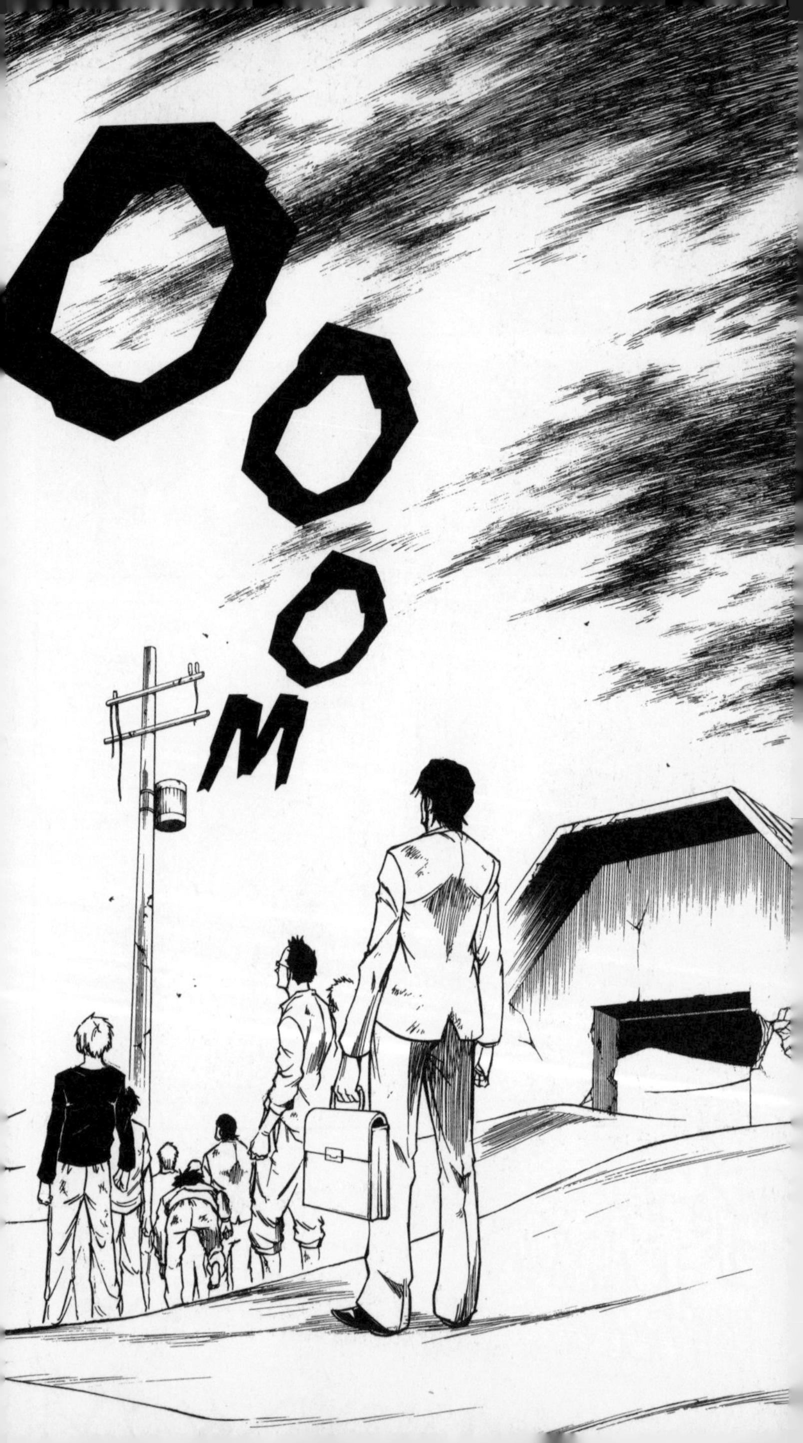
DOOOM

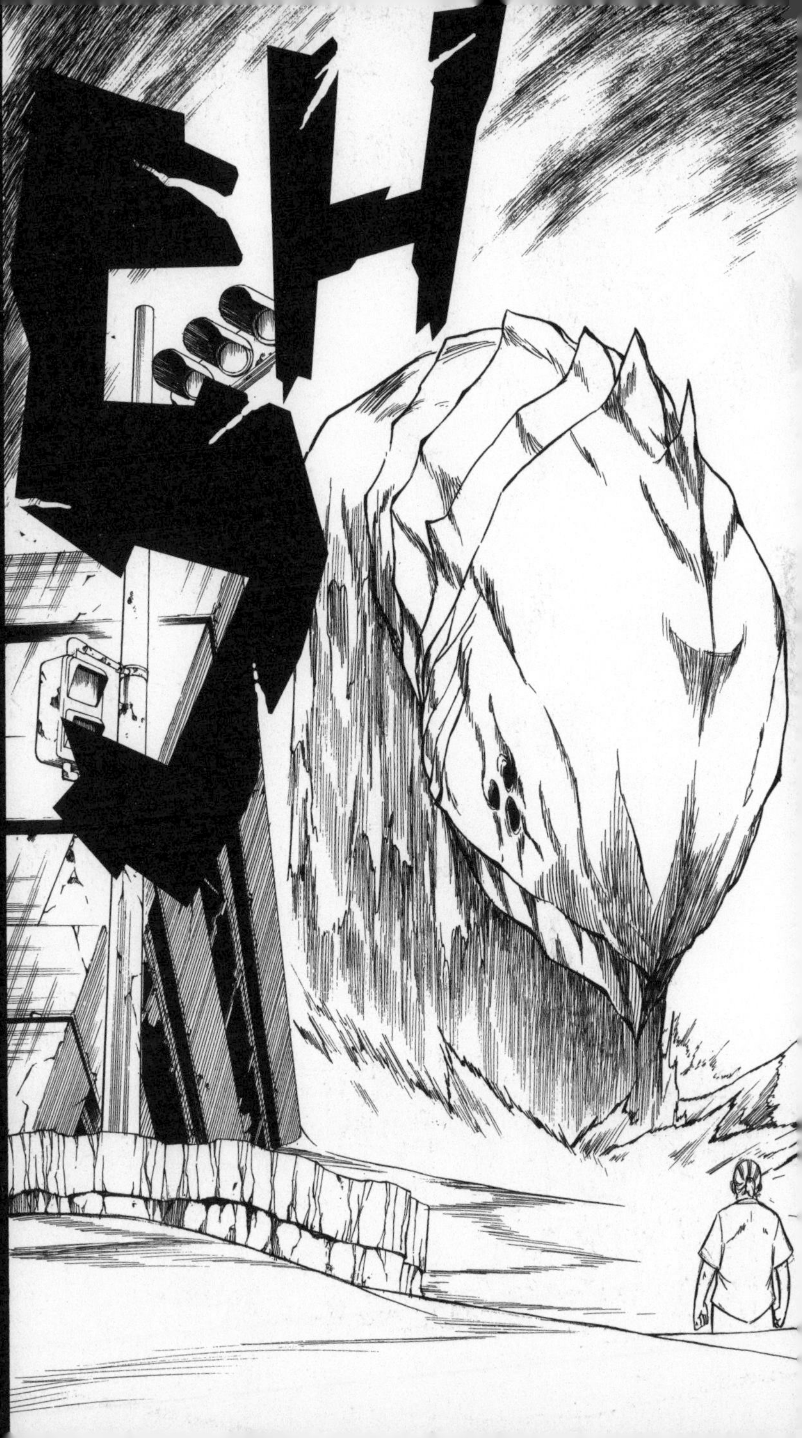

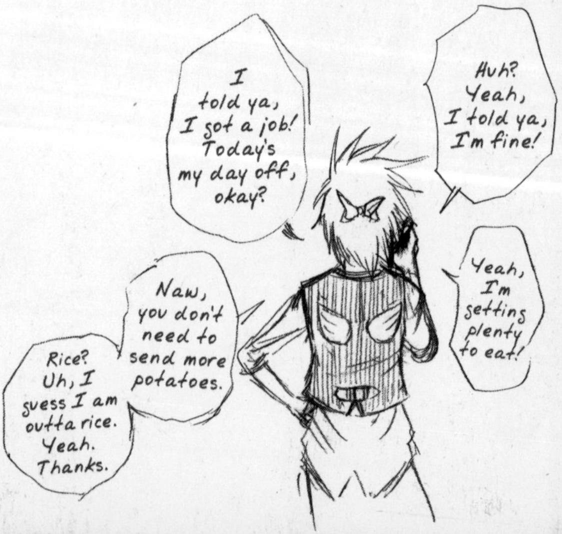
Huh? Yeah, I told ya, I'm fine!
I told ya, I got a job! Today's my day off, okay?
Yeah, I'm getting plenty to eat!
Naw, you don't need to send more potatoes.
Rice? Uh, I guess I am outta rice. Yeah. Thanks.

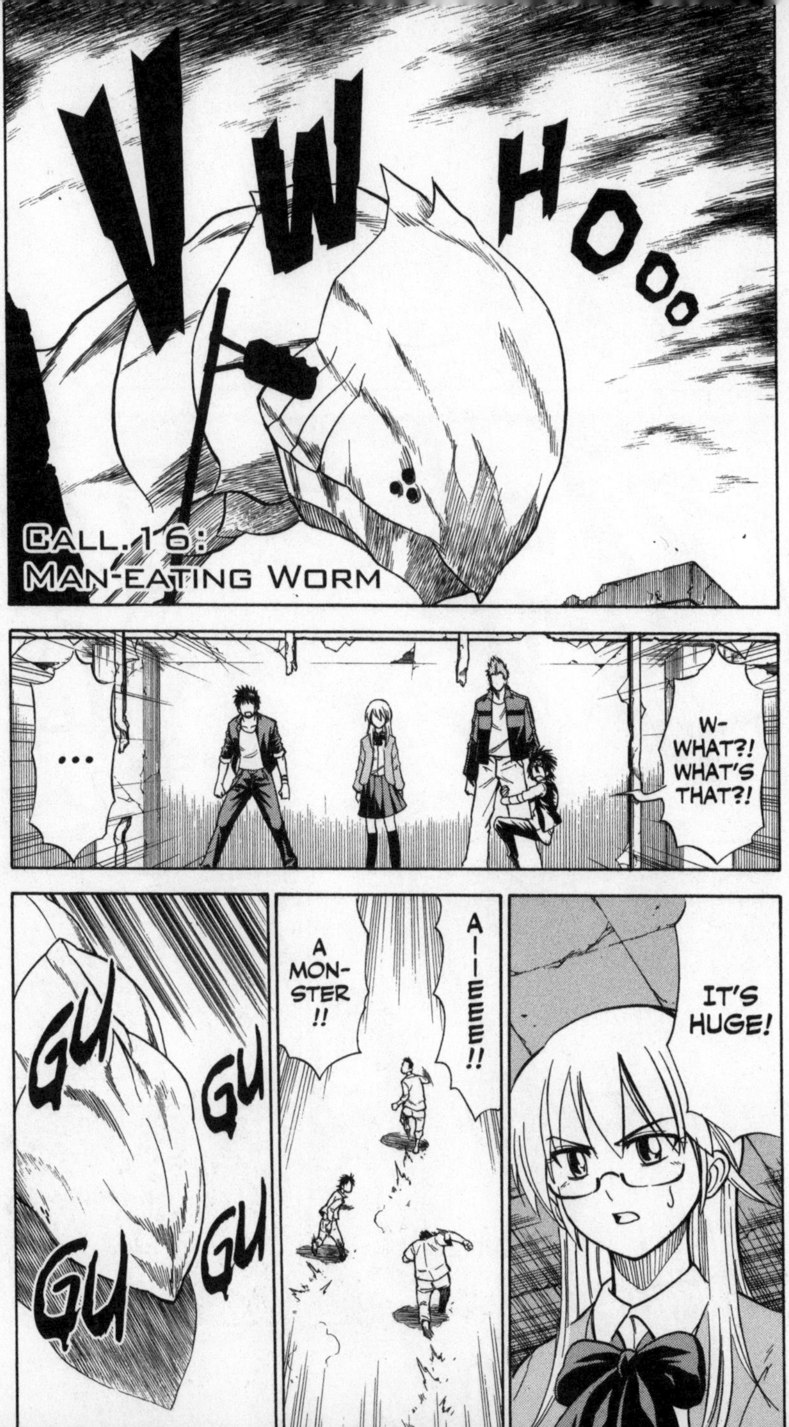
VWHOOO
CALL. 16:
MAN-EATING WORM
W- WHAT?! WHAT'S THAT?!
...
IT'S HUGE!
AIIEEE!!
A MON-STER!!
GU GU GU GU

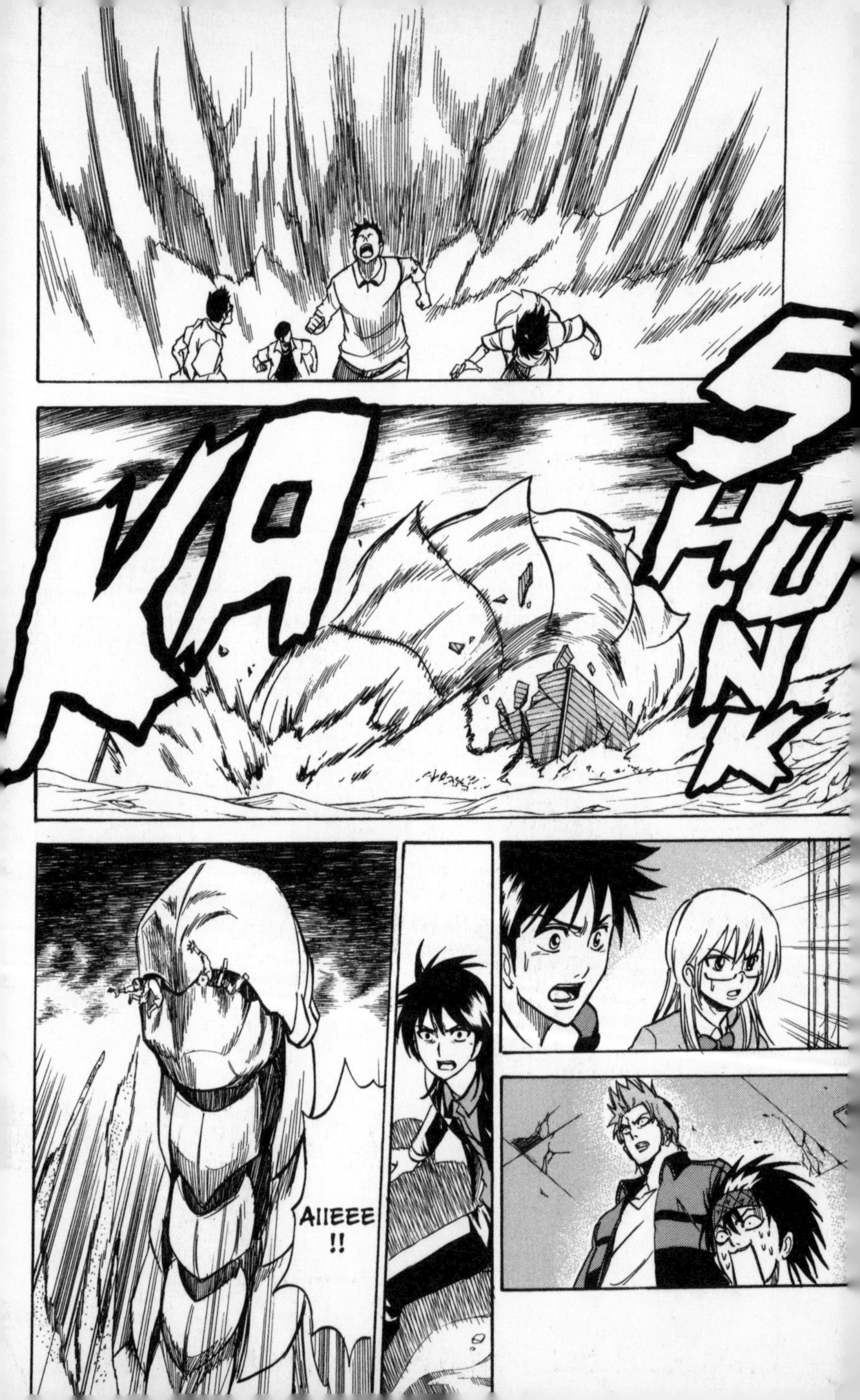
SHUNK
AIIEEE !!

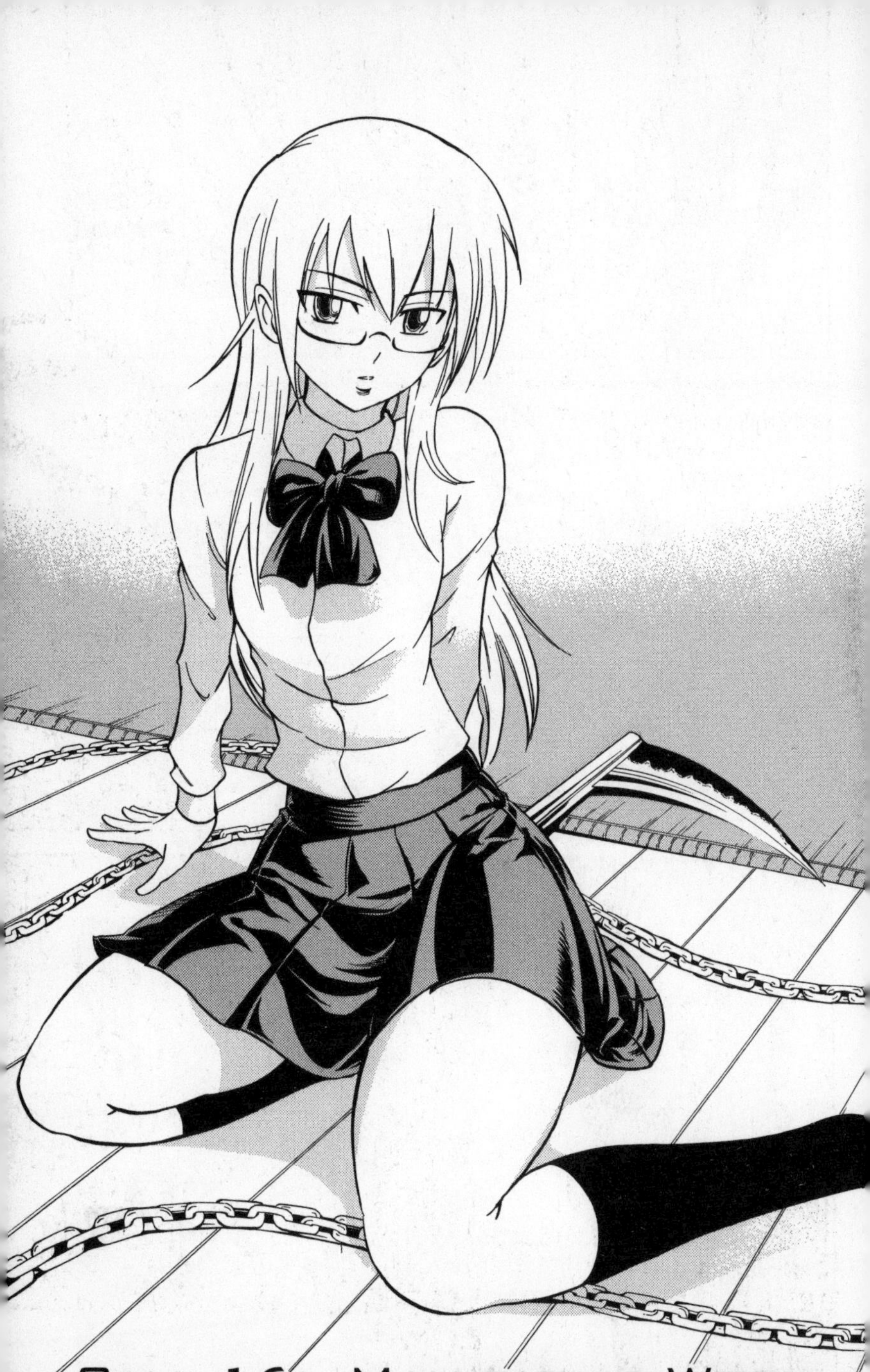

Call.16: Man-eating Worm

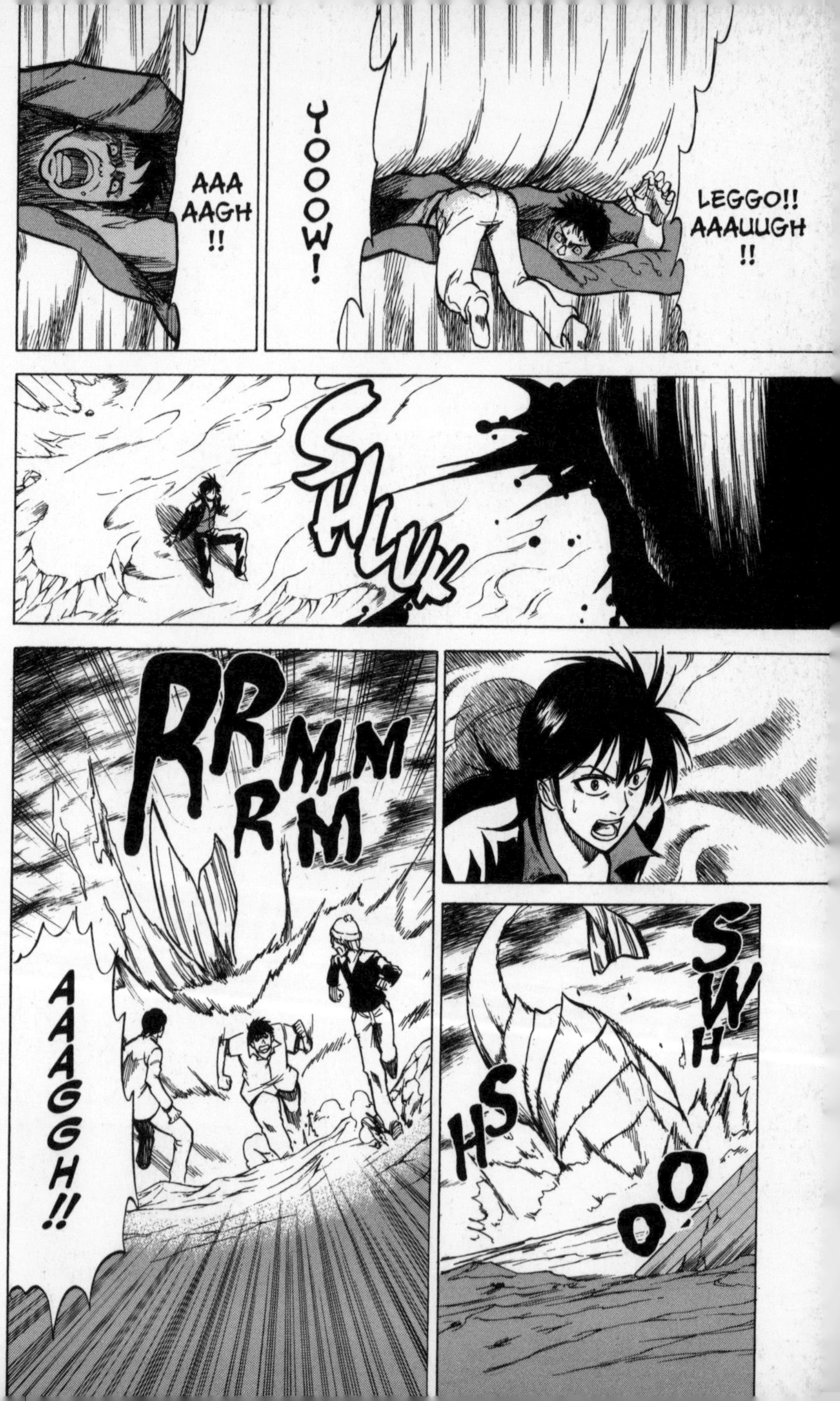
LEGGO!! AAAUUGH !!
YOOOOW!
AAA AAGH !!
SHLUK
SWHOOOSH
RRMM RM
AAAGGGH!!

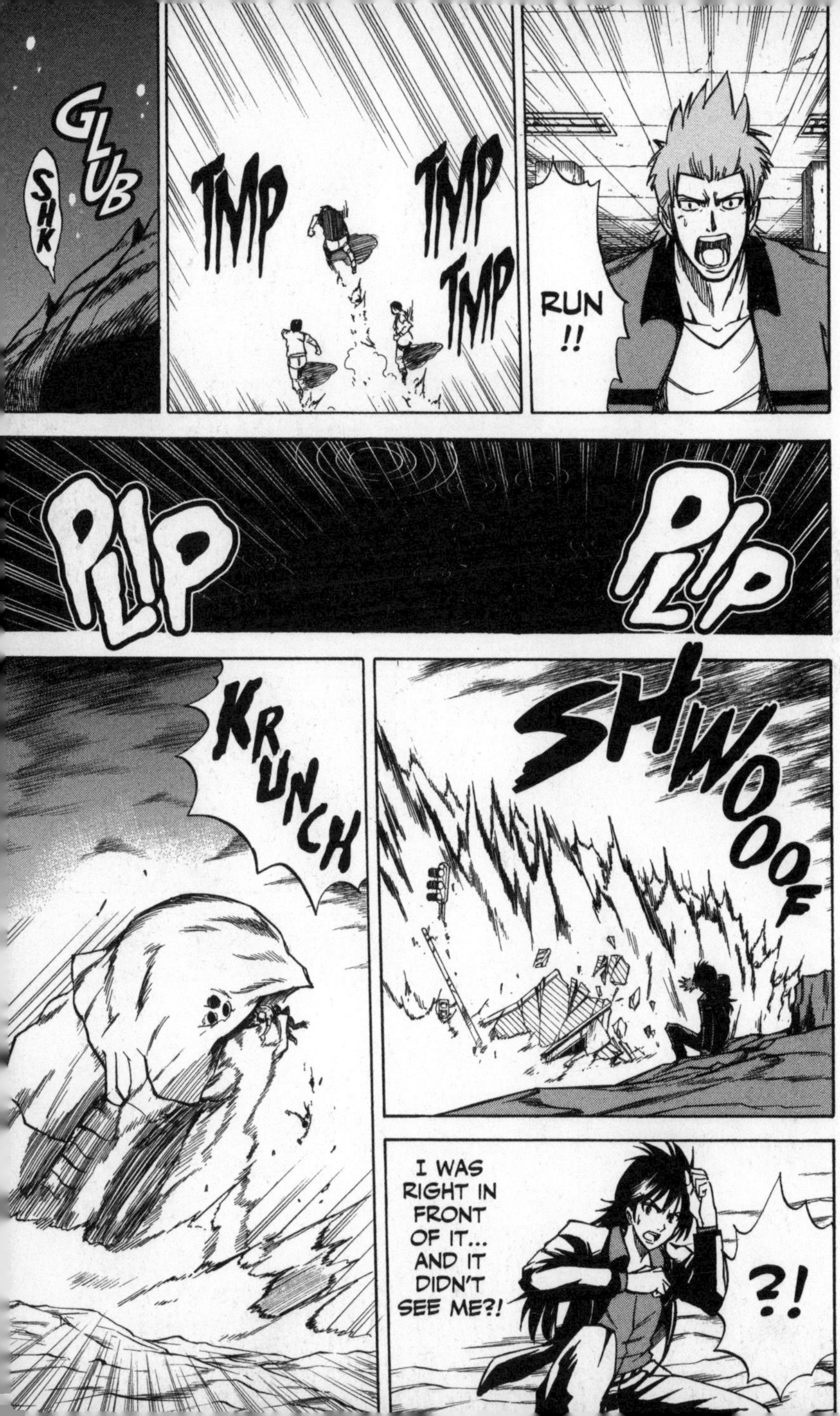
RUN !!
TMP
TMP
TMP
TMP
GLUB
SHK
PLIP
PLIP
SHWOOOF
I WAS RIGHT IN FRONT OF IT... AND IT DIDN'T SEE ME?!
?!
KRUNCH

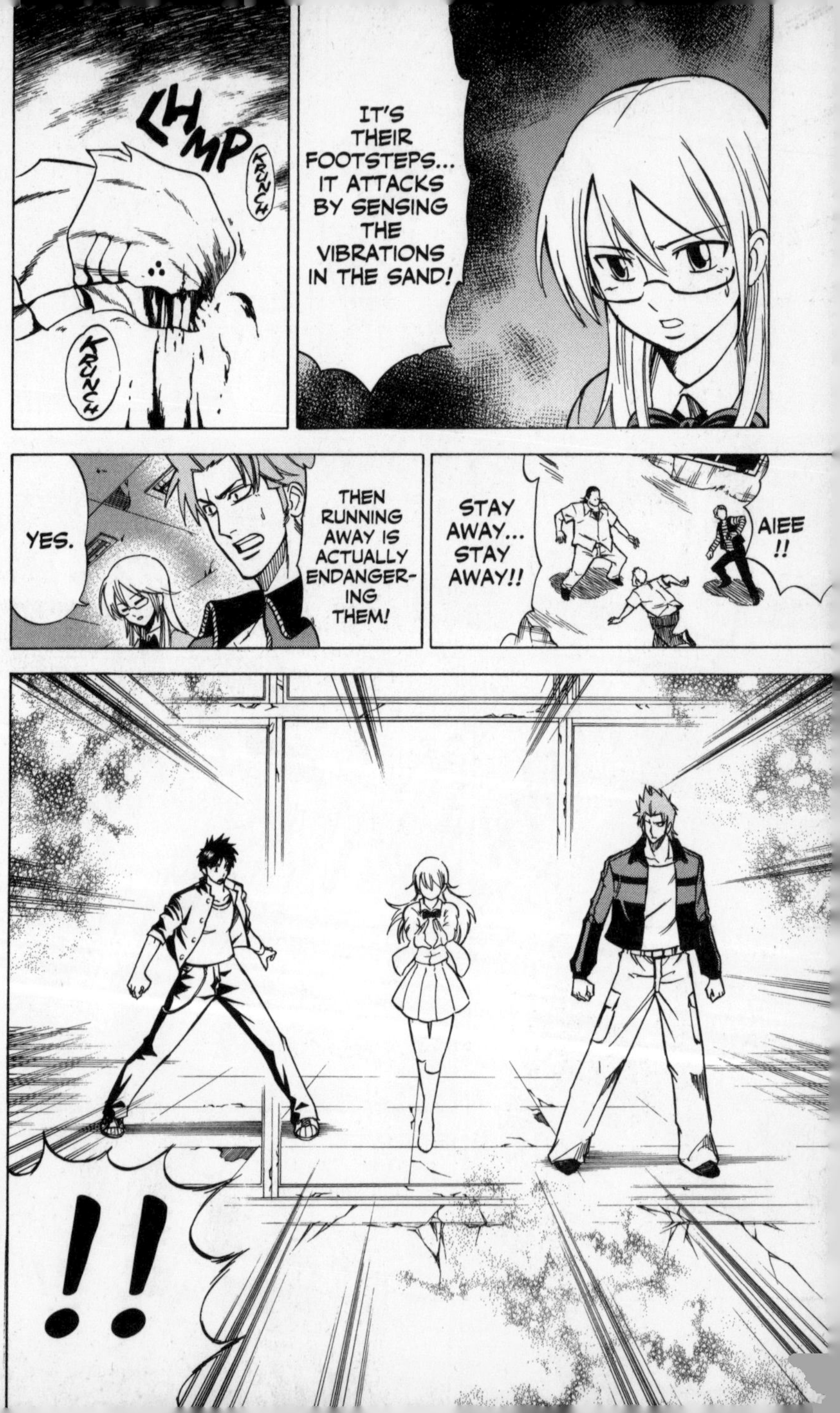
IT'S THEIR FOOTSTEPS... IT ATTACKS BY SENSING THE VIBRATIONS IN THE SAND!
CHMP
KRUNCH
KRUNCH
AIEE !!
STAY AWAY... STAY AWAY!!
THEN RUNNING AWAY IS ACTUALLY ENDANGERING THEM!
YES.
!!

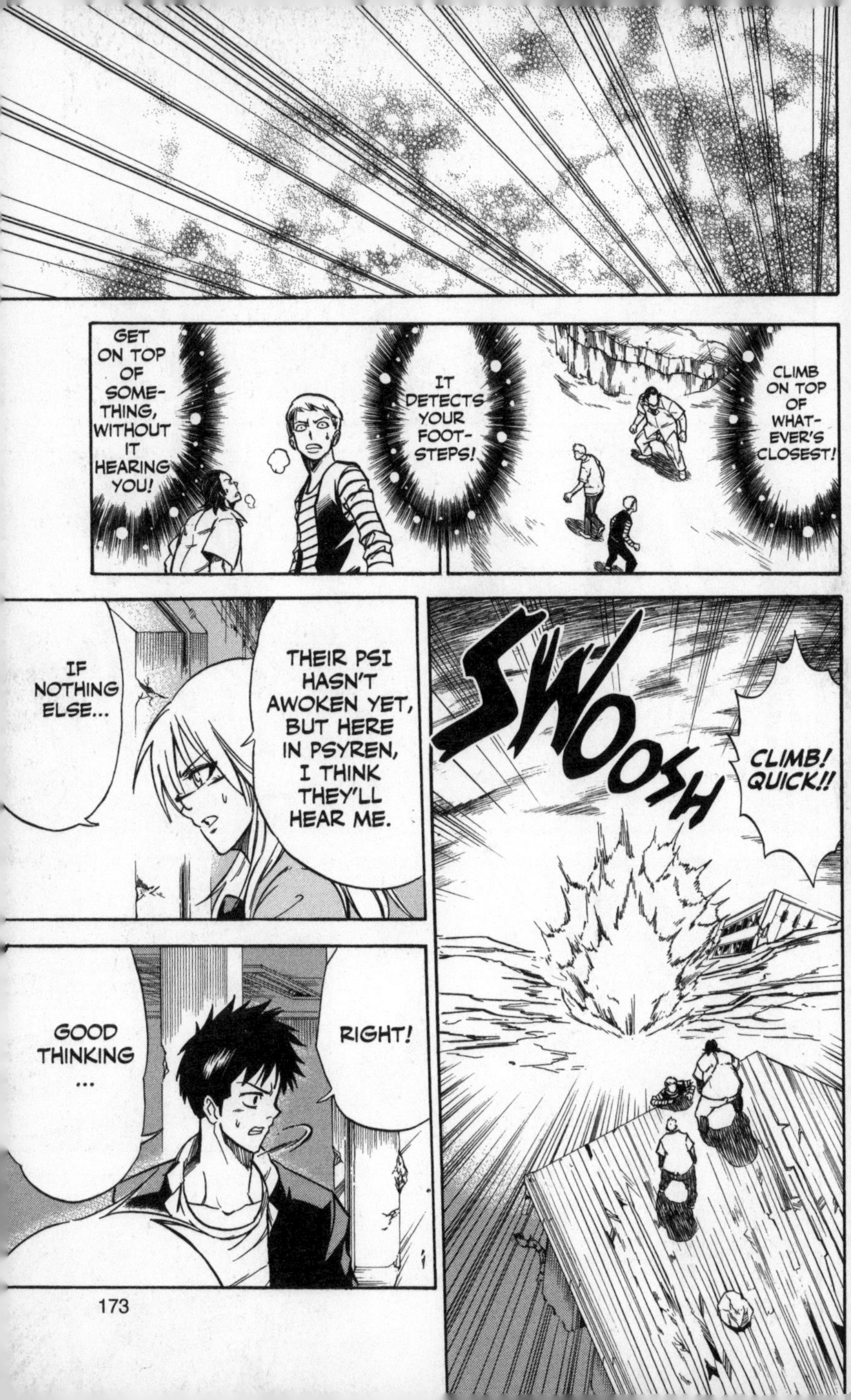
CLIMB ON TOP OF WHATEVER'S CLOSEST!
IT DETECTS YOUR FOOTSTEPS!
GET ON TOP OF SOMETHING, WITHOUT IT HEARING YOU!
SWOOSH
CLIMB! QUICK!!
THEIR PSI HASN'T AWOKEN YET, BUT HERE IN PSYREN, I THINK THEY'LL HEAR ME.
IF NOTHING ELSE...
RIGHT!
GOOD THINKING ...

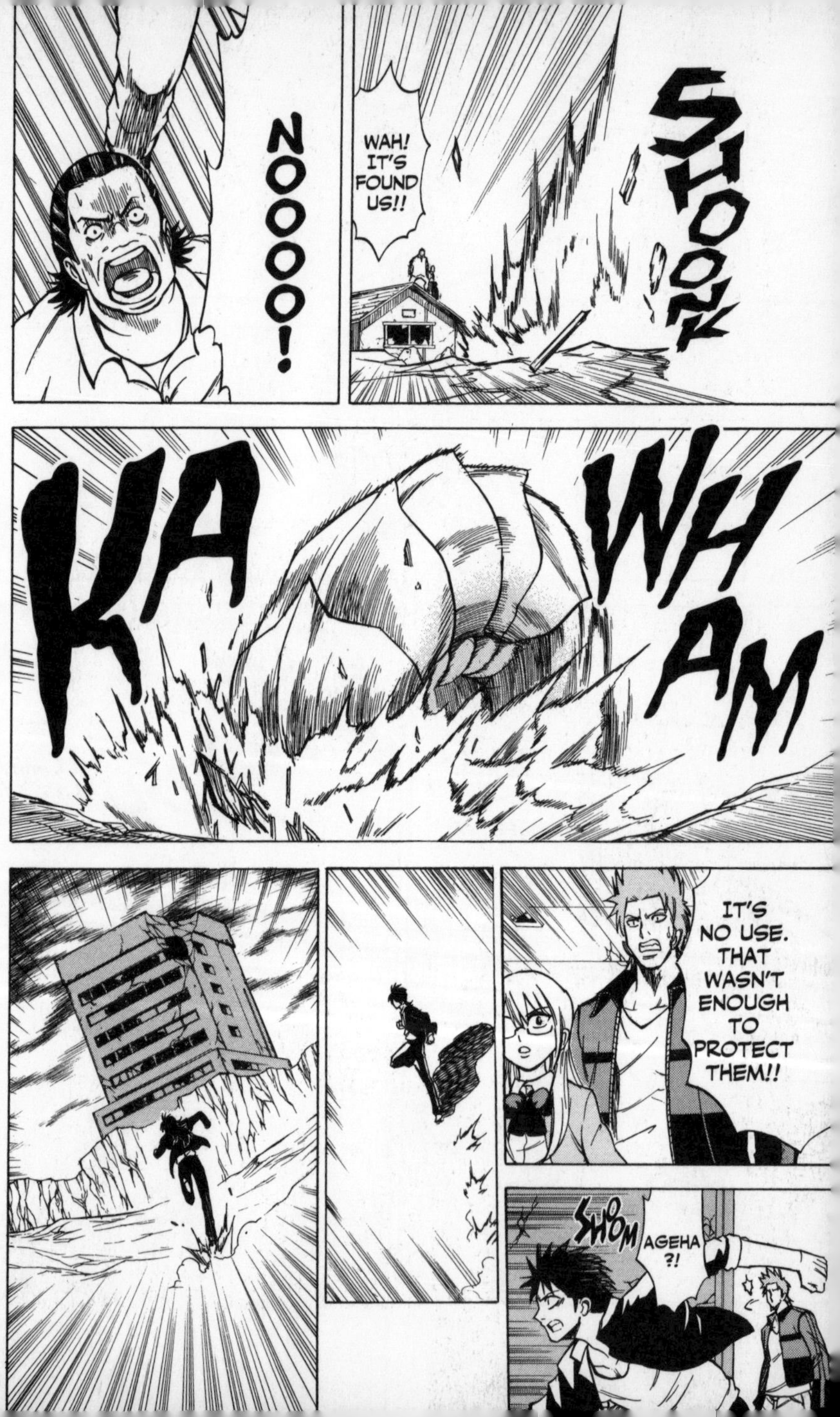
SHOOK
WAH! IT'S FOUND US!!
NOOOOO!
KA WHAM
IT'S NO USE. THAT WASN'T ENOUGH TO PROTECT THEM!!
SHOM
AGEHA ?!

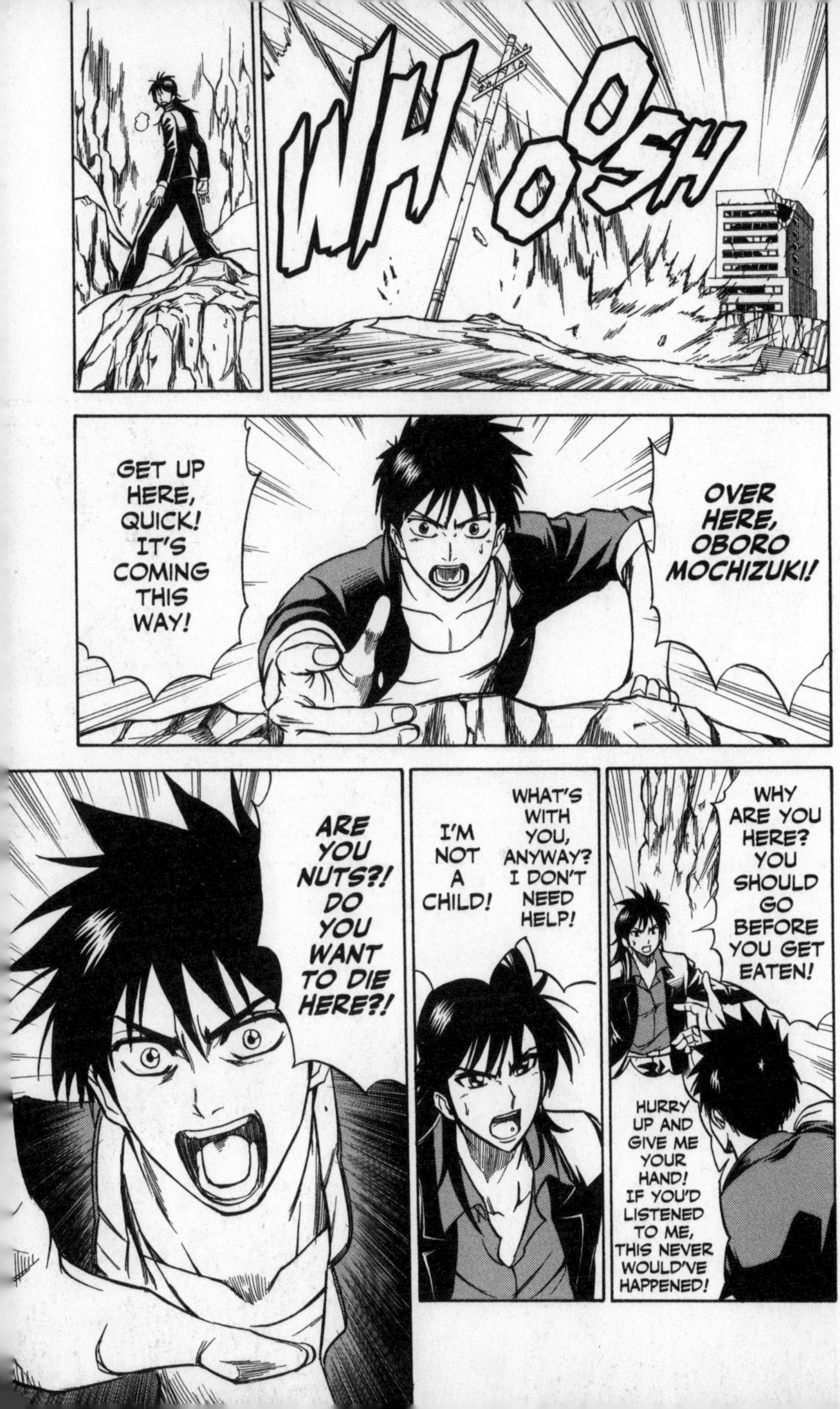
WHOOSH
OVER HERE, OBORO MOCHIZUKI!
GET UP HERE, QUICK! IT'S COMING THIS WAY!
WHY ARE YOU HERE? YOU SHOULD GO BEFORE YOU GET EATEN!
HURRY UP AND GIVE ME YOUR HAND! IF YOU'D LISTENED TO ME, THIS NEVER WOULD'VE HAPPENED!
WHAT'S WITH YOU, ANYWAY? I DON'T NEED HELP!
I'M NOT A CHILD!
ARE YOU NUTS?! DO YOU WANT TO DIE HERE?!

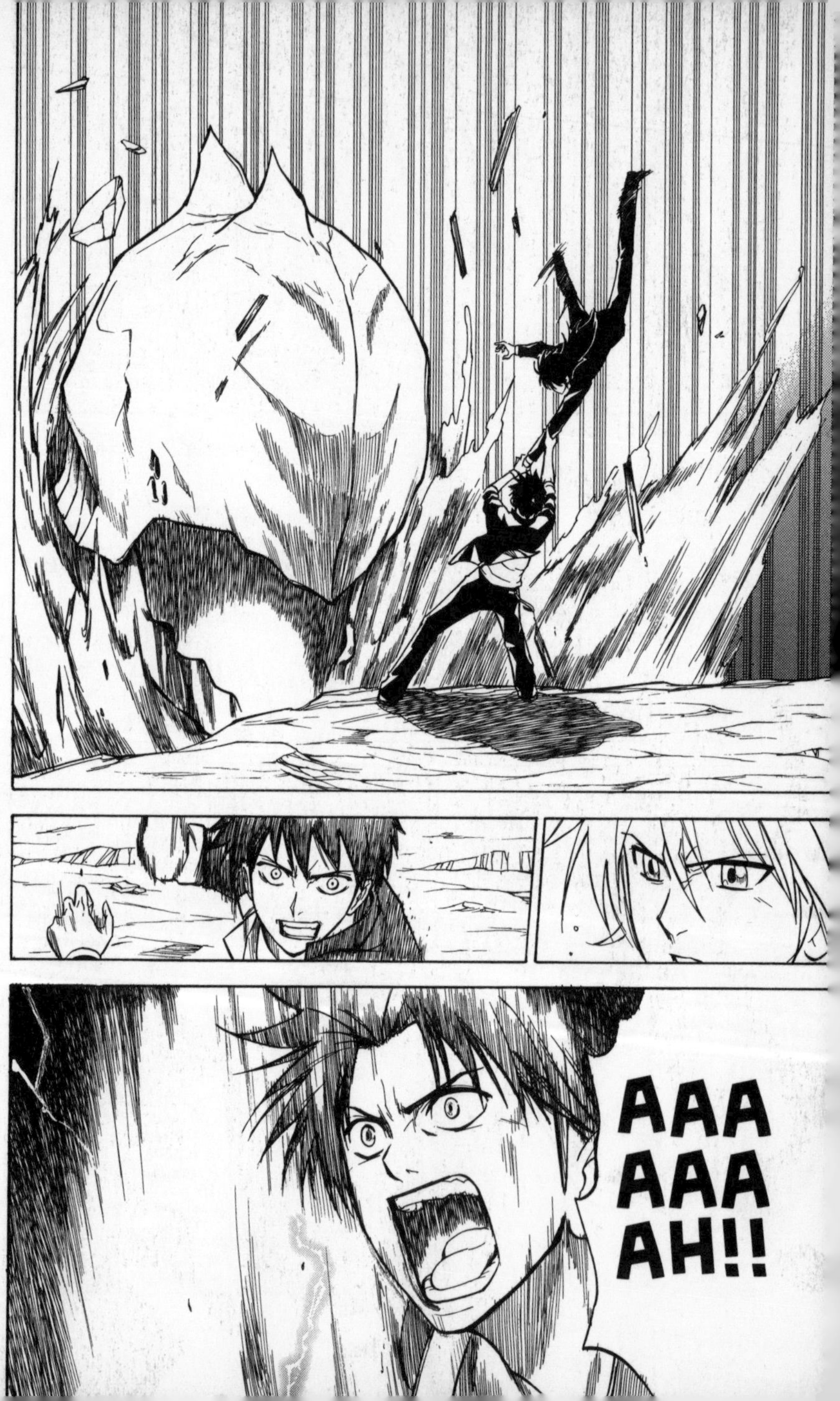
AAA
AAA
AH!!

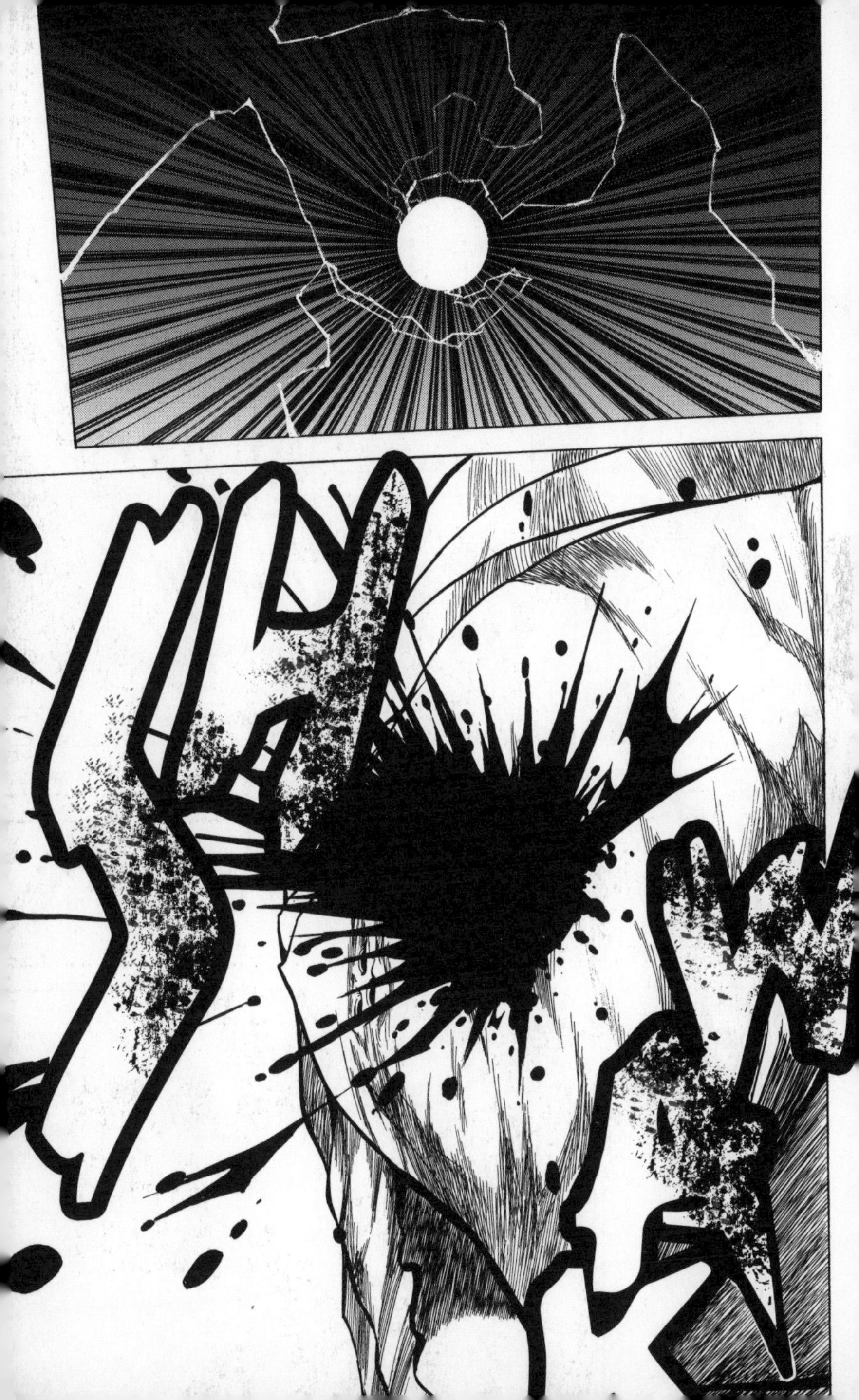

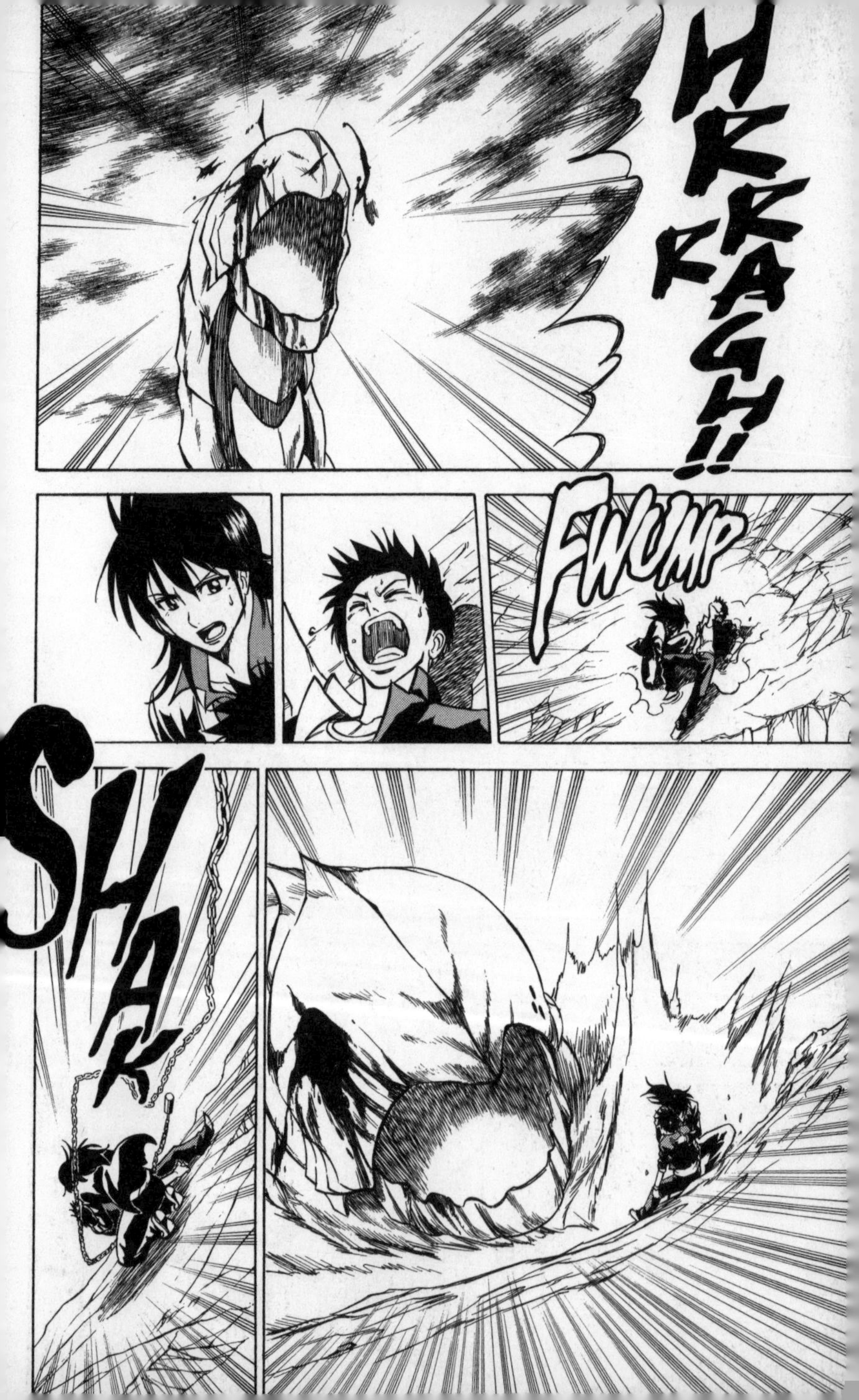
HKRRRAGH!!
FWUMP
SHAK

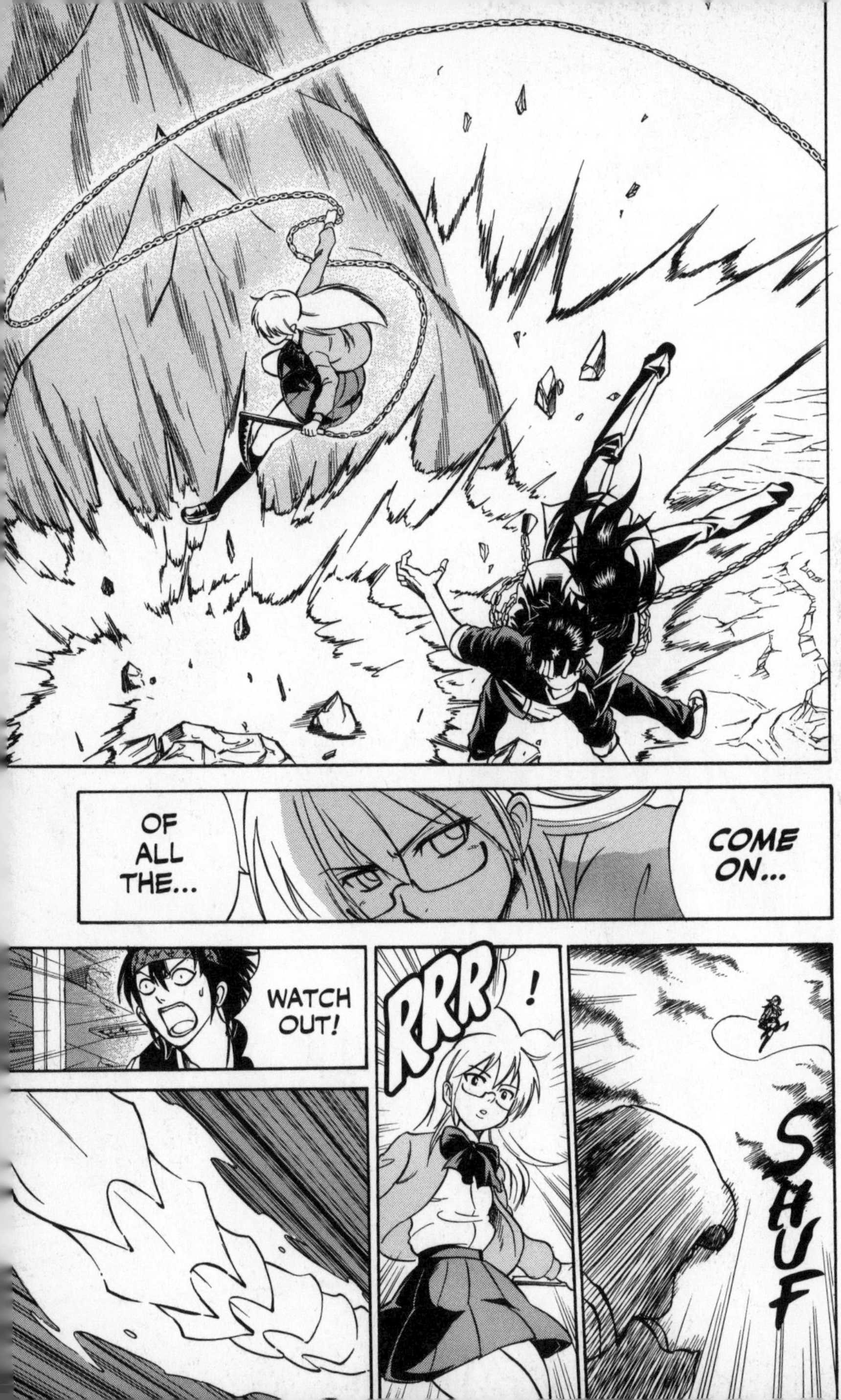
COME ON...
OF ALL THE...
SHUF
RRR !
WATCH OUT!

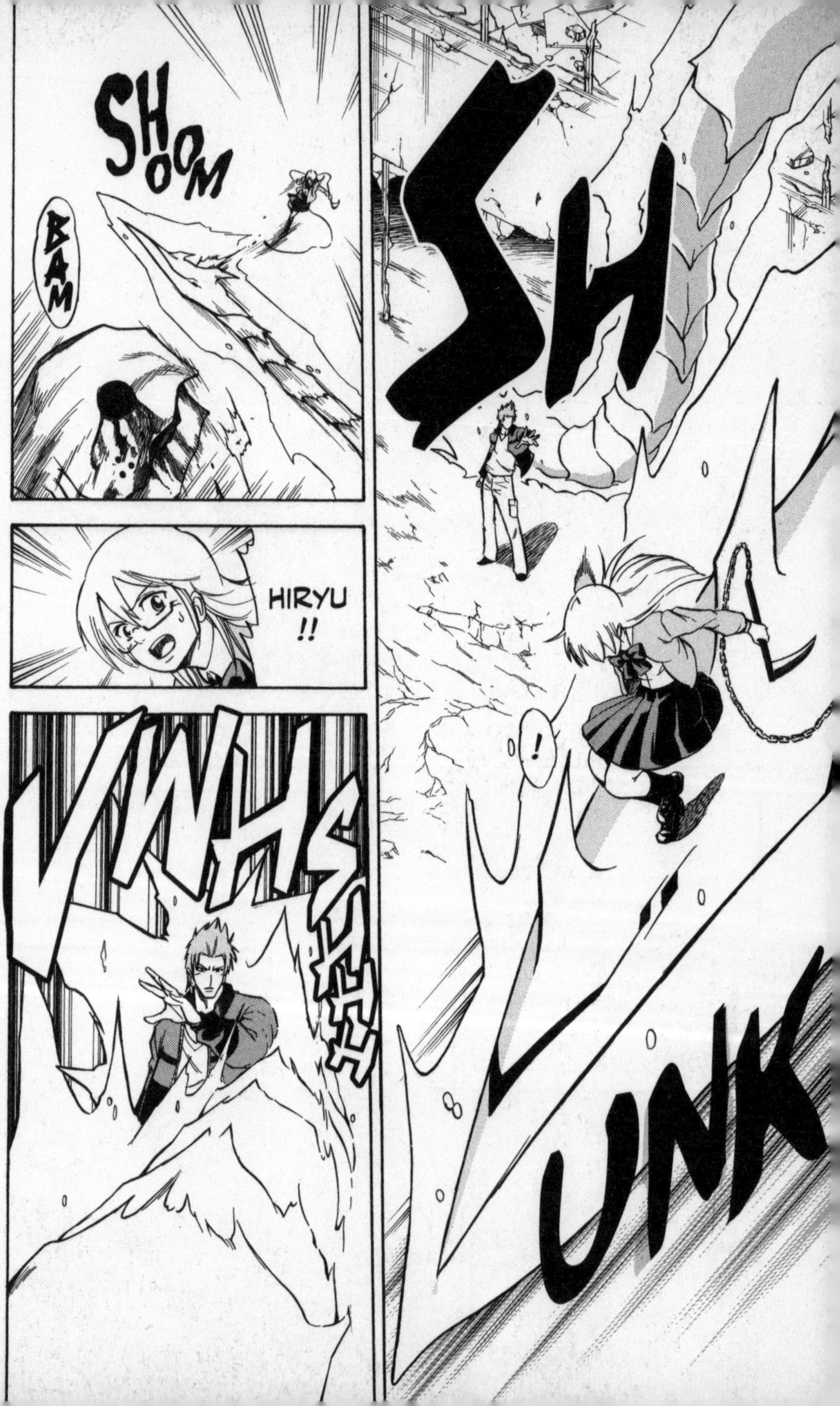
SH
!
UNK
SHOOM
BAM
HIRYU !!
WHS

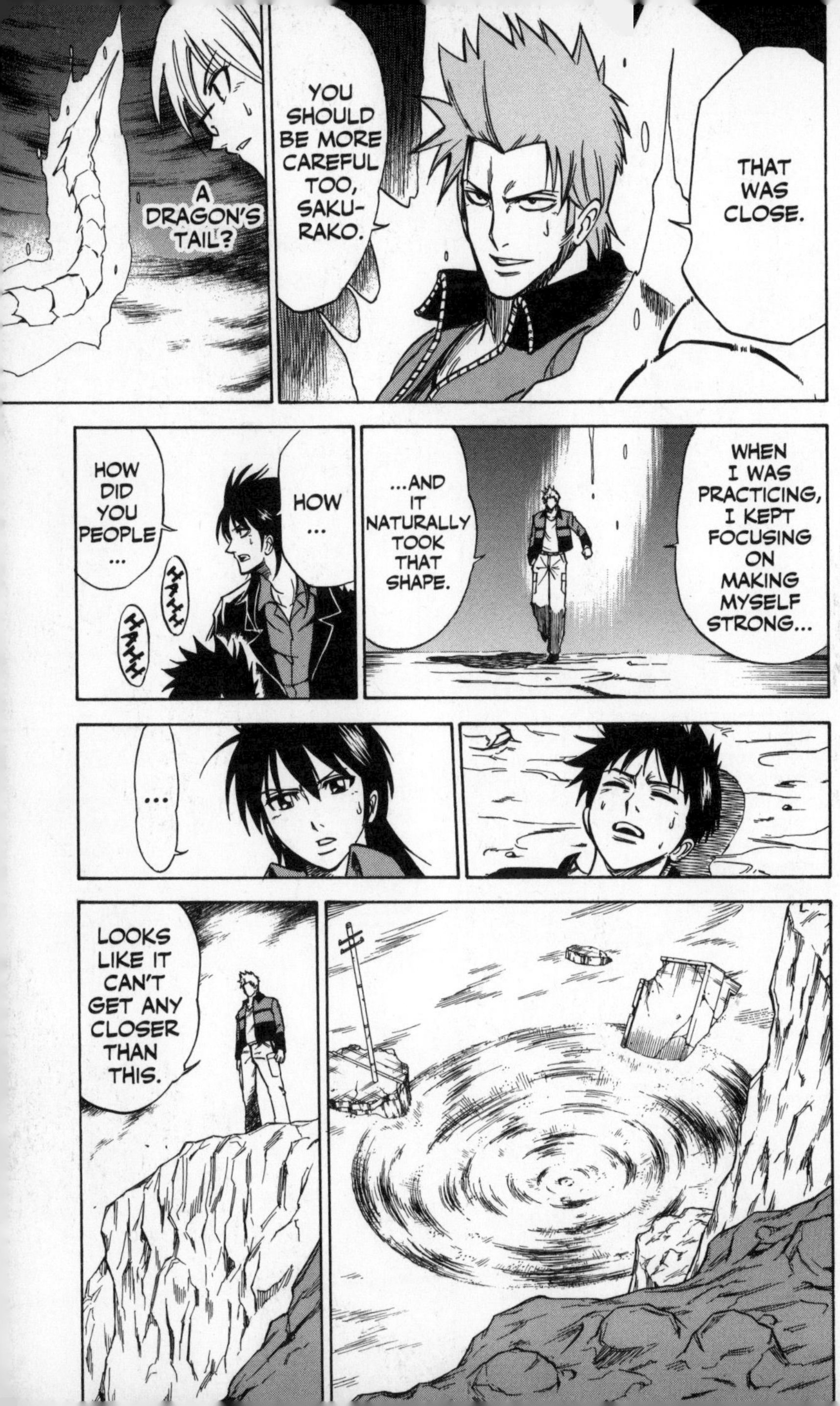
THAT WAS CLOSE.
YOU SHOULD BE MORE CAREFUL TOO, SAKU-RAKO.
A DRAGON'S TAIL?
WHEN I WAS PRACTICING, I KEPT FOCUSING ON MAKING MYSELF STRONG...
...AND IT NATURALLY TOOK THAT SHAPE.
HOW ...
HOW DID YOU PEOPLE ...
...
LOOKS LIKE IT CAN'T GET ANY CLOSER THAN THIS.

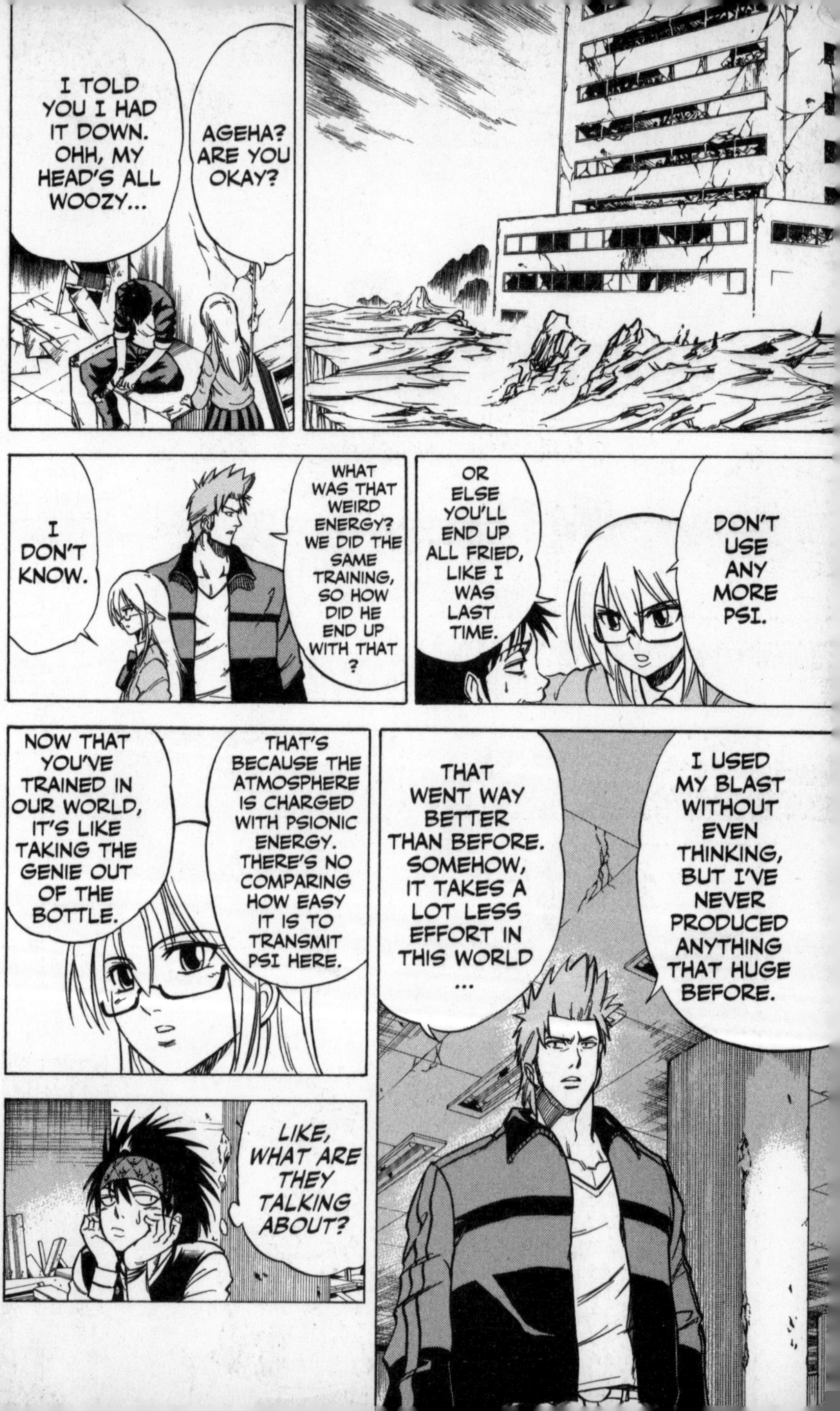
AGEHA? ARE YOU OKAY?
I TOLD YOU I HAD IT DOWN. OHH, MY HEAD'S ALL WOOZY...
DON'T USE ANY MORE PSI.
OR ELSE YOU'LL END UP ALL FRIED, LIKE I WAS LAST TIME.
WHAT WAS THAT WEIRD ENERGY? WE DID THE SAME TRAINING, SO HOW DID HE END UP WITH THAT?
I DON'T KNOW.
I USED MY BLAST WITHOUT EVEN THINKING, BUT I'VE NEVER PRODUCED ANYTHING THAT HUGE BEFORE.
THAT WENT WAY BETTER THAN BEFORE. SOMEHOW, IT TAKES A LOT LESS EFFORT IN THIS WORLD...
THAT'S BECAUSE THE ATMOSPHERE IS CHARGED WITH PSIONIC ENERGY. THERE'S NO COMPARING HOW EASY IT IS TO TRANSMIT PSI HERE.
NOW THAT YOU'VE TRAINED IN OUR WORLD, IT'S LIKE TAKING THE GENIE OUT OF THE BOTTLE.
LIKE, WHAT ARE THEY TALKING ABOUT?

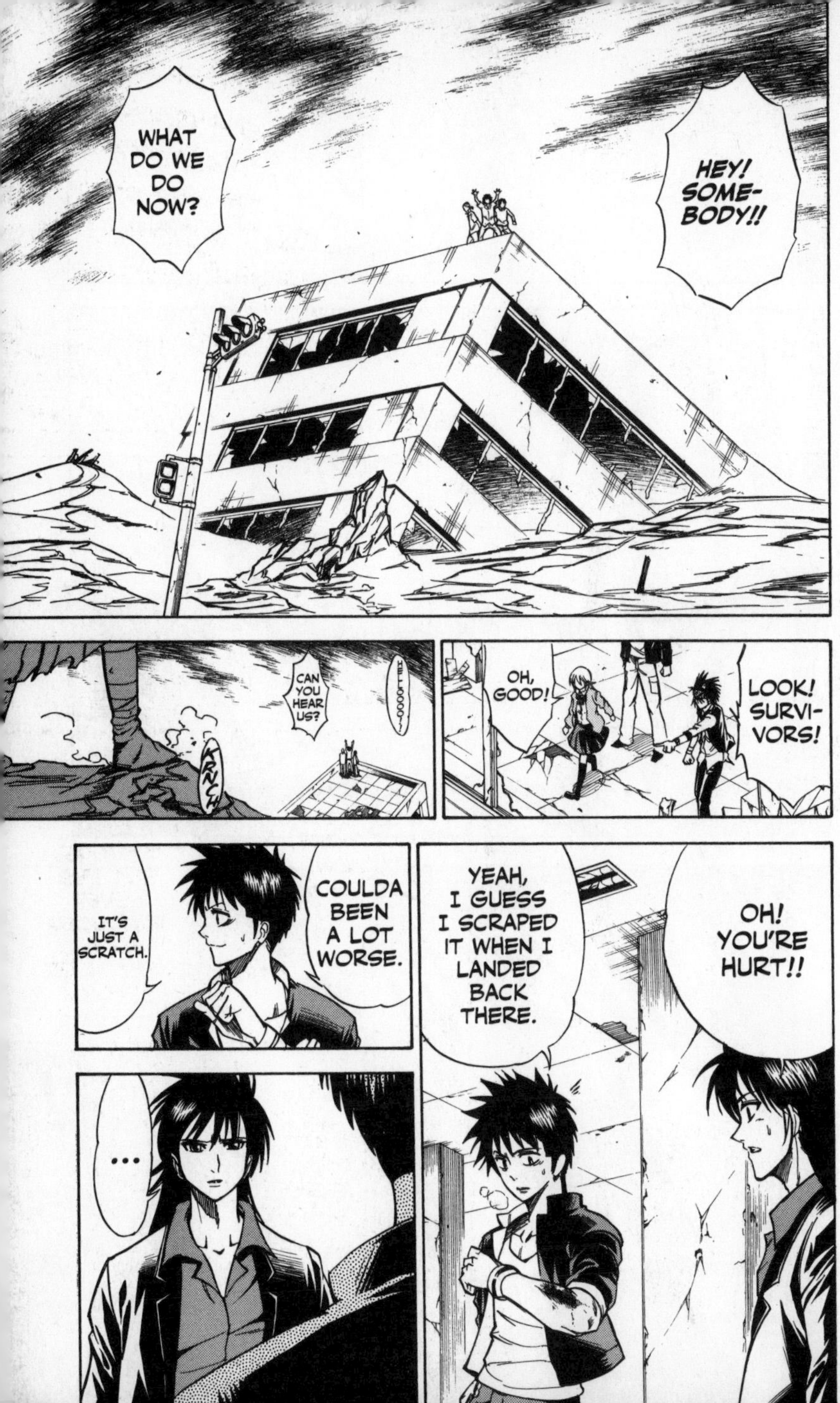
HEY! SOME-BODY!!
WHAT DO WE DO NOW?
LOOK! SURVI-VORS!
OH, GOOD!
HELLOOOO?!
CAN YOU HEAR US?
KRNCH
OH! YOU'RE HURT!!
YEAH, I GUESS I SCRAPED IT WHEN I LANDED BACK THERE.
COULDA BEEN A LOT WORSE.
IT'S JUST A SCRATCH.
...

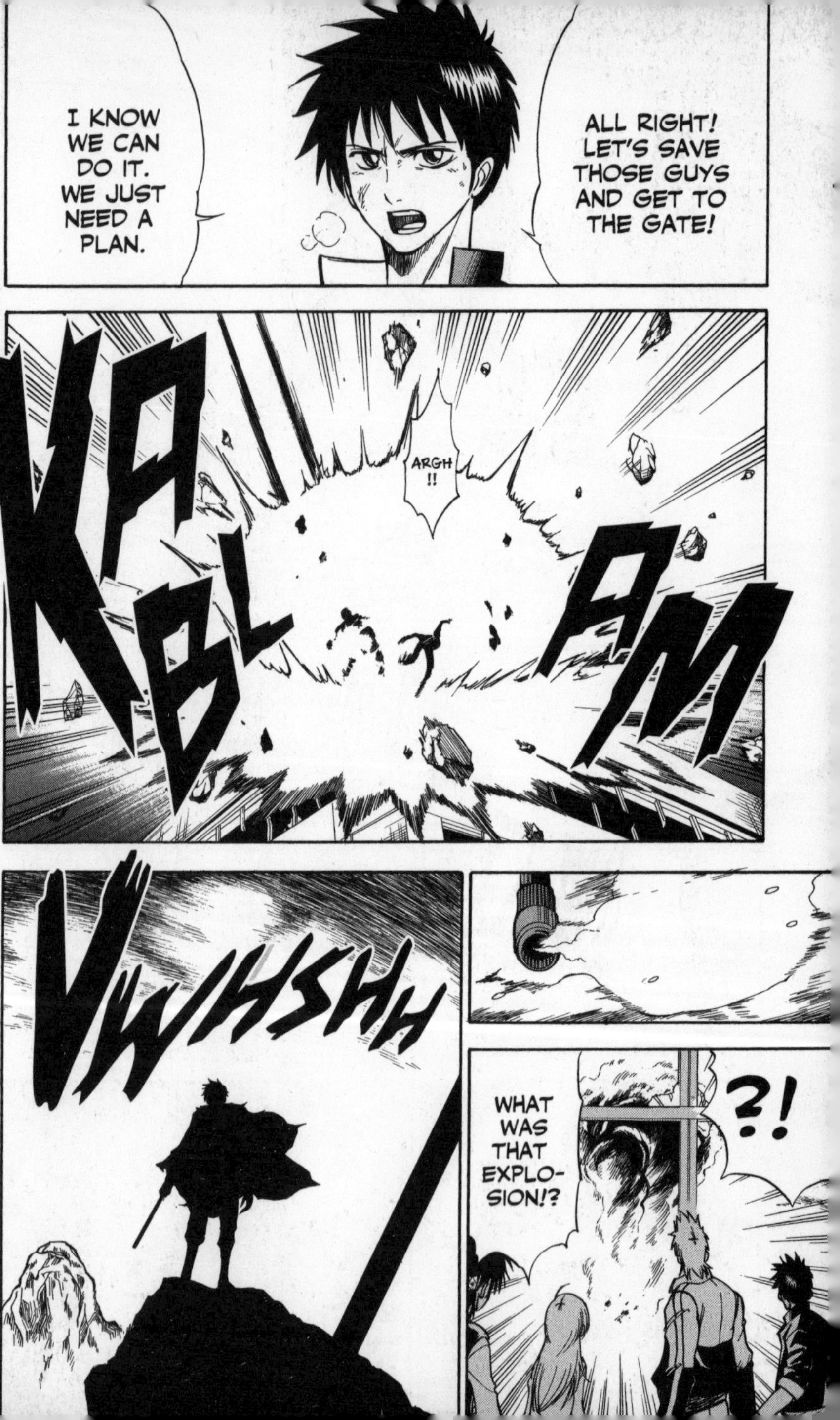
ALL RIGHT! LET'S SAVE THOSE GUYS AND GET TO THE GATE!
I KNOW WE CAN DO IT. WE JUST NEED A PLAN.
KABLAM
ARGH !!
?!
WHAT WAS THAT EXPLOSION!?
VWHSHH

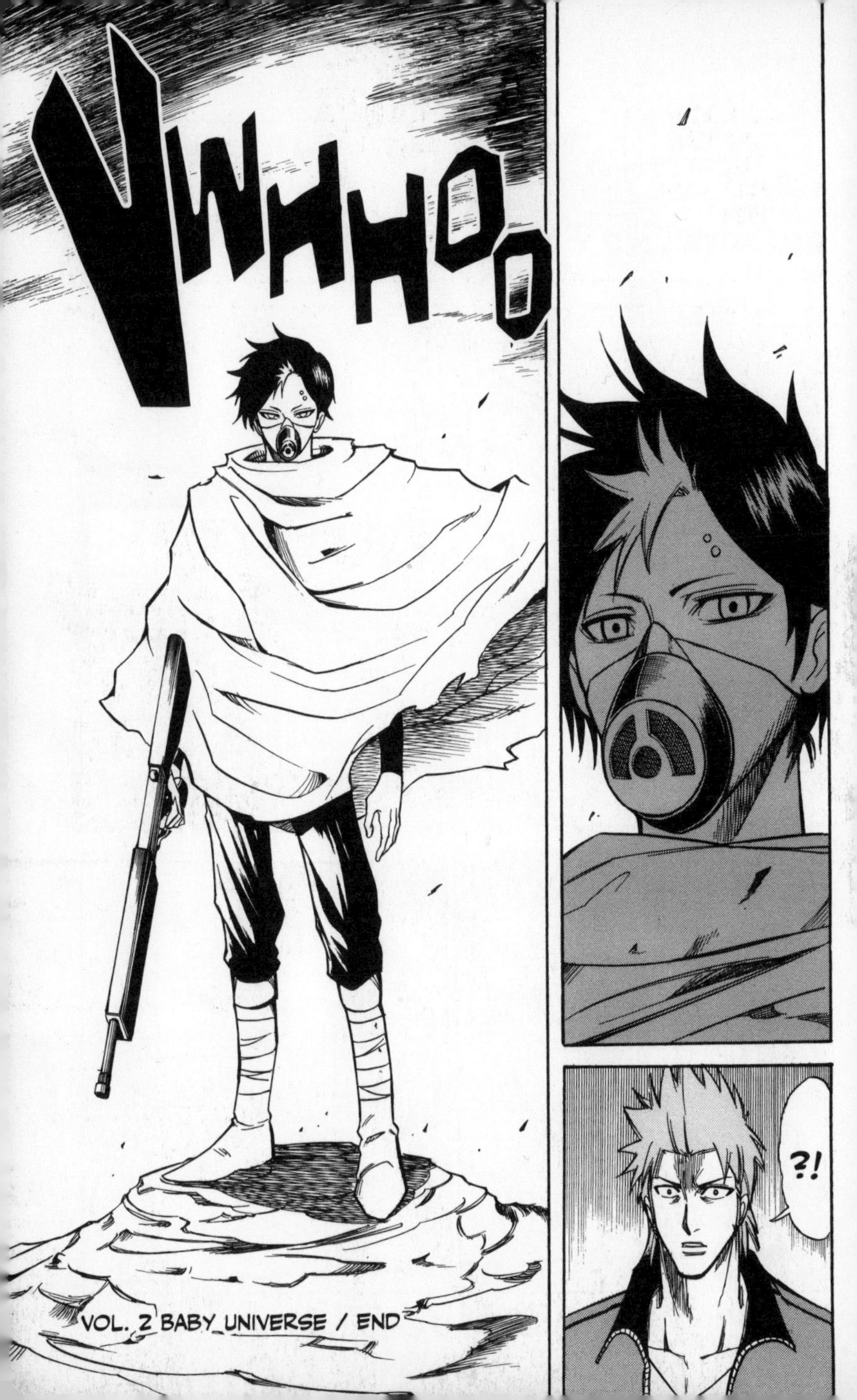
?!
VWHHOO
VOL. 2 BABY_UNIVERSE / END

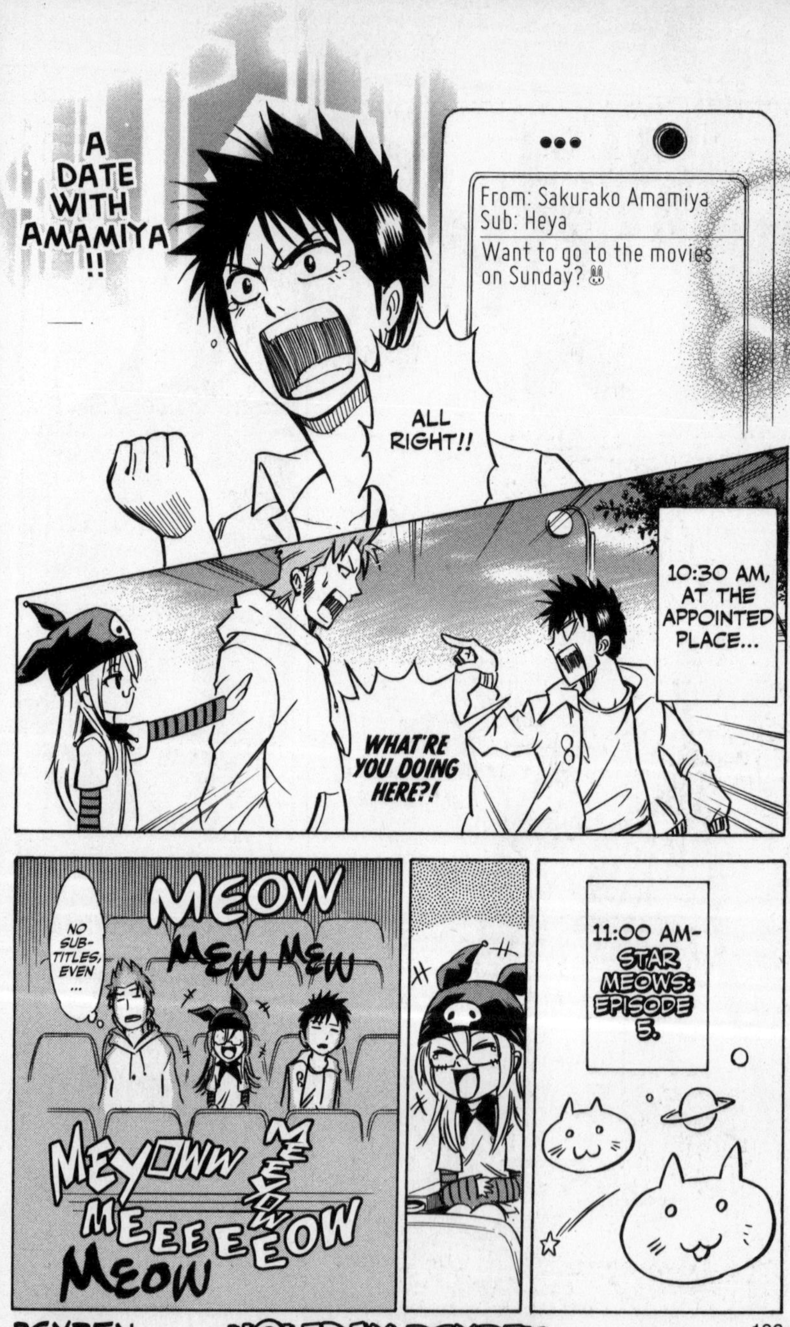
From: Sakurako Amamiya
Sub: Heya
Want to go to the movies on Sunday?
ALL RIGHT!!
A DATE WITH AMAMIYA!!
—
10:30 AM, AT THE APPOINTED PLACE...
WHAT'RE YOU DOING HERE?!
11:00 AM- STAR MEOWS: EPISODE 5.
MEOW
MEW MEW
NO SUB-TITLES, EVEN ...
MEYOWW
MEYOWW
MEEEEEEOW
MEOW

PSYREN BONUS STORY: HOLIDAY PSYREN

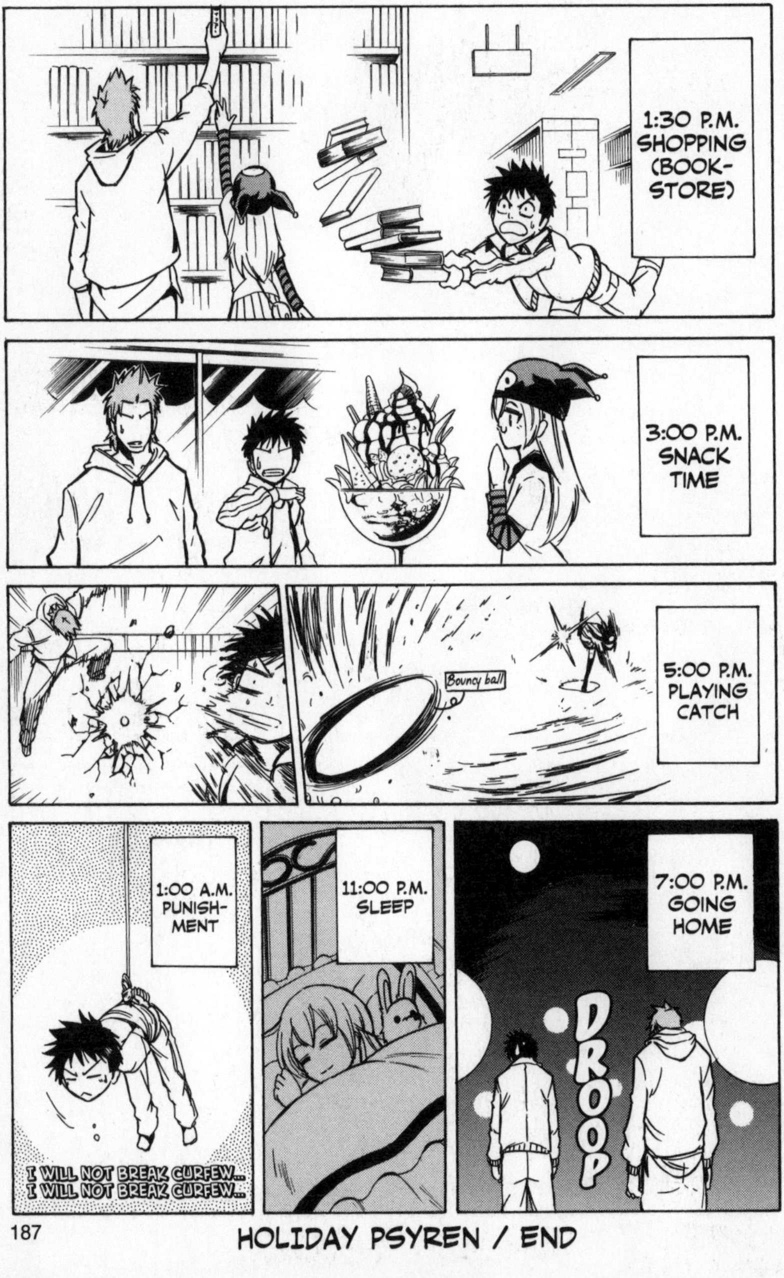
1:30 P.M. SHOPPING (BOOK-STORE)
3:00 P.M. SNACK TIME
5:00 P.M. PLAYING CATCH
Bouncy ball
7:00 P.M. GOING HOME
DROOP
11:00 P.M. SLEEP
1:00 A.M. PUNISH-MENT
I WILL NOT BREAK CURFEW...
I WILL NOT BREAK CURFEW...

HOLIDAY PSYREN / END

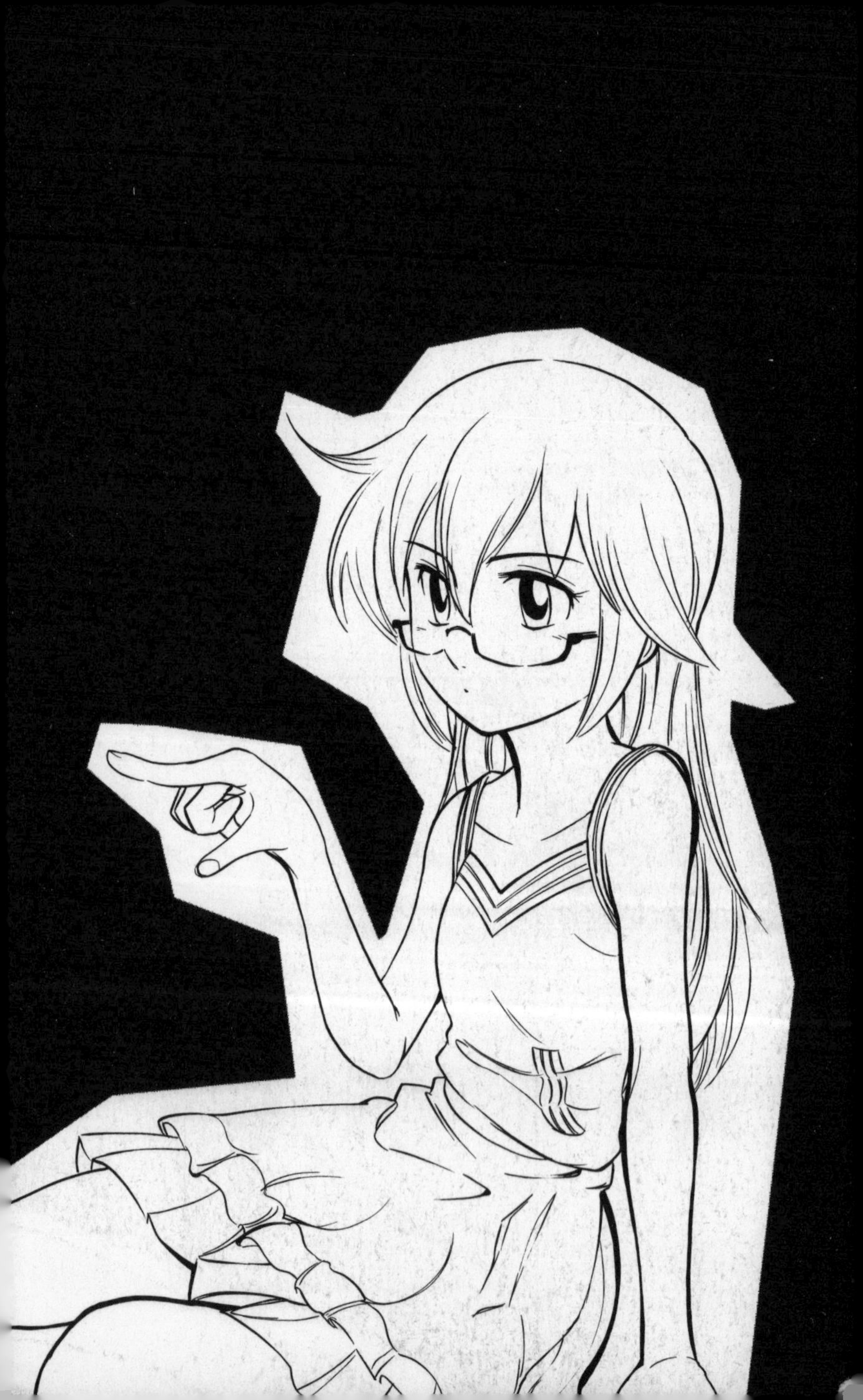

Afterword

GREETINGS. THIS IS TOSHIAKI
IWASHIRO.

THANK YOU SO MUCH FOR READING
VOLUME 2!

IT REALLY MAKES ME HAPPY TO HAVE
THE OPPORTUNITY TO DO THIS WORK
AND SEE THE FRUIT OF MY LABORS
TAKE SHAPE IN BOOK FORM.

RIGHT NOW, THE ASSISTANTS HELPING
ME WITH MY WORK ARE ALL NEWBIES
AT *JUMP*. THERE ARE A LOT OF
OPPORTUNITIES TO GET SINGLE-
CHAPTER MANGA PUBLISHED IN THE
MAIN *JUMP* MAGAZINE, SO EVERYONE
SCRAMBLES TO DRAW STORYBOARDS
AND GET THEM IN BEFORE THE
DEADLINE. I JUGGLE THEIR
SCHEDULES TO GIVE THEM DAYS
OFF WHILE WE PULL TOGETHER THE
PSYREN MANUSCRIPT.

SOMETIMES THEY SHOW UP FOR WORK
WITH THEIR EYES GLAZED OVER OR
CRAZED-LOOKING. IT DOES MAKE
THINGS ROUGH, BUT THEY DO KEEP
THINGS LIVELY AT WORK. I'M
DETERMINED TO WORK HARD AND
KEEP UP WITH THEIR ENERGY!

TOSHIAKI IWASHIRO

JUNE 2008

IN THE NEXT VOLUME...

KA-CHA

DRAGON

Ageha returns to the treacherous Psyren world, where he and his
fellow players are instantly under attack. To survive, they'll have to
use every resource they can. But Ageha's crew are showing signs
of fever, meaning their psionic powers are awakening at the worst
possible time!

Available MARCH 2012!